LCT709
LCA671

VIKING

John Pimlott

Foreword by
Alan Bullock

The Viking Atlas of World War II

VIKING

VIKING

Published by the Penguin Group
Penguin Books Ltd, 27 Wrights Lane, London W8 5TZ, England
Penguin Books USA Inc., 375 Hudson Street, New York, NY 10014, USA
Penguin Books Australia Ltd, Ringwood, Victoria, Australia
Penguin Books Canada Ltd, 10 Alcorn Avenue, Toronto, Ontario, Canada M4V 3B2
Penguin Books (NZ) Ltd, 182–190 Wairau Road, Auckland 10, New Zealand

Penguin Books Ltd, Registered Offices: Harmondsworth, Middlesex, England

First published by Viking 1995
1 3 5 7 9 10 8 6 4 2

Printed in Great Britain by Bath Press Colourbooks, Glasgow, Scotland

A CIP catalogue record for this book is available from the British Library

ISBN 0-670-86527-3

In our new planes, with our new crews, we bombed
The ranges by the desert or the shore,
Fired at towed targets, waited for our scores –
And turned into replacements and woke up
One morning, over England, operational.
It wasn't different: but if we died
It was not an accident but a mistake
(But an easy one for anyone to make).
We read out mail and counted up our missions –
In bombers named for girls, we burned
The cities we had learned about in school –
Till our lives wore out; our bodies lay among
The people we had killed and never seen.
When we lasted long enough they gave us medals;
When we died they said, "Our casualties were low."
They said, "Here are the maps"; we burned the cities.

from *Losses*
Randall Jarrell (1914–1965)

Contents

"The Sinking of the Bismarck", painted by C.E. Turner.

Foreword

No other event in human history can compare with World War II in the number of participants, the cost in human lives and physical destruction or the scale of its consequences.

There is no doubt about who started the war. In *Mein Kampf*, published in the mid-1920s, Hitler wrote:

> *"When we speak of* Lebensraum *(living space) for the German people, we must think principally of Russia and the border states subject to her. Destiny itself seems to wish to point the way for us here."*

Hitler had no idea of how or when he would achieve his objective, but he had no doubt that it could only be by war. At a cabinet meeting on 8 February 1933, a week after coming to power, he declared, "This has to be the dominant thought always and everywhere: everything for the armed forces." When he put Goering in charge of the Four-Year Plan in 1936, his secret directive was to have the German armed forces and economy ready for war in four years. In presenting the plan to the German cabinet, Goering reiterated: "It starts from the basic premise that the showdown with Russia is inevitable."

In the winter of 1937/38, Hitler felt strong enough to take the initiative. In March 1938 he annexed Austria; in March 1939, he broke up the Czechoslovak state. The Poles were certain to fight for their independence but were defeated in less than a month (September 1939) at the cost of no more than 11,000 German dead. In the summer of 1940 it took only six weeks, at a cost of no more than 27,000 German dead, to defeat the French and drive the British off the European continent.

These were the preliminaries. Hitler covered himself against intervention from the east by the Soviet–Nazi Pact, guaranteeing Russia's neutrality. Once the preliminaries were secured, however, he began preparations for his real objective, the invasion of the Soviet Union (21/22 June 1941).

We still do not appreciate the extent to which the fighting in the east was the core of the European war. It was fought on a scale and with a violence which was unknown elsewhere in the European and Mediterranean theaters, at least until the Anglo–U.S. invasion of June 1944 (three years after the German attack on Russia). The Russian victory at Stalingrad alone, a battle which lasted from 1 September 1942 to 2 February 1943, cost 2 million Russian lives and 800,000 German. The comparative table of lives lost on page 13 makes clear how far Russian and German losses on the Eastern Front overshadow those suffered by any other nation except China.

The German success in 1940–41 made a great impression on the Japanese. In the summer of 1941 they decided to switch from concentrating on their four-year-old war with China to the conquest of the British, French and Dutch colonial empires in South East Asia, hoping to safeguard themselves against American intervention by knocking out the U.S. Navy in Pearl Harbor (7 December 1941). At one stroke, the European war became a world war, a development confirmed by Hitler's declaration of war on the United States (11 December 1941).

Germany and Japan inflicted heavy blows on the Allies in 1941–42, but once they failed to achieve the knock-outs on which they had counted, the superior manpower and economic strength of America, Russia and Britain began to tell. By the beginning of 1943 the Germans and Japanese had lost the initiative, never to recover it. Hitler, who had begun the war, committed suicide on 30 April 1945 but showed no remorse for the horrors he had let loose on the world. The war in Europe ended eight days later; the war in Asia continued for another three months, ending on 15 August 1945, nine days after the dropping of the first atomic bomb on Hiroshima.

The scale of the physical destruction and loss of life of a war which extended to three continents and all the oceans defeats the imagination. The total number of lives lost (including those who were massacred or died in prisoner-of-war, concentration and extermination camps) is put at about 40 million for Europe, with another 15–20 million for Asia, the Middle East and Africa. For the first time the civilian loss of life (the majority of them women and children) exceeded the military. Many more millions were uprooted either by deportation, conscription for forced labor or by flight from the war zones; this process continued after the fighting ended, when several million Germans and Japanese were evicted from their homes.

The application of technology brought about a trans-

Adolf Hitler at a triumphal parade in Berlin, 1939.

formation of warfare. The difference between the use of air power at the beginning and at the end of the war – culminating in the dropping of the atomic bomb – was revolutionary. So was the use of armored forces (5000 tanks took part in the Battle of Kursk), rockets, radar and wireless, submarines and the replacement of the battleship by the aircraft carrier.

Equally revolutionary was the transformation of national economies. The increased scale of organization and the rise in productivity on both sides made this the biggest sustained economic effort in history. This continued after the war, switching from war production to making good the damage. The wartime experience made possible the extraordinary economic recovery of Western Europe, West Germany and Japan as well as the sustained economic ascendancy of the United States.

Amongst the social consequences of the war the change with the biggest long-term effect, as in World War I, was the involvement of women, many serving in the armed forces, many more taking the place of men in industry, agriculture, transport offices, and public services. Taken together, the two world wars contributed more to the emancipation of women than any other episode in history.

Whoever won the war, the world was bound to be changed irrevocably. This time Germany was not only defeated but divided and occupied. The Soviet Union made major territorial acquisitions in Europe and Asia, and ended the war in occupation of half Europe, including Eastern Germany which joined the other East European states in forming a Soviet-dominated communist bloc. The alliance between the Soviet Union and the Western powers did not survive the defeat of Germany and was followed by the so-called Cold War between the Soviet bloc and the NATO powers, led by the U.S.A., in the second half of the twentieth century.

In the Far East, Japan lost all its conquests, was occupied by the Americans and had to face the emergence of a united communist China. Elsewhere the revolutionary impact of the war created independence movements and brought the end of the European colonial empires in the post-war period, often after bitter fighting, and the emergence of the Third World.

Not until 1989–91, with the demolition of the Berlin Wall and the reunification of Germany, with the withdrawal of Russian troops from Eastern Europe and the collapse of communist rule in the Soviet Union, were the consequences of World War II finally dispelled.

Alan Bullock
St Catherine's College
Oxford

ESTIMATED LOSS OF LIFE IN WORLD WAR II

Country	Military Losses	Civilian Losses	Total Losses
USSR (1941–45)	c. 8.7 million	c. 16 million	c. 25 million
Germany (1939–45)	3,250,000	3,600,000	6,850,000
UK (1939–45)	326,000	62,000	388,000
France	340,000	470,000	810,000
Poland	123,000	c. 6 million (1)	c.6,123,000
Yugoslavia	300,000	1,400,000 (3)	1,706,000
Hungary			840,000 (2)
Greece			520,000
Romania			460,000
Austria			480,000
Italy			410,000
Czechoslovakia			400,000
All other European states			425,000
TOTAL ALL EUROPEAN STATES			**c.43 million**
U.S.A. (All Fronts including the Pacific, 1941–45)			296,000
Japan			2 million
China			c.15 million
TOTAL ALL FRONTS			**c. 60 million**

Notes: (1) Of whom c. 3 million were Polish Jews
(2) Of whom c. 540,000 were Hungarian Jews
(3) Including partisans

"I was horrified when I saw the map. We're quite alone, without any help from outside. Hitler has left us in the lurch. Whether this letter gets away depends on whether we still hold the airfield. We are lying in the north of the city. The men in my battery already suspect the truth, but they aren't so exactly informed as I am. So this is what the end looks like. Hannes and I have no intention of going into captivity; yesterday I saw four men, who'd been captured before our infantry re-occupied a strong-point. No, we're not going to be captured. When Stalingrad falls you will hear and read about it. Then you will know that I shall not return."

Anonymous German soldier

The grave of a U.S. soldier in Normandy, August 1944. The note has been pinned to it by local people as a mark of respect.

Chronology

1919
April 28 League of Nations founded
June 28 Signing of Treaty of Versailles

1921
July 29 Hitler becomes president of National Socialist Party

1923
Nov 8 Hitler jailed after failure of Munich Putsch

1924
Jan 21 Death of Lenin
April 6 Large Fascist majority in Italian elections

1925
July 18 Publication of *Mein Kampf*

1926
Sept 8 Germany admitted to League of Nations

1929
Oct 24 Wall Street Crash

1930
Sept 14 German Election: Nazi Party becomes second largest party in Germany

1931
Sept 18 Japanese troops invade Manchuria

1932
Nov 8 Roosevelt elected U.S. President

1933
Jan 30 Hitler becomes Chancellor of coalition government
March 21 First concentation camp opened at Oranienburg outside Berlin
March 23 Enabling Act gives Hitler dictatorial powers
March 27 Japan leaves League of Nations
July 14 Nazi party declared only party in Germany
Oct 14 Germany leaves League of Nations

1934
June 29/30 Night of the Long Knives: Nazi purge of the SA
Aug 19 Hitler becomes Führer
Oct Long March of the Chinese Communists begins

1935
March 16 Hitler reneges on disarmament clauses of Treaty of Versailles and introduces conscription
Sept 15 Jews stripped of German citizenship rights by Nuremburg laws
Oct 3 Italian forces invade Ethiopia

1936
March 7 German troops re-occupy demilitarized Rhineland
May 9 Italian annexation of Ethiopia
July 8 Civil war breaks out in Spain
Oct 1 Franco declared head of Spanish state

1937
April 27 Guernica badly damaged in raid
June 11 Stalin's purge of Red Army generals begins
July 7 Sino–Japanese war begins

1938
March 12/13 Germany announces an "Anschluß" (union of Austria and Germany)
Aug 12 German mobilization
Oct 1–5 German troops occupy Sudetenland; Czech government resigns
Nov 3 Japan announces a "New Order" in Asia
Nov 9 "Kristallnacht": widespread German attacks on Jews

1939
Jan 26 Franco's troops seize Barcelona
Feb 27 Britain and France recognize Franco's government
March 15–16 Germany dismembers Czechoslovakia
March 28 Spanish Civil war ends
Aug 31 British fleet mobilizes; evacuations from London begin
Sept 1 Germany invades Poland and annexes Danzig
Sept 3 Britain, France, New Zealand and Australia declare war on Germany
Sept 4 First RAF attacks on German Navy
Sept 5 U.S.A. proclaims its neutrality. German troops cross Vistula
Sept 10 Canada declares war on Germany. Battle of Atlantic begins
Sept 17 U.S.S.R. invades Poland
Sept 27 Surrender of Warsaw
Sept 29 Partition of Poland
Nov 30 U.S.S.R. invades Finland. "Winter War" begins
Dec 13 Battle of the River Plate
Dec 14 U.S.S.R. expelled from League of Nations

1940

JANUARY
8 Rationing begins in Britain

MARCH
12 Treaty of Moscow ends the "Winter War"
16 Germany bombs Scapa Flow naval base
28 Allied War Council decides to lay mines off Norway
30 Japanese set up puppet Chinese government in Nanking

APRIL
9 Germany invades Denmark and Norway

MAY
1 Norway surrenders
10 Germany invades Netherlands, Belgium, Luxembourg and France. Churchill becomes Prime Minister
15 Holland surrenders
26 Evacuation of Allied troops from Dunkirk begins
28 Belgium surrenders

JUNE
3 Germans bomb Paris. Dunkirk evacuation ends
10 Italy declares war on Britain and France
14 Germans enter Paris
18 U.S.S.R. begins occupation of Baltic States
28 Britain recognizes de Gaulle as Free French leader
30 Germany begins occupation of Channel Islands

JULY
1 U-boats increase attacks on merchant ships in the Atlantic
5 Vichy government breaks off relations with Britain
10 First phase of Battle of Britain begins
23 U.S.S.R. annexes Lithuania, Latvia and Estonia

AUGUST
3–19 Italy occupies British Somaliland
13 "Adlertag" (Eagle Day) – German bombing offensive against British airfields and aircraft factories begins
15 Air battles and daylight raids over Britain
17 Hitler declares blockade of British Isles
23/24 First air raids on central London
25/26 First RAF raid on Berlin

SEPTEMBER
3 Hitler plans invasion of Britain (Operation *Sealion*)
7 Beginning of the Blitz
13 Italians invade Egypt
15 Heavy German air raids on London, Southampton, Bristol, Cardiff, Liverpool and Manchester
16 U.S. Conscription Bill passed
22 Japanese forces enter Indo-China
27 Tripartite Pact signed by Germany, Italy and Japan

OCTOBER
7 German troops enter Romania
12 Operation *Sealion* postponed until Spring 1941

18 Burma Road reopened
28 Italy invades Greece

NOVEMBER
11/12 Taranto raid cripples Italian fleet
14/15 German bombing of Coventry
22 Greeks defeat Italian 9th Army

DECEMBER
9/10 Wavell's Western Desert Offensive against the Italians begins
23 Eden becomes British Foreign Secretary
29/30 Massive air raid on London

1941

JANUARY
6 Australians seize Bardia from Italians
22 Tobruk falls to British and Australians

FEBRUARY
6 Australian troops seize Benghazi
7 Beda Fomm falls to British
11 British forces advance into Italian Somaliland
12–14 Rommel arrives in Tripoli
25 Mogadishu falls to British forces

MARCH
4 British Commando raid on Lofoten Islands
7 British forces begin to arrive in Greece
27 Coup in Yugoslavia overthrows pro-Axis government

APRIL
3 Pro-Axis regime set up in Iraq
6 German invasion of Yugoslavia and Greece
17 Yugoslavia surrenders to Germany
27 Greece surrenders to Germany
30 Iraqi forces attack British bases and embassy

MAY
1 German attack on Tobruk repulsed
10 Hess flies to Scotland
10/11 Heavy German bombing of London in climax of the Blitz. RAF raid on Hamburg
15 Operation *Brevity* in Egypt
24 Sinking of the *Hood* by the *Bismarck*
27 Sinking of the *Bismarck*
30 Iraqi revolt collapses

JUNE
4 Pro-Allied government installed in Iraq
8 Allies invade Syria and the Lebanon
22 German attack on U.S.S.R. (Operation *Barbarossa*) begins
28 Germans capture Minsk

JULY
3 Stalin calls for "scorched earth" policy
10 Germans cross the River Dnieper
12 Mutual Assistance Agreement between Britain and U.S.S.R.
14 Ceasefire in Syria
21 Japan begins occupation of southern French Indo-China
26 Roosevelt freezes Japanese assets in U.S.A. and suspends relations
31 Hitler orders measures for the "desired final solution of the Jewish question"

AUGUST
1 U.S. oil embargo against "aggressor" states announced
12 Roosevelt and Churchill sign Atlantic Charter
20 Siege of Leningrad begins

SEPTEMBER
3 First use of gas chambers at Auschwitz
19 Germans take Kiev
29 Massacre of 33,000 Jews at Kiev

OCTOBER
2 Operation *Typhoon*, the German advance on Moscow, begins
16 Germans take Odessa
24 Germans take Kharkov
30 Germans reach Sevastopol

NOVEMBER
13 HMS *Ark Royal* sunk off Gibraltar by U-boat
20 Germans take Rostov
27 Soviet troops retake Rostov

DECEMBER
5 German attack on Moscow abandoned
7 Japanese bomb Pearl Harbor
8 U.S.A. and Britain declare war on Japan
10 Japan begins invasion of the Philippines
11 Germany declares war on U.S.A.
16 Rommel begins retreat to El Agheila
25 Hong Kong surrenders to the Japanese

1942

JANUARY
1 Declaration of the United Nations signed by 26 Allied nations
13 Germans begin U-boat offensive along east coast of America
16 Japanese invade Burma
21 Rommel's counter-offensive from El Agheila begins
26 First American forces arrive in Britain

FEBRUARY
1 U.S. air attack on Japanese bases on Gilbert and Marshall Islands
7 Japanese land on Singapore Island
15 British surrender at Singapore
19 Japanese air raid on Darwin, Australia
27/28 Allied force destroyed in Battle of Java Sea

MARCH
1 Soviet offensive in the Crimea
8 Japanese capture Rangoon
9 Dutch East Indies surrender
27/28 Commando raid on St. Nazaire docks
30 End of Soviet counter-offensive

APRIL
2 New Japanese offensive on Bataan
10 "Bataan Death March" begins
18 Surprise U.S. bomber raid on Tokyo
23 "Baedeker" raids begin against cathedral cities in Britain
29 Japanese cut Burma Road and take control of central Burma

MAY
1 Japanese take Mandalay in Burma
4–8 Battle of the Coral Sea
5 Japanese advance into China
8 German summer offensive begins in the Crimea
10 Surrender of U.S. forces in Philippines
26 Rommel begins offensive against Gazala Line
30 1000-bomber RAF raid on Cologne

JUNE
2–11 Siege of Bir Hakeim
4–16 Battle of Midway
5 Germans besiege Sevastopol
7 Japan invades Aleutian Islands
18 Second siege of Tobruk by Axis troops begins
30 Rommel reaches El Alamein

JULY
1–30 First Battle of El Alamein
3 Germans take Sevastopol
5 Soviet resistance in the Crimea ends
9 Germans begin drive towards Stalingrad
22 First deportations from Warsaw Ghetto to concentration camps. Treblinka extermination camp opened
31 Germans cross the River Don

AUGUST
8 U.S. Marines take Henderson Field on Guadalcanal
9 Gandhi, Nehru and other Indian leaders arrested. Riots in India
12–15 First Moscow Conference
17 First all-American air attack in Europe
19 Anglo-Canadian raid on Dieppe
23 Massive air raid on Stalingrad
30 (to Sept 1) Battle of Alam Halfa. Rommel driven back

SEPTEMBER
12–14 Battle of "Bloody Ridge" on Guadalcanal
13 Battle of Stalingrad begins

27 British/Indian troops begin offensive into Arakan, Burma

OCTOBER

11/12 Battle of Cape Esperance, off Guadalcanal

18 Hitler issues order to execute all British Commandos taken prisoner

23 Operation *Lightfoot* opens Second Battle of El Alamein

26 Battle of Santa Cruz, off Guadalcanal

NOVEMBER

1 Operation *Supercharge*: Allies break through Axis lines at El Alamein

4 Axis troops begin retreat

8 Operation *Torch*, the U.S. invasion of North Africa, begins

11 Germans and Italians invade Southern France

19 Soviet counter-offensive at Stalingrad begins

30/31 Naval Battle of Tassafaronga, off Guadalcanal

DECEMBER

2 The nuclear age is born when Professor Enrico Fermi sets up an atomic reactor in Chicago

13 Rommel withdraws from El Agheila

16 Italians defeated by Soviet troops on River Don

17 Eden tells House of Commons of mass executions of Jews by Nazis. U.S. declares that these crimes will be avenged

28 Hitler withdraws Army Group A from Caucasus

31 Battle of the Barents Sea

1943

JANUARY

3 Germans begin withdrawal from Caucasus

10 Soviets begin offensive against Germans in Stalingrad

14–24 Casablanca Conference, Roosevelt demands "unconditional surrender"

18 Siege of Leningrad lifted

23 Eighth Army takes Tripoli

27 First USAAF bombing raid on Germany, at Wilhelmshaven

FEBRUARY

1–8 Japanese evacuate Guadalcanal

2 Last Germans surrender at Stalingrad

8 Soviet troops take Kursk

13 Chindits enter Burma

14–25 Battle of Kasserine Pass

16 Soviets re-take Kharkov

MARCH

1–4 Battle of Bismarck Sea

2 Germans begin withdrawal from Tunisia

15 Germans re-capture Kharkov

16–20 Climax of Battle of Atlantic: 27 merchant ships sunk by U-boats

20–28 8th Army breaks through Mareth Line, Tunisia

25 Chindits withdraw to India

APRIL

6/7 Axis forces in Tunisia begin withdrawal toward Enfidaville

19 Warsaw Uprising begins

20 Massacre of Jews from Warsaw Ghetto begins

MAY

7 Allies take Tunis

12 Japanese take Maungdaw in Burma: end of first Arakan offensive

13 Axis troops surrender in North Africa

16/17 The RAF Dams Raid on the Ruhr

22 Dönitz suspends U-boat operations in the North Atlantic

JUNE

1 U.S. begins submarine war against Japanese shipping

10 "Pointblank" directive to improve Allied bombing strategy issued

11 Himmler orders liquidation of all Polish ghettos

16 Allied air raids on Guadalcanal

21 Allies land on New Georgia

30 Operation *Cartwheel* against Japanese on Rabaul

JULY

5 Germans begin last offensive against Kursk

9/10 Allied landings on Sicily

19 Allies bomb Rome

22 Palermo captured by Americans

24 RAF bombing raid on Hamburg begins Battle of Hamburg

25/26 Mussolini arrested and Fascist government dissolved. Badoglio takes over and establishes martial law

27/28 Air raid causes firestorm in Hamburg

AUGUST

5 Soviet troops take Orel and Belgorod

6/7 Battle of Vella Gulf, Solomon Islands

12–17 Germans evacuate Sicily

17 First U.S. raid on Schweinfurt-Regensburg

23 Soviet troops recapture Kharkov

28 Japanese resistance on New Guinea ends

SEPTEMBER

8 Italian surrender announced

9 Allied landings at Salerno and Taranto

11 Germans occupy Rome

12 Germans rescue Mussolini

22 Soviet troops cross River Dnieper

23 Mussolini re-establishes Fascist government

OCTOBER

1 Allies enter Naples

13 Italy declares war on Germany. Second U.S. raid on Schweinfurt

19–30 Second Moscow Conference

NOVEMBER

1 U.S. Marines land on Bougainville, Solomon Islands

2 Battle of Empress Augusta Bay

6 Russians recapture Kiev

18 RAF air raid begins on Berlin

20 U.S. troops land on Makin and Tarawa Atolls, Gilbert Islands

22–26 First Cairo Conference

28–30 Teheran Conference

DECEMBER

3–7 Second Cairo Conference

24–26 Soviet troops launch offensives on Ukrainian front

25/26 Battle of North Cape: *Scharnhorst* sunk

1944

JANUARY

6 Soviet troops advance into Poland

9 British/Indian troops recapture Maungdaw in Burma

17 First attack towards Cassino

22 Allied landings at Anzio

27 Leningrad relieved after 900-day siege

FEBRUARY

1–7 U.S. troops take Kwajalein and Majura Atolls in Marshall Islands

15–18 Aerial bombardment of Monte Cassino destroys monastery

17/18 U.S. air raid destroys Japanese naval base at Truk

29 German counterattack against Anzio beachhead

MARCH

1 Chindits re-enter Burma

4 Soviet troops begin offensive on Belorussian front. First major daylight raid on Berlin by Allies

15 Japanese offensive toward Imphal and Kohima launched. Second Allied attempt to capture Monte Cassino begins

29 Battle of Imphal begins

APRIL

4–20 Japanese siege of Kohima

8 Soviet troops begin offensive to liberate Crimea

18 Japanese launch Operation *Ichi-Go*

MAY

9 Soviet troops recapture Sevastopol

11 Allies attack Gustav Line

12 Germans surrender in Crimea

15 Germans withdraw to Adolf Hitler Line

25 Germans retreat from Anzio

JUNE
5 Allies enter Rome
6 D-Day landings
9 Soviet offensive against Finnish front begins
13 First V-1 raid on Britain
14 First B-29 Superfortress raid on Japan
15 U.S. Marines take Saipan, Mariana Islands
19/20 Battle of the Philippine Sea
22 Operation *Bagration*, the Soviet summer offensive, begins
27 U.S. troops capture Cherbourg

JULY
3 "Battle of the Hedgerows" in Normandy
8 Japanese begin withdrawal from Imphal
9 British and Canadian troops capture Caen
18 Operation *Goodwood* begins: U.S. troops take St Lô
21 U.S. Marines land on Guam
24 U.S. Marines land on Tinian. Soviet troops liberate first concentration camp at Maidenak
25–30 Operation *Cobra* begins in Normandy. U.S. troops break out west of St Lô
28 Soviet troops take Brest-Litovsk. U.S. troops take Coutances

AUGUST
1 Warsaw Uprising begins
3 Myitkyina falls to Chinese/U.S. troops after 2½ months siege
7 German counterattack towards Avranches begins
12 German counterattack fails
15 Operation *Dragoon*, the Allied invasion of Southern France, begins
19 Resistance Uprising in Paris
19/20 Soviet offensive in Balkans begins with attack on Romania
25 Liberation of Paris
29 Slovak Uprising begins
30 Soviet troops capture Ploesti in Romania
31 Soviet troops take Bucharest

SEPTEMBER
1–4 Arras, Verdun, Dieppe, Artois, Rouen, Abbeville, Antwerp and Brussels liberated by Allies
4 Finland and U.S.S.R. agree to a ceasefire
13 U.S. troops reach Siegfried Line
17–26 Operation *Market Garden*
26 Soviet troops occupy Estonia

OCTOBER
2 Warsaw Uprising ends. Polish Home Army surrenders
9–19 Third Moscow Conference
10–29 Soviet troops capture Riga
11 Air raids against Okinawa
12–18 Allied air raids against Formosa
14 Allies liberate Athens
20 U.S. invasion of Leyte
21 Germans surrender at Aachen
23–25 Battle of Leyte Gulf
30 Last use of gas chambers at Auschwitz

NOVEMBER
11 Bombardment of Iwo Jima by U.S. Navy
20 French troops drive through "Belfort Gap" to reach Rhine
24 French capture Strasbourg

DECEMBER
4 Civil War in Greece: Athens placed under martial law
15 U.S. troops land on Mindoro, Philippines
16–25 Battle of the Bulge in the Ardennes
27 Soviet troops besiege Budapest

1945

JANUARY
1–17 Germans withdraw from the Ardennes
4 British occupy Akyab in Burma
9 U.S. troops land at Lingayen Gulf on Luzon, Philippines
16 Allies eliminate Ardennes salient
17 Soviet troops capture Warsaw
26 Soviet troops liberate Auschwitz

FEBRUARY
3 U.S. forces enter Manila
13/14 Dresden destroyed by firestorm after Allied bombing raids
19/20 U.S. troops land on Iwo Jima
22 Operation Clarion: attacks on German communications network

MARCH
2 Tito sets up Communist government in Romania
3 U.S. and Filipino troops capture Manila
6 Germans begin their last offensive of the war – to defend the oilfields of Hungary
7 Allies take Cologne and establish a bridge across the Rhine at Remagen
9/10 Bombing raid on Tokyo opens a series of attacks on Japanese cities
30 Soviet troops capture Danzig

APRIL
1 U.S. troops invade Okinawa. U.S. troops encircle German troops in Ruhr
7 Battle of East China Sea
12 Allies liberate Buchenwald and Belsen concentration camps. President Roosevelt dies: Truman becomes President
16 Soviet troops begin final offensive on Berlin
18 German forces in Ruhr pocket surrender
26–28 Mussolini captured and hanged by partisans
29 U.S. troops liberate Dachau concentration camp
30 Red Army reaches Reichstag; Hitler commits suicide

MAY
2 German troops in Italy surrender
3 British/Indian troops capture Rangoon
5 Ceasefire in the West
7 Unconditional surrender of all German forces to Allies
8 VE Day
20 Japanese begin pulling back from Chinese bases
23 German High Command and Provisional Government imprisoned

JUNE
5 Allied powers partition Germany and Berlin, and assume government of Germany
22 Resistance on Okinawa ends
26 United Nations World Charter of Security signed in San Francisco
30 Luzon campaign ends

JULY
1 U.S., British and French troops move into Berlin
5 Liberation of Philippines declared
10 1000-bomber raid against Japan begins
16 First atomic bomb test in Mexican desert.Potsdam Conference begins
26 Atlee succeeds Churchill as British Prime Minister

AUGUST
6 First atomic bomb dropped on Hiroshima
8 U.S.S.R. declares war on Japan and invades Manchuria
9 Atomic bomb dropped on Nagasaki
14 Japanese accept Allied surrender terms
15 VJ Day
30 British forces reoccupy Hong Kong

SEPTEMBER
2 Japanese sign surrender agreement
5 British troops land in Singapore
9 Japanese sign surrender in China
13 Japanese sign surrender in Burma

OCTOBER
24 United Nations comes formally into existence

NOVEMBER
20 Nuremburg war crimes trials begin
29 Yugoslavia declared a "Federal People's Republic"

Key to Maps

Size of Military Units

ARMY GROUP NAME	or	XXXXX 1	or	XXXXX 1	Army group
ARMY NAME	or	XXXX 1	or	XXXX 1	Army
I CORPS	or	XXX I	or	XXX I	Corps
		XX			Division
		X			Brigade
		III			Regiment
		II			Battalion

- Infantry
- XX Armored
- XX Motorized
- XX Parachute/air landing
- Artillery
- Cavalry

Army Movements

- Attack or advance
- Retreat or withdrawal

Earliest date/ time			Latest date/time	
				Front line
				Unit
				Attack

National colors

Austrian	French	Portuguese
Belgian	German	Romanian
British and Commonwealth	Iraqi	Serbian
Bulgarian	Italian	Soviet
Chinese	Japanese	Turkish
Dutch	Norwegian	United States
Finnish	Polish	

General military symbols

- Headquarters
- Headquarters second level
- Heavy AA guns
- Coastal defense guns
- Coastal defense gun (alternative)
- Light AA guns
- Anti-aircraft gun site
- Machine-gun post
- Mobile gun
- AA machine-gun
- Steel 'Hedgehogs'
- u/c Under construction
- Barbed wire
- Concrete shelter
- Dugout
- Trenches
- Artillery observation post
- Batteries
- Heavily fortified defensive line
- Defensive line
- Incomplete or second-class defensive line
- Field work
- Resistance point
- Mined area
- Parachute landing
- Parachute landing area/Drop Zone/DZ
- Armored concentration
- Bridge/pass
- Anti tank ditch/defense
- Raid/bombing/attack/naval bombardment
- Oil field

Headquarters airfield

Sector airfield

Airfield/airbase

Radar station (low level)

Radar station (high level)

Radar range (low level)

Radar range (high level)

Observer corps site

Balloon barrage

Wireless transmitter

Radio beacon

Air attack

Fighter patrol

Bomber

Bomber (alternative)

Fighter

Glider

Searchlight batteries

Airdropped torpedo

Nightfighter area

Smokescreen

Mines (sea)

Minefield (sea)

Ship attacked and sunk

Ship sunk (alternative)

Naval troops (unit strengths vary)

XXXX Army boundary

XXX Corps boundary

XX Division boundary

Warships

Aircraft carrier

Battleship

Cruiser

Destroyer

Submarine

FORCE Y *Strasbourg* (Battleship) *Neptune* (Cruiser) — Surface group

Other symbols used on maps

Urban area

Town / settlement

International border

Provincial border

Major road

Road (alternative)

Canal

Railway

Mountain

Mountain (alternative)

Forest

Swamps

Beaches

Rocks

B. Jacobs
1933

PART I
The Inter-War Period, 1919–1939

World War I (1914–1918) left a number of legacies. At one level, there was an understandable desire to avoid such a nightmare again, particularly among those European states that had suffered substantial losses in both men and material. This was manifested in calls for disarmament and international cooperation, based on a "new world order" that had at its center the League of Nations, established in 1920. But there was also a steady growth in political extremism, reflecting the enormous social changes triggered by the conflict and the unsatisfactory nature of the peace settlement that emerged between 1919 and 1921. At the same time, the military lessons of the war could not simply be forgotten. The impact of new technology, on land, at sea and especially in the air, altered the way in which force could be used for political ends, offering alternatives to the attritional deadlock of 1914–18 which made that bloodbath seem an aberration. To the optimists, it may have been "the war to end all wars", but to many it was merely one more step in man's inexorable journey to Armageddon.

These emotions and beliefs became apparent very quickly. In countries such as Britain and France, where the victory of 1918 seemed small recompense for the human losses incurred, war-weariness was shown in calls for rapid demobilization and disarmament. Indeed, the British Army – over three million strong in 1918 – was reduced to pre-war levels and returned to the "proper soldiering" of colonial policing so quickly that much of the hard-won experience of the war years was forgotten. Moreover, as the peacetime period progressed, the desire to avoid a repetition of the recent conflict did not diminish. Memoirs of the war abounded, many of them stressing the suffering, hardship and waste involved, while the new medium of film portrayed the reality of trench deadlock to the next generation. To the survivors of 1914–18, there was little glory to be found in war. Small wonder, therefore, that when Britain and France entered a new conflict in 1939, they did so not with the jingoism of 1914 but with an air of resigned determination.

But not everyone felt the same. In Germany, Austria and Hungary for example, the suffering of 1914–18 had been made worse by defeat and by the imposition of swingeing peace terms by the Allies. The peace settlement of 1919–21 was in many ways a disaster, breeding resentment and opening the way to more extreme political views. However well meaning the Allied leaders, they ignored many of the pressures that had been building up in Europe since the 19th century, not least in terms of nationalism, and their redrawing of the map created more problems than it solved. It may have seemed a good idea to reduce the size of Germany and to split Austria and Hungary, creating new states that would act as buffers, but the inclusion within states such as Poland, Czechoslovakia and Yugoslavia of ethnic groups which felt that they belonged elsewhere merely stored up trouble for the future. In addition, there was a feeling, particularly among many Germans, that the peace settlement had been imposed unfairly, reflecting Allied desires for revenge rather than for lasting peace. When this was added to economic pressures created by the demand for reparations, leading to hyper-inflation and its attendant social problems, it was hardly surprising that Adolf Hitler should find a ready audience for his political beliefs. The fact that he was also able to exploit a fear of communism spreading from the east was just one more legacy of World War I, for without that conflict the Bolshevik Revolution of 1917 would not have occurred when it did, feeding on the enormous hardships suffered by the Russian people. Once two such diametrically opposed

Adolf Hitler painted by Jacobs.

"The Doormat", cartoon by Low depicting Japan's rising militarism (1932).

political ideologies – fascism and communism – emerged, a major clash was inevitable.

According to the peace settlement, conflict should have been avoidable by recourse to the League of Nations as an international body for debate and diplomacy. Its failure, apparent in the early 1930s when both Japan and Italy got away with naked aggression against Manchuria and Abyssinia respectively, was one of the key factors in preparing the way for renewed conflict. In very simple terms, the League lacked "teeth", for although it could impose economic penalties on aggressor states, it had no way of ensuring that these were carried out effectively. The refusal of the U.S. Senate to ratify the peace settlement denied the League any form of official American backing and left it in the hands of states such as Britain and France that were too weak to ensure its success. As fascism flexed its muscles in the 1930s, it did so in an international vacuum and, with each "victory", grew more adventurous. Hitler's expansionism could have been stopped as early as 1936; that it was not and was instead "appeased" by British and French leaders intent on avoiding another European bloodbath, made war unavoidable.

The fact that any future war would be a bloodbath was widely believed as the 1930s progressed. Despite attempts through the League of Nations and other international bodies to outlaw the worst manifestations of new technology – not least strategic bombing and gas – it was apparent from events in China and Spain that these had little effect when it came to actual conflict. Trench deadlock might be avoidable, particularly if the lessons of 1918 concerning all-arms cooperation and inter-service links were remembered, but the trend towards making war on civilian populations was reinforced by the sack of Shanghai and the bombing of Guernica. By 1939 the widespread fears of bombing using both high explosives and gas were shown by British plans for the evacuation of children and young mothers from the major cities and by the issue of gas masks to all members of the population. Indeed, many people believed firmly that as soon as war began, enemy bombers would hit cities with impunity, causing enormous casualties. For these reasons, few in Britain or France were keen on war when it finally came in 1939, although the aggressive nature of fascism had by then made it difficult to find an alternative.

Nazi Party Brownshirts parade on Party Day at Nuremburg, 1933.

The Peace Settlement 1919–23

In January 1919, two months after the defeat of Germany in the First World War, the Allies convened a Peace Conference in Paris to decide the post-war territorial settlement. The defeated powers were not represented, leaving major decisions to be made by the Allies. Their redrawing of the map was to sow the seeds for future conflict.

By the Treaty of Versailles (28 June 1919), attempts were made to prevent future German aggression by weakening the state and creating buffers around it. In eastern Europe, Poland was recreated and awarded the "Danzig Corridor", a strip of former German land that gave the Poles access to the sea and isolated East Prussia. In the west, Germany was forced to cede Alsace and Lorraine to France, northern Schleswig to Denmark, and Eupen and Malmedy to Belgium. The Saarland was placed under international rule for 15 years and its coalfields given to France; the Rhineland was occupied by Allied troops and demilitarized. At the same time, Germany's economic power was diminished by taking away her overseas colonies and insisting that she pay reparations.

By the Treaty of St Germain (10 September 1919), Austria-Hungary lost Bohemia (including the Sudetenland) to the newly formed Czechoslovakia, with Galicia being ceded to Poland, and Trieste, Istria and the South Tyrol to Italy. By the Treaty of Trianon (4 June 1920), Hungary was split away from Austria and stripped of nearly two-thirds of its pre-war territory to help to create both Czechoslovakia and Yugoslavia. Under the terms of the Treaty of Neuilly, signed on 27 November 1919, Bulgaria lost territory to Greece.

The treaty with Turkey was signed at Sèvres on 10 August 1920. Substantial parts of the former Ottoman Empire in the Middle East were given to France and Britain as "mandates" to be prepared for eventual independence. Attempts by Greece, Britain and Italy to occupy parts of Turkey itself provoked a nationalist revolt necessitating a second treaty, which gave the Turks improved peace terms but did not alter the settlement in the Middle East.

Many of these territorial changes led to deep resentment and, to police the settlement, the League of Nations was created. America did not join the League, leaving it in the hands of countries such as Britain and France, seriously weakened by the losses of the First World War. The settlements were seriously flawed.

U.S. President Woodrow Wilson, photographed during his attendance at the Paris Peace Conference in 1919. Wilson's own proposal for peace, the "Fourteen Points", had been announced as early as January 1918, but had met with little enthusiasm from the Allies.

2/Europe-Political
1914 – 1919
Borders 1914
Borders after the 1919 peace treaties
Territory lost by Germany
Territory lost by Austro-Hungary
Territory lost by Bulgaria
Territory lost by Russia /USSR
Demilitarized zones
0
400 km
0
200 miles
N
NORWAY
SWEDEN
FINLAND
ESTONIA
LATVIA
LITHUANIA
DENMARK
NETHERLANDS
BELGIUM
LUX.
GERMANY
POLAND
East Prussia
CZECHOSLOVAKIA
AUSTRIA
HUNGARY
SWITZ.
FRANCE
ITALY
YUGOSLAVIA
ROMANIA
BULGARIA
ALBANIA
GREECE
TURKEY
UNION OF SOVIET SOCIALIST REPUBLICS
White Russia
Ukraine
Bessarabia
Serbia
Monte-Negro
Saarland
NORTH SEA
BALTIC SEA
GULF OF FINLAND
Skagerrak
Kattegat
Ligurian Sea
Tyrrhenian Sea
Adriatic Sea
AEGEAN SEA
Trondheim
Bergen
Oslo
Umeå
Sundsvall
Vaasa
Kuopio
L. Onega
Petrozavodsk
L. Ladoga
Åland
Helsinki
Leningrad (St. Petersburg)
Örebro
Stockholm
L. Väner
L. Vätter
Göteborg
Jönköping
Tallinn
L. Peipsi
Novgorod
Pskov
Gottland
Öland
Riga
Daugavpils
R. Dvina
Vitebsk
Copenhagen
Malmö
Bornholm (Denmark)
Kaunas
Wilno
1920
Königsberg
Danzig
Lübeck
Rostock
Hamburg
Bremen
Amsterdam
The Hague
Stettin
Grodno
Minsk
Berlin
Hannover
Bialystok
Gomel
Poznan
R. Vistula
Warsaw
Brest-Litovsk
1921
R. Pripet
R. Dnieper
R. Elbe
R. Oder
R. Rhine
Antwerp
Dortmund
Lille
Brussels
Leipzig
Lódz
Cologne
Bonn
Dresden
Lublin
R. Meuse
Frankfurt
Wiesbaden
Reims
Prague
Kiev
R. Seine
Kraków 1919/20
Pilzen
Brno
Lwow
1919/20
R. Dniester
Stuttgart
R. Danube
Bratislava
Munich
Basel
Zurich
Salzburg
Vienna
Debrecen
Kishinev
Berne
Geneva
Lausanne
R. Inn
Graz
Budapest
Tisza R.
Lyons
R. Drau
Cluj
Szeged
Milan
Trieste
Zagreb
Timişoara
R. Rhône
Venice
Po R.
Ploesti
Turin
Genoa
Bologna
Bucharest
Nice
Marseilles
Belgrade
Florence
Sarajevo
R. Danube
Varna
Corsica
Ajaccio
Sofia
Rome
Skopje
Istanbul
Bari
Tirana
Naples
Salonika
Taranto
Sardinia
Cagliari

The Depression 1929 – 1939

The First World War was expensive, not just in manpower but also in money. Combatant powers had diverted huge sums into the war effort, boosting armaments production but neglecting more peaceful industries. Traditional trading patterns were upset, stockpiles of raw materials run down and factory machinery overused. Despite a boom in 1919–20 as countries scrambled to replace material used up during the war, the world economy soon began to suffer. Countries that had over-produced to meet the demands of conflict suddenly found that they had a surplus on their hands; this led to recession as prices fell on glutted markets. In addition, countries such as Britain and France were saddled with enormous war debts, chiefly to the U.S.A. while the imposition of reparations on Germany by the terms of the Versailles Treaty left a vacuum in the middle of Europe. The Germans had little incentive to produce wealth that merely went into the pockets of the victors.

By 1923 the German Mark had fallen dramatically in value, from 275 to the U.S. dollar in May 1922 to 16,667 to the dollar a year later, and an international conference, triggered largely by a Franco-Belgian occupation of the Ruhr to seize debt-payments in kind, introduced a revised repayment scheme in 1924 (the Dawes Plan). Initially, this appeared to work, but the benefits could not last. In April 1930 the Young Plan tried to reschedule reparations yet again, but with German unemployment rising alarmingly, there was little choice but to cancel the debt entirely. This was done at the Lausanne Conference in July 1932. Britain and France, still under obligation to repay their war debts to the U.S.A., grew increasingly resentful, raising tariff barriers against the import of American goods and suffering the consequences when U.S. import tariffs were introduced in retaliation.

In such circumstances, the countries that should have been controlling the world economy were too weak and divided to do so effectively. This became apparent in the late 1920s, when the world economy virtually collapsed, heralding a period of high unemployment and social unrest known as "the Depression". The first signs appeared in the U.S.A. where, on 24 October 1929 ("Black Thursday"), the New York stock exchange ceased to function. Share prices, pushed up to unnatural heights by speculation, suddenly fell, leading to panic as investors tried desperately to sell before the shares became completely worthless. Much of the speculation had been financed by bank loans and, as the banks called in the debts, companies collapsed and money bcame difficult to raise. Prices of commodities fell as no-one could afford to buy, leading to hardship in the commodity-producing countries. As exports declined, countries tried to escape the spiral by borrowing money from international banks, only to find that their new debts often canceled out declining national profits. Money that should have been used for domestic industry or welfare, countering the effects of unemployment now that traditional methods of production had collapsed, had to be diverted, making the social problems worse. By 1932, unemployment in Germany was affecting more than 25 percent of the workforce, and the figures for Britain and the U.S.A. were not far behind.

With little chance of international co-operation, it had to be left to individual countries to deal with the Depression. In the U.S.A. Franklin D. Roosevelt was elected President in 1932 on the basis of a "New Deal" that involved increased government interference in economic matters, while in both Britain and France there was a dramatic swing to the political right, characterized by restrictions on wages and government spending. Similar policies were introduced in Italy and, after Hitler's rise to power in 1933, in Germany, enhancing the appeal of fascism. It was an unforeseen, long-term consequence of the First World War.

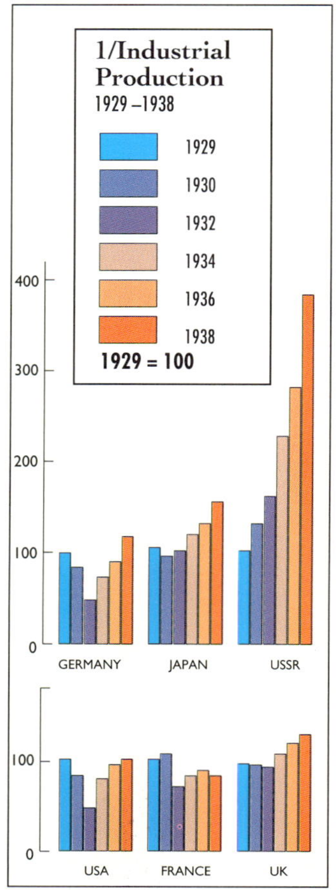

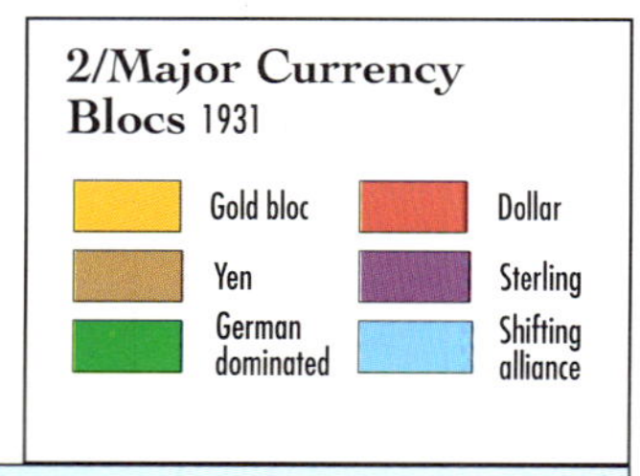

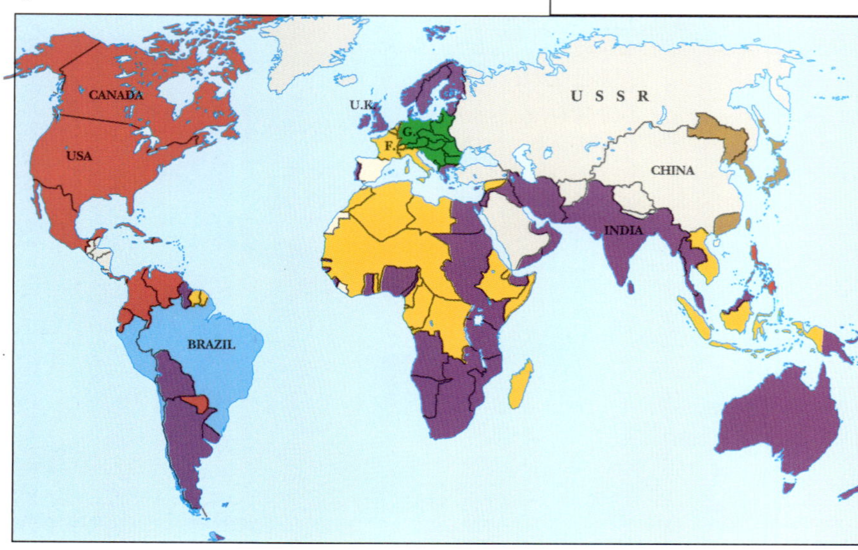

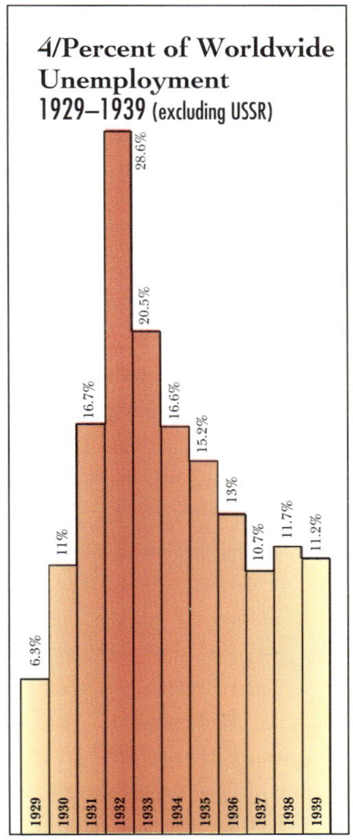

Unemployed Americans line up for cheap food in Bryant Park, New York in 1931. Many farmers finding that they no longer had a market for their produce, destroyed it – though thousands of jobless Americans found themselves reduced to destitution and want. Similar scenes could be viewed throughout the west.

"We are at the dead season of our fortunes. Our power of feeling or caring beyond the immediate questions of our own material well-being is temporarily eclipsed."

J.M. Keynes, British Economist

Communism and Fascism 1917 – 1934

The most important European state to be excluded from the peace settlement of 1919–23 was Russia. The reasons were simple: the Bolshevik (Communist) Revolution of 1917 had led to a separate treaty between Russia and Germany at Brest-Litovsk in March 1918, while the First World War was still being fought elsewhere, and the spread of communist ideas into eastern Europe and Germany after the war led to fears among the other powers. By the early 1920s, Russia was regarded as a "pariah" state, to be contained and marginalized.

This was not difficult to do. In the aftermath of the revolution, Russia had dissolved into civil war. Although Allied troops were sent to support the "White" factions against the communist "Reds", the latter's victory by mid-1920 led to Allied withdrawal. A Polish attack on Russia was similarly defeated by the Red Army, allowing Lenin to consolidate his power. He created the Union of Soviet Socialist Republics (USSR) in 1922 and gave precedence to domestic affairs, designed to increase economic strength of the state. When he died in 1924, a power struggle ensued, and it was not until 1929 that Joseph Stalin emerged as undisputed leader.

Stalin concentrated on building "socialism in one country", aiming to force Soviet industry to catch up with that of the capitalist West. His creation of collective farms and a succession of Five-Year Plans to improve heavy industry led to enormous human suffering – it is estimated, for example, up to 10 million peasants died during enforced collectivization – but Soviet industry did improve in the 1930s. By then, Stalin had begun to show a greater interest in international affairs, raising the spectre in many European minds of a spread of communism, destroying the existing instruments of government and condemning the people to the sort of hardship associated with left-wing totalitarianism.

But communism was not the only form of extreme politics to emerge during the inter-war period. As early as October 1922 in Italy, Benito Mussolini, leader of the *Fasci di Combattimento* (or Fascist Party) had seized power by marching on Rome. His mixture of charismatic oratory and authoritarian, right-wing policies appealed to many in Europe, especially those who feared the spread of communism and deplored the weakness of existing democratic governments, not least in their inability to deal effectively with post-war economic crises. This was particularly the case in Germany, where pro-communist groups had tried to seize power as early as 1919 and the newly-created Weimar Republic had been blamed for both economic hardship and the severity of the Versailles peace settlement. In 1923 Adolf Hitler, leader of the small National Socialist German Workers' (Nazi) Party, attempted a coup in Bavaria that led to his imprisonment and drew attention to his right-wing ideals. These ideals were further disseminated through his book *Mein Kampf* ("My Struggle"), written while he was in prison. His emphasis on the need to restore German "greatness", principally through overthrowing the Weimar Republic, ridding the country of Jews and other "non-Aryans" and defying the terms of Versailles, began to gain popularity in the early 1930s as Germany virtually collapsed under the economic crisis of the Depression.

The Nazis won substantial gains in the 1932 elections, becoming the largest single party in the *Reichstag* (parliament), and on 30 January 1933 Hitler was appointed Chancellor of Germany. Once in power, he moved swiftly to impose his rule, arresting political opponents and gaining unprecedented rights for himself and his party. By August 1934, when he assumed the title of *Führer* ("Leader"), the Nazis had created a dictatorship. Laws were enacted against the Jews, censorship imposed and rival political parties banned. These were not unpopular policies. At the same time, Hitler began to look for ways to reverse the Versailles settlement. It was the beginning of the road to renewed war in Europe.

Adolf Hitler photographed with General Ludendorff in 1923. The support of such eminent figures lent much credibility to the Nazi movement.

> *"It is blood that moves the wheels of history."*
>
> Benito Mussolini c.1919

1/The League of Nations
Founded 1920

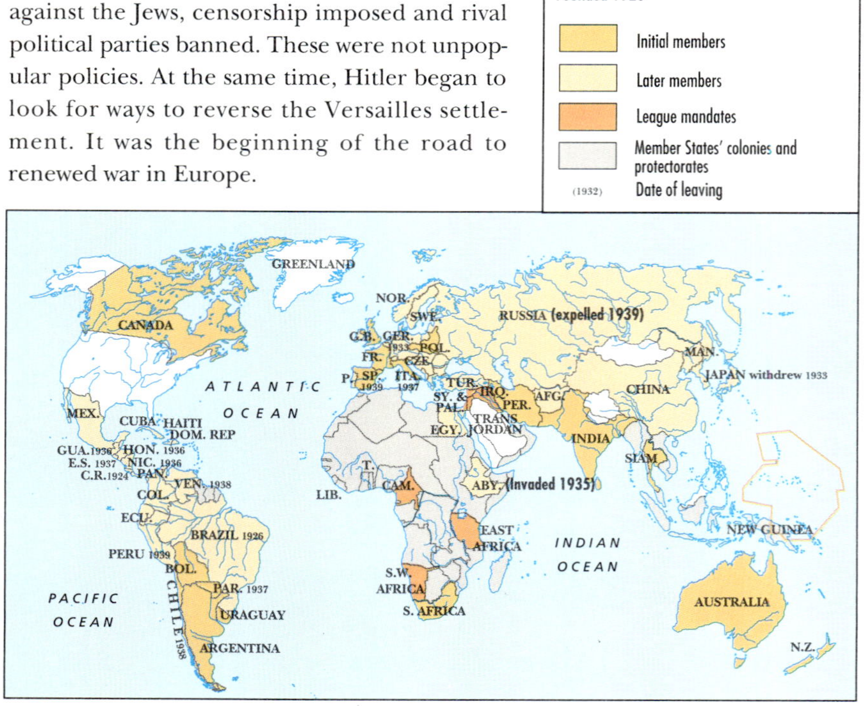

2/Europe Political
1934–35

- German–Polish Non-Aggression Pact, 1934
- Rome protocols, March 1934
- Franco–Soviet & Soviet–Czech pact, May 1935 (also '36–'37)

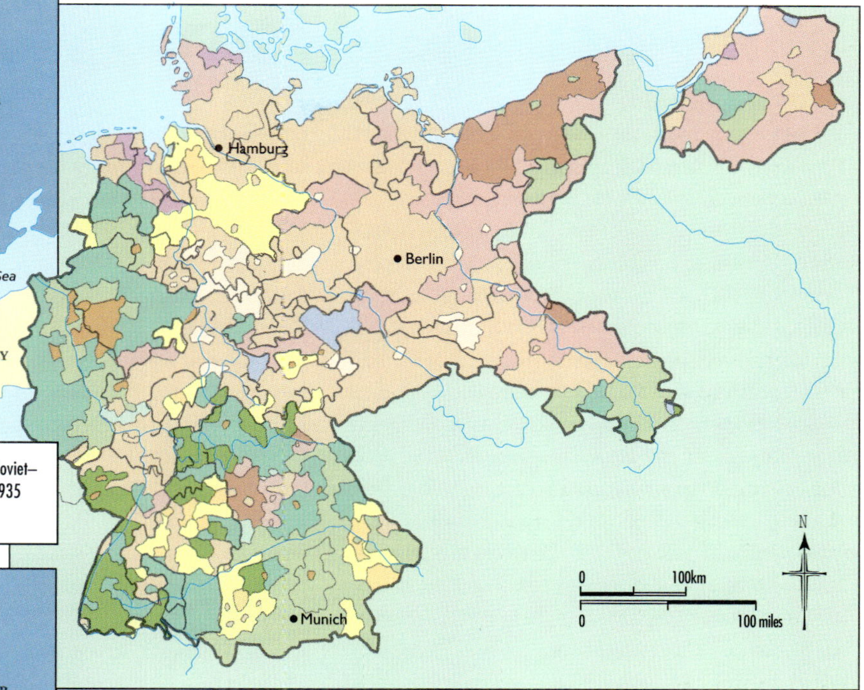

5/Germany Political
20 May 1928

- **SPD** (Social Democrats) 29.8%
- **Zentrum BVP** (Center; Bavarian People's Party) 15.2%
- **DNVP** (Nationalists) 14.3%
- **NSDAP** (National Socialists) 2.6%
- **KPD** (Communists) 10.6%
- **DVP** (German People's Party) 8.1%
- **Bauernpartei; Landbund** (Peasants' Party; Provincial Alliance) 5.1%
- **DDP** (Democrats) 4.3%
- **Mittelstand** (Middle–Class) 4.6%
- **Others** 4.2%

Proportional representation gives other parties (not shown) a share of representation in the Reichstag

3/Europe Political
1936–37

- Axis, Nov 1936–May 1939
- Neutrality declaration, 1936
- Franco–Soviet/Soviet–Czech pact 1937–37
- Anglo–Egyptian Treaty, 1936 (Egypt off map)

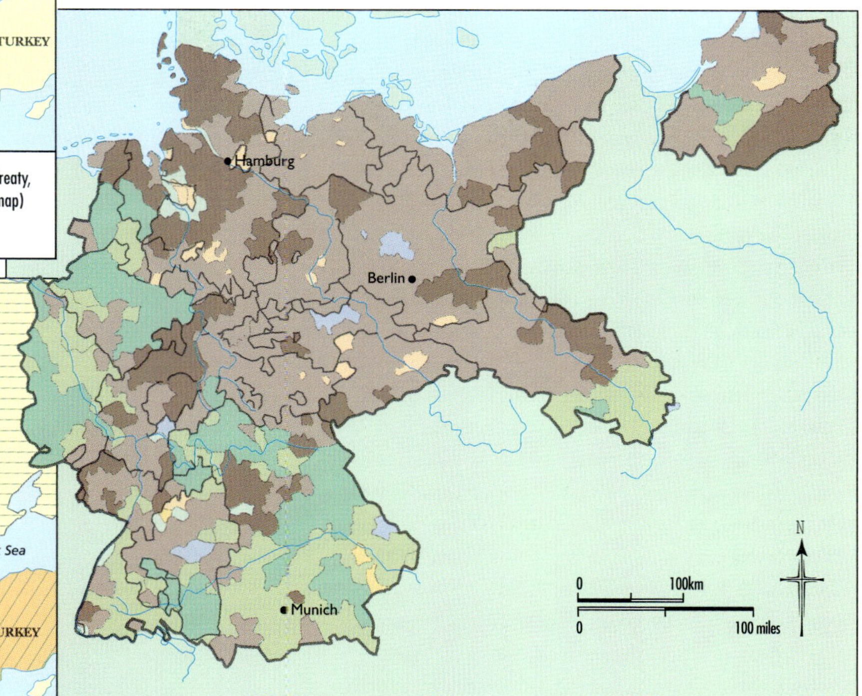

4/Europe Political
1938–39

- Copenhagen Neutrality Declaration, July 1938
- British and French guarantees for Poland, Greece, Turkey and Romania, 1939
- Anglo–Franco–Polish & Anglo–Franco–Turkish alliances, September 1939
- Anglo/French Staff Talks, Apr '36, May '38, Mar–June '39
- German/Soviet Non Aggression Pact, 1939

6/Germany Political
6 Nov 1932

- **SPD** (Social Democrats) 20.4%
- **Zentrum BVP** (Center; Bavarian People's Party) 15%
- **DNVP** (Nationalists) 8.3%
- **NSDAP** (National Socialists) 33.1%
- **KPD** (Communists) 16.9%
- **Bauernpartei; Landbund** (Peasants' Party; Provincial Alliance) 2.5%
- **DVP** (German People's Party) 1.9%
- **Staatspartei** (Official Party) 1%
- **Others** 0.9%

Proportional representation gives other parties (not shown) a share of representation in the Reichstag

Sino–Japanese Rivalry SEPTEMBER 1931 – DECEMBER 1941

Reasons for Sino–Japanese rivalry pre-dated World War I, reflecting both the weakness of China and, in the aftermath of Japanese victory over the Russians in 1904–05, the growing strength of Japan. China, riven by civil strife and dominated by outside powers such as Britain, the U.S.A. and Germany, which enjoyed unprecedented rights over Chinese trade and occupied key ports, suffered a revolution in 1911. Led by Sun Yet-sen, this took power away from the last of the Manchu emperors but soon found itself opposed by local warlords, who defied any attempt at central government. When Sun died in 1925, his National Party (*Kuomintang*) became much more militaristic and, led by Chiang Kai-shek, began to extend its influence by force. At the same time, communism emerged as an alternative political philosophy, put forward most effectively by Mao Tse-tung in south-central China in the late 1920s. Gaining support from the enormous peasant class, the communists posed a threat to *Kuomintang* control, leading to campaigns against them by Chiang in the early 1930s. By then, China was virtually ungovernable.

Such weakness attracted Japanese attention. Being an island nation, Japan depended for much of its economic power on imports of raw materials and exports of finished products to docile markets. China offered both. During World War I, Japan seized German assets and bases in China and, at the post-war peace conference, received international backing for their retention, much to the dismay of the Chinese delegation, which refused to sign the Versailles Treaty. This isolated China from world politics, allowing the Japanese to extend their economic influence unopposed. By the later 1920s, certain factions in Japan, led by the military, responded to the collapse of Chinese political control by arguing that it was in Japanese interests to seize the raw materials and markets it needed. On 30 September 1931, Japanese troops marched into Manchuria, completing their occupation of the province by early February 1932 having encountered little Chinese military resistance. Such was the popularity of the conquest in Japan that the military faction began to dominate domestic policies, fueled by a widespread feeling that Japan had been unfairly treated by the international community. In response to the invasion of Manchuria, Japan was widely condemned (although no other action was taken against her). Believing that her fate lay in her own hands, Japan withdrew from the League of Nations in February 1933, and, three years later, forged an alliance (the Anti-Comintern Pact) with Germany. On 5 June 1937, a new pro-military government took power in Tokyo. In July 1937, Japanese forces responded to a relatively minor clash with Chinese troops at the Marco Polo Bridge outside Peking by invading northern China, occupying Tientsin on 30 July and Peking itself on 8 August. A few days later fighting broke out in Shanghai and, as the Japanese poured in reinforcements, a major war developed. It was to continue until August 1945.

The fighting in China between 1937 and 1941 (when it widened out considerably in the aftermath of Japanese attacks on U.S., British and Dutch possessions in the Pacific and Far East) was bitter, made infinitely worse by Japanese racism. Two separate campaigns were fought, to the south of Peking and around Shanghai respectively, until, in early 1938, a Japanese offensive linked the two theaters. Thereafter, Japanese troops moved west, into central China, gradually slowing down as terrain and Chinese resistance posed problems. Continued prosecution of the war alarmed other powers, increasing the isolation of Japan and paving the way to a wider conflict.

Mao Tse-tung speaking at the third anniversary of the founding of the Chinese People's Anti-Japanese and Political College in Yenan, 1939. From 1940 there was an uneasy and often broken truce between the Communists and Chiang Kai-shek's nationalists, based around Chungking, 500 miles to the south. Between the two armies existed remnants of warlord armies whom the Japanese could cooperate with or exploit.

A Japanese tank enters Chengteh in the province of Jehol, 1933.

1/Chinese Warlords 1926

2/The Expansion of Japan
1920–1941

The Road to War in Europe MARCH 1935 – AUGUST 1939

The failure of the League of Nations to deal effectively with the Japanese invasion of Manchuria augured ill for the future security of the world and particularly of Europe. In the absence of collective international action, fascist expansionism could not be countered, and as early as 1935, when Mussolini ordered Italian troops to invade Abyssinia (Ethiopia), the weakness of the League was manifest. Although economic sanctions were imposed on Italy, most members of the League chose to ignore them. By 1936 Abyssinia was firmly in Italian hands, posing a threat to British and French possessions in North and East Africa.

Hitler watched these developments with interest. Once in power, he began systematically to test the League, particularly the British and French, in an effort to overturn the Versailles Treaty and reunite those parts of Germany that had been handed over to other states. Only then would Germany be strong enough to support his main policy – the occupation of vast areas of eastern Europe as *Lebensraum* ("living space") for the Nazi master race. In 1935 Hitler openly defied Versailles by reintroducing conscription to the German armed forces, and a year later he sent his troops to reoccupy the demilitarized Rhineland. Although they protested, neither Britain nor France made any move to stop him. Indeed, when Neville Chamberlain became Prime Minister of Britain in 1937, he initiated a policy known as "appeasement", designed to negotiate over Hitler's demands.

By then, the League had been further tested, this time over international aid to the rival factions in the Spanish Civil War. This had its origins in July 1936 when a right-wing coalition of conservatives and army officers ("Nationalists") carried out a coup in Spanish Morocco and then, under the command of General Francisco Franco, invaded mainland Spain, attacked positions held on behalf of the existing left-wing government ("Republicans"), and thereby initiated a bitter civil war that was to continue until April 1939. During the conflict, Franco was openly supported by both the Italians and Germans, the latter providing not only transportation from Morocco to Spain but also a *Kondor Legion* of troops, tanks, artillery and aircraft. Their use, not least in the bombing of the

Members of the Spanish Foreign Legion – which formed part of Franco's Nationalist army – are photographed in company with an armed nurse.

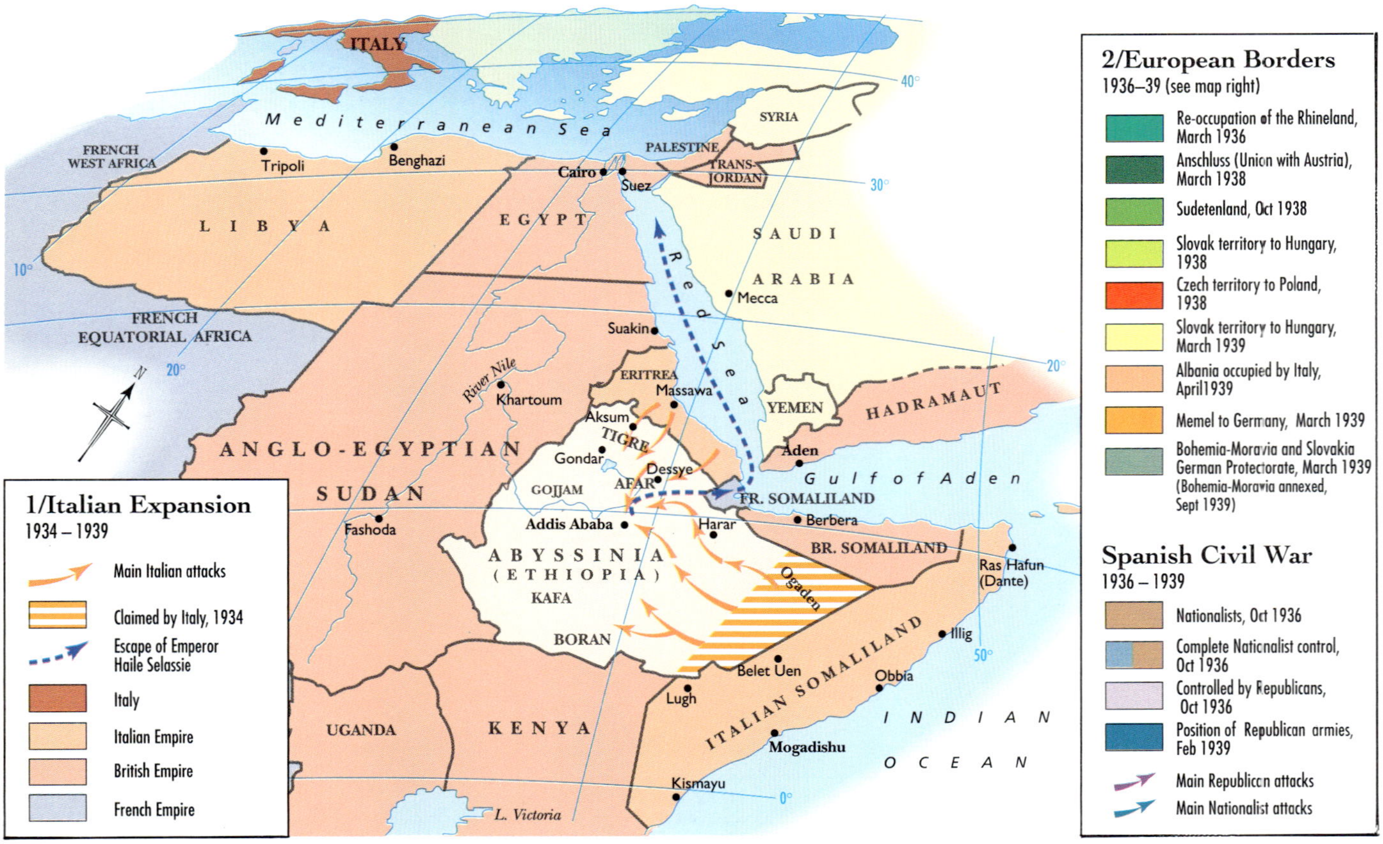

Basque town of Guernica in April 1937, did much to engender fears elsewhere in Europe about the growing strength of Hitler's armed forces. By comparison, the Republicans received little direct aid; some equipment was provided by the Soviets, and "International Brigades" of left-wing volunteers were raised, but the impact was small. Britain and France, intent on non-intervention, stood on the sidelines, rendering the League of Nations impotent.

Such ineffectiveness was noted by Hitler, who began to increase pressure for the expansion of the *Reich.* On 12 March 1938 he sent troops into Austria and imposed an *Anschluss* (union with Germany). Then in the summer of 1938, Hitler turned his attention toward Czechoslovakia, demanding the right of the Sudetenland to be ruled by Germany. A conference was called in Munich to discuss the issue and, in the absence of any Czech representative, an agreement was signed in late September which dismembered Czechoslovakia. Six months later, Hitler sent his troops into Prague to seize the rest of the country, while Mussolini, taking advantage of crises elsewhere, invaded Albania. On 22 May 1939, Hitler and Mussolini concluded a full-scale alliance – the "Pact of Steel".

These moves finally mobilized the British and French, who began actively to prepare for possible war. They also issued guarantees to Poland, Greece and Romania, promising military assistance if any of them was attacked. Hitler, with his eyes on Poland, countered such promises by approaching the Soviets. Stalin, aware of his own weakness and annoyed that he had not been consulted over Czechoslovakia, agreed to a pact, signed on 23 August 1939, which effectively partitioned Poland. Hitler was free to make his move, even though it was guaranteed to result in war with the Western Allies.

"How horrible, fantastic, incredible it is, that we should be digging trenches and trying on gas-masks here because of a quarrel in a faraway country between people of whom we know nothing."

Neville Chamberlain

European Armed Forces in 1939

The major European powers – Britain, France, Germany, Italy and the Soviet Union – prepared for war in the late 1930s. By the time it broke out in September 1939, all five countries were more or less on a war footing, having pursued deliberate policies of rearmament in response to existing conflicts or to perceived threats. However, the size and effectiveness of those armed forces varied considerably, as did the doctrines with which they would go to war. The balance of forces was unequal.

Of the five, Germany had done most to create modern forces capable of fighting a new style of war. Hitler's decision to flout the terms of the Versailles Treaty and reintroduce conscription in 1935 had not caused any reaction from Britain or France, enabling him to expand his army from 100,000 men to 730,000 in less than four years. At the same time, he authorized the recreation of the Luftwaffe – again, in defiance of Versailles – and increased its size from 36 to more than 8000 combat aircraft, while ordering the construction of new battleships and submarines. In the process, defense expenditure was increased from less than a billion *Reichsmarks* in 1932 to more than 17 billion by 1939.

But size alone did not make the German armed forces a threat. One of the advantages enjoyed by Hitler was that he was effectively starting from scratch, creating forces that were not saddled with out-of-date ideas or clogged with reactionary generals. Such ideas and officers did undoubtedly exist – the reluctance of some members of the General Staff to accept the concept of *blitzkrieg* in 1939–40 proves that – but the opportunity to experiment was there. The first of the panzer divisions was created as early as 1935, comprising a balanced "mix" of armor, mechanized infantry, artillery, airpower and engineers, and although the bulk of the German Army remained dependent on marching infantry and horse-drawn transport, its spearheads gained the full potential of mobility at a time when most of their projected enemies were virtually static. When it is added that by 1935 the Luftwaffe was concentrating on the role of close support to ground forces rather than strategic bombing of enemy cities, it can be seen that inter-service links were strong. This was further reflected in the equipment available. The early panzers may have been small and only lightly armored by the standards of 1944–45, but they were fast and mechanically quite reliable; in the air, the Junkers Ju-87 *Stuka* may have been obsolete when pitted against modern interceptors like the Spitfire, but its impact on ground troops without air cover could be devastating. When all these factors were taken together – the panzers and their supporting arms probing for and then exploiting lines of least resistance to unhinge and paralyze enemy defenses – the results could be dramatic. Many of the ingredients of *blitzkrieg* had been tested in Spain during the civil war (1936–39), giving the Germans recent combat experience.

Hitler's emphasis on his ground and air forces reflected both his own experience of war and the difficulties inherent in creating a large ocean-going navy quickly. Even if he had been a strong advocate of naval power, it was unlikely that enough could have been achieved in terms of ship-building by 1939. As it was, his preference for land campaigns left the navy less prepared for war than its commanders would have liked. They may have taken possession of powerful "pocket battleships" by 1939, and the U-boat arm was by no means weak, but the navy was up against the British and French – two of the strongest naval powers of the time. When war began the German Navy felt that it was not fully prepared.

This problem appeared to be solved, at least in part, by the alliance with Italy, for the Italian Navy boasted 240 major warships by 1939. These were confined to the Mediterranean, but their presence there would divert British and French naval forces away from the North Atlantic, balancing the odds for the Germans in what was clearly going to be a decisive theater. Unfortunately, the Italian Navy was intimidated by the British and French Mediterranean fleets and did not achieve the results required, not least because Mussolini declined to declare war until June 1940. His reluctance was perhaps understandable, for of all the major powers Italy was least prepared for war in 1939. Not only were her armed forces committed to East and North Africa, far distant from the main theater of conflict, but their reputation was not impressive. The invasion of Abyssinia (Ethiopia) in 1935–36 was widely seen as having been achieved by sheer weight of numbers rather than military expertise, and the Italian Army particularly was known to contain men whose commitment to war-fighting was low. Nevertheless, with 400,000 soldiers available, backed by an air force with recent combat experience in both Abyssinia and Spain, the Italian forces could not be ignored.

The unknown quantity in 1939 was the Soviets. Not only was it unclear which side Stalin would support – the Soviet-German Pact of late August 1939 came as quite a shock to the rest of Europe – but the fighting prowess of the Soviet armed forces was untested. Since the Bolshevik victory in the civil war of the early 1920s, Stalin had undoubtedly used the forces as instruments of politicization, ensuring loyalty from a disparate people by ordering conscription that included political education as well as military training. Moreover, in 1937 Stalin had displayed his fear of military power by instigating widespread purges of the officer class, weakening leadership and command potential. However, the Soviet forces were strong – nearly two million men in the army alone by 1939, backed by more than 10,000 combat aircraft – and they were known to have indulged in experiments that implied a degree of sophistication. During maneuvers in the mid-1930s, for example, Soviet armored formations had shown off their mobility, while parachutists had been used to seize strongpoints in the "enemy" rear, Like Hitler, Stalin was not a sea-going animal – the Soviet Navy in 1939 comprised only 100 warships, many of them coastal protection vessels – but no-one could afford to dismiss his land and air capabilities.

That left the British and French, both of whom had been forced to rearm quickly once the threat from Germany became apparent in the late 1930s. The French suffered from a number of problems, many of which were legacies of World War I. Although they maintained an army of 500,000, a significant proportion were tied to static defenses along the border with Germany, manning the Maginot Line as an elaborate "trench system" designed to deter attack. Other formations were stationed abroad, in Indo-China, the Middle East and Africa, to protect French colonies, leaving relatively few to adopt the sort of mobile operations that modern war was demanding. Some French officers, notably Charles de Gaulle, were aware of the new methods, but they could do little to prepare the forces in time, particularly as French politicians preferred a defensive strategy. One of the results of such preference was the lack of a large air force: by 1939 the French had just over 300 combat aircraft, tied to support of defensive ground forces. Only the navy was strong, reflecting the French need to secure sea-lanes worldwide, although the total of 161 major warships was divided between the Mediterranean and Atlantic theaters, lacking concentration. Throughout the armed forces, there was a reluctance for war, based on memories of 1914–18.

Britain suffered from similar problems. As soon as World War I ended, the British Army returned to its peace-time size and duties, being reduced from more than three million men to less than 500,000 in a matter of months. By the 1930s, this figure had been reduced further to a total of less than 250,000 regulars, many of whom were strewn around the world in defense of the Empire. In the aftermath of the Munich Crisis in late 1938 the army was increased – in May 1939 conscription was reintroduced and the size of the Territorial Army doubled – but these figures were illusory, disguising the real lack of recent combat experience in a European setting. Nor had the lessons of World War I been heeded, for although some experiments with tanks (a British invention) had been conducted between 1927 and 1934, they had been curtailed to save money and condemned as inappropriate to colonial policing. The same was true of the Royal Air Force, for although its size was impressive in 1939 – a total of 7900 combat aircraft – many of the designs were obsolete and many were earmarked for strategic bombing, leaving too few to support ground forces. As with the French, Britain's real strength lay at sea, where the Royal Navy enjoyed a superiority in experience and expertise over all its European rivals. With 290 major warships available, many of which could be concentrated in the Atlantic or Home Waters as long as the French remained active in the Mediterranean, the Royal Navy was a force that its enemies could not ignore.

Conscripted in 1939–40 into a Scottish regiment in an expanding British Army, this group is made up of the new citizen soldiers typical of many nations. It includes artists, artisans, mechanics and musicians. By 1945 only two had survived – the man on the left and the man with the guitar.

PART II
The Axis Ascendant

Reasons for Axis success between September 1939 and June 1942 are not difficult to find. The eagerness with which many Germans went to war, intent on reversing the defeat of 1918, contrasted sharply with the attritions of resignation seen in both Britain and France, where lack of preparation for war had reflected political desires to avoid a repetition of 1914–18. By the same token, when Japanese aggression was added in late 1941, it was aimed principally against a country, the U.S.A., that had chosen to remain aloof from the problems of the world since the end of the previous conflict. In addition, the methods of warfare employed by the Axis powers were, in most cases, far superior to those of the Allies, enabling substantial gains to be made at little real cost. In retrospect, the seeds of Axis defeat may be discernable during these early months, but at the time the Germans and Japanese seemed to be unstoppable.

Hitler's war between 1939 and 1941 has been aptly described as "total war by instalments", with each campaign carefully planned to be short and decisive before moving on to the next. In the early stages this worked well, helped by a style of warfare, known as *blitzkrieg*, which depended on speed and mobility to achieve results. In Poland, it took less than a month to gain complete victory, and there is little doubt that the outcome would have been the same regardless of Soviet involvement. The German combination of air superiority and fast-moving armored spearheads, seeking out and exploiting "lines of least resistance", confused and paralyzed the Poles, while their dependence on obsolete horsed cavalry merely highlighted the tragedy. One result of the campaign was an Anglo-French declaration of war on Germany, but this had little immediate effect. Hitler was able to pause to recover strength, then choose the next theater of conflict, this time Scandinavia. Once Denmark had been taken and Norway invaded, the Allies were already stretched; when the Germans attacked France and the Low Countries in May 1940, they were also outfought. The panzer attack through the "impassable" Ardennes was a master-stroke, catching the Allies wrong-footed, and when this coincided with advances into Holland and Belgium, there was little alternative but withdrawal.

There were weaknesses to *blitzkrieg*, however, many of which became apparent when Hitler, after another pause, turned his attention towards the Soviet Union in June 1941. The attack on France and the Low Countries had enjoyed the advantage of achievable objectives, allowing the panzers to stop after a short campaign. In the east, things were different, for with objectives that were up to 700 miles beyond the start-line, the armored spearhead encountered problems that proved to be insurmountable. Not only were they drawn deep into the Soviet Union, where deteriorating weather destroyed momentum, but their supply and support echelons could not keep up. Soviet counterattacks in late 1941 may not have led to German defeat, but they ensured that Hitler could no longer afford to fight by instalments. He was now committed to a fight to the death.

The same was true elsewhere. Italian failures in both the Balkans and North Africa in 1940 and early 1941 drew German forces into those theaters, stretching resources, while the failure of the Luftwaffe to prepare the way for an invasion of Britain in the summer of 1940 left a thorn in the Germans' western flank. Thus, although the string of German victories in 1939, 1940 and 1941 was impressive, none was taken to its full potential. In the west, coun-

Benito Mussolini photographed in 1941.

German troops in Paris after the capitulation of France, 1940.

tries may have fallen like ripe plums but the continued defiance of Britain meant that Hitler could not afford to devote his full attention to the east, particularly as he also needed to divert troops to the Balkans and North Africa. Finally, although German efforts at sea were equally impressive, not least in terms of a U-boat campaign against Allied shipping, the lack of coordination between the submarine and surface elements of the German fleet enabled the British to hold on until joined by the immense potential of the U.S.A. Once the Americans began to mobilize their industry and manpower, there was little that Hitler could do to match them.

None of this should be allowed to disguise the very real nature of Allied defeats in the early years of the war. Both Britain and France displayed weaknesses in 1940 that were a clear reflection of their lack of political, economic and military preparation for war, and although the British could take some comfort from their ability to face the threatened German invasion and to defeat the Italians in North and East Africa, their recovery from the early disasters was slow. It was made infinitely worse by the sudden Japanese attack in late 1941, when it became obvious that survival in Europe and the Mediterranean had been ensured by a neglect of possessions in the Far East. The rapid fall of Malaya, Hong Kong, Singapore and Burma showed just how stretched the British really were and how dependent on the Americans they were likely to become. Once the war became global, Britain was effectively out of her league.

The same could be said of the Japanese, for although their gains in late 1941 and early 1942 were extensive, their armed forces were left with an empire that was too large to hold against a power with the potential of the U.S.A. Just as the Germans were overstretched and vulnerable by 1942, so were the Japanese, and both were pitted against embryonic superpowers. The Axis had escalated the war to one of totality, in which the aim became the complete destruction of enemy states using all human and material resources available, seeking out and destroying the enemy wherever he could be found. In these circumstances, regardless of initial victories, neither Berlin nor Tokyo had the means to fight such a war indefinitely; in terms of manpower, access to resources and industrial wealth, their enemies held the advantage, and the fact that Britain, the Soviet Union and the U.S.A. still survived meant that the balance was already tilting away from the Axis powers. The war still had to run its bloody course, but by mid-1942 its outcome, despite appearances, was already laid down.

A German U-boat shells a British merchantman. Painted by H.R. Butler.

The Greater German Reich

During the 1930s Hitler created a unique position of authority for himself: head of state, head of government, head of party and supreme commander, all combined in the title of Führer of the German People. But it was the fact that Adolf Hitler was the Führer that gave the office its authority and he was determined not to see it institutionalized or defined. The Weimar constitution was never formally replaced; the constitutional rights of the citizen were only "suspended" by emergency decree, never repealed. The sole constitutional basis of the Nazi regime was a single law, the Enabling Act, passed by the Reichstag in March 1933, giving the Cabinet the power to enact laws. As the Cabinet met less and less frequently, not at all after February 1938, this meant Hitler; in fact laws were soon replaced by decrees.

But Hitler was not interested in the day-to-day business of government, and more and more withdrew from it, concentrating on his long-term interests of foreign policy, re-armament and war. He left the more powerful of the Nazi leaders – Goering, Himmler, Ley, Goebbels – free, not only to build up rival empires, but to feud with each other and with the established ministries in a continuing fight to take over parts of each others' territory. The result has been variously described as "authoritarian anarchy", "permanent improvization", "administrative chaos" – very different from the outside world's picture of a monolithic totalitarian state.

Such a state of affairs suited Hitler very well. His chief lieutenants competed for his support and turned to him for decisions, while he retained the freedom to make arbitrary interventions, whenever he chose to, so keeping the civil service unsure of his intentions. At the same time, Hitler outflanked it by setting up special agencies for tasks he regarded as urgent, in effect creating an alternative state. The three most powerful of these agencies were the Four Year Plan headed by Goering – which absorbed an increasing share of the German economy and eventually the economies of the occupied countries as well; the fusion of the police and the Gestapo (secret police) with Himmler's black-shirted SS security corps – so removing the police function and the power of coercion from the state and placing it in the hands of a body unknown to the constitution and responsible only to Hitler himself; and Ley's Labor Front.

With the war, Hitler began to lose confidence in Goering and set up a new Reich ministry for armament and munitions, headed first by Fritz Todt and then by Albert Speer. In 1942 Goering suffered another loss when the recruitment of millions of prisoners of war and foreign workers to provide labor for the war economy was given to Fritz Sauckel. As Goering lost power, Himmler's steadily grew, giving him responsibility for racist policy (including the extermination of the Jews), an SS army, the Waffen SS, more than 900,000-strong and as well or better equipped than the regular army, and an economic empire based on the concentration, and labor camps.

On coming to power, Hitler swept away the existing federal structure of Germany, replacing the state by thirty-two *Gaue* (or party districts), each headed by a Nazi party *Gauleiter* appointed by the Führer, who was at the same time the local representative of the state (*Reichstatthalter*), just as Hitler was head of the Nazi Party and of the German Reich.

The annexation of Austria and the break up of the Czechoslovak and Polish states in 1938–39 led to the creation of 7 Austrian *Gaue*, the Sudetenland, and Danzig-West Prussia and the Wartheland.

In accordance with Hitler's long-term plans, Bohemia and Moravia were destined to become part of the *Lebensraum* ("living space") of the German people. As a first step Bohemia and Moravia were made a protectorate under

Adolf Hitler photographed at a Nazi rally in Dortmund in 1933.

German control and brought into the Greater German Reich. But for the duration of the war the contribution the skilled Czech population under German direction could make to the German war economy took priority over their resettlement to the east.

The racist Germanization of Eastern Europe was entrusted to Himmler and the SS. If it had to be postponed in Bohemia and Moravia, Himmler was given a free hand with the much larger Slav and Jewish population of Poland. His plans were carried out with great brutality, in two stages. The first involved executing the Polish leadership, local as well as national, and forcing Jews and Poles out of the newly-annexed territories (West Prussia and Wartheland) into the General Government (occupied Polish territory incorporated into the German Reich). The second stage involved "the Final Solution of the Jewish problem" in the extermination camps sited in the General Government, and drafting in ethnic Germans to replace the Poles, who were to be reduced to slave labor. The Germanization of Poland, however, was cut short by the return of the Red Army which drove the Germans out by the beginning of 1945.

Reichsmarshall Hermann Goering, painted by Hugo Lehmann.

Hitler's Europe – November 1942

With hindsight, November 1942 can be seen as the peak of Hitler's success. In the East, at the beginning of the month, the German Army had reached Stalingrad and the Caucasus; German control of the rest of continental Europe and North Africa was unchallenged. By the end of the month, however, though hardly recognizable at the time, the tide had turned. First in North Africa, where the British and Americans had landed at one end and defeated Rommel at the other, and then at Stalingrad, where the Russians had surrounded the German Sixth Army. It took another two and a half years to complete Hitler's defeat, in the process replacing German with Soviet occupation of Eastern and Central Europe.

Apart from the five neutral countries, Spain, Portugal, Switzerland, Sweden and Turkey, in November 1942 the whole of continental Europe in one form or another was occupied by, or dependent on, Nazi Germany. Its core was the Greater German Reich including Bohemia-Moravia and Poland which were to be Germanized in Hitler's New Order. The people of Eastern Europe were regarded as *Untermenschen*, "sub-humans", and were treated accordingly.

Eastern Europe, including Russia west of the Urals, was earmarked for Hitler's objective of a German racist empire which was to be colonized by ethnic Germans. All Jews were to be eliminated and all Slavs not required to form a slave population to serve the Germans were to be deported. Until this could be realized, occupied Russia was divided into two Reichskommissariats, Ostland (the Baltic States and Belorussia) and the Ukraine, governed by two Nazi veterans and *Gauleiters*, Heinrich Lohse and Erich Koch, and three zones of Western Russia under German military administration. Following the decision to exterminate the Jewish population of Europe, numbering 10.5 million, about 6 million Jews were either massacred, or put to death in the extermination camps in Poland.

Besides a number of strategic areas such as Salonika and Crete, Germany also remained in occupation of half of Croatia and of Serbia, where the partisan forces led by Tito maintained their guerrilla warfare and emerged victorious at the end of the war.

The peoples of Western Europe were regarded as Aryans and there were no plans for deportation and resettlement comparable with those for the East. Until 11 November 1942, France was divided into an occupied and an unoccupied zone. With an eye to the threat of an Allied invasion, the occupied zone was placed under German military administration; in the unoccupied zone a French government, with its capital at Vichy, was allowed to enjoy the illusion of independence until the Allied landing in North Africa, when it too was occupied and brought under German military administration.

Both Denmark (until 1943) and Norway, although under military occupation, were allowed to retain governments of their own, under German supervision. Holland was placed under a German civil administration, Belgium with the two French departments of Nord and Pas-de-Calais (again with an eye to invasion) under a German military administration. The majority of the peoples of Western Europe, for practical reasons, collaborated. The heaviest burden on them was the constantly increasing demands of the Germans on their industry and agriculture and the conscription of labor.

Italy, as Germany's principal ally (to be occupied by the Germans in 1943 after Mussolini's fall), had already acquired Albania and in 1941, after Yugoslavia's defeat, was rewarded with the occupation of a large share of her territory as well as the occupation of Greece.

Germany's other allies (Hungary, Romania and Bulgaria) received territory at the expense of Yugoslavia, Greece and the Soviet Union. Slovakia, separated from the Czech lands,

A Dutch anti-Nazi cartoon depicting Hitler, Goering and Goebbels as the Riders of the Apocalypse.

became a German protectorate with its own government.

In practice, Hitler's Europe was a series of improvizations. In addition to the uncertainties of war, throughout the eastern half of Europe there was a perpetual conflict between meeting the demands of the German war economy from the occupied countries and Hitler's and Himmler's pressure to drive out or dispossess the native Slav population and replace them with ethnic Germans. The chance to win the cooperation of the Ukrainians, for example, was thrown away by the insistence of *Gauleiter* Koch that they were *Untermenschen*, who could only be ruled with the knout.

Even after the occupation of the whole of France, Laval and other French collaborators still hoped that France might save its national identity by becoming Germany's foremost partner in Hitler's new European order. As for the smaller countries Hitler assumed that after victory Denmark, Norway, the Low Countries and a broad band of territory in north-east France as well as Alsace Lorraine would be incorporated in the Greater German Reich.

Such proposals depended upon German victory. Once the possibility of that was removed, in 1943, Hitler's planned New Order was consigned to the trashcan of history.

German–Soviet Invasion of Poland

SEPTEMBER – OCTOBER 1939

The German invasion of Poland began at dawn on 1 September 1939. It caught the Poles largely unprepared, for although some form of attack had been anticipated, Polish mobilization had been slow and the deployment of existing forces was poor. The bulk of the Polish Army, about one million strong, with 475 tanks, over 2800 artillery pieces and 445 aircraft available, was deployed close to the borders of East Prussia, Pomerania, Silesia and Slovakia, with reserves in the center of the country to protect the approaches to Warsaw. Commanded by Marshal Edward Smigly-Rydz, it lacked mobility and its command structure was over-centralized, leaving it with few options once battle was joined. Some forces had also to be kept back in case of a Soviet attack from the east.

The Germans were much stronger, fielding more than 1.5 million men, 2511 tanks, nearly 10,000 artillery pieces and 1393 combat aircraft. They were divided into two separate formations: Army Group North (General Fedor von Bock) in Pomerania and East Prussia, tasked with seizing the Polish Corridor and threatening Warsaw from the north, and Army Group South (General Gerd von Rundstedt) in Silesia and Slovakia, tasked with destroying Polish forces on the border before approaching Warsaw from the west and south. The initial intention was to break through and encircle enemy armies along the River Vistula, exploiting their inherent lack of mobility. As the campaign developed, this was altered to a deeper encirclement on the River Bug. In both cases, the emphasis was on speed of advance, but the campaign was not pure *blitzkrieg*; German panzer and light divisions were not concentrated, being used instead to enhance the fighting power of conventional infantry.

However, certain aspects of the campaign did give warning of what was to come. On the morning of 1 September, German aircraft carried out pre-emptive strikes against Polish airfields, designed to destroy the Polish Air Force and seize air superiority. Although these attacks were not universally successful – enough of the Polish Air Force survived to inflict significant damage on the Luftwaffe, which was to lose over 500 aircraft destroyed or badly damaged during the four-week campaign – they did allow the ground forces to begin their advance free from air interference. In the north, the Polish Corridor was breached by 5 September, opening up communications between Pomerania and East Prussia for the first time since 1920; further east, Roznan was taken on the same day, raising the possibility of an armored thrust toward Brest-Litovsk. Meanwhile, Army Group South had penetrated border defenses, exploiting gaps between Polish armies, and was close to capturing both Krakow and Tarnow. By 7 September, elements of the German Tenth Army were within 40 miles of Warsaw.

Polish attempts to consolidate were rendered impossible by the pace of the German advance. The Polish Poznan Army did manage to mount a spirited counterattack along the River Bzura on 9 September, which caused some problems for von Rundstedt, but a swift redeployment of German units reversed the situation. By 16 September, the Bzura "pocket" had been contained and, under heavy air attack, the remains of the

A smiling Hitler salutes his troops as they advance into Poland. The Poles could muster almost as many infantry as the Germans but their line was too far spread to resist the lightning assaults launched on 1 September.

1/Planned German Offensive 31 August 1939

Poznan Army collapsed two days later. By then, the Soviets had committed two Fronts (army groups) to an advance from the east, meeting little resistance. As German armies closed in on Warsaw from north and south, subjecting the city to deliberate terror-bombing, the campaign drew to a close. Warsaw surrendered on 27 September, although the government had by then withdrawn to Romania, intent on continuing the fight now that Britain and France, having declared war on Germany on 3 September, were directly involved. By then, the Polish armed forces had ceased to exist – although 100,000 Poles escaped, nearly 700,000 had been captured and nearly 200,000 killed or wounded. Soviet casualties numbered some 2600, but the campaign had cost the Germans about 15,000 killed and 30,000 wounded.

Poland was split between the Germans and Soviets along the line of the River Bug, with Hitler incorporating the Polish Corridor and Teschen region into Germany, leaving the rest of the western zone to be administered by a civilian body known as the Government-General. The Soviets occupied the eastern zone, including Galicia and the Polish Ukraine, and took the opportunity to consolidate their positions in the Baltic States – by 10 October, Estonia, Latvia and Lithuania, now effectively surrounded, had been forced to accept "mutual assistance pacts" with Moscow that were no more than excuses for Soviet occupation.

"I was shocked at what had become of the beautiful city I had known – ruined and burnt-out houses, starving and grieving people. Warsaw was a dead city."

Walter Schellenberg, German Foreign Intelligence Service

A Heinkel He-111 disgorges its bomb load over a Polish city. Despite the Luftwaffe's pre-emptive raids against Polish airfields, the bombers still met with fierce opposition from what remained of Poland's ill-equipped airforce.

The Winter War NOVEMBER 1939 – MARCH 1940

The ease with which the Soviets extended their influence into the Baltic States in October 1939 helped to persuade Stalin that the time was ripe for further expansion. On 12 October, he approached the Finns with the offer of a treaty that would cede eastern Karelia to Finland in exchange for concessions on the Karelian Isthmus, north of Leningrad, and in the Gulf of Finland. Having witnessed Soviet actions in eastern Poland and the Baltic States, the Finns were understandably wary, fearing that the treaty would be just the beginning of "Sovietization" of their country. On 13 November the negotiations fell through, triggering a Soviet attack on Finland, soon to be known as the "Winter War", that was initially disastrous for the Soviet Army.

Soviet plans were ambitious, based on an assumption that the Finns would be unable to mount a viable defense. Over 600,000 men were deployed along the border, divided into four armies. In the far north, the Soviet Fourteenth Army was poised to advance toward Petsamo, after which it would move south to reinforce the Ninth Army, aiming to advance across the center of Finland to the Gulf of Bothnia, bisecting the country. Meanwhile, further south, the Eighth Army was to assault Finnish positions around Lake Ladoga, diverting attention from the main attack, by the Seventh and Thirteenth Armies, into the Karelian Isthmus, threatening Viipuri. The campaign was not expected to be lengthy – chiefly because the Finns had no more than 150,000 soldiers available, with virtually no armor or heavy artillery support.

This proved to be a costly error of judgment. The Soviet armies were not co-ordinated and the attacks began at just about the worst time of year, when the weather in southern Finland, although cold, was not sufficiently severe to freeze the lakes or rivers to an extent that would allow them to be used as avenues of advance for armored or mechanized formations. In addition, the cloud cover was low, precluding the use of air support, while the Finns, although outnumbered, were determined to defend their state. Thus, despite apparent Soviet successes in the first few days after the war began on 30 November, the fighting quickly assumed a deadly attritional nature as Finnish troops, familiar with the terrain and climate, consolidated their positions. In the far north, Petsamo fell to the Soviets, while further south elements of Ninth Army pushed forward to seize Suomussalmi and Kuhmo, but progress was slow around Lake Ladoga and halted completely in the Karelian Isthmus when men of the Seventh Army came up against prepared defenses on the Mannerheim Line. A set-piece attack against the Line was broken up by the Finns in late December.

By then, the Soviet plan had collapsed. In the north and center, Finnish ski-troops blocked forest tracks and mounted guerrilla-style attacks

Camouflaged Finnish machine-gunners train their weapons on the Soviet invaders. Despite possessing only antiquated equipment, the Finns were able to offer unexpectedly stout resistance, even managing to immobilize many Soviet tanks with nothing more than makeshift bottle bombs known as Molotov Cocktails.

A church in the Finnish capital, Helsinki, is destroyed by incendiary bombs dropped by the Red Air Force.

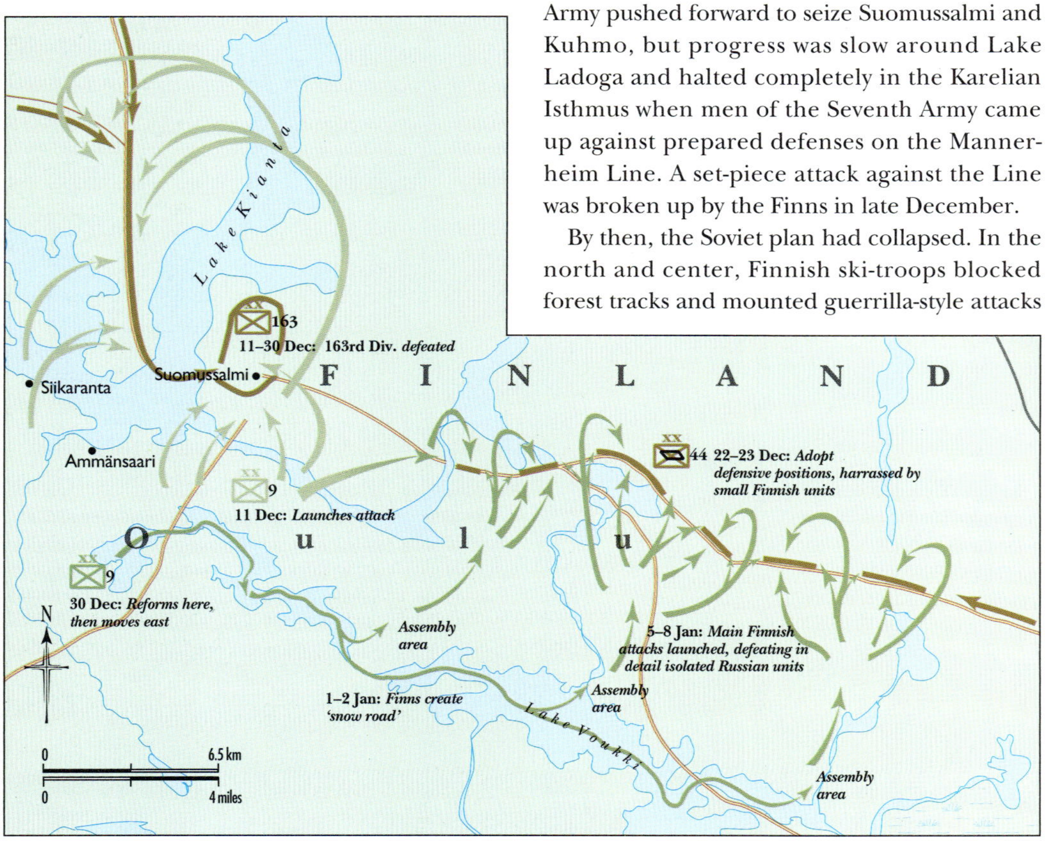

1/Battle of Suomussalmi
11 December 1939 – 8 January 1940

11–28 Dec 1939
Soviet front line
Finnish attacks

5–8 January 1940
Finnish attacks

to split Soviet forces into small and vulnerable pockets; between 11 December 1939 and 8 January 1940, two Soviet Rifle Divisions were destroyed around Suomussalmi in this way. But the Finnish advantage could not be exploited, enabling the Soviets to regroup. When they resumed the offensive in February, their armies were better co-ordinated, more suitably equipped and fresh; by comparison, the Finns had been reduced to less than 100,000 men and were close to exhaustion. The Finnish government had already recognized the reality of the situation – they opened new negotiations with Moscow as early as 29 January, seeking a settlement – although this did not prevent a series of Soviet attacks which breached the Mannerheim Line and, by early March, entered Viipuri. The Treaty of Moscow ended the Winter War on 2 March 1940.

Inevitably, Soviet demands were greater than in October 1939. Not only was a new border established in the Karelian Isthmus, but islands in the Gulf of Finland were secured, along with territory around Salla and in the far north. The Soviets even secured the right to station troops at Hanko, in south-western Finland. But the costs had been high. It is estimated that the Soviets suffered nearly 600,000 casualties and made an enemy of Finland for the future. From the Finnish point of view, the Treaty of Moscow appeared to be the beginning of Soviet pressure to take over the state entirely, and although the Finnish Army had fought extremely well, it had been effectively destroyed in the second phase of the war. The only hope for Finland's security in the future was to seek allies who would divert the Soviet Union's attention and allow a Finnish recovery of lost territories. By mid-1940, the Finns were actively pursuing association with the newly victorious Germany.

> *"It happened in the initial fighting in December that the Russians would advance in close formation, singing, and even hand in hand, against the Finnish minefields, apparently indifferent to the explosions and the accurate fire of the defenders. The fatalistic submission which characterized the infantry was astonishing."*
>
> **Marshal Mannerheim**

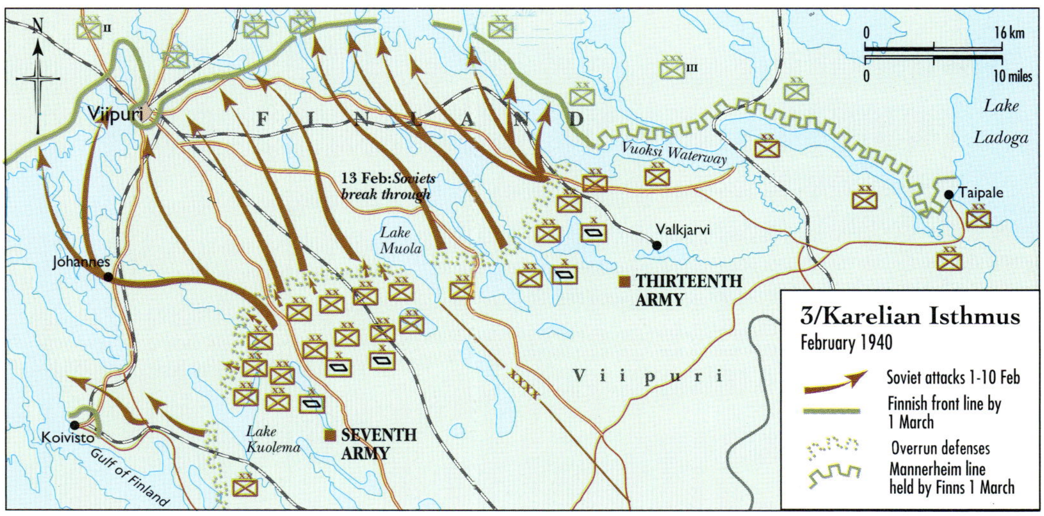

The Phoney War SEPTEMBER 1939 – APRIL 1940

The British and French responded to the invasion of Poland by declaring that "a state of war" existed between themselves and Germany from 3 September 1939. Neither of the democracies was in any position to help the Poles, whose defeat and occupation could only be watched from afar. Instead, they concentrated on protecting the borders of France against possible German attack, a strategy that was, by definition, inactive. As fall turned to winter, journalists dubbed it a "Phoney War" or "sitzkrieg". Some even speculated that Germany was deterred by the strength of Allied defenses.

On paper, those defenses were formidable. Since 1929, the French had spent enormous amounts of money building the Maginot Line to protect their border with Germany. A succession of casemates, interspersed every five miles or so by powerful fortresses, was constructed of concrete and equipped with artillery pieces of every description. Forests of barbed-wire and mines were planted in front of the fortresses, the garrisons of which could survive for weeks. By early 1940 the French had 14 divisions manning the Maginot Line, with another 88 available for operations elsewhere. A British Expeditionary Force (BEF), commanded by Lord Gort, was deployed to northern France in October 1939, comprising four more divisions, and this number was steadily increased to nine by May 1940. By then, the Allies had some 3100 tanks and 2000 combat aircraft available.

The Maginot Line extended only as far as the Belgian border since it was felt to be too provocative to build such defenses along a frontier with a neutral state. This in itself was not disastrous – the static defenses along the German border could be held by second-rate divisions, leaving the better and more mobile formations to concentrate in the north-east, where a repeat of the 1914 Schlieffen Plan was widely anticipated. Once this began, the bulk of Allied forces would move north into Belgium ("Plan D"), ready to destroy the enemy assault. But the plan was flawed. Allied command co-ordination was poor; the tanks were "penny-packeted" to support the infantry, precluding their use as a maneuver arm; co-operation between air and ground forces was weak; and morale declined as the Phoney War progressed. The pre-war emphasis on the Maginot Line had led to a dangerous degree of complacency and inactivity, while the memory of the First World War, in which the French had lost 1.5 million men, weighed heavily on the consciences of commanders: such suffering had to be avoided, almost at any cost.

Without realizing it, the Allies had predicted German moves exactly. As early as 27 September 1939 Hitler, aware that he needed to defeat Britain and France before he could turn against the Soviets, called for planning to begin for an attack on the West, with a provisional start-date in November. His planning staff advocated a repeat of the Schlieffen Plan, with the main German forces attacking through the Netherlands and Belgium to swing round Paris and catch the Maginot Line in the rear. Known as *Fall Gelb* (Plan Yellow), this was accepted chiefly because it was felt that the new mobility of German spearhead units, equipped with tanks and half-tracks, could avoid the problems of 1914, when foot-slogging infantry proved incapable of covering the enormous distances involved. Because of the need to build up German forces in the West and to avoid the winter weather, Hitler agreed to postpone the offensive until the spring of 1940.

By then, the plan had been compromised. In late January a Luftwaffe staff officer, carrying *Fall Gelb* documents, crash-landed in Belgium. His brief-case was returned to Berlin, but the Belgians, understandably, read its contents and passed the information on to the Dutch, British and French. Hitler, afraid of this, accepted a revised plan (known as *Sichelschnitt*, or "cut of the scythe") put forward by General Erich von Manstein, chief of staff to Army Group A facing Belgium in the east. He advocated an attack by Army Group B in the north to trigger Allied moves into Belgium, upon which panzer divisions of Army Group A would infiltrate the Ardennes region and push through to the Channel coast, cutting Allied forces off from their support in France. Encircled, the Allies would have no choice but to surrender or die. The attack was scheduled to start on 10 May 1940, by which time the Germans had 133 divisions in the West (almost the same number as the Allies when Belgian and Dutch formations were added), about 2400 tanks, many of them concentrated in panzer divisions, and up to 4200 combat aircraft. Before then, however, other campaigns had taken place.

The plans for the Maginot Line had their origin in the bloody battles which were fought around the fortress of Verdun in 1916. Although a brilliant feat of engineering, the Maginot Line was effectively rendered obsolescent by the development of mobile armored columns.

"It had in it something of the 'boos' howled out by the spectators at a prize-ring when the two contestants are not putting on as bloody an exhibition as they have paid to witness."

Sumner Welles,
U.S. Under-Secretary of State

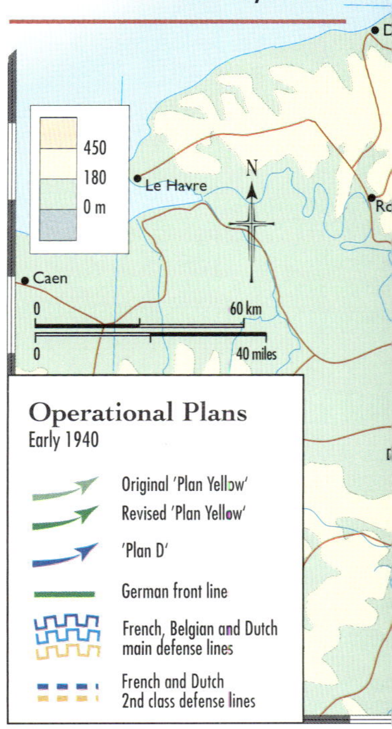

Soldiers of the British Expeditionary Force march into Fort de Sainghain on the Franco–Belgian border. Inactivity and cold, damp weather conditions placed considerable strain upon the morale of both French and British troops awaiting the anticipated German onslaught.

Battle of the Atlantic SEPTEMBER 1939 – APRIL 1940

While Allied troops waited for German attacks in France, the war followed a more active path at sea. When hostilities began, Britain and France seemed to enjoy overwhelming advantages. Despite the vulnerability of British maritime trading routes the Royal Navy was large (12 battleships/battlecruisers, six aircraft carriers, 58 cruisers, 201 destroyers and escorts, and 69 submarines) and specifically designed to protect the sea-lanes. In addition, the French Navy was available to help protect the route through the Suez Canal to the Far East. By comparison, the German Navy in 1939 comprised only four battleships, seven cruisers, 34 destroyers and torpedo boats, and 57 submarines (U-boats). If they were to stand any chance of defeating the Allies, they had to sink between them an estimated 750,000 tons of merchant shipping a month over a 12-month period.

This was a tall order, but one that the Kriegsmarine attempted to carry out, using commerce raiders, U-boats and mines. Before the war began, key elements of the navy were sent out into the Atlantic to avoid any Allied blockade and threaten trading routes. On 3 September, two armored cruisers, the *Deutschland* and *Admiral Graf Spee* (deployed to the North and South Atlantic respectively on 21 August), began to prey on merchant ships that were, at this stage, unprotected by Royal Navy escorts. The *Deutschland* did not enjoy a great deal of success but the *Graf Spee* posed much more of a threat, forcing the British to set up "hunting groups" of warships to cover both the South Atlantic and Indian Oceans. It was one of these groups, Force G based in the Falkland Islands and comprising two heavy cruisers (*Cumberland* and *Exeter*) and two light cruisers (*Ajax* and *Achilles*), that finally engaged the *Graf Spee* 150 miles off the River Plate on the east coast of Latin America on 13 December 1939, although not before the German warship had sunk nine merchantmen totaling 50,000 tons. In the Battle of the River Plate, *Exeter* was badly hit (*Cumberland* was detached from Force G at the time), but *Graf Spee* suffered enough damage to persuade her captain to seek shelter in the neutral Uruguayan port of Montevideo. Unable to stay there long without breaching international laws of neutrality and convinced that the British had stationed a large fleet offshore, Captain Lansdorff took his ship out of harbor on 17 December and scuttled her. It was a rare triumph for British arms in the dark days of 1939.

The other threats to British trade were more difficult to counter. As soon as war began, German ships and aircraft planted mines, including the new "magnetic" or influence mine, around the coasts of Britain. Although an influence mine was disarmed and dismantled on 23 November, after which ships were "degaussed" to render them non-magnetic, 128 ships (a total of nearly 430,000 tons) were sunk by mines between September 1939 and April 1940; at one point, the Port of London was effectively closed because of the threat. However, as British minesweeping techniques improved and German attention was diverted elsewhere, these successes could not be sustained.

The greatest threat was that posed by the U-boats. Despite their limited numbers and Britain's rapid introduction of a convoy system, the very nature of submarine warfare, involving surprise attacks almost anywhere throughout the oceans, meant that the U-boats were sure to enjoy some success. It was the merchantmen that suffered the most: between September 1939 and March 1940 a total of 222 merchant ships were sunk by submarine, for a loss of 17 U-boats. The merchant losses were severe, but at no time during this early period of the war did sinkings even approach the 750,000 tons a month deemed necessary by the Kriegsmarine. In addition, the Royal Navy, although stretched, did manage to protect a significant proportion of ships by introducing the convoy system. The war at sea assumed an uneasy balance.

The 16,000-ton pocket battleship Graf Spee *at the time of being scuttled outside the port of Montevideo. Fearing that his ship and its equipment would fall into enemy hands, Captain Langsdorff ordered that the ship's torpedoes be detonated in the magazines. Two days later Langsdorff shot himself in Buenos Aires.*

> *"You English are hard. You do not know when you are beaten. The* Exeter *was beaten, but would not know it!"*
>
> **Captain Langsdorff**

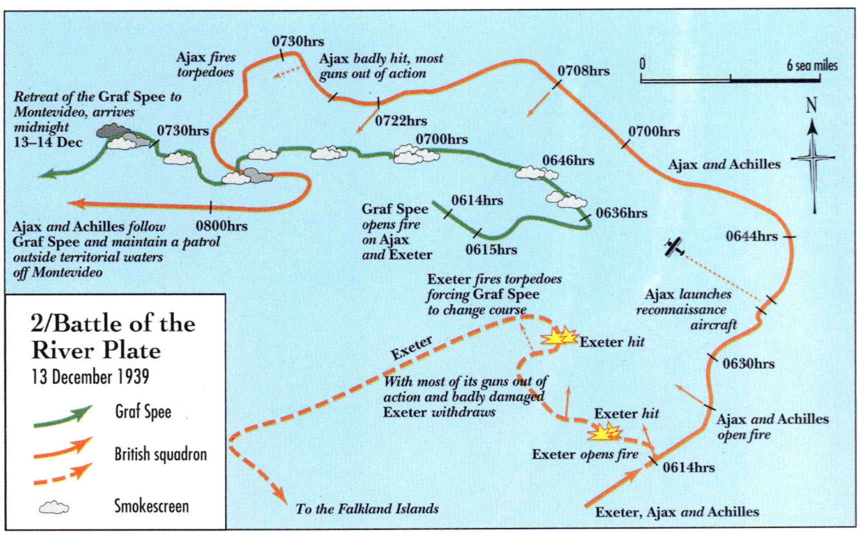

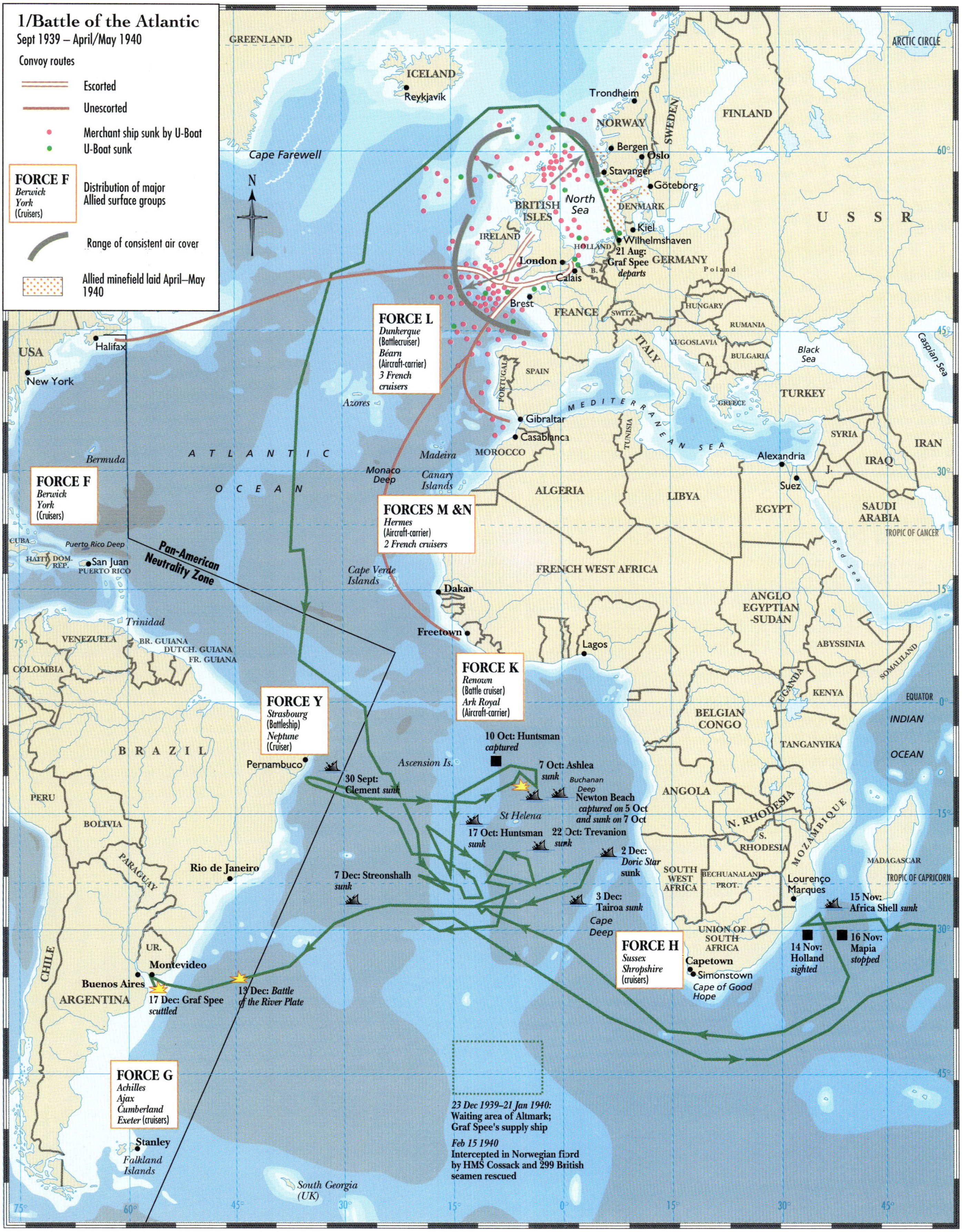

1/Battle of the Atlantic
Sept 1939 – April/May 1940
Convoy routes
Escorted
Unescorted
Merchant ship sunk by U-Boat
U-Boat sunk
FORCE F Berwick York (Cruisers)
Distribution of major Allied surface groups
Range of consistent air cover
Allied minefield laid April–May 1940
GREENLAND
ICELAND
Reykjavik
Cape Farewell
Trondheim
NORWAY
SWEDEN
FINLAND
Bergen
Oslo
Stavanger
Göteborg
North Sea
DENMARK
BRITISH ISLES
IRELAND
Kiel
Wilhelmshaven
HOLLAND
21 Aug: Graf Spee departs
London
Calais
B.
GERMANY
Poland
U S S R
ARCTIC CIRCLE
Brest
FRANCE
SWITZ.
HUNGARY
RUMANIA
YUGOSLAVIA
BULGARIA
ITALY
Black Sea
Caspian Sea
FORCE L Dunkerque (Battlecruiser) Béarn (Aircraft-carrier) 3 French cruisers
USA
Halifax
New York
SPAIN
PORTUGAL
Azores
TURKEY
GREECE
MEDITERRANEAN SEA
Gibraltar
Casablanca
TUNISIA
SYRIA
IRAQ
IRAN
Alexandria
Suez
ATLANTIC OCEAN
Bermuda
Madeira
MOROCCO
Monaco Deep
Canary Islands
ALGERIA
LIBYA
EGYPT
SAUDI ARABIA
J.
TROPIC OF CANCER
Red Sea
FORCE F Berwick York (Cruisers)
FORCES M &N Hermes (Aircraft-carrier) 2 French cruisers
CUBA
Puerto Rico Deep
HAITI
DOM. REP.
San Juan
PUERTO RICO
Pan-American Neutrality Zone
Cape Verde Islands
Dakar
FRENCH WEST AFRICA
ANGLO EGYPTIAN -SUDAN
Freetown
Lagos
Trinidad
VENEZUELA
BR. GUIANA
DUTCH. GUIANA
FR. GUIANA
COLOMBIA
ABYSSINIA
SOMALILAND
FORCE K Renown (Battle cruiser) Ark Royal (Aircraft-carrier)
KENYA
UGANDA
EQUATOR
FORCE Y Strasbourg (Battleship) Neptune (Cruiser)
BELGIAN CONGO
INDIAN OCEAN
10 Oct: Huntsman captured
TANGANYIKA
BRAZIL
Pernambuco
Ascension Is.
7 Oct: Ashlea sunk
Buchanan Deep
30 Sept: Clement sunk
Newton Beach captured on 5 Oct and sunk on 7 Oct
ANGOLA
PERU
St Helena
N. RHODESIA
MOZAMBIQUE
BOLIVIA
17 Oct: Huntsman sunk
22 Oct: Trevanion sunk
S. RHODESIA
PARAGUAY
2 Dec: Doric Star sunk
Rio de Janeiro
SOUTH WEST AFRICA
BECHUANALAND PROT.
MADAGASCAR
TROPIC OF CAPRICORN
7 Dec: Streonshalh sunk
Lourenço Marques
3 Dec: Tairoa sunk
15 Nov: Africa Shell sunk
Cape Deep
UNION OF SOUTH AFRICA
14 Nov: Holland sighted
16 Nov: Mapia stopped
FORCE H Sussex Shropshire (cruisers)
UR.
CHILE
Montevideo
Capetown
Simonstown
Cape of Good Hope
Buenos Aires
ARGENTINA
17 Dec: Graf Spee scuttled
13 Dec: Battle of the River Plate
FORCE G Achilles Ajax Cumberland Exeter (cruisers)
23 Dec 1939–21 Jan 1940: Waiting area of Altmark; Graf Spee's supply ship
Feb 15 1940 Intercepted in Norwegian fiord by HMS Cossack and 299 British seamen rescued
Stanley
Falkland Islands
South Georgia (UK)
75°
60°
45°
30°
15°
0°
15°
30°
45°

Denmark and Norway APRIL – JUNE 1940

One of the results of the trade war at sea was that both the Allies and Germans directed their attention toward neutral Scandinavia. To the Allies, German access to Swedish iron ore, shipped out of the Norwegian port of Narvik, was clearly a matter for concern, and if this could be disrupted, the German war economy would suffer. Other factors were added – not least the Allied desire to send military aid, through Norway and Sweden, to Finland while that country was engaged in the "Winter War" against Hitler's ally, Russia – but German trade was the key target. By the same token, German interest in the region had an economic emphasis, not just to secure the iron-ore needed but also to seize naval bases closer to the North Atlantic. If Norwegian and Danish ports could be captured, U-boats and surface raiders would be able to dominate the North Sea and move more easily into the North Atlantic.

One of the bizarre results of these arguments was that both sides decided to intervene in Scandinavia simultaneously. During the night of 7/8 April 1940, British warships began to lay mines in the approaches to Narvik, only to be disrupted by the discovery that a German naval task force had entered the North Sea. It was presumed that the Germans intended to break out into the North Atlantic, but early on 9 April the true nature of the expedition became apparent: a German invasion of Denmark and Norway was under way. Codenamed Operation *Weserübung*, it was an ambitious undertaking, ordered by Hitler on 19 February and designed to be over before the assault on France and the Low Countries began on 10 May. Substantial forces were deployed – the whole of the Kriegsmarine's surface fleet (less three cruisers), 28 U-boats, over 500 combat aircraft and eight divisions of troops – in what was the first tri-service campaign in German history. In addition, for the first time airlanding and parachute forces were to be used to secure airfields and cities, in the hope that this would disrupt Danish and Norwegian defenses to such an extent that both countries would collapse quickly. In the event, the Danes surrendered on 9 April after the Germans threatened to bomb Copenhagen, but Norway put up a stiffer fight, aided by Allied naval, air and ground units.

On 9 April, the Germans secured a number of key positions in Norway, including Narvik, Trondheim, Bergen, Stavanger and Kristiansand, but naval losses began to mount. The cruiser *Blücher* was sunk as it approached Oslo, and, on 10 April, the light cruiser *Königsberg* was destroyed by land-based aircraft. More significantly, in two engagements on 10 and 13 April, British warships entered Narvik fjord to cripple the entire German force of 10 destroyers. A number of merchantmen, ploughing between Germany and Norway, were also sunk, although this did not prevent the invading force from receiving the supplies and reinforcements it needed, chiefly because airborne troops had secured important airfields at Oslo and Sola, enabling transport aircraft to land virtually unopposed. British units were rushed to northern and central Norway, landing by sea at Namsos on 14 April and Andalsnes four days later, but the Allies had to accept that southern Norway had been lost. Despite gallant efforts, the Norwegian Army could not prevent German advances to take Oslo and to link up with their troops in Bergen and Trondheim. Clashes occurred between British and German forces around Lillehammer on 20 April, but it was soon clear that central Norway could not be held by the Allies. Andalsnes was evacuated on 1 May and Namsos two days later.

This left just the north where, for a time, it looked as if the Allies (now including French and Free Polish units) might secure Narvik. Unfortunately, landings were delayed until 24 April, allowing the Germans time to consolidate, and a major assault was not initiated until 13 May, by which time Allied attention had been diverted by the opening of the German assault on France and the Low Countries. Thus, although Narvik was secured on 28 May, it was abandoned on 9 June after being deliberately destroyed. As King Haakon and his government fled into exile, the campaign came to an ignominious end for the Allies. It had cost them 5300 dead since 9 April, for no strategic benefit. By comparison, the Germans had lost 5700 dead and had gained access to the ports and airfields they needed. At sea, the campaign had been equally costly to both sides – the Allies lost 12 warships and six submarines, while the German losses were 13 warships and six U-boats – but the German victory, coming at the same time as that in France, was a severe blow to Allied morale.

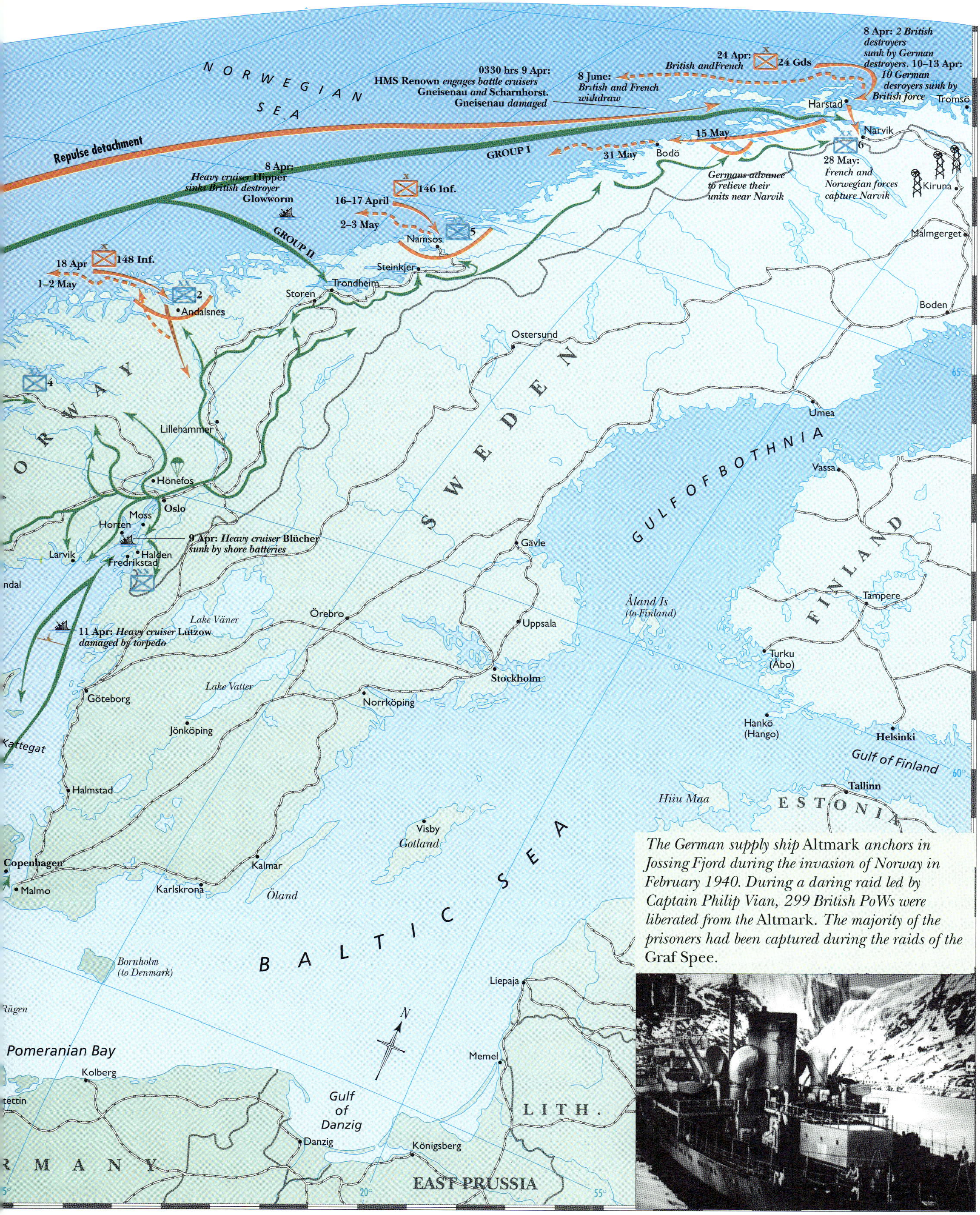

The German supply ship Altmark *anchors in Jossing Fjord during the invasion of Norway in February 1940. During a daring raid led by Captain Philip Vian, 299 British PoWs were liberated from the* Altmark. *The majority of the prisoners had been captured during the raids of the* Graf Spee.

Blitzkrieg in the West MAY – JUNE 1940

The German attack in the West began in the early hours of 10 May 1940 with pre-emptive air attacks on Anglo-French airfields, designed to destroy aircraft on the ground and achieve a measure of air superiority. This not only contributed to Allied surprise but also allowed the Luftwaffe to provide reconnaissance, close air support, and air-transport to ground forces, while denying the same facilities to the enemy. At the same time, elements of Army Group B, commanded by von Bock, moved into the Low Countries as if carrying out a refined version of the 1914 Schlieffen Plan. This coincided exactly with Allied expectations, drawing the bulk of their mobile forces, including the BEF, into Belgium in accordance with Plan D. In reality von Bock's attack was an elaborate feint.

Of far more significance was the advance of von Rundstedt's Army Group A through the "impassable" Ardennes, in accordance with von Manstein's *Sichelschnitt* plan. The Ardennes was not ideal country, forcing the seven panzer divisions to advance slowly along narrow, forest-lined roads, but Allied obsession with the north and lack of adequate defenses in the Ardennes gave von Rundstedt's troops vital time to deploy. Late on 12 May, lead units of General Hermann Hoth's XV Panzer Corps had reached the River Meuse to the north of Dinant and, 24 hours later, General Erwin Rommel's 7th Panzer Division was across, threatening the rear of the French formations guarding what had been seen as only a secondary theater. To Rommel's south, General Georg-Hans Reinhardt's XLI Panzer Corps and General Heinz Guderian's XIX Panzer Corps crossed at Monthermé and Sedan respectively on 14/15 May, unhinging the French defenses entirely. Allied air attacks tried to destroy the bridgeheads over the Meuse but suffered crippling losses. By early on 15 May, the panzers were free to advance at speed toward the Channel coast.

As the Allies tried desperately to regroup, von Bock maintained the pressure to tie them firmly to the fighting in Belgium, so that the panzers of Army Group A had virtually a free passage to the coast, severing Allied links between their frontline units and reserves. By 21 May the Allied armies in Belgium were effectively surrounded. They began to withdraw toward the coast at Dunkirk, where plans were already in train for a naval evacuation. By then, the Dutch and Luxembourgers had surrendered and all attempted counterattacks against the panzers had failed. Belgium capitulated on 28 May.

Between 26 May and 4 June over 338,000 Allied troops were picked up from the beaches at Dunkirk. Any hope of redeploying them south of the panzer advance was made impossible by the abandonment of their heavy equipment and low morale. Furthermore, as soon as Dunkirk had been taken, the bulk of the combined formations of Army Groups A and B turned south. They met little real resistance from the demoralized French Army. Paris fell on 14 June and, on the 22nd, the French government sought surrender terms. A ceasefire came into effect on 25 June, little more than six weeks after the start of the German attack. It was a stunning victory, made possible by the combination of surprise and momentum known as *blitzkrieg*. Casualties had not been light – German losses totaled 137,000 – but the results were dramatic. France had been knocked out of the war and Britain left virtually undefended. With the coastal areas of France and the whole of the Low Countries occupied, Hitler could afford to turn his forces east to face the Soviets. An invasion of Britain was all that was needed to secure his western flank entirely, and in June 1940 that seemed a simple affair.

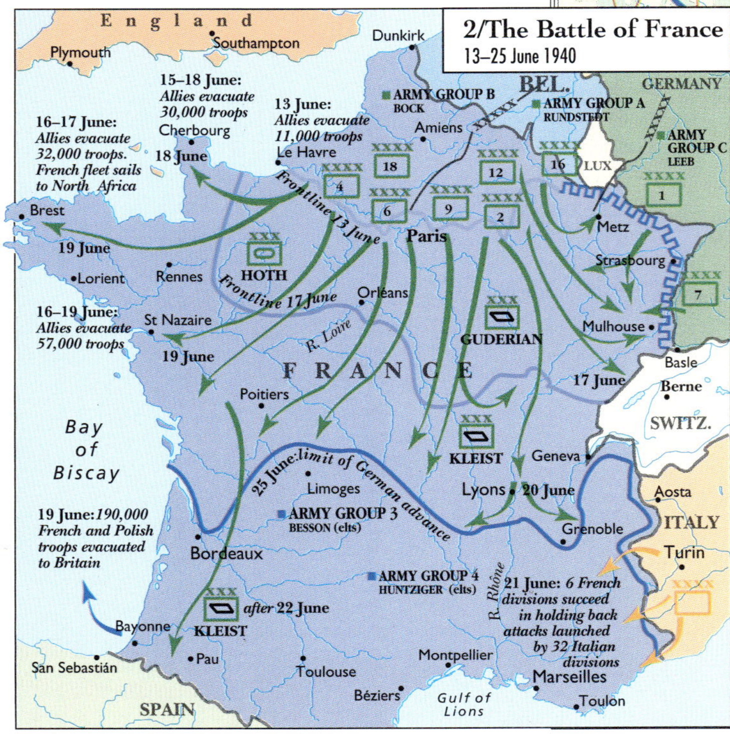

2/The Battle of France
13–25 June 1940

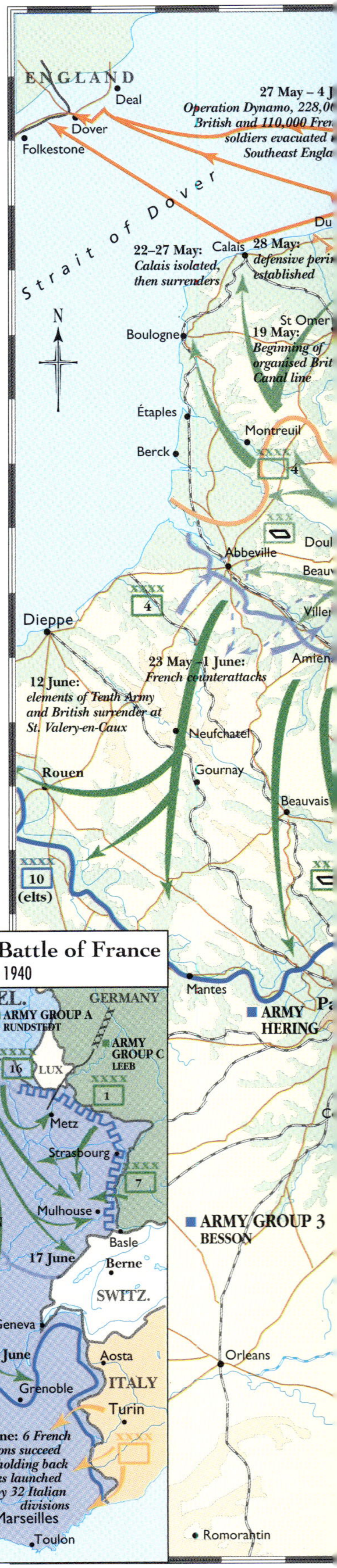

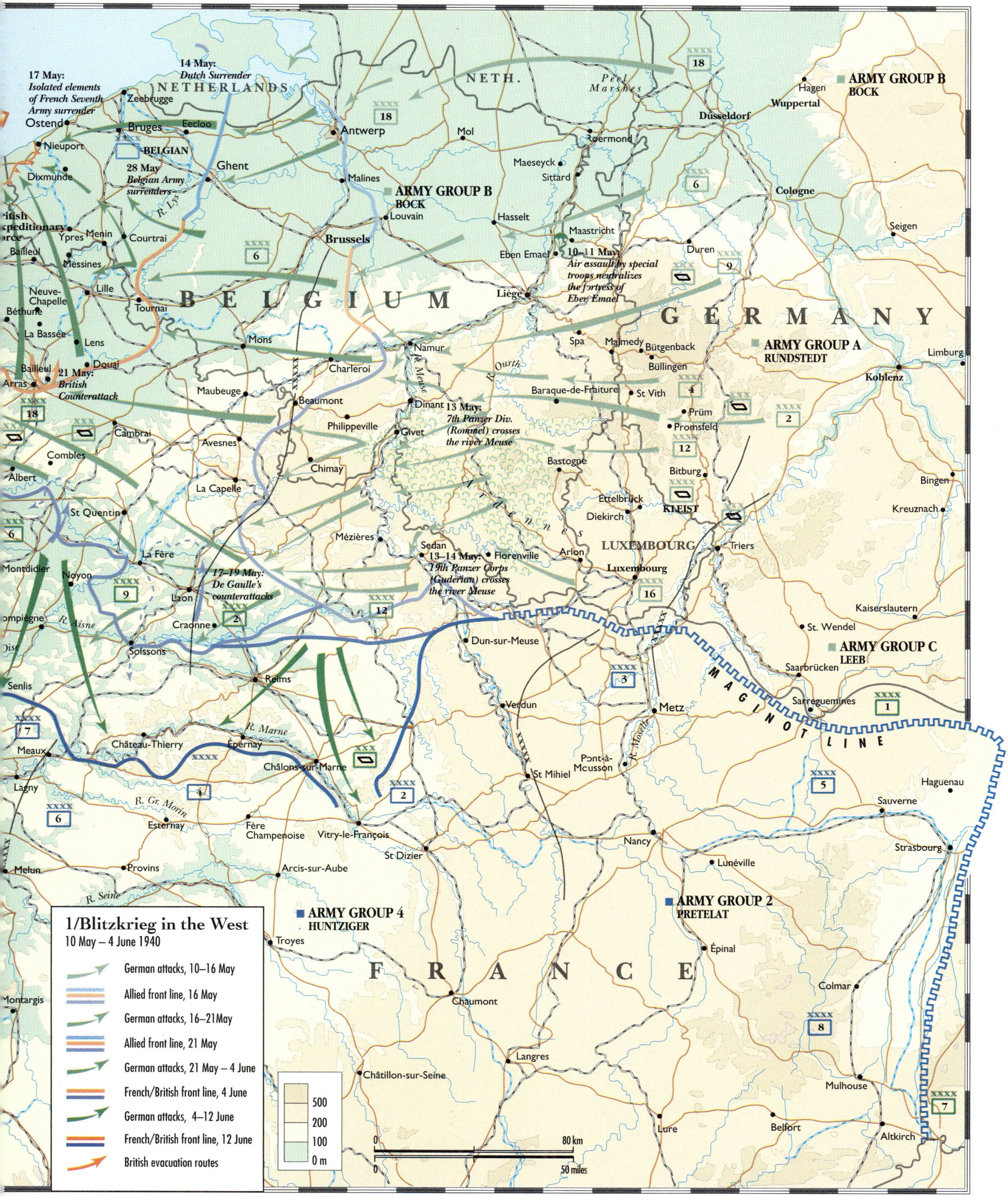
1/Blitzkrieg in the West
10 May – 4 June 1940
German attacks, 10–16 May
Allied front line, 16 May
German attacks, 16–21May
Allied front line, 21 May
German attacks, 21 May – 4 June
French/British front line, 4 June
German attacks, 4–12 June
French/British front line, 12 June
British evacuation routes
500
200
100
0 m
0
80 km
0
50 miles
14 May:
Dutch Surrender
17 May:
Isolated elements
of French Seventh
Army surrender
28 May
Belgian Army
surrenders
21 May:
British
Counterattack
10–11 May:
Air assault by special
troops neutralizes
the fortress of
Eben Emael
13 May:
7th Panzer Div.
(Rommel) crosses
the river Meuse
13–14 May:
19th Panzer Corps
(Guderian) crosses
the river Meuse
17–19 May:
De Gaulle's
counterattacks
NETHERLANDS
NETH.
BELGIAN
BELGIUM
GERMANY
LUXEMBOURG
FRANCE
MAGINOT LINE
ARMY GROUP B
BOCK
ARMY GROUP A
RUNDSTEDT
ARMY GROUP C
LEEB
ARMY GROUP 4
HUNTZIGER
ARMY GROUP 2
PRETELAT
KLEIST
Peel Marshes
Ardennes
R. Lys
R. Meuse
R. Ourthe
R. Aisne
R. Marne
R. Gr. Morin
R. Seine
R. Moselle
Zeebrugge
Ostend
Nieuport
Dixmunde
Bruges
Eecloo
Ghent
Antwerp
Malines
Mol
Louvain
Brussels
Hasselt
Maeseyck
Sittard
Roermond
Maastricht
Eben Emael
Liège
Düsseldorf
Wuppertal
Hagen
Cologne
Seigen
Duren
Ypres
Menin
Courtrai
Bailleul
Messines
Lille
Neuve-Chapelle
Béthune
La Bassée
Lens
Tournai
Douai
Arras
Mons
Charleroi
Namur
Maubeuge
Beaumont
Dinant
Philippeville
Givet
Cambrai
Avesnes
Combles
Albert
Chimay
La Capelle
St Quentin
Spa
Malmedy
Bütgenback
Büllingen
Baraque-de-Fraiture
St Vith
Prüm
Promsfeld
Bastogne
Bitburg
Ettelbrück
Diekirch
Arlon
Luxembourg
Triers
Limburg
Koblenz
Bingen
Kreuznach
Kaiserslautern
St. Wendel
Saarbrücken
Sarreguemines
Mézières
Sedan
Florenville
La Fère
Montdidier
Noyon
Laon
Craonne
Soissons
Senlis
Reims
Dun-sur-Meuse
Verdun
Metz
Château-Thierry
Épernay
Châlons-sur-Marne
Meaux
Lagny
Esternay
Fère Champenoise
Vitry-le-François
St Dizier
St Mihiel
Pont-à-Mousson
Nancy
Lunéville
Haguenau
Sauverne
Strasbourg
Melun
Provins
Arcis-sur-Aube
Troyes
Épinal
Colmar
Chaumont
Langres
Châtillon-sur-Seine
Mulhouse
Lure
Belfort
Altkirch
Montargis

The Battle of Britain JULY – OCTOBER 1940

Hitler delayed his decision to order an invasion of Britain (codenamed Operation *Sealion*) until 16 July 1940, partly because he expected Britain to sue for peace after Dunkirk and partly because of the practical problems of gathering an invasion fleet. Furthermore, the continued existence of the RAF meant that any attempt to mount an invasion would be heavily opposed from the air. In such circumstances, Reichsmarschall Goering's offer to Hitler of a short aerial campaign designed to achieve both air and naval supremacy was readily accepted.

But the Luftwaffe lacked the aircraft needed for such a campaign, while the delay in the decision to prepare for invasion allowed the RAF to recover from its losses in France. This meant that when the Battle of Britain began in July, the two sides were roughly equal in terms of numbers of aircraft, and their fighters were similar in capability. However, the British did enjoy three key advantages: radar early warning, an ability to keep reserves beyond the range of German attack, and the fact that they were operating over home territory.

The Luftwaffe began with attacks on shipping and port installations. Such attacks were not crucial to British survival, allowing Air Chief Marshal Dowding, C-in-C Fighter Command, to commit his fighters sparingly. By the end of this phase of the battle the RAF had destroyed 297 aircraft for a loss of 175. Goering reassessed his strategy, shifting his attacks to RAF airfields, control centers and radar sites in an effort to destroy Dowding's command. Between 12 August and 5 September he came close to success, as RAF losses mounted and Dowding was forced to commit a dwindling Fighter Command to the protection of its own infrastructure. By the end of this phase, the RAF had lost a further 446 aircraft to the Luftwaffe's 493 and was running desperately short of pilots.

At this point Goering made a crucial error. Convinced that the Luftwaffe was succeeding, and aiming to demoralize the British people, he ordered the bombers to concentrate on London. This decision tied the Luftwaffe to a specific and predictable target. On 15 September, Dowding was able to concentrate his fighters against attacks on the capital, inflicting losses of 56 aircraft on an exhausted enemy. By then, the balance of losses had shifted firmly in favor of the RAF and although the battle was to continue until the end of October, the crisis had been passed. On 16 September, his thoughts turning toward Russia, Hitler ordered a postponement of *Sealion*. Britain had survived.

An RAF pilot dismounts from his Hawker Hurricane during the Battle of Britain. The fatigue of constant combat is clearly delineated on the face of this young pilot and on his tunic he bears the ribbon of the Distinguished Flying Cross.

"I wondered idly what he was like, this man I would kill. Was he young, was he fat, would he die with the Führer's name on his lips, or would he die alone … I would never know."

Richard Hillary, RAF pilot

1/Operation 'Sea Lion' German Invasion Plans

2/The Battle of Britain
July–October 1940
Fighter Command Group HQ
Sector airfield
RAF group boundary
RAF sector boundary
High level radar station
Low level radar station
Balloon barrage
Observer corps center station
Anti-aircraft artillery (site with number of guns)
Luftflotte HQ
Luftflotte boundary
Fliegerkorps boundary
VIII
Fliegerkorps
Limit of German fighter range
Main direction of German air attacks on Adler Tag (Eagle Day), Aug 13
0
50 km
0
40 miles
N
LUFTFLOTTE 5
bomber attacks
from bases in
Norway and Denmark
High level radar range
Low level radar range
NORTH
SEA
UNITED
KINGDOM
Wales
Fighter Command 13 Group
Fighter Command 12 Group
Fighter Command 11 Group
Fighter Command 10 Group
Fighter Command HQ
Stanmore
Carlisle
R. Tyne
R. Tees
Middlesbrough
Catterick
Church Fenton
Blackpool
Bradford
Leeds
Hull
Manchester
Liverpool
Stockport
Ringway
Sheffield
Kirton-in-Lindsey
R. Trent
Watnall
Derby
Nottingham
Digby
Ternhill
Wolverhampton
Leicester
Wittering
Aberystwyth
Birmingham
Coventry
R. Severn
R. Ouse
Cambridge
Norwich
Coltishall
Ipswich
Martlesham
Harwich
Debden
North Weald
Gloucester
Pembrey
Swansea
Bibury
R. Thames
Oxford
Northolt
Hendon
Stapleford
London
Hornchurch
Rochford
Filton
Cardiff
Bristol
Bath
Colerne
Bristol Channel
Croydon
Gravesend
Manston
Kenley
Biggin Hill
West Malling
East Church
Detling
Hawkinge
Lympne
Dover
Middle Wallop
Boscombe Down
Thorney Island
Westhampnett
Southampton
Gosport
Portsmouth
Brighton
Exeter
Warmwell
Isle of Wight
Roborough
Plymouth
English Channel
L M K G J F E Z Y A B C D W
Flushing
Ostend
Antwerp
The Hague
Rotterdam
Dunkirk
Ghent
R. Schelde
LUFTFLOTTE 2
Brussels
BELGIUM
IX
Calais
Oye-Plage
Calais-Marck
Coquelles
Wissant
Fiennes
Caffier
Boulogne
Samer
Devres
St-Omer
Arques
Lille
R. Lys
Etaples
Le Touquet
Montreuil
Campagne
Berck-sur-Mer
Arras
Crécy-en-Ponthieu
Cambrai
Tramecourt
Abbeville
R. Somme
Dieppe
Amiens
Rosieres-en-Santerre
Couvron
Laon
Montdidier
I
Cherbourg
Cherbourg-Ouest
Deauville
Le Havre
Rouen
Beauvais
Compiegne
Clermont
Guernsey
Jersey
Carquebut
Crépon
Caen
Cormeilles-en-Vexin
R. Seine
Evreux
Beaumont-le-Roger
St-André-de l'Eure
Saint-Cloud
Paris
Orly
Villacoublay
Dreux
IV
Dinard
St Malo
LUFTFLOTTE 3
VIII
Alençon
V
FRANCE
Dinan
Rennes
1000
500
0 m
54°
52°
50°
48°
2°
0°
2°
4°

The Blitz SEPTEMBER 1940 – MAY 1941

Victory in the Battle of Britain did not mean that German attacks ceased. The Luftwaffe was still powerful enough to pose a threat to British cities, conducting a strategic bombing campaign, popularly known as "The Blitz", that was designed to demoralize the British people and undermine Britain's capacity to produce war-related goods by hitting factories, dockyards and urban housing. The campaign began on 24/25 August 1940, when German bombers, aiming for targets in the Thames estuary, hit populated areas in the East End of London, and was to continue in unrestricted form until May 1941, when Hitler transferred bombers to eastern Europe in preparation for the invasion of Russia. During that time, cities throughout the British Isles were subjected to essentially night-time raids, forcing people to take shelter and to endure the indiscriminate nature of aerial bombardment. The experience was not unexpected – by 1940 everyone in Britain had been issued with a gas-mask, children and young mothers had been evacuated from the major cities and attempts made to defend key centers using searchlights and anti-aircraft guns – but the scale of the attacks still shocked the country.

To begin with, the Luftwaffe concentrated on London, flying daylight raids in which the bombers were escorted by fighters. The RAF victory on 15 September forced Goering to rethink and gradually it became the norm for the bombers to appear, unescorted, at night over a variety of targets. This meant that their attacks were far less precise and that the civilian population suffered as bombs, aimed into the darkness, hit houses instead of factories. By the end of September 6953 civilians had been killed. More worryingly, the defenses around key cities had proved inadequate. Searchlights swept the night skies in desperate pursuit of aircraft they could only hear, anti-aircraft guns fired indiscriminately and night-fighters, lacking radar, failed to locate their quarries. These problems came to a head on the night of 14/15 November 1940, when 439 German bombers, spearheaded by pathfinder aircraft using a sophisticated radio direction beam known as *X-Gerät*, dropped 503 tons of high explosive and over 30,000 incendiaries on Coventry. The raid killed 568 people and left 1256 badly injured; more than 60,000 buildings were destroyed or damaged. What made it worse in retrospect was that British code-breakers at Bletchley Park in Buckinghamshire had warned that a major raid was imminent, but in the absence of further information, the authorities had presumed that it would be against London.

The raids continued elsewhere. By Christmas 1940 Birmingham, Sheffield, Liverpool and Manchester had been badly hit, and other cities had begun to feel the weight of Luftwaffe attacks. Nor was London spared. On the night of 29/30 December, 130 German bombers visited the city, dropping incendiaries that left an area between St Paul's Cathedral and the Guildhall a sea of flames. By the end of the year, Britain was under siege.

The country survived partly through improvements to air defenses – by early 1941 searchlights and anti-aircraft guns were connected to special radars that could predict the height and direction of the bombers, while night-fighters, similarly equipped with radar, enjoyed some success – and partly because the ordinary people refused to crack. It became a matter of pride to continue "business as usual" and a matter of basic revenge to ensure that war-production did not falter. The raids continued into the spring of 1941 – one of the worst was on the night of 10/11 May, when more than 1400 civilians were killed in London – but by then it was obvious that Britain was not about to collapse. As the Germans prepared for their invasion of Russia, the pressure eased. Some raids continued to be mounted, but the worst was over.

For many, London's numerous underground railway stations became the only place of safe refuge from the 18,000 tons of high-explosive bombs dropped by the Luftwaffe during the Blitz's six-month duration.

"The feeling was something you had never experienced before – the excitement and dash of fire-engines arriving to help from so far away, and the oily, evil smell of fire and destruction, with its lazy, insolent rhythm."

New Recruit, Middlesex Regiment

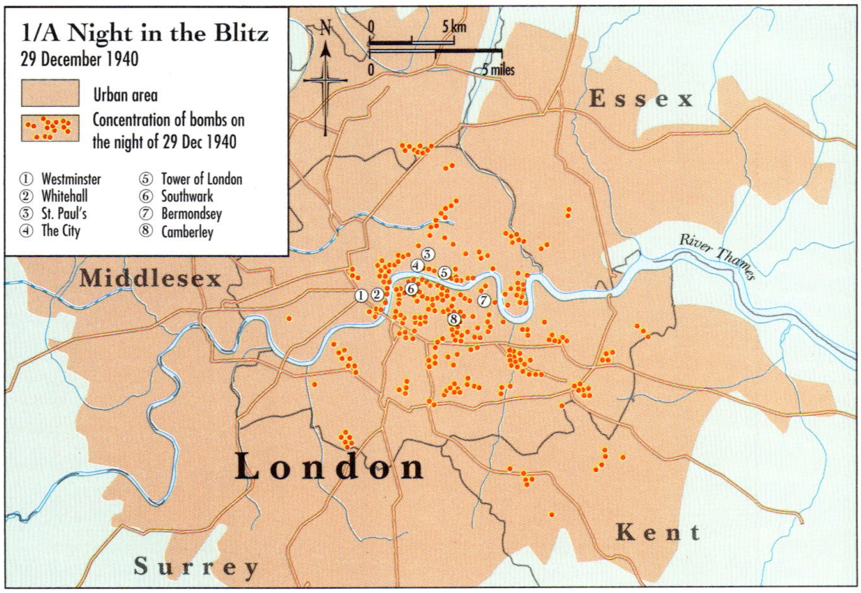

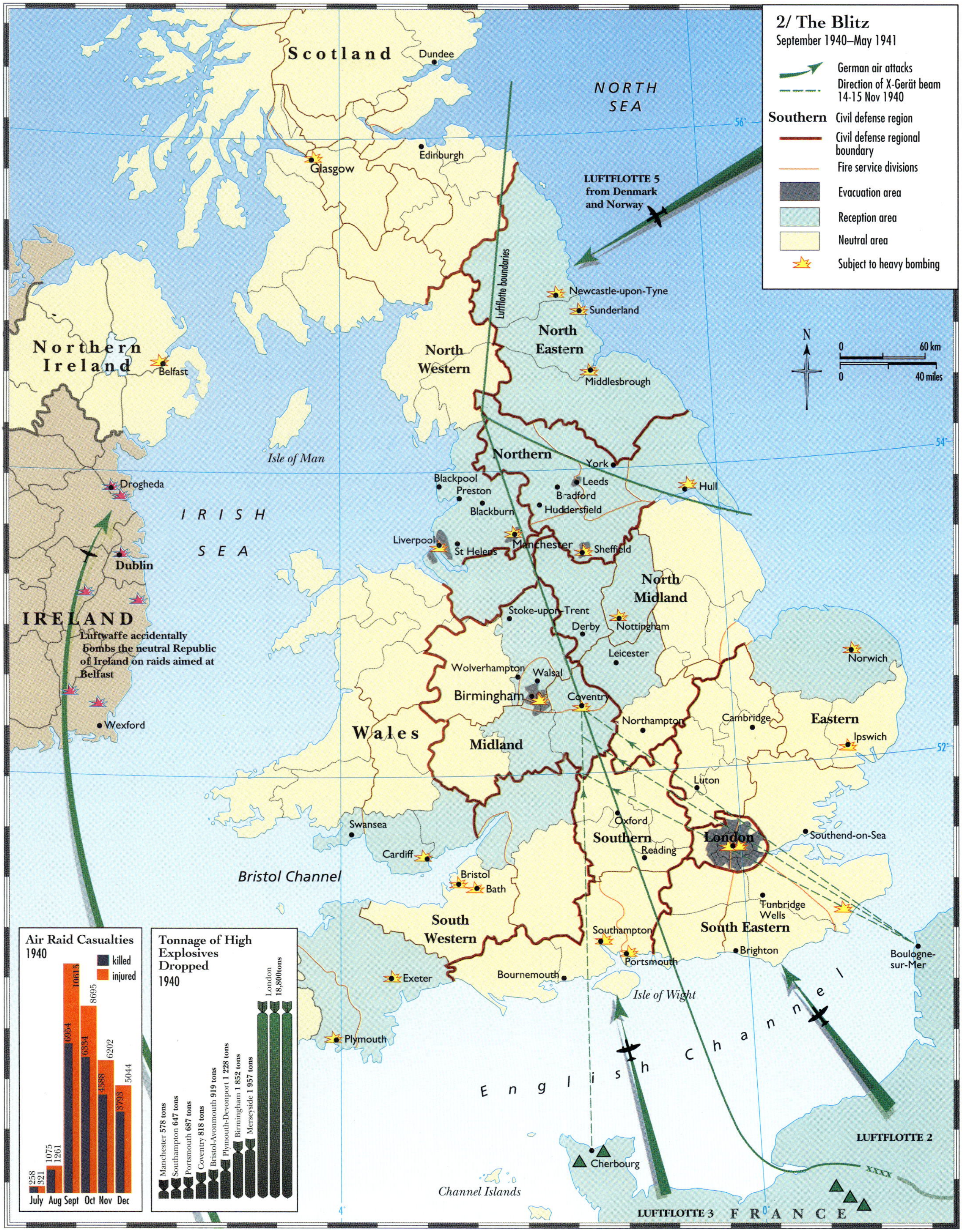
2/ The Blitz
September 1940–May 1941
German air attacks
Direction of X-Gerät beam 14-15 Nov 1940
Southern Civil defense region
Civil defense regional boundary
Fire service divisions
Evacuation area
Reception area
Neutral area
Subject to heavy bombing
0 60 km
0 40 miles
N
Scotland
Dundee
NORTH SEA
Edinburgh
Glasgow
LUFTFLOTTE 5 from Denmark and Norway
Luftflotte boundaries
Newcastle-upon-Tyne
Sunderland
North Eastern
North Western
Northern Ireland
Belfast
Middlesbrough
Isle of Man
Northern
York
Blackpool
Preston
Leeds
Bradford
Huddersfield
Hull
Blackburn
Drogheda
IRISH SEA
Liverpool
St Helens
Manchester
Sheffield
Dublin
North Midland
IRELAND
Luftwaffe accidentally bombs the neutral Republic of Ireland on raids aimed at Belfast
Stoke-upon-Trent
Derby
Nottingham
Norwich
Leicester
Wolverhampton
Walsal
Birmingham
Coventry
Wexford
Wales
Midland
Northampton
Cambridge
Eastern
Ipswich
Luton
Swansea
Oxford
London
Southend-on-Sea
Southern
Reading
Cardiff
Bristol Channel
Bristol
Bath
Tunbridge Wells
South Western
Southampton
South Eastern
Portsmouth
Brighton
Boulogne-sur-Mer
Exeter
Bournemouth
Isle of Wight
Plymouth
English Channel
Cherbourg
LUFTFLOTTE 2
Channel Islands
LUFTFLOTTE 3
FRANCE
56°
54°
52°
4°
0°
Air Raid Casualties 1940
killed
injured
July 258 321
Aug 1075 1261
Sept 6954 10615
Oct 6334 8695
Nov 4588 6202
Dec 3793 5044
Tonnage of High Explosives Dropped 1940
Manchester 578 tons
Southampton 647 tons
Portsmouth 687 tons
Coventry 818 tons
Bristol-Avonmouth 919 tons
Plymouth-Devonport 1 228 tons
Birmingham 1 852 tons
Merseyside 1 957 tons
London 18,800tons

Bombing of Germany SEPTEMBER 1940 – FEBRUARY 1942

When hostilities began the RAF believed firmly in a theory of strategic bombing, using aircraft to hit precise industrial targets in daylight to undermine the enemy's ability to manufacture modern weapons. To begin with, however, RAF Bomber Command lacked both the political backing and the means with which to initiate such a campaign. British politicians, wary of the power of the Luftwaffe, did not want to begin something that might result in devastating retaliation, while Bomber Command itself fielded no more than 300 aircraft, many of which were unsuited to a campaign against Germany. What little bombing took place – against shipping in the North Sea in late 1939 – proved to be disastrous: on 14 December, for example, five out of a force of 12 Vickers Wellington bombers failed to return and, four days later, 12 out of 22 were lost. The only "success" proved to be leaflet raids at night over Germany. By January 1940 more than 65 million leaflets had been dropped with no aircraft losses to enemy action.

It was the leaflet raids that helped to persuade the Air Staff to shift from daylight to night-time bombing, but the transition was by no means straightforward. As the Phoney War was replaced by fighting in Scandinavia, France and the Low Countries, many of the bombers had to be transferred to support ground forces, while the introduction of night bombing raised obvious problems of accuracy as crews found it virtually impossible to navigate in the dark. In addition, no-one seemed to be clear about the type of targets to go for. Although there was an ostensible emphasis on oil as a known weakness of the German war-economy, other priorities kept emerging, ranging from the need to hit invasion barges in July 1940 to calls for the bombing of U-boat bases and construction yards in an effort to relieve the pressure on merchant convoys in the Atlantic. By late 1940, it was obvious that the bombing campaign was not succeeding.

This was reinforced by scientific analysis of the raids over Germany. In August 1941 over 600 photographs, taken by night bombers in June and July, were studied in an effort to test their reported accuracy. The conclusions were depressing: far from the aiming point being the 50 yards around a target that precision bombing required, it was anything up to five miles in diameter, and that in only about a third of the cases studied. Despite the development of new, heavier bombers, the bombing campaign was costing more than it was achieving. Prime Minister Winston Churchill, alarmed at the heavy cost (on the night of 7/8 November 1941, for example, 37 aircraft were lost over Berlin and Mannheim), ordered the campaign to be suspended for the winter, with a clear implication that vast improvements would have to be made before it could be resumed.

Some of those improvements were already in the pipeline. Bomber production was increasing and the first of the radar aids to navigation (known as "Gee") was about to be introduced, but it was apparent that the real problem lay in the aims of the campaign. If the RAF was only dropping bombs in the general vicinity of a target, it seemed logical to make that target bigger, going for the entire urban complex rather than just the factories within it. City bombing had already been tried – on 12/13 March 1941 Bremen had been hit with some success – and this led the way to a new Bombing Directive, issued on 14 February 1942. It specified a number of German cities that were to be bombed in their entirety, with particular emphasis on civilian centers, the destruction of which, it was argued, would undermine German morale. The Area Bombing Directive represented a practical solution to the problems of night-bombing, but ushered in a totally new campaign of urban destruction, success in which would depend on the creation of an enormous bombing force.

An RAF Blenheim bomber was sent to report on the German Navy base at Wilhelmshaven one hour after Britain had entered the war. Subsequent daylight raids on shipping were ineffective and energies were directed instead to leaflet raids. On the first night of the war over 5 million leaflets denouncing Germany's leaders were showered onto Germany.

Bombing Statistics 1940–42

Bomber Production

	Germany	Britain	United States
1940	2,852	3,488	—
1941	3,373	4,668	—
1942	4,502	6,253	12,627

These figures include all bomber types.

Bomber Losses

	Germany	Britain	United States
1940	1,653	494	—
1941	1,814	914	—
1942	2,338	1,400	30

German losses are for all bomber types and from all causes. British and American losses are for aircraft involved in operations from only British bases against Europe, all causes.

Bomb Tonnage

	Luftwaffe on UK	RAF on Germany and Occupied Europe	USAAF on Germany and Occupied Europe
1940	36,844	13,033	—
1941	21,848	31,704	—
1942	3,260	45,561	1,561

Figures for UK are for Bomber Command flying from British bases; figures for USA are for 8th Air Force flying from British bases.

Battle of the Atlantic JUNE 1940 – JUNE 1942

The fall of Norway and France in June 1940 had a profound effect on the Battle of the Atlantic. Not only was the Royal Navy left alone to face enemy naval threats, but the German U-boats were able to move to Brittany, from where, between July and October 1940, they enjoyed the first of their "Happy Times", sinking 217 merchant ships for virtually no loss. The British found it impossible to divert warships from the task of preventing an invasion, leaving many of the convoys vulnerable. Admiral Karl Dönitz, commander of the U-boat fleet, introduced new tactics, including the effective use of radio by individual submarines to report convoy sightings, upon which others would home in on the target in a "Wolf Pack", while the Luftwaffe devoted Focke-Wulf Fw-200 Condor long-range bombers to the battle. In October 1940, for example, Convoy SC7, sailing from Canada to Britain, lost 20 out of 35 merchant ships to a "Wolf Pack"; four months later Convoy HG53, from Gibraltar, lost five ships to Condor attack. The Royal Navy responded with extra escort vessels and with the deployment of fighter aircraft on board merchant ships or light carriers, but the threat of blockade was very real.

It was made more so by the actions of German surface ships. Some of these, disguised as neutral or Allied vessels, enjoyed some success but the real threat lay with more formidable warships. Two German battlecruisers – *Scharnhorst* and *Gneisenau* – roamed the North Atlantic in early 1941, sinking a further 22 merchantmen. They were followed in May by the battleship *Bismarck* and heavy cruiser *Prinz Eugen*, leading to one of the most dramatic naval actions of the war. As Admiral Gunther Lütjens took the German warships through the Denmark Strait on 23 May, elements of the British Home Fleet were already deployed. Shadowed by the heavy cruisers *Norfolk* and *Suffolk*, the Germans seemed to be entering a trap, closed as the battleships *Hood* and *Prince of Wales* steamed to intercept. But *Bismarck* was a powerful ship: at 6 a.m. on 24 May she fired salvoes at *Hood* which sent the British battleship to the bottom along with over 1400 of her crew. The British stood away, allowing *Bismarck* and *Prinz Eugen* to sail into the North Atlantic, shadowed by heavy cruisers. Unknown to the British, *Bismarck* had suffered damage, forcing Lütjens to make for St Nazaire, and when he split his force, sending *Prinz Eugen* south, contact was lost. It was by chance that a Catalina flying-boat found the German battleship on 26 May, upon which Fairey Swordfish torpedo-bombers were launched from the carrier *Ark Royal* in a desperate attempt to slow the warship down. They succeeded, leaving *Bismarck* without proper steering. Early on 27 May the British closed in, battering the enemy with shell-fire before finishing the job with torpedoes. Over 2000 German sailors perished.

But this was an isolated incident, disguising the very real problems faced by the British as the U-boats continued to take a heavy toll. Some respite was gained when the Americans, although neutral, agreed to escort convoys in the western Atlantic, but even when the U.S.A. joined Britain in the conflict in December 1941, the balance was not redressed. In the second of their "Happy Times", during the early months of 1942, U-boats roamed freely along the east coast of the U.S.A. sinking unescorted merchant ships, and it was not until the adoption of the convoy system by Britain's allies that things improved. Morale was further undermined in February 1942 when *Scharnhorst* and *Gneisenau*, with *Prinz Eugen* in attendance, suddenly made a dash for Germany through the Channel, all Royal Navy efforts to prevent such an audacious move proving unsuccessful. America's entry into the war may have given the potential for improvement but the Battle of the Atlantic was far from won.

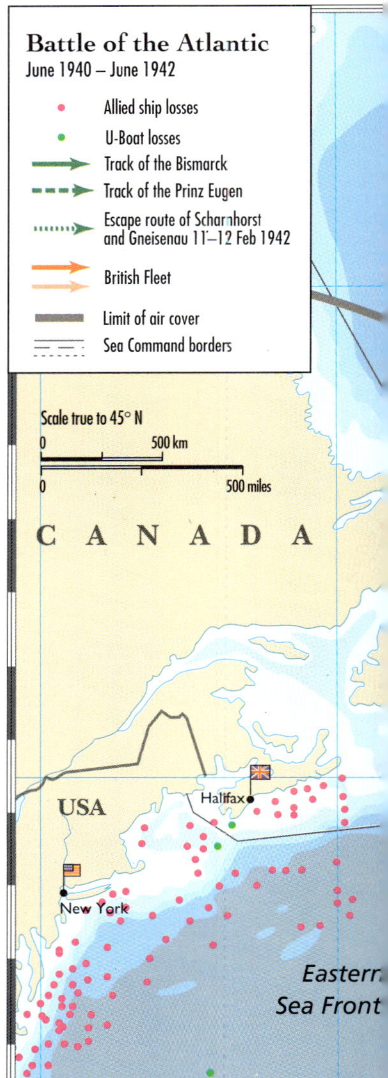

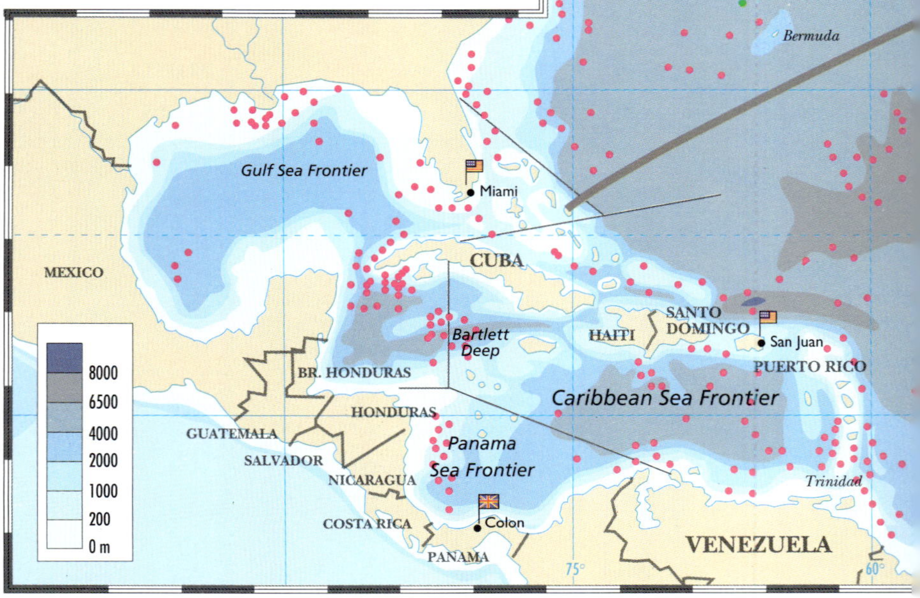

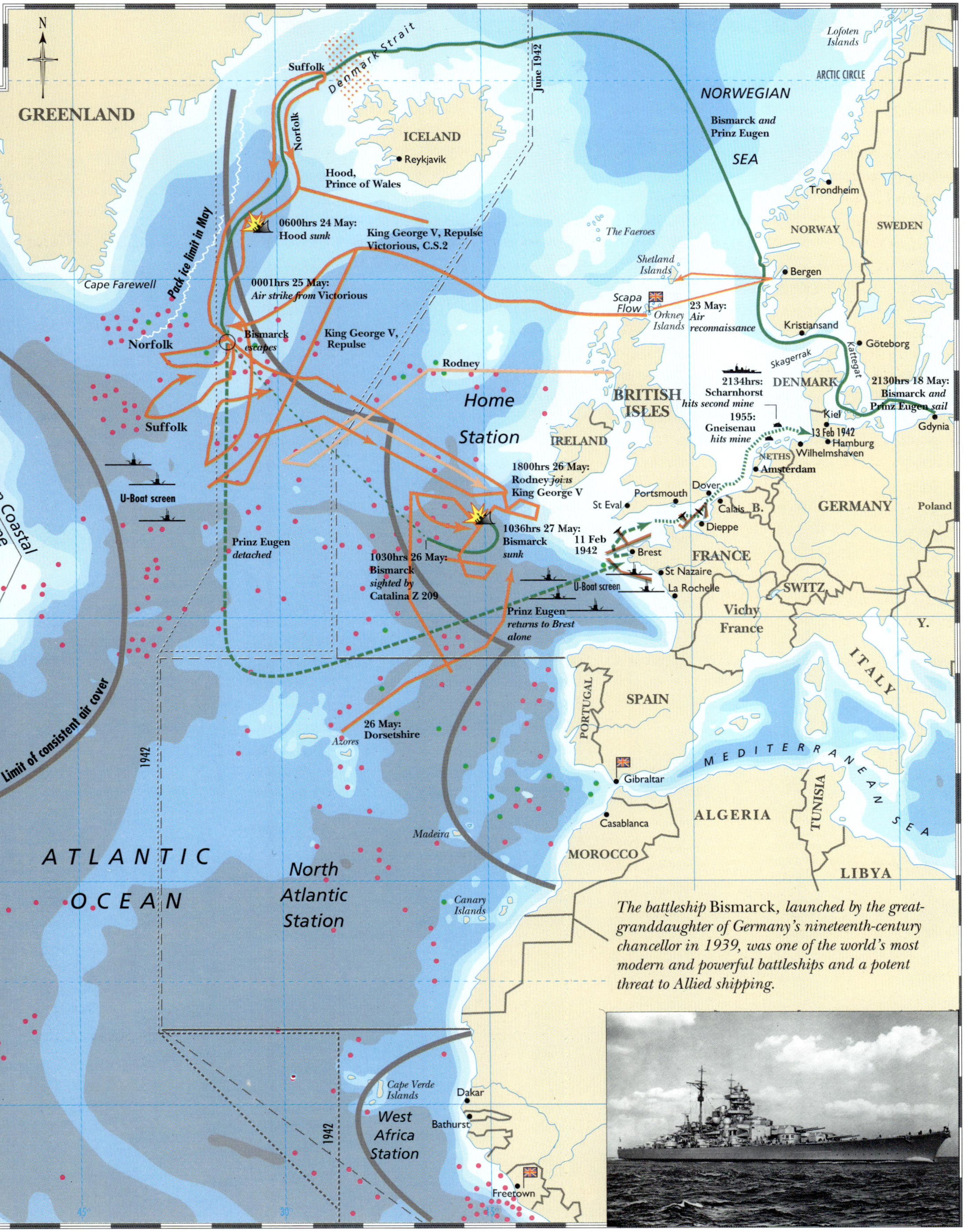

The battleship Bismarck*, launched by the great-granddaughter of Germany's nineteenth-century chancellor in 1939, was one of the world's most modern and powerful battleships and a potent threat to Allied shipping.*

War in East Africa JUNE 1940 – NOVEMBER 1941

Italy declared war on Britain and France on 10 June 1940, sending troops into France on the 21st, one day before the French surrender. Any hopes that this would ensure a voice in the "new Europe" were quickly dashed as Hitler imposed terms on France without reference to Mussolini. But Italy could look elsewhere for gains and it was in Africa that the best hopes of expansion lay. More than 250,000 of Mussolini's soldiers were stationed in Libya, facing a British force in Egypt of only 36,000; in Abyssinia (Ethiopia), he had a further 350,000 men to pit against 21,500 British troops in Sudan, Kenya, Aden and British Somaliland. In July 1940, the Italians captured border posts in Kenya and Sudan, followed a month later by an all-out invasion of Somaliland. In September, six Italian divisions crossed into Egypt, advancing 60 miles in four days.

General Sir Archibald Wavell, British C-in-C Middle East, gave priority to Egypt and waited until January 1941 before ordering a counterattack in East Africa. On 19 January, the 4th and 5th Indian Divisions, commanded by Major-General William Platt, crossed the border from Sudan into Eritrea, threatening Abyssinia from the north. By the beginning of February, Platt's men had advanced more than 100 miles, only to find their way blocked by a steep escarpment close to the town of Keren. Amid bitter fighting in oppressive heat, it was not until 27 March that the Italian defenses could be prised apart, opening the way to the important Red Sea port of Massawa, taken on 8 April.

Meanwhile, on 11 February another British force, under Lieutenant-General Alan Cunningham, advanced into Italian Somaliland, capturing Mogadishu on 25 February before thrusting deep into Abyssinia from the south. Crossing the Ogaden Desert, Nigerian troops entered Jijiga unopposed on 17 March, where they were joined by a third British force, which had liberated British Somaliland from Aden. Together, they faced a formidable natural fortress around Harar, although in the event the Italians withdrew after putting up little more than a token fight. Diredawa fell on 28 March, opening the route to the Abyssinian capital, Addis Ababa. Cunningham's men, having advanced 1700 miles in less than eight weeks, took the city on 6 April, enabling Emperor Haile Selassie to return in triumph.

Meanwhile, the Italian garrison at Addis Ababa had withdrawn north to link up with forces still facing Platt's men in northern Abyssinia and their commander, the Duke of Aosta, decided to make a stand at Amba Alagi, a formidable mountain stronghold. Indian troops attacked Amba Alagi from the north on 3 May, but it was not until elements of Cunningham's army arrived from the south that Aosta recognized the hopelessness of his position. He surrendered on 19 May. Clearing-up operations continued until November 1941, ending a brilliant British campaign. Possession of Eritrea, Abyssinia and Italian Somaliland ensured that the vital trade and supply route through the Red Sea was firmly in British hands.

Lieutenant-General Alan Cunningham's army, which included troops from Nigeria, the Gold Coast, and East and South Africa, covered over 1700 miles (2700 kilometers) in less than eight weeks in their advance on the Abyssinian capital Addis Ababa. Despite the heat and the rough terrain, they succeeded in defeating an army many times their size.

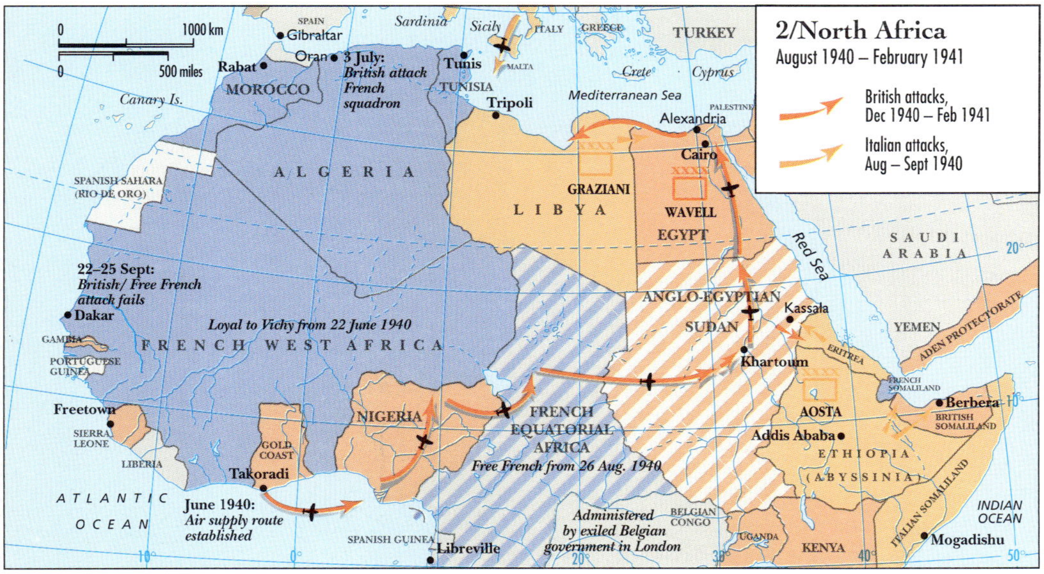

"Lord, how we sweated and toiled to master those monstrous heights, and yet the dry humour common to the sturdy Yorkshireman continued to flow freely. Between their puffs and grunts, one caught such apt and expressive remarks as: 'Think we're bloody mountain goats' and 'We'll be sprouting horns soon'."

A British Infantry Officer

SAUDI-ARABIA
YEMEN
ADEN PROTECTORATE
ANGLO-EGYPTIAN SUDAN
ERITREA
Red Sea
Farasan Is.
Gulf of Aden
San a
Haura
Mocha
Aden
Candala
Massawa
Keren
Kassala
Asmara
5 IND
4 IND
Jan–Feb 1941: British forces re-take Kassala and Gallabat
GIDEON FORCES
Tigre
Gallabat
Gondar
Amba Al gi
Lake Tana
Amhara
Dessie
FRENCH SOMALILAND
(From 5 Aug 1940: Loyal to Vichy)
Djibouti
19 Aug 1940: British evacuation
Karan
Berbera
Jul–Aug 1940: Italian attacks
BRITISH SOMALILAND
Diredawa
Jijiga
Harar
29 Mar 1941
5 May 1936: Italians capture capital city
Ghimbi
Addis Ababa
6 April 1941: Liberated by British troops
Galla
Jimma
6 Aug 1940
Ogaden
Galladi
Walwal
14 Apr 1936
Claimed by Italy
Soddu
ETHIOPIA (ABYSSINIA)
14 Apr 1936
Obbia
ANGLO EGYPTIAN SUDAN
Negelli
Lavello
Mega
25 Feb 1941
Belet Uen
Lugh
Lake Rudolf
Moyale
1 SA
15 July 1940: British recapture Moyale
ITALIAN SOMALILAND
INDIAN OCEAN
Villagio Ducas degli Abruzzi
Mogadishu
UGANDA
KENYA
R. Juba
22 Feb 1941
FORCE F
Royal Navy Support Force
Wajir
Brava
Tanaland
1 SA
11 AFRICAN
12 AFRICAN
Kismayu
14 Feb 1941: Occupied
11 Feb 1941: British attacks launched
Lake Victoria
TANGANYIKA
3000
2000
1000
500
200
0 m
16°
12°
8°
4°
0°
36°
40°
44°
48°
N
0 200 km
0 100 miles
1/Abyssinia, Conquest and Liberation
1934–1941
Italian attacks and advances
Ethiopian counterattacks
Emperor Haile Selassie escapes, 2 May 1936
British attacks from January 1941

The Western Desert JUNE 1940 – FEBRUARY 1941

Britain's Western Desert Force, commanded by Major-General Richard O'Connor, was in no position to prevent an Italian advance into Egypt in September 1940. Comprising little more than 36,000 men, the Force had responded positively to the Italian declaration of war in June by mounting raids across the border into Libya, but once Marshal Rodolfo Graziani, under direct orders from Mussolini, decided to advance into Egypt, there was no choice but to withdraw. The Italian Tenth Army seemed set to push forward as far as Cairo and Alexandria, threatening the Suez Canal.

But after advancing only 60 miles, Graziani halted his army and ordered it to dig in, creating a series of fortified camps that extended southwards from the coast at Sidi Barrani. It was an opportunity that O'Connor did not waste. After consultations with Wavell, he mounted an elaborate "raid", codenamed Operation *Compass*, on the camps, beginning at dawn on 9 December. Men of the 4th Indian Division, supported by 50 Matilda tanks, infiltrated gaps between the Italian positions, while 7th Armored Division looped round the south to take Buq Buq in the enemy rear. As infantry and tanks swept into camps at Nibeiwa, Tummars and Point 90, the Italians broke and ran, only to find their escape route blocked by 7th Armored. By 11 December over 38,300 Italians had surrendered to a numerically inferior force.

Egypt was now secure, but O'Connor had not finished his campaign. Gaining permission from Wavell to extend the scope of the "raid", he invaded Cyrenaica, the eastern province of Libya, giving the enemy no chance to recover. Despite losing 4th Indian Division, transferred to East Africa, he sent its replacement, the 6th Australian Division, along the coast road in close pursuit of Graziani's shattered force, while ordering 7th Armored to sweep through the desert in a wide outflanking move. The advance was not always straightforward – the Italian fortress of Bardia, 15 miles inside Libya, only fell after heavy fighting – but it was inexorable. Once Bardia had fallen on 6 January 1941, the Australians raced on to take El Adem and, on the 22nd, to seize Tobruk, an important supply port. As O'Connor prepared his force for the next stage of the attack, towards Benghazi, Graziani decided to abandon Cyrenaica, pulling back in the direction of Sirte, where he intended to make a stand in defense of Tripolitania, Libya's western province.

O'Connor now faced a race against time, for

Enjoying a respite in the campaign, a member of the British Western Desert Force plays with a tame monkey, 'Private Whiskey'.

"The battlefield was an amazing sight. It was strewn with broken and abandoned equipment, tattered uniforms, piles of empty shell and cartridge cases. It was littered with paper, rifles and bedding."

Cyril Joly, Tank Commander

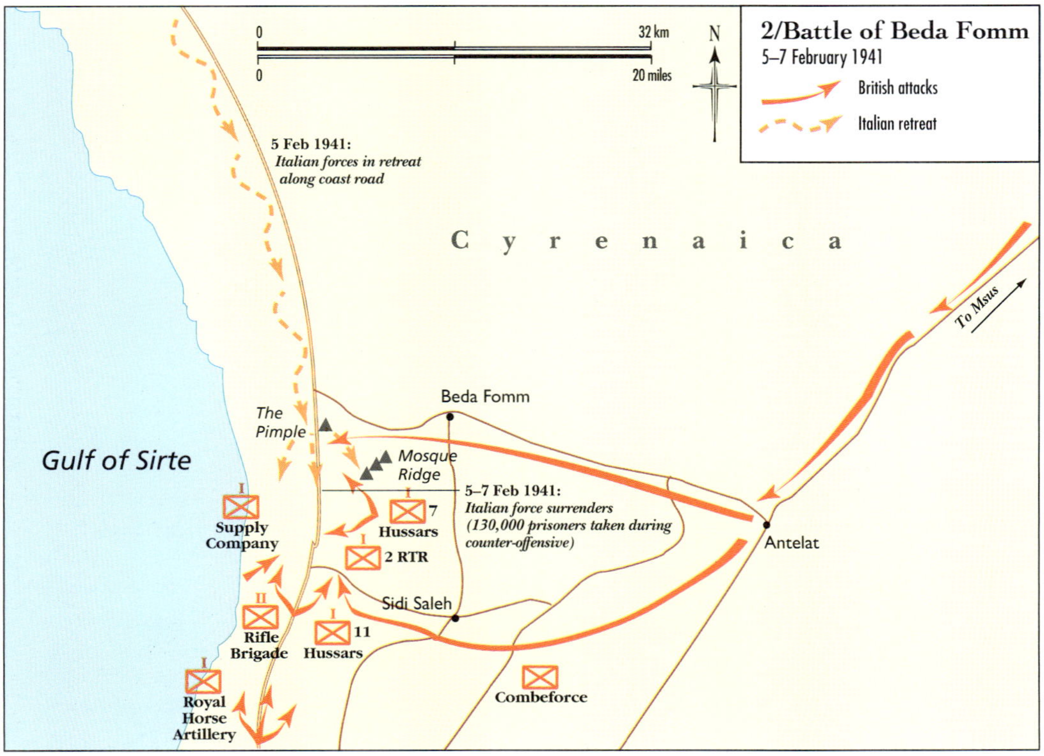

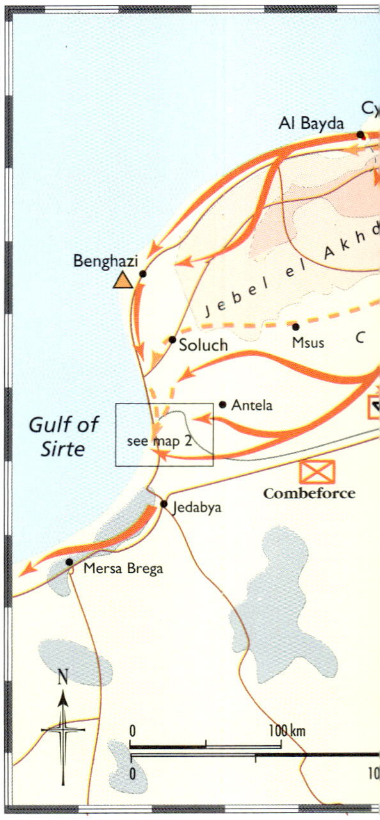

if he could not trap the remaining Italians before they reached their destination, they might recover sufficiently to mount a counter-offensive against what was, in reality, a minute British/Imperial force. In early February he ordered 7th Armored Division to push west, across the base of the Cyrenaican "bulge" through Mechili and Msus to reach the coast at Beda Fomm, while the Australians continued to pursue the enemy along the coast road through Derna and Benghazi. 7th Armored sent a force of armored cars, trucks and light tanks across seemingly impassable terrain to reach Beda Fomm late on 5 February, arriving just 30 minutes before the first of the retreating Italian columns appeared along the coast road from the north. Realizing that they were trapped, the Italians tried desperately to force a way through, but were held by 7th Armored. On 7 February, as Australian troops entered Benghazi, the Italians surrendered, allowing British troops to push on as far as El Agheila on the Gulf of Sirte. O'Connor's "raid" had lasted less than two months and, at a cost of about 2000 casualties, had defeated an entire Italian army. More than 130,000 prisoners were taken. O'Connor wanted to push on, into Tripolitania, but was stopped by Wavell, under pressure from Churchill to transfer troops to the Balkans. The British victory was about to be wasted.

"Further down the road I saw some Australians with a pile of Italian paper money and it soon became fashionable to light a cigarette with a fifty or a hundred lire or to post an autographed note back to Australia. Useless in Tobruk, these same notes were real money in Benghazi, as the troops ruefully discovered."

Chester Wilmot, war correspondent

Italian prisoners-of-war produce their military identification. After the initial success of their offensive, the Italian army was caught completely by surprise by O'Connor's audacious counterattack. The heavily-armored, though slow moving, British Matilda tank proved particularly effective against the Italian fortified positions, and kept the Italians off balance.

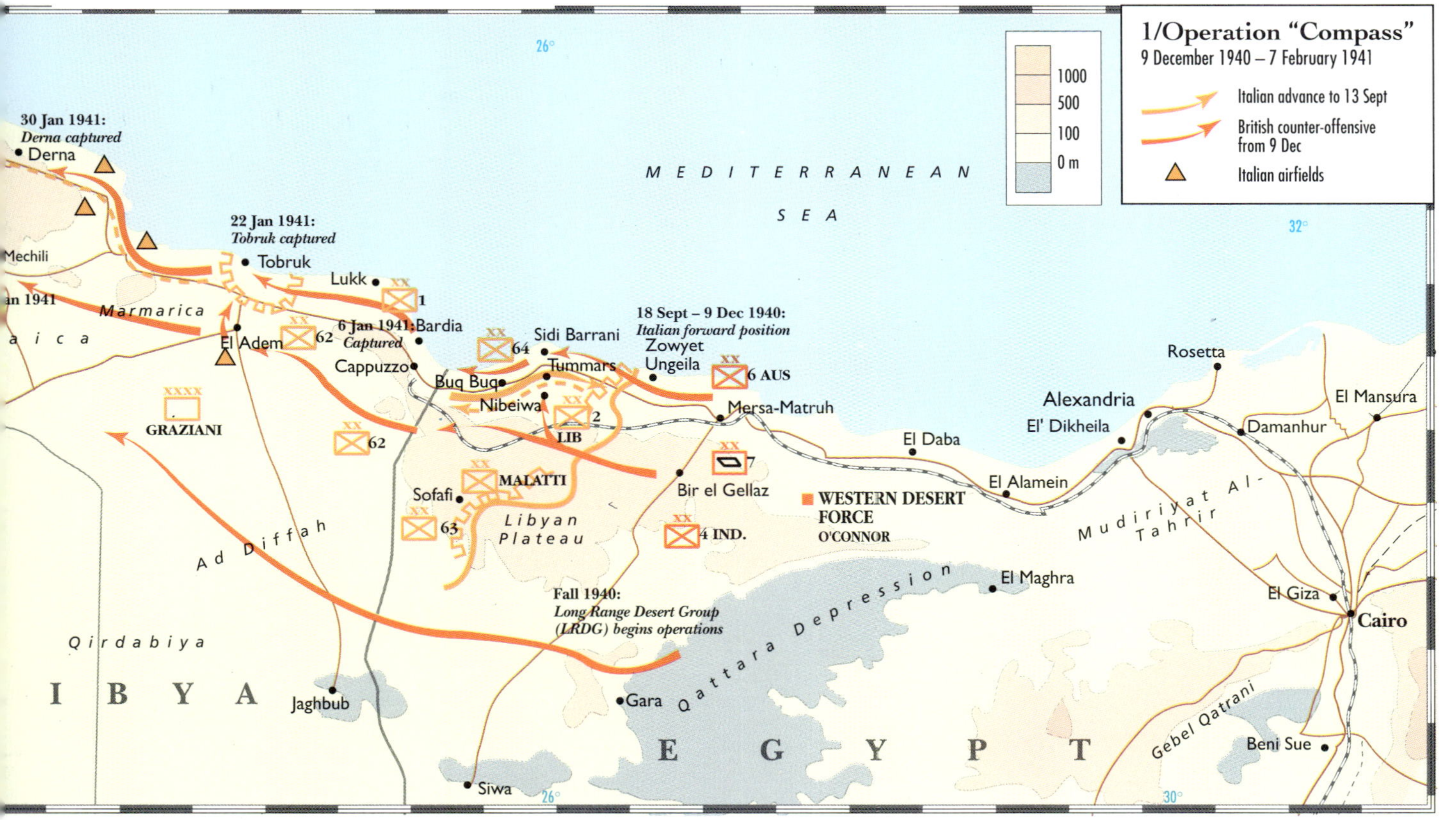

The Conquest of Greece APRIL – MAY 1941

Responsibility for the German invasion of Greece lay with Field Marshal Wilhelm List's Twelfth Army, massed in Bulgaria. Hitler's decision to invade Yugoslavia as well as Greece, taken on 27 March, meant that XL Panzer Corps had to be diverted towards Skopje, leaving the initial attack on Greece to be carried out by XVIII Corps. Its units attacked and, more significantly, outflanked the Aliakhmon Line in Macedonia on 6 April. Three days later, German troops were in Salonika.

This left the Metaxas Line further south, manned by the British/Dominion 'W' Force, dangerously exposed. XL Panzer Corps, having entered Skopje on 8 April, exploited south over "impassable" terrain to enter the Monastir Gap, advancing behind Greek forces in Albania and outflanking 'W' Force. On 12 April, the British withdrew to positions around Mount Olympus and then, when they too became compromised, to the Thermopylae Line, protecting the approaches to Athens. By 20 April, with Yugoslavia defeated and the Greek Army collapsing, Field Marshal Sir Archibald Wavell, C-in-C Middle East, reluctantly authorized a withdrawal from Greece. Evacuation by sea began on 22/23 April and continued for five nights; of the 62,500 troops committed to Greece, over 50,000 were saved, but they lost most of their heavy equipment.

About 27,000 of the evacuees were sent to Crete. Codebreakers at Bletchley Park in Buckinghamshire, England, reading German Enigma messages, were able to say with certainty that an attack by airborne troops was imminent, and this was passed to Freyberg via Ultra. With nearly 30,000 British and Dominion troops available, plus about 14,000 Greeks and innumerable Cretan guerrillas, Freyberg should have offered a strong defense, but he had no air

Major-General Freyberg VC deployed 30,000 British and Commonwealth troops in the defense of Crete. Spread out to defend all possible landing zones, the Allies fought hard but German airpower eventually forced their evacuation.

> *"We have beaten off the attack of an enemy battalion. One of our battalions drops as reinforcements into the battle area. A 3.7 cm anti-tank gun lands near me. It came down supported by five parachutes. A little further off a motorcycle combination crashes to the ground and is totally wrecked. The 'chutes did not open."*
>
> **from the personal diary of Adolf Strauch, Fallschirmjäger, 22 May 1941**

support and was convinced that an airborne assault would be a preliminary to a more conventional seaborne invasion.

About 15,000 German airborne troops of XI Fliegerkorps under Major-General Kurt Student were to land along the north coast of the island. As soon as airfields had been secured, men of the 5th Mountain Division would be flown in by Junkers Ju-52 transports. Other troops of the same division would arrive by sea, together with heavy equipment and light tanks.

The attack, codenamed *Operation Merkur,* began early on 20 May. It did not go well. Around Maleme, elements of the Sturmregiment landed in the middle of a New Zealand battalion and were virtually wiped out, while men of the 3rd Regiment were soon bogged down in "Prison Valley" to the south of Canea. When the second wave arrived in the afternoon, they too made little headway. By the morning of 21 May, however, British confusion had led to the abandonment of Hill 107, overlooking Maleme airfield. Student, realizing this, ordered Ju-52s carrying reinforcements to land under artillery fire. By the end of the day over 650 extra men had arrived.

Freyberg remained obsessed about a seaborne landing. When flotillas carrying mountain troops from Greece were dispersed by the Royal Navy during the night of 21/22 May, he thought the battle was over. It was not. As more German reinforcements arrived by air, the Allies failed to co-ordinate counterattacks and their defenses cracked. British troops at Heraklion were evacuated by sea on 28/29 May, by which time the main evacuation further south had begun. It ended on 1 June. *Operation Merkur* remains the only strategic airborne operation in history.

Fallschirmjäger drop to earth around the Cretan port of Heraklion. One of the Ju-52 transport aircraft, hit by ground fire, becomes part of the huge loss of aircraft in Operation Merkur, *along with around 6500 men killed and wounded.*

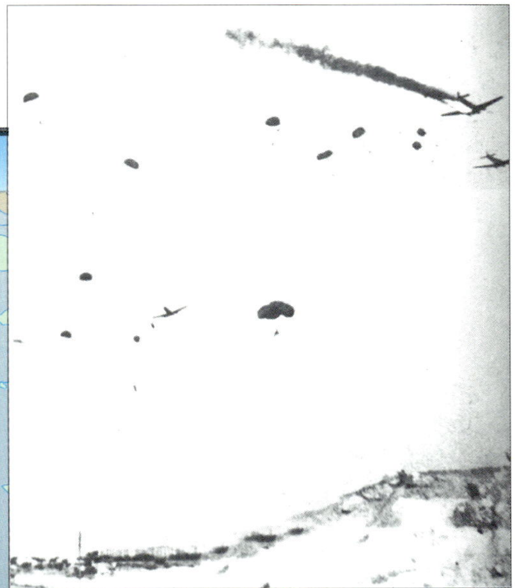

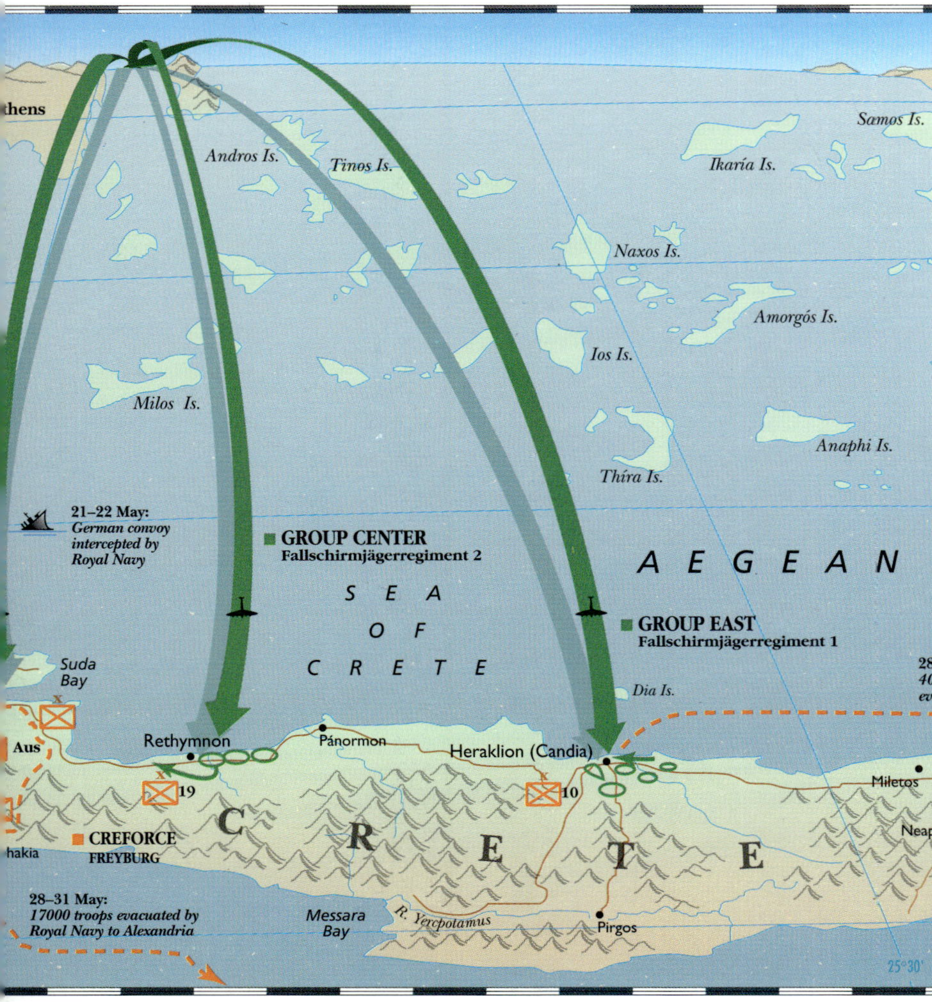

The Western Desert MARCH – JUNE 1941

The crushing Italian defeat in Cyrenaica in early 1941 alarmed the Germans. They recognized that a British victory could lead to an escalation of the war in the eastern Mediterranean – the right flank of any attack into Russia. Hitler's response was to offer military aid to the Italians in Libya, hoping that this would bolster their defense. On 12 February 1941, less than a week after the Battle of Beda Fomm, Lieutenant-General Erwin Rommel arrived in Tripoli under direct orders from Hitler to recapture Cyrenaica. Two days later, the first German troops – spearhead units of the *Deutsches Afrika Korps* – arrived by sea.

Rommel and his men rapidly transformed the situation. The British were at the end of a supply line that stretched back as far as the Nile Delta, and had lost a proportion of their more experienced units to the defense of the Balkans. Thus, when Rommel decided to take the offensive in late March 1941, establishing forward positions at the Marada Oasis and El Agheila, he quickly realized that his enemy was weak. Although ostensibly subject to orders from the Italian C-in-C North Africa, General Italo Gariboldi, and aware that the Libyan theater was not first priority among German planners currently putting the final touches to the projected invasion of Russia, Rommel was not the sort of general to miss an opportunity. On 31 March, he attacked Mersa el Brega and, when that fell after stiff fighting, pushed on to attack Agedabia, triggering a British retreat. As one Italo-German motorized column followed the coast road, retaking Benghazi, Barce and Derna in early April, another swept through the desert to sever the road well in the rear at Gazala. It was an exact reversal of O'Connor's success in February, although he was not to witness it. On 6 April both he and Lieutenant-General Philip Neame were captured when their staff car was overrun by German troops.

Once the two Axis columns linked up at Gazala, the British had no choice but to pull back. On 11 April Bardia fell, followed four days later by Sollum, just over the border in Egypt. Lieutenant-General Sir Noel Beresford-Pierse, brought from East Africa to command the Western Desert Force, hastily reorganized his men into infantry and armor "boxes" close to the border, while mobile, all-arms "Jock" Columns (named after their commander, Lieutenant-Colonel "Jock" Campbell) harassed the enemy's forward units. By this time, Rommel was suffering from serious supply problems – his truck convoys had to drive from Tripoli to deliver much-needed fuel and ammunition – and was intent on capturing Tobruk, held by the 9th Australian Division. The port was surrounded, well to the rear of the Axis front-line, but could be sustained by sea. Rommel attacked Tobruk on 14 April, only to be repulsed by British and Australian artillery. A second, more co-ordinated assault, supported by Stuka dive-bombers, began on 30 April, but made little headway. As losses mounted, Rommel called off the attack on 4 May, preferring to lay siege to the town. It was to hold out, denying Axis forces the forward supply base they so desperately needed, until relieved by the British toward the end of the year.

*Still wearing the **Afrika Korps'** original issue of tropical helmet and shorts, Rommel jumps down from a captured British Crusader tank during the early days of his campaign in the Western Desert.*

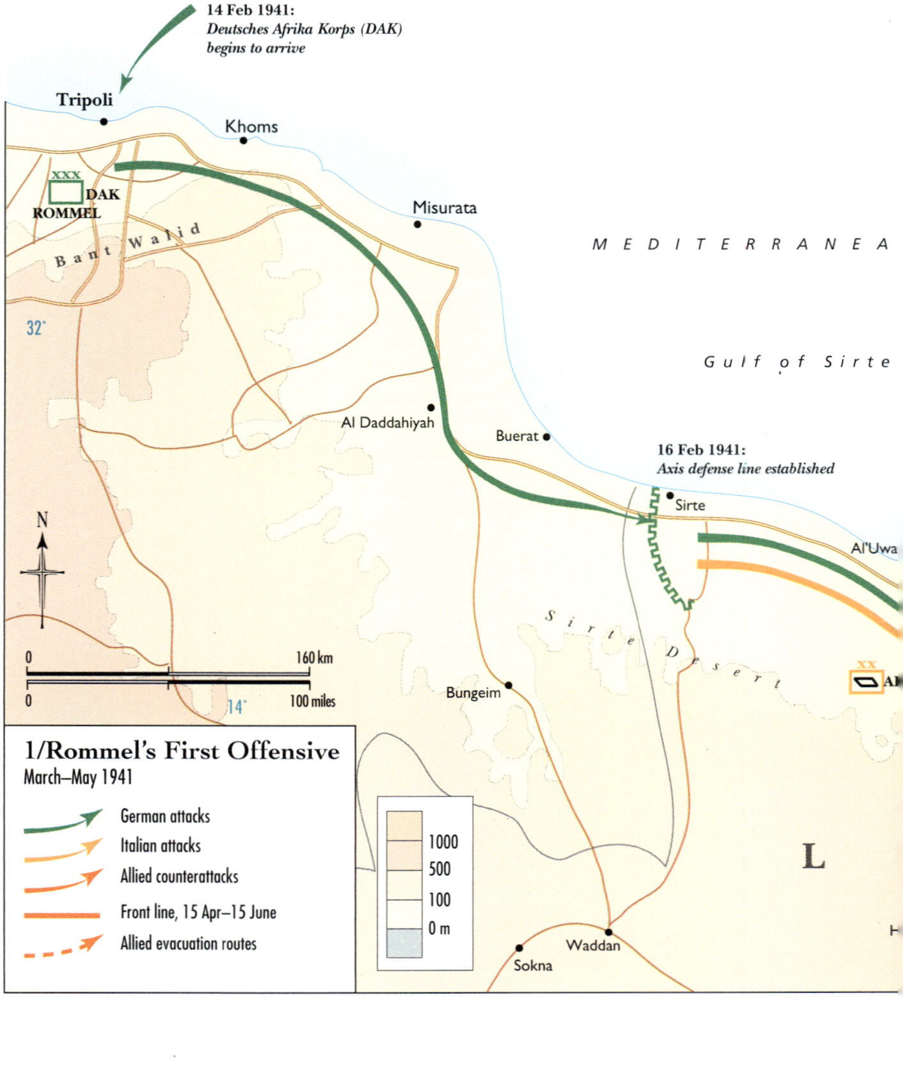

1/Rommel's First Offensive
March–May 1941

Meanwhile General Wavell, C-in-C Middle East, had ordered Beresford-Pierse to prepare for a counterattack, even though Western Desert Force was still weak. This materialized on 15 May as the aptly-named Operation *Brevity*, which took Halfaya Pass on the Egyptian-Libyan border, only to lose it again once Rommel reacted. By late May, both sides had paused to absorb reinforcements – Rommel received the bulk of 15th Panzer Division, while the British took delivery of 400 new tanks – and the war devolved, temporarily, into a stalemate. It was during this period that the British Long Range Desert Group (LRDG), founded in 1940, began to conduct reconnaissance missions deep behind enemy lines. In the summer of 1941 it was joined by the Special Air Service (SAS), dedicated to long-range raiding. By then, the next stage of the campaign had begun.

> *"If the struggle were not so brutal, so entirely without rules, one would be inclined to think of the romantic idea of a knight's tourney."*
>
> **Lieutenant Schorm, Afrika Korps**

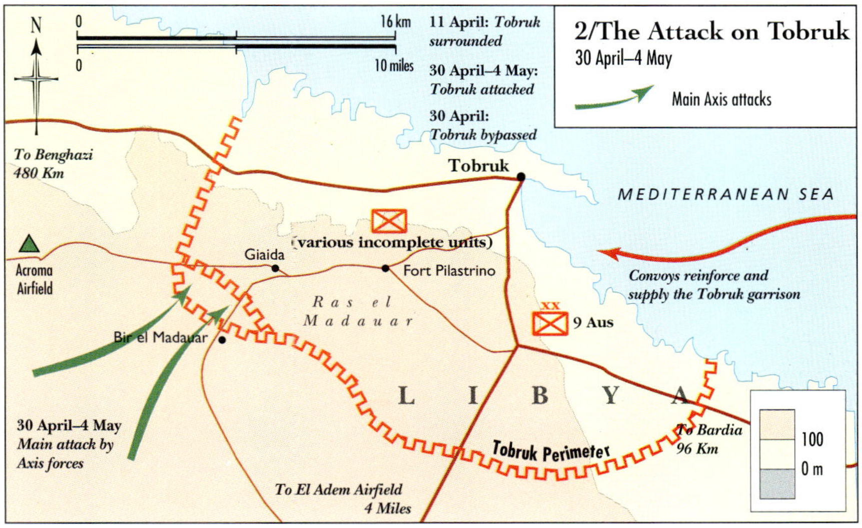

Members of the British Long Range Desert Group in an American-built Chevrolet truck. In a theater of war in which lax dress-codes had become the rule rather than the exception, the members of the LRDG were renowned for their flamboyance.

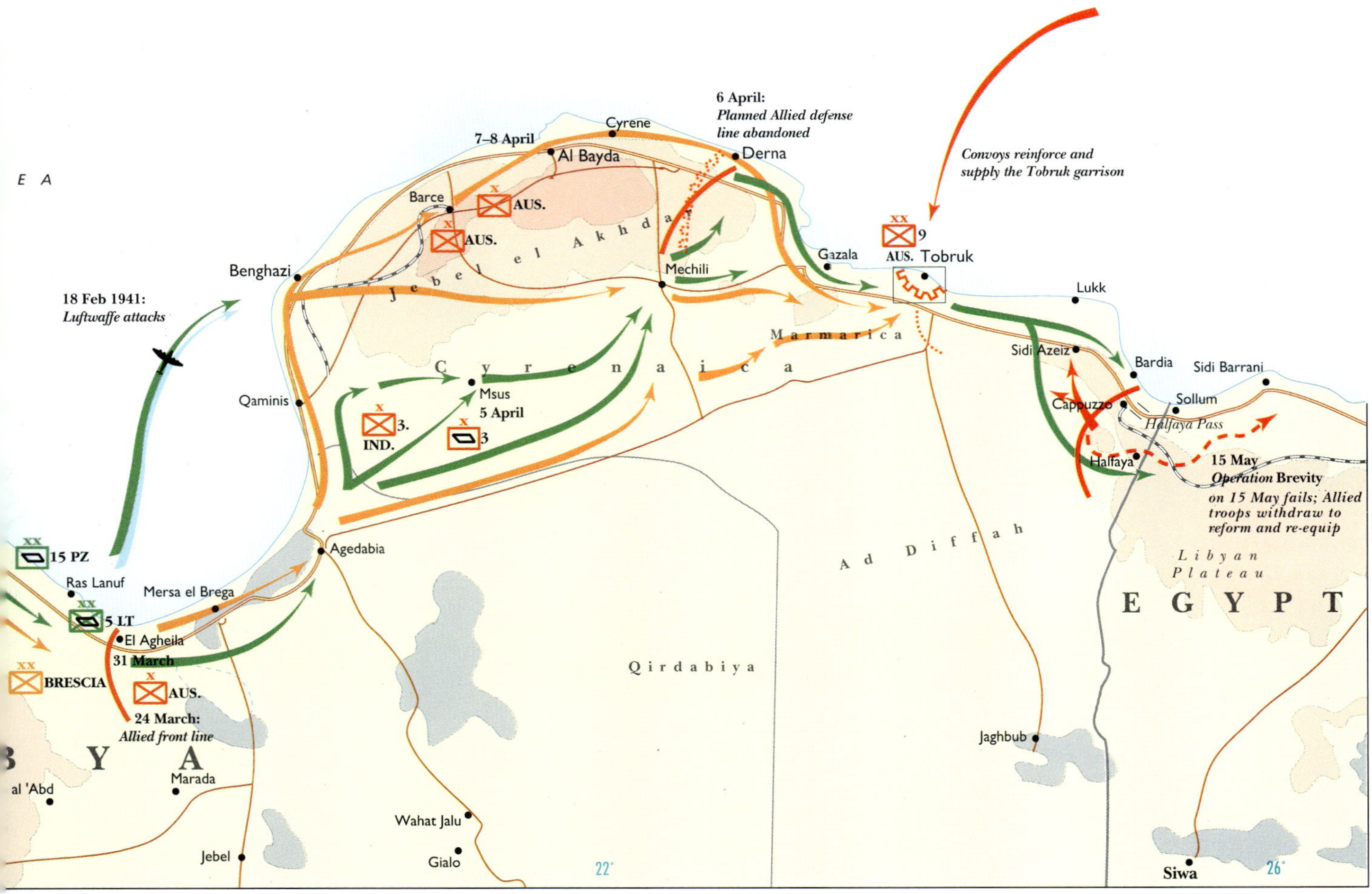

Iraq, Syria and Iran APRIL – SEPTEMBER 1941

By mid-May 1941, the British were having to deal with a plethora of separate campaigns throughout the Middle East and eastern Mediterranean. In the Balkans, the German invasion of Yugoslavia and Greece had necessitated a British withdrawal to Crete, which was about to be attacked from the air, while in North Africa Rommel had advanced from El Agheila to the Egyptian border in less than a month and was laying siege to the port of Tobruk. At the same time the campaign in East Africa, although close to victory, continued to demand attention. As if Wavell did not have enough on his plate as C-in-C Middle East, he also faced severe problems in Iraq, Lebanon and Syria. The British/Imperial forces under his command were seriously overstretched.

The crisis in Iraq – a nominally independent country containing British garrisons – began in late April 1941 when Rashid Ali, the pro-fascist prime minister, objected to the arrival of the 10th Indian Division, sent to secure the oilfields around Basra. When his objections were ignored, he ordered his troops to surround the British airbase at Habbaniya, about 50 miles west of Baghdad. On 2 May RAF bombers hit the Iraqi positions, after which Habbaniya came under artillery fire. Wavell, under intense pressure from London, reluctantly agreed to commit troops to the relief of the airbase, although it was not until 11 May that "Habforce", created from units of the 1st British Cavalry Division in Palestine, began to move into Iraq. They arrived at Habbaniya on 18 May, having crossed desert terrain in temperatures of over 120°F, only to find that the Iraqis were already withdrawing. "Habforce" moved on to take Baghdad, while 10th Indian Division pacified the area around Basra. Rashid Ali fled to Persia (Iran).

Meanwhile, the Free French, under General Charles de Gaulle, had been exerting pressure on the British to support an invasion of Lebanon and Syria, parts of the French Empire now under the control of the collaborationist government at Vichy. Again, Wavell (for understandable reasons) was not keen, but was overruled by Churchill, who recognized the strategic implications of possible German deployment to the Vichy-controlled territories. In late May, Wavell earmarked 7th Australian Division (less one brigade) and elements of 1st Cavalry Division to Operation *Exporter*, which began on 8 June when about 34,000 British/Imperial and Free French troops advanced along the coast road toward Beirut and, further inland, across mountains into Syria. Initially, some success was achieved, but by 13 June the advance had bogged down, enabling the Vichy-French forces to mount a counterattack, principally around Merjuyun, which led to heavy fighting. Nevertheless, Allied strength proved superior and, as Beirut came under heavy air bombardment, the Vichy-French began to lose the initiative. Reinforced by "Habforce" and 10th Indian Division from Iraq, and by two brigades of the British 6th Division from Palestine, the Allies resumed the advance on 23 June, by which time the Vichy authorities had decided to abandon Damascus. As defensive positions to the south of Beirut fell, a ceasefire was negotiated. On 14 July the Acre Convention officially ended a campaign that had cost the Allies about 4700 men killed, wounded, or captured but had secured the strategically important area to the rear of British positions in Egypt.

Within a month, the British were on the move again, this time into Iran, a neutral country which was

> *"...with the wantonness of a boy destroying some harmless bird for 'sport', I contributed my share towards the never-ending story of man's inhumanity to man."*
>
> **John Verney, British Infantryman**

needed as a route for Western supplies to a beleaguered Soviet Union. On 7 August 1941 arrangements for a joint intervention were finalized with the Soviets, and on 24/25 August the country was invaded. Three Soviet mechanized columns advanced from the Caspian Sea toward Tabriz, Rasht Qazvin and Teheran, while a much smaller British force came in from the south across the River Euphrates. The Shah put up only a token resistance, ordering a ceasefire on 28 August, although this did not prevent him having to abdicate in favor of his son, Mohammed Reza Pahlavi, when the Allies demanded it. Teheran in turn was occupied on 17 September.

Mediterranean Naval War JUNE 1940 – NOVEMBER 1942

Italy's entry into the war and the defeat of France in June 1940, transformed the naval situation in the Mediterranean, leaving the British badly over-stretched in their efforts to protect the vital trade and communications route that ran from Gibraltar, through Malta, to the Suez Canal. The Italian navy and air force threatened to sever the connection between Gibraltar and Alexandria, while the surrender of the French fleet not only deprived the Royal Navy of much-needed support but also, by implication, boosted Axis strength. One of the first British responses was to call for the disarming of French ships, but when this was refused by the new Vichy government, a British naval force was sent to destroy them. On 3 July 1940, a British attack on the French base at Mers el Kebir in Algeria disabled two battleships.

This, however distasteful, allowed the British to maintain a presence in the Mediterranean, but it was by no means a secure one. As early as 11 June 1940 the island of Malta, strategically placed to threaten the Axis supply line to Libya, came under air attack, beginning a siege that was to last until late 1942, and the Italian fleet began to venture out from its bases. On 9 July, the commander of the British Mediterranean Fleet, Admiral Sir Andrew Cunningham, caught an Italian force off Calabria and inflicted damage on the enemy flagship *Giulio Cesare*; ten days later his ships sank the cruiser *Bartolomeo Colleoni* off northern Crete. More dramatically, on the night of 10/11 November a two-wave assault by Fairey Swordfish torpedo-bombers hit the Italian base at Taranto, destroying the battleship *Conte de Cavour* and badly damaging two others. For the first time, the British felt confident enough to send a small troop convoy through the Mediterranean to Alexandria, in the course of which an attack by two battleships off Cape Spartivento was driven off. The Italian navy seemed to be on the defensive.

It was at this moment that Hitler decided to help his ally by sending aircraft to Sicily. They enjoyed

The Italian battleship Littorio *rests in shallow water after the British* Fairey Swordfish *attack on Taranto harbor.*

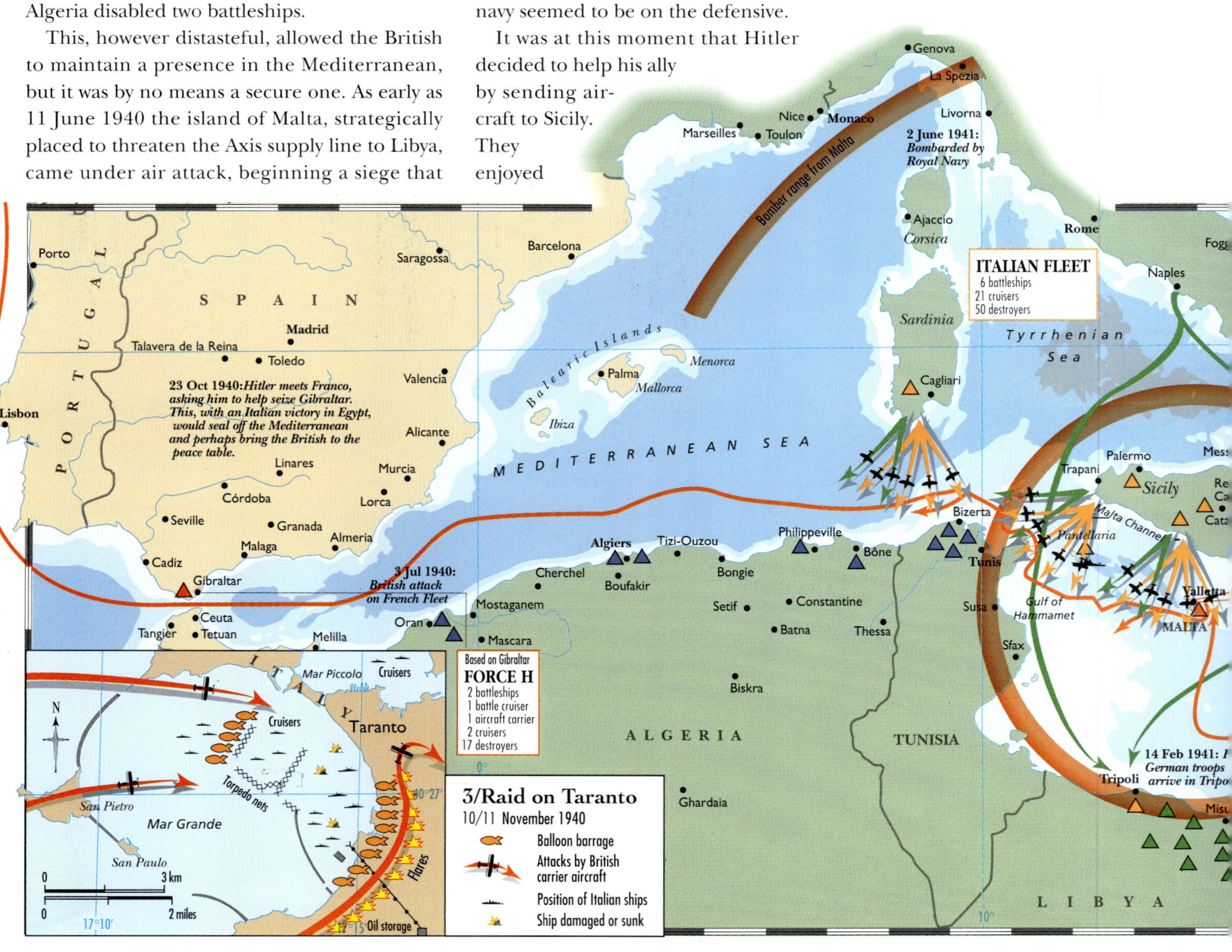

The Vittorio Veneto *fires on the British fleet at Cape Matapan. This battle effectively eliminated the Italian navy in the conflict which had commenced in the Adriatic, Ionian and Aegean seas. Over 2400 Italian sailors were drowned during the engagement.*

"None of us really thought we would come out of it alive"

A *Swordfish* pilot after Taranto

immediate success, crippling *Illustrious* on 10 January 1941, sinking the cruiser *Southampton* the following day, and increasing the pressure on Malta. The Italian navy again ventured out to protect convoys to Libya, only to be caught by Cunningham off Cape Matapan on 28/29 March. In a running battle, the British destroyed three cruisers and two destroyers. It marked the end of the Italian menace, but the Luftwaffe was still capable of inflicting enormous damage, sinking three British cruisers and six destroyers in less than ten days during May 1941. On a more positive note, a special convoy codenamed *Tiger*, did manage to reach Alexandria in May, delivering tanks and aircraft, but this was a lucky gamble. With Malta under sustained attack and the Royal Navy fighting for survival, the war in the Mediterranean seemed to be going the Axis way.

But Hitler's attack on Russia in June 1941 diverted Luftwaffe strength, allowing the British to reinforce Malta and to begin the laborious task of interdicting Rommel's supply route from Italy. This was effective – in October 1941 about 63 percent of Axis supplies were sunk in the Mediterranean – but by December German aircraft had reappeared to hit Malta with even greater force. The island's defenses were maintained precariously and supply convoys continued to fight through at great cost. It was not until the tide had begun to turn in North Africa in October/November 1942, that the Mediterranean was relatively clear for British shipping. It had been a hard-fought battle.

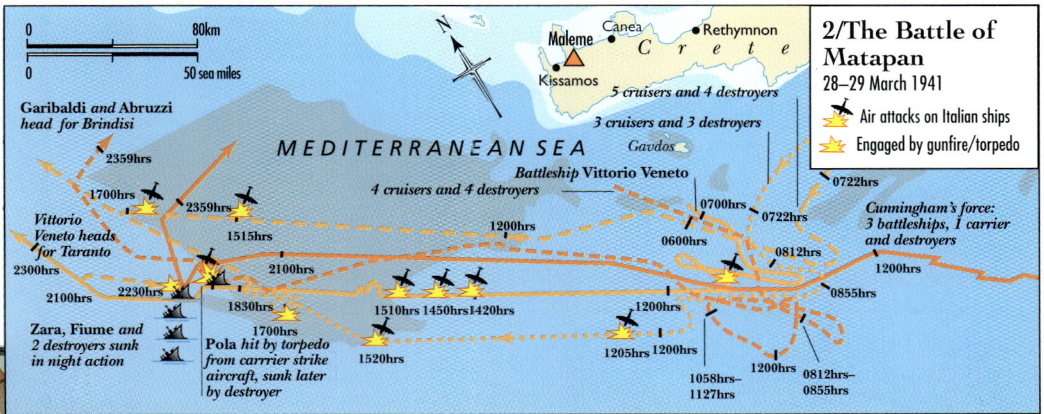

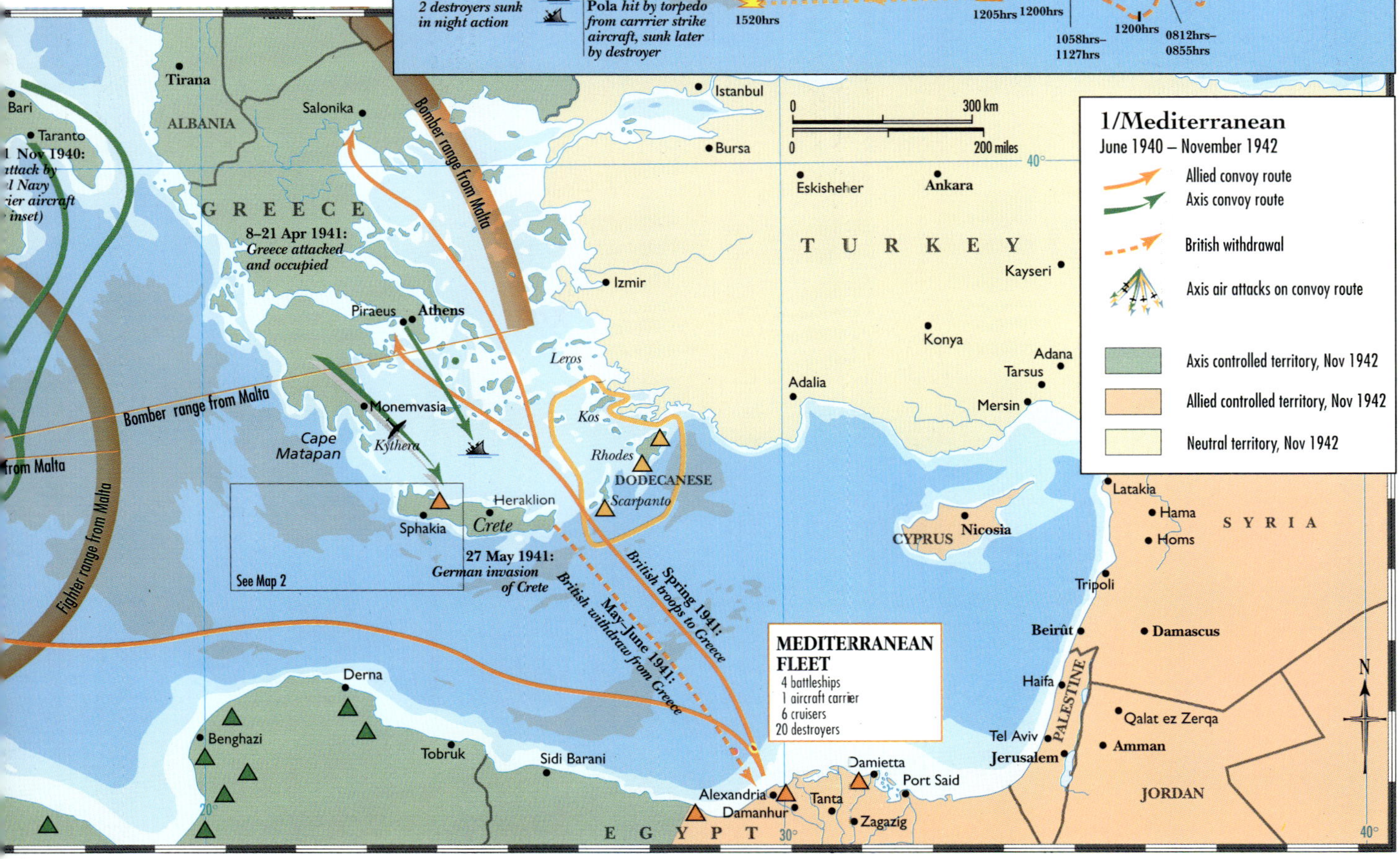

The Western Desert JUNE – DECEMBER 1941

One of the results of the arrival of Convoy Tiger at Alexandria in May 1941 was that Wavell felt strong enough to mount another attack on Rommel's positions along the Egyptian-Libyan border, despite the recent failure of Operation *Brevity*. On 15 June Wavell sent heavy tanks and 4th Indian Division forward to attack Halfaya Pass, while 7th Armored Division tried to loop round to the left to outflank the Axis positions. Known as Operation *Battleaxe*, the engagement lasted only two days, coming to an end when Rommel counterattacked with 15th Panzer Division. *Battleaxe* cost the British 91 tanks and nearly 1000 casualties; it also cost Wavell his job as C-in-C Middle East. Prime Minister Winston Churchill, convinced that Wavell was tired out, had him transferred to India and replaced by General Sir Claude Auchinleck. He set about transforming Western Desert Force into Eighth Army, the command of which was given to Lieutenant-General Sir Alan Cunningham, hero of the East African campaign.

The war in North Africa settled into a stalemate as both sides absorbed reinforcements and waited for supplies. Meanwhile, Tobruk remained under siege. The Australians were relieved by sea and replaced by Indian, South African, Polish and British troops in a series of audacious night operations, and Axis pressure was increased significantly in October 1941, but the port held out. Its relief by land became the aim of Eighth Army operations in November, under the codename Operation *Crusader*. Cunningham's plan, put into effect on 18 November 1941, was to tie down Axis forces on the border using the infantry of XIII Corps, while the armor of XXX Corps – 453 tanks of the 4th, 7th and 22nd Armored Brigades – looped round to the left to advance on Tobruk, tempting the 272 tanks of the 15th and 21st Panzer Divisions into a set-piece battle around the airstrip at Sidi Rezegh. Once the panzers had been defeated, British/Imperial infantry would advance, squeezing the enemy between themselves and the armor at Sidi Rezegh, prior to an advance into Tobruk itself.

To begin with, the plan seemed to work. Despite heavy rain which turned the desert to mud, British tanks managed to seize Sidi Rezegh on 19 November, clashing with Italian armor at Bir el Gubi, while the infantry of XIII Corps advanced toward Sollum. Rommel, intent on attacking Tobruk, did not react immediately, but when it became obvious that a major battle was developing, he committed both his panzer divisions to Sidi Rezegh. This was what Cunningham had planned, although in the event a lack of co-ordination between the three British armored brigades meant that they clashed with the panzers piecemeal. Sidi Rezegh was back in Axis hands by 22 November, upon which the panzers pushed forward into the gap between XXX and XIII Corps, destroying the 5th South African Infantry Brigade. By then, the battlefield was chaotic, leading Rommel to make a rare mistake. On 24 November he ordered his remaining 106 tanks to disengage and race for the Egyptian-Libyan border, convinced that nothing more than infantry stood between him and the Nile Delta. The advance enjoyed some success, but was irrelevant, allowing the British armor to recover sufficiently to link up with the Tobruk garrison. By then, Auchinleck had relieved Cunningham of his command, replacing him with Major-General Neil Ritchie.

Once Tobruk had been relieved, Rommel's main force was dangerously exposed. Although he recognized the problem and recovered sufficiently to impose heavy losses on the New Zealand Division around Sidi Rezegh on 1 December, he could do nothing to prevent a British/Imperial entry into Tobruk on the 10th. Short of supplies and aware that his panzers had been badly mauled, he decided to withdraw, retreating methodically westward to El Agheila. As Derna, Barce and Benghazi changed hands yet again, it looked as if Axis forces had suffered a major defeat.

*A German PzKfw IV tank of the **Afrika Korps**, called by Rommel 'the hard core of the motorized army'. The panzers proved far superior to any British tank and their 1 1/4 inch-thick armor was practically immune to the British 2-pounder anti-tank guns.*

"It was a frightening and awesome spectacle – the dead and dying strewn over the battlefield, in trucks and Bren-carriers, in trenches and toppled over in death, others vocal with pain and stained by red gashes of flowing blood or the dark marks of old congealed wounds."

Lieutenant Cyril Joly, Tank Commander, at Sidi Rezegh

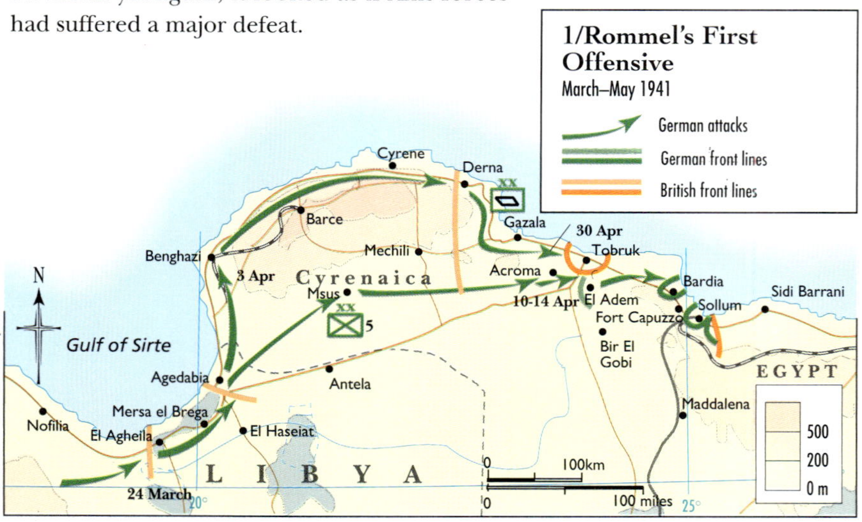

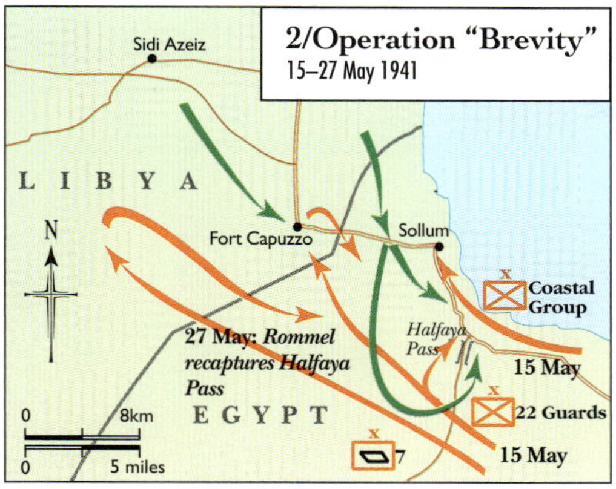

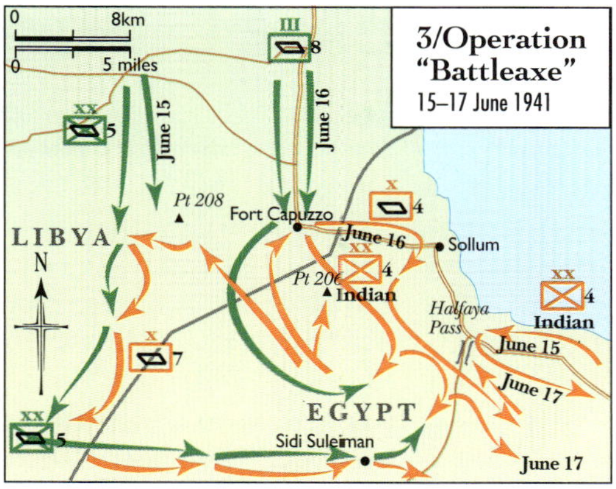

Afrika Korps field artillery in action near Tobruk, 1941.

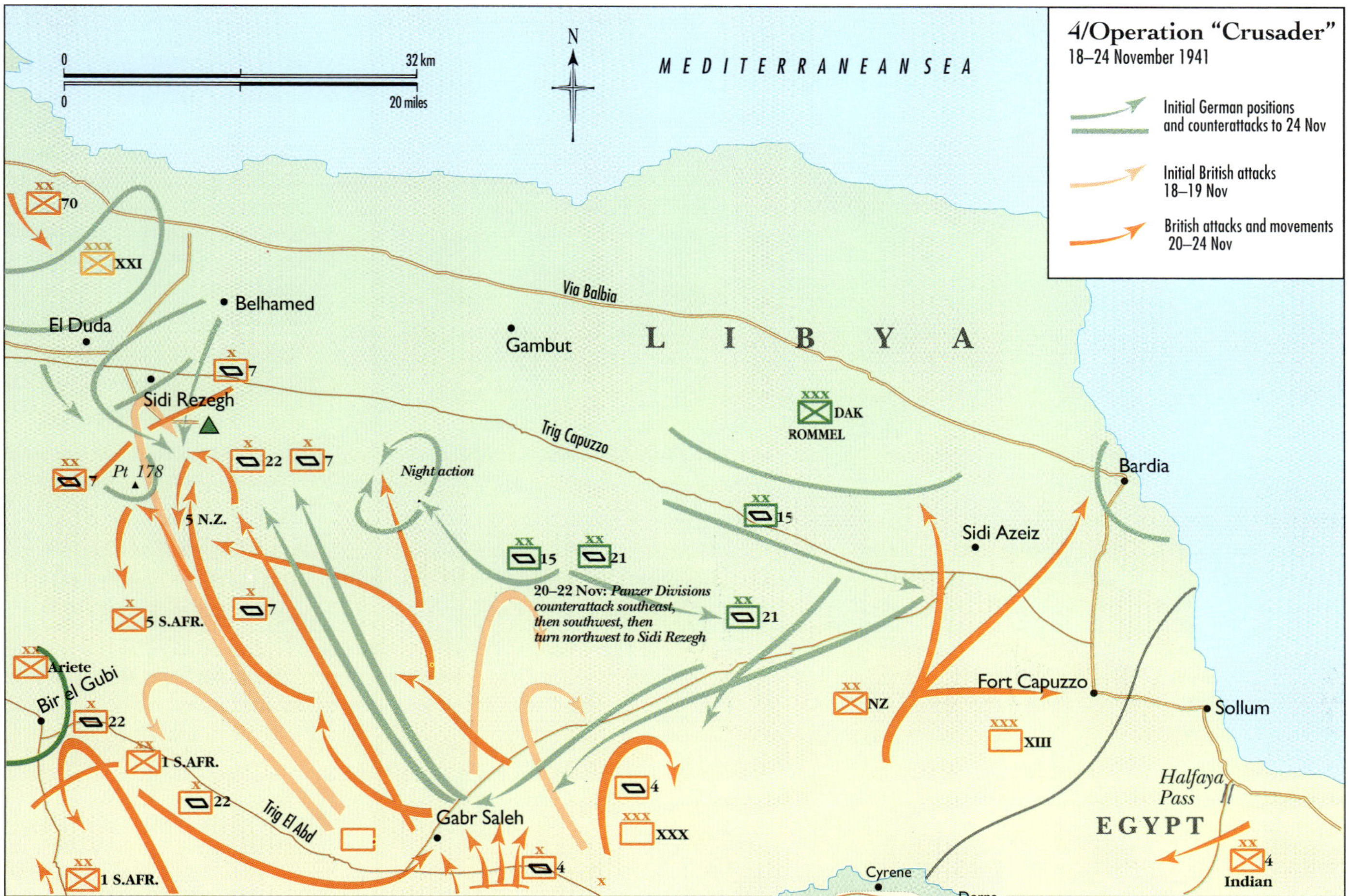

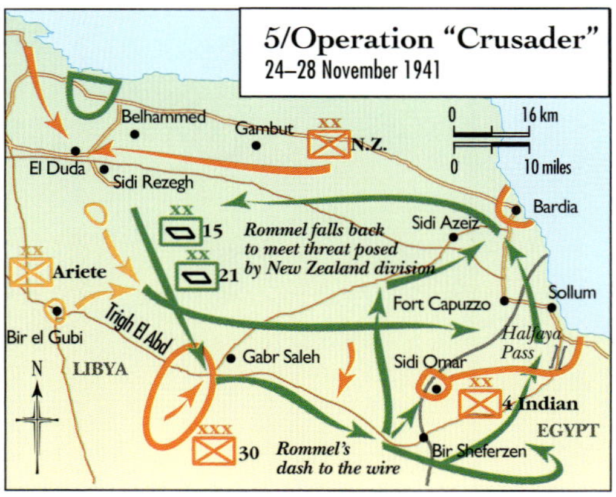

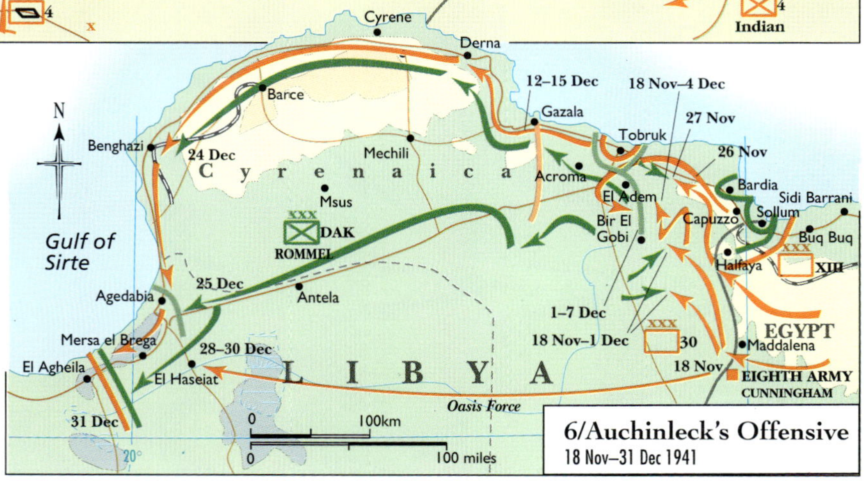

The Western Desert JANUARY – JUNE 1942

Rommel did not remain on the defensive for long once he reached El Agheila in late December 1941. Realizing that Auchinleck's forces were at the end of a stretched supply line, he took advantage of the arrival of replacements to carry out a surprise counteroffensive. Beginning on 21 January 1942, he sent a feint toward Mechili while committing the bulk of his forces along the coast road to Benghazi. Ritchie's Eighth Army fell back to the Gazala Line, a series of strongholds (or "boxes") and minefields that stretched south from Gazala to the Free French fortress at Bir Hacheim. Short of fuel, Rommel paused to build up strength.

He resumed the offensive on 26 May, when the Italian X and XXI Corps attacked the north end of the Gazala Line. Meanwhile, Rommel led the 15th and 21st Panzer and 90th Light Divisions, with the Italian Ariete and Trieste Divisions, on a wide outflanking move to the south, aiming to take Bir Hacheim before pushing north, behind the Gazala Line, to the coast, surrounding the bulk of Eighth Army. The plan did not go smoothly. In the north, the British XIII Corps blunted the Italian assault, while in the south Rommel failed to take Bir Hacheim and encountered unexpected opposition from XXX Corps. By 28 May Rommel was on the defensive. He pulled his mobile forces into an area known as the "Cauldron", with their backs to British minefields. It looked like they were surrounded.

Poor co-ordination by Eighth Army allowed Rommel to survive and recover. As his engineers cleared the minefields, Ritchie's formations mounted ill-prepared attacks that were seen off in succession.

By 1 June, Rommel was strong enough to destroy a "box" held by the British 150th Brigade; two days later, he sent the Trieste and 90th Light Divisions to resume the assault on Bir Hacheim. The Free French fought magnificently, but on 10 June the panzers finally penetrated the northern perimeter. Refusing to surrender, about 2700 of the garrison escaped to the west. His southern flank secured, Rommel mounted increasingly violent and effective attacks out of the "Cauldron" toward El Adem and Tobruk. British armored attacks were systematically destroyed by panzers and 88 mm antitank guns, while less mobile units were crushed or forced to retreat. By 14 June, the battle had swung Rommel's way and Ritchie ordered a withdrawal toward Tobruk.

Garrisoned by 35,000 men, Tobruk's defenses had not been maintained and Ritchie appears to have been unclear in his orders to the garrison commander, who was not prepared to withstand the Axis attack when it began on 20 June. The rest of Eighth Army was in no position to help and, as the port came under sustained attack, the defenses crumbled. Tobruk fell on 21 June, yielding stockpiles of fuel and giving Rommel a vital supply port for his advance into Egypt.

Meanwhile, Auchinleck sacked Ritchie and took personal command of Eighth Army. He decided that a far better defensive position lay further back, at El Alamein, only 150 miles from Cairo.

Tobruk was defended largely by South Africans under the command of Maj. Gen. Henry Belsazar Klopper. To both the British and the Germans Tobruk had come to represent British resistance and many felt that it should be held to the last man.

"My fiancée would read that I had died a hero's death for the Fatherland. And what would that mean? That I was just a bloody mess in the sand at an unidentified spot near an unimportant point in the desert called Acroma."

Lieutenant Heinz Werner Schmidt

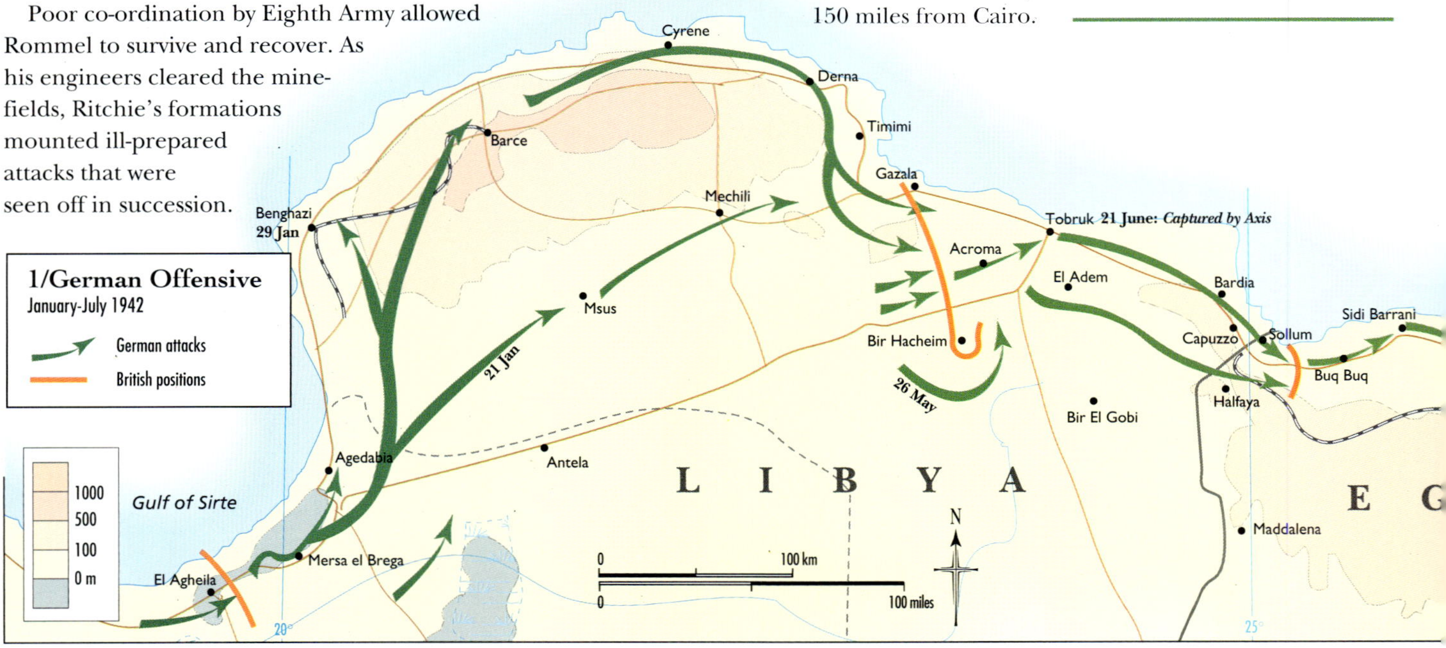

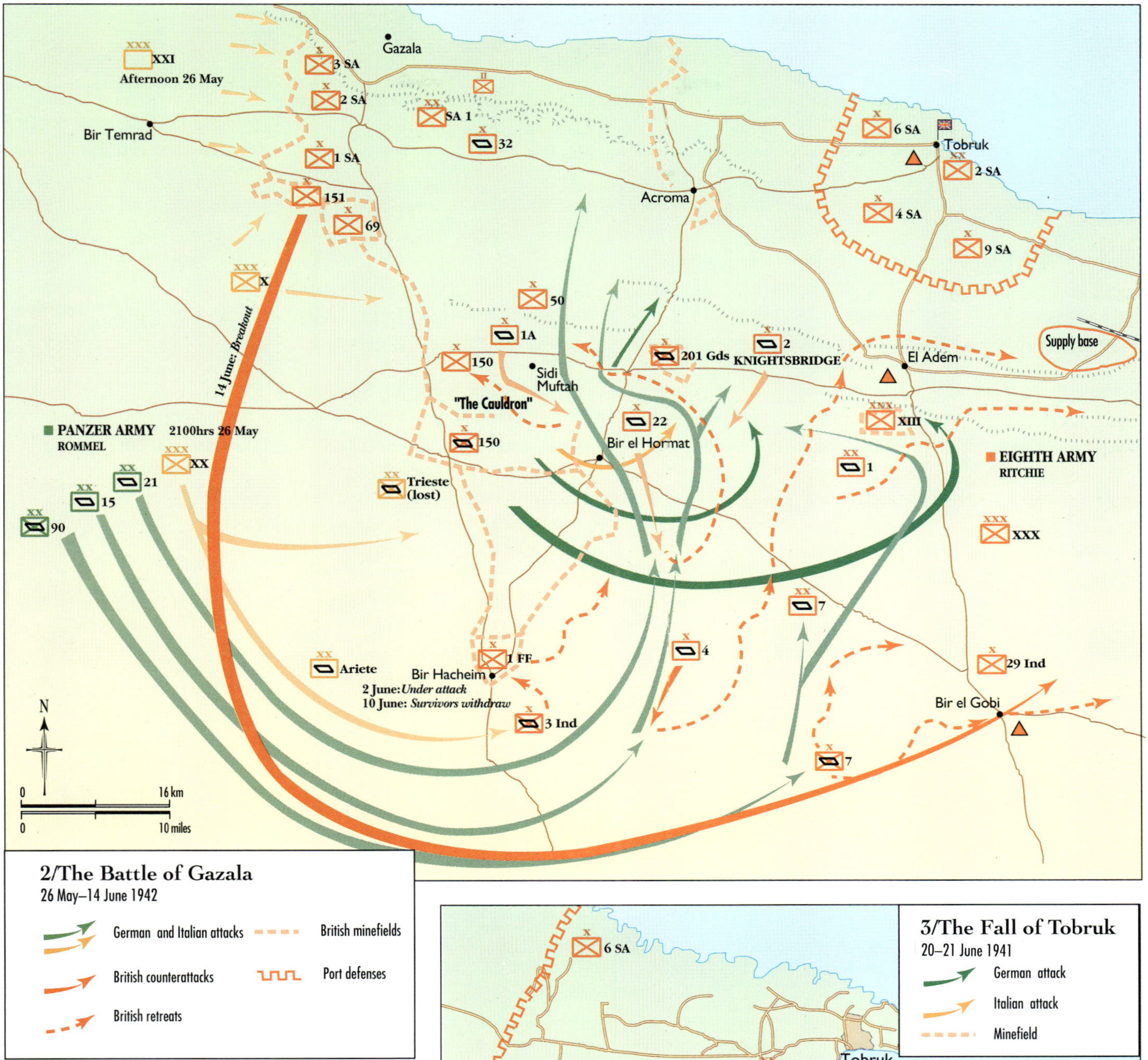

2/The Battle of Gazala

26 May–14 June 1942

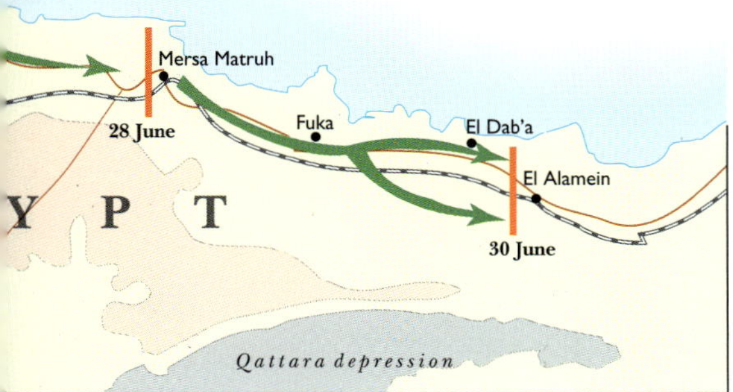

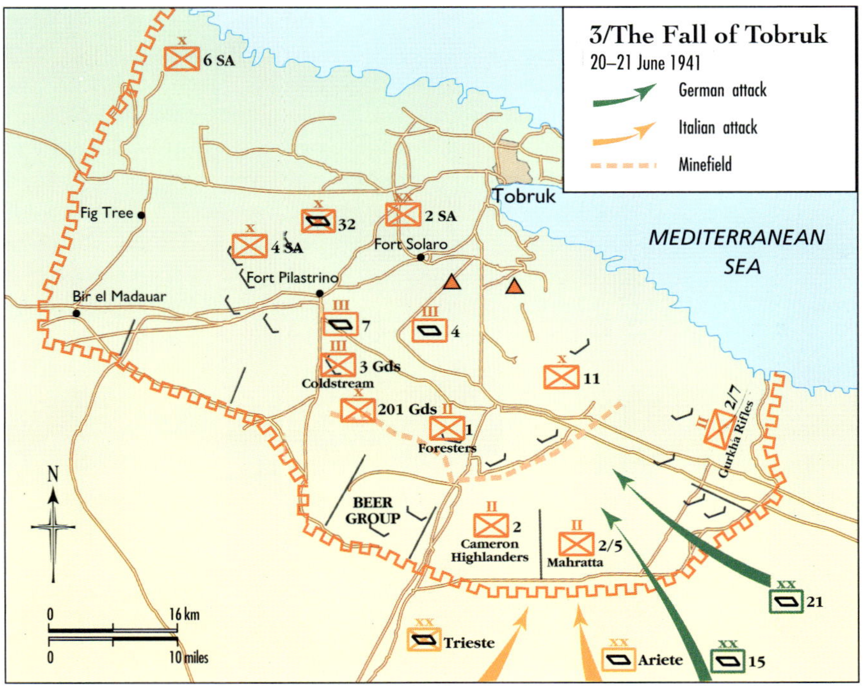

3/The Fall of Tobruk

20–21 June 1941

Operation Barbarossa 1 JUNE – AUGUST 1941

The German invasion of Russia began at 3 a.m. on 22 June 1941. A massive artillery bombardment caught the Russian forces by surprise and, as the Luftwaffe targeted enemy airfields, destroying an estimated 2000 Russian aircraft in the first 48 hours to achieve air superiority, the ground forces attacked. It was the largest single campaign of the war, involving over three million Axis troops against almost five million Russians, and one of the most ambitious. Hitler's intention was to advance deep into western Russia to seize Leningrad in the north, Smolensk (and eventually Moscow) in the center, and the whole of the Ukraine in the south. By these means he intended to destroy communism at its root, gain *Lebensraum* ("living space") in the east, and seize the resources of grain and oil so vital to the German war effort. He came close to success.

The directive for Operation *Barbarossa* was issued as early as 18 December 1940. Army Group North under Field Marshal Ritter von Leeb, comprising three panzer, two motorized and 24 infantry divisions, was to advance out of East Prussia to take the Baltic states of Lithuania, Latvia and Estonia, before linking up with the Finns around Leningrad. Army Group Center, under Field Marshal Fedor von Bock, comprising one cavalry, nine panzer, six motorized and 33 infantry divisions, was to attack eastwards toward Moscow, but pause once it had reached Smolensk. Army Group South, under Field Marshal Gerd von Rundstedt, comprising five panzer, three motorized and 34 infantry divisions, plus Romanian formations, was to push into the Ukraine, aiming for Rostov. The Russians had eleven full armies (about 200 divisions) packed close to the border, but they were poorly organized and badly commanded, reflecting the demoralization caused by Stalin's recent "purges".

Initial German advances were stunning. In the north, General Erich Hoepner's 4th Panzer Group reached Daugavpils and seized crossings over the River Dvina on 26 June, having advanced almost 200 miles in five days. By 14 July, the tanks were within 80 miles of Leningrad. Further south, panzers belonging to General Hermann Hoth's 3rd and General Heinz Guderian's 2nd Panzer Groups carried out a double envelopment, surrounding the Russian Tenth Army and closing pincers around Minsk by 29 June. These two pockets alone yielded 290,000 Russian prisoners. By 1 July, the panzers had crossed the River Berezina and, on the 16th, Guderian took Smolensk, trapping substantial enemy forces to the west of the city. But the Germans already had problems that were to prevent complete success. Co-operation between Army Groups Center and South was impossible because of the Pripet Marshes – an area of forests and swamp to the north-west of Kiev – and communications all along the front, from the Baltic to Romania, were poor. As the panzers advanced, they broke up existing roads, while the Russian railway system, using a different gauge to that of the rest of Europe, needed rebuilding if it was to carry bulk supplies. This made the task of the infantry divisions difficult – they moved on their feet, at a much slower pace than the tanks, and soon lagged, exhausted, behind the spearhead units – while supplies were so short that fuel had to be airlifted forward as early as 23 June. In the north, the Germans lost momentum in the forests of the Baltic states; in the south, von Rundstedt's force faced unexpected resistance from the Russian Fifth Army, equipped in part with the new T-34 tank. With each delay Stalin recovered his balance.

It was at this point, in mid-July, that German debates about strategy came to a head. When *Barbarossa* had first been planned, the generals had favored a drive on Moscow, with attacks toward Leningrad and Rostov as secondary, arguing that if Moscow fell, so would the communist state. Hitler disagreed, preferring to concentrate on Leningrad and the Ukraine, but with the fall of Smolensk, the generals presumed that Moscow would become the main objective. It did not. On 19 July, Hitler ordered the attack in the center to become an infantry affair once Smolensk had been cleared, with Hoth's panzers diverting north to assist in the capture of Leningrad and Guderian's forces moving south to skirt the Pripet Marshes and link up with von Rundstedt to encircle Russian armies around Kiev. Despite further pressure from the generals, this plan prevailed, although the need to rest the panzers and to clear the Smolensk pocket – it eventually yielded another 300,000 prisoners – delayed the start of the offensive until 25 August.

Time was beginning to run out.

"I have decided again today to place the fate and future of the Reich and our people in the hands of our soldiers. May God aid us, especially in this fight."

Adolf Hitler,
22 June 1941

German and Soviet Command Structures at 22 June 1941

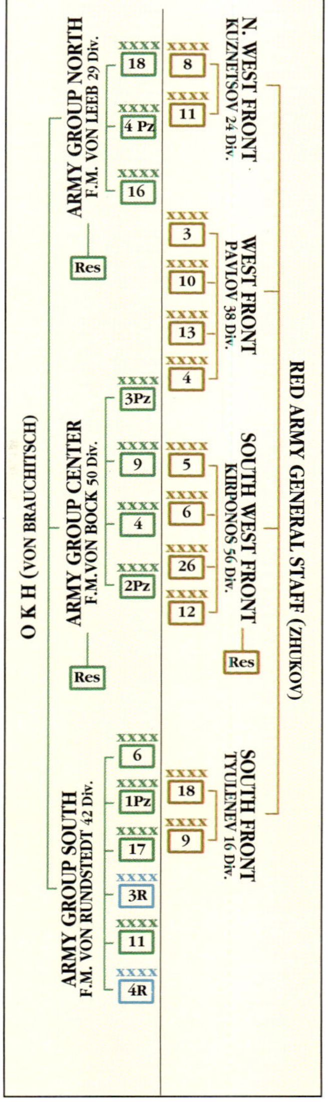

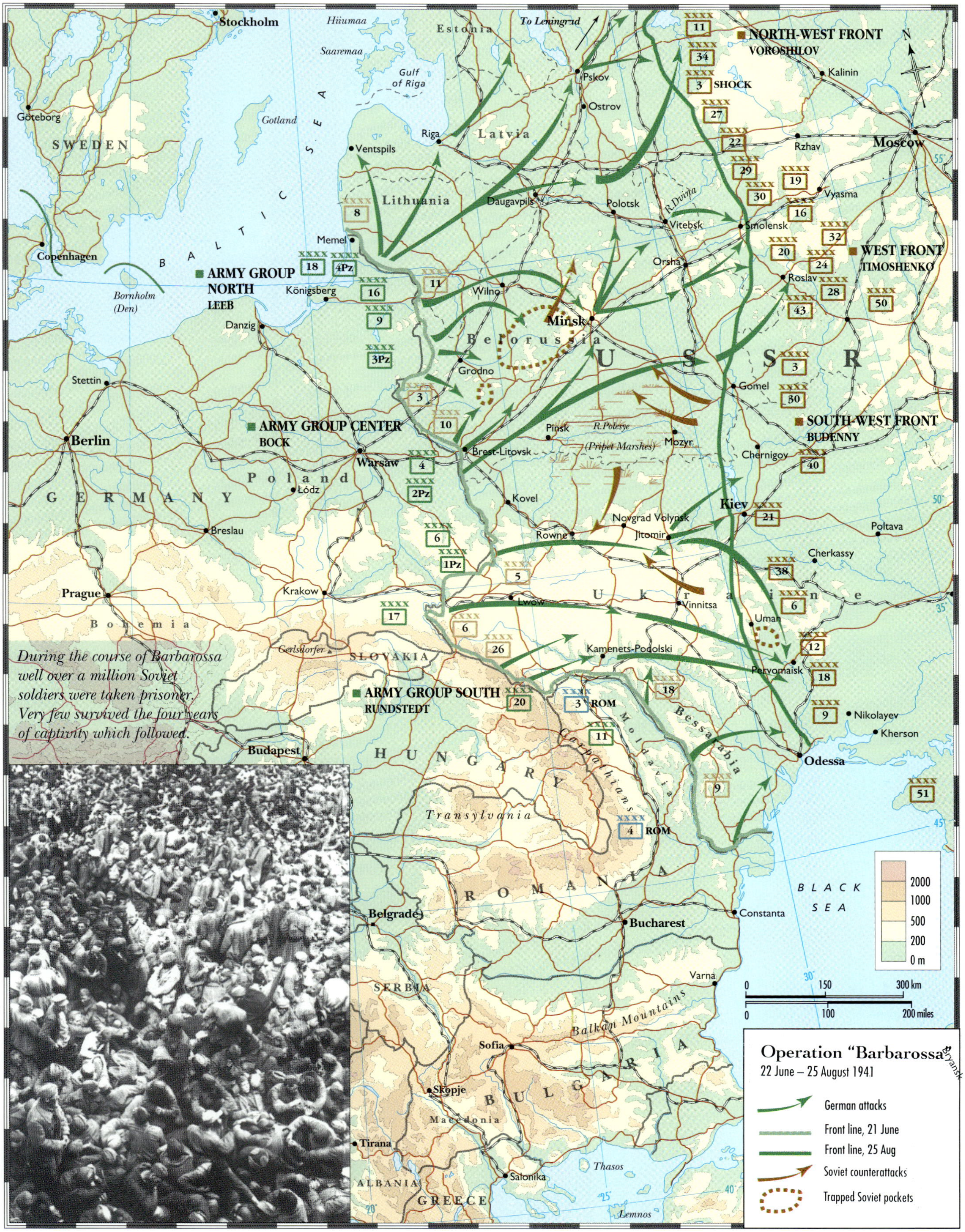

During the course of Barbarossa well over a million Soviet soldiers were taken prisoner. Very few survived the four years of captivity which followed.

Operation Barbarossa II AUGUST – OCTOBER 1941

Hitler's decision to divert the panzers of Army Group Center away from the thrust toward Moscow, made on 19 July, took more than a month to implement. By then, the crises that had occasioned the decision had largely passed. Army Group North managed to advance from the River Luga on 8 August, seizing Novgorod on the 16th and Chudovo four days later, without the benefit of Hoth's 3rd Panzer Group. Indeed, Leningrad itself came under direct artillery fire on 1 September, beginning a siege that was to last until January 1944. Similarly, Army Group South achieved a breakthrough on 3 August, when 1st Panzer Group and Seventeenth Army met at Pervomaisk to encircle substantial Soviet forces around Uman, well before Guderian's 2nd Panzer Group had even begun its drive south. Yet Hitler insisted on the diversion being carried out, leaving the advance on Moscow effectively stalled. It was, in retrospect, a turning-point in the opening campaign on the Eastern Front.

Stalin certainly expected the thrust against Moscow to continue, committing scarce reserves to the Bryansk Front in August. They were not needed immediately. On 25 August Guderian began to move south, advancing parallel to the River Desna, with the Pripet Marshes to his west. He encountered little opposition, although he was aware that he would have to cross the Desna – a sprawling, marshy river some 1000 yards wide – at Novgorod Severskiy before aiming for Kiev and contact with Army Group South. By the end of August, lead elements of 6th Panzer Division had seized a wooden bridge at Novgorod Severskiy, opening up the route south. Rainstorms delayed progress but on 16 September Guderian's panzers linked up with those of von Kleist's 1st Panzer Group at Likhvitsa, 120 miles east of Kiev. The Soviet armies defending the city were encircled. Their commanders had pleaded with Stalin to authorize a withdrawal before it was too late, but he had prevaricated. By the time he gave his permission early on 17 September, the trap had been sprung. Kiev fell on 19 September; a further 210,000 Soviet troops marched into captivity. Less than three weeks later, they were joined by another 106,000, trapped as von Kleist's panzers raced ahead toward the Sea of Azov to link up with the Eleventh Army which then turned south into the Crimea, pushing the Soviets back into the fortress-city of Sevastopol, while the rest of von Rundstedt's Army Group advanced eastward to Rostov.

By then, Hitler had shifted his priorities yet again. As early as 6 September he issued another directive, ordering the infantry of Army Group Center to resume the advance on Moscow, aided by Guderian's Second Panzer Army (as 2nd Panzer Group was now known) as soon as it could be disengaged from the Kiev battle. In similar fashion, Hoth's Third and Hoepner's Fourth Panzer Armies would aim for Moscow from the north now that they were no longer needed around Leningrad. Codenamed Operation *Taifun* (*Typhoon*), this was to be the final push of the campaigning season. With Leningrad besieged and the Ukraine in Axis hands, the chances of victory seemed high.

But problems were already multiplying. After three months of relentless fighting, the strain on both men and vehicles was beginning to tell. In addition, logistic problems had not eased. The railway system, deliberately destroyed by retreating Soviet troops and under growing attack from partisans, could only be rebuilt slowly, forcing the Germans to depend on trucks and horse-drawn wagons to carry supplies forward. They were obliged to use roads which were, in most cases, little more than cart tracks, impeding progress. Finally, the decision to divert tanks of Army Group Center to north and south had given Stalin the respite he so desperately needed. Moscow may have been vulnerable by early October 1941, but it was defended.

Marshal Semyon Budenny, who was placed in command of all southern Soviet forces in July 1941. Though a professional soldier who had served in the Tsar's cavalry, Budenny owed his position to acquaintance with Stalin and political reliability rather than to proven ability. Taken completely by surprise by Guderian's panzer advance, Budenny was relieved of command within two months of his appointment.

Soviet infantry armed with PPSh submachine guns defend the ruins of Leningrad. Soviet clothing and equipment was specifically designed for winter warfare and gave the soldiers a considerable advantage over their German opponents.

Operation "Barbarossa"
26 August – October 1941
Front line, end of August
German attacks
Front line, early October
Soviet counterattacks
Trapped Soviet pockets
0 130 km
0 80 miles
N
1500
1000
500
200
100
0 m
SWEDEN
Stockholm
Åland
Turku
FINLAND
Tampere
Mikkeli
Helsinki
Gulf of Finland
Tallinn
Kohtla-Järve
Leningrad
Gatchina
Lake Ladoga
Petrozavodsk
Lake Onega
Olonets
Vytegra
Bielo-Osero
Tikyin
Vologda
ESTONIA
Hiiu maa
Saare maa
Gotland
BALTIC SEA
Pärnu
Lake Peipus
Tartu
Novgorod
Gulf of Riga
Ventspils
Riga
LATVIA
Jelgava
ARMY GROUP NORTH LEEB
Pskov
Ostrov
Lake Ilmen
Kholm
Rezekne
Daugavpils
Memel
Königsberg
Elbing
PRUSSIA
LITHUANIA
Kaunas
Wilno
FOURTH PANZER ARMY HOEPNER
GERMANY
Poland
Grodno
R. Niemen
Bialystok
Minsk
Borisov
Orsha
Vitebsk
R. Dvina
Smolensk
Mogilev
Roslavl
Belorussia
Warsaw
Siedlce
Brest-Litovsk
Baranowicze
Pinsk
ARMY GROUP CENTER BOCK
Bobruisk
R. Dnieper
Mozyr
Gomel
R. Pripet
Klintsy
R. Desna
Briansk
Lublin
Kowel
Luck
Jaroslav
Novgorod Severskiy
Brody
Lwow
Tarnopol
Zhitomir
Kiev
Nieshin
Konotop
Sumy
Romny
Berdichev
ARMY GROUP SOUTH RUNDSTEDT
Vinnitsa
R. Dniester
HUNGARY
Uman
Cherkassy
Ukraine
Kremenchug
Poltava
Czernowitz
Satu Mare
ARMY GROUP SOUTH RUNDSTEDT
Butosani
R. Prut
Balta
Pervomaisk
Kirovo
Dnepropetrovsk
Bessarabia
Kishinev
Cluj
Jassi
ROMANIA
Sibiu
Brasov
Bender
Tiraspol
Odessa
Nikolayev
Kherson
Nikopol
Zaporozhe
Melitopol
Galatz
Ismail
Ploesti
Craiova
Bucharest
Mouth of the Danube
Gulf of Karkinitski
Crimea
Simferopol
Sevastopol
Constanta
BLACK SEA
R. Danube
Sea of Azov
Kerch
Taman
Krasnodar
Novorossiisk
Maikop
Voroshilov
Vinodyelnoe
Kropotkin
Proletarskaya
Rostov
Azov
Taganrog
Novo Cherkassk
R. Don
Mariupol
Stalino
Makyeevka
Lugansk
Pavlograd
Izyum
Zmiev
R. Donets
Kharkov
Belgorod
Ostrogoshsk
Pavlovsk
R. Don
Ust Medviedtsa
Kursk
Voronezh
SOUTH-WEST FRONT BUDENNY
Balashov
Orel
Mtsensk
Eletz
Michurinsk
Tambov
Riashk
WEST FRONT TIMOSHENKO
Tula
Kaluga
Shatsk
Ryazan
Spask
R. Oka
Kasimov
Temnikov
Serpukhov
Kolomna
Arsamas
Moscow
Vyazma
Rzhev
Tver
Vladimir
Kovrov
Gorki
USSR
Russia
Kineshma
Kostroma
Yaroslavl
Rybinsk
Bieshetzk
NORTH-WEST FRONT VOROSHILOV
SHOCK
ROM

Operation Typhoon OCTOBER – DECEMBER 1941

General Heinz Guderian's Second Panzer Army began the assault towards Moscow (Operation *Typhoon*) on 30 September 1941 with a sudden shift of direction northeastwards to Orel, some 75 miles behind the Soviet front line. The fall of Orel on 3 October, and a simultaneous attack by Guderian to link up with Second Army around Bryansk, caught the Soviets by surprise. This was exacerbated by a pincer move further north by the Third and Fourth Panzer Armies to trap substantial forces around Vyazma, directly to the west of Moscow. The Bryansk and Vyazma pockets together yielded another 663,000 Soviet prisoners, but these disasters did lead Stalin to appoint General Georgi Zhukov as commander of the capital's defenses. It was an astute move.

When Zhukov took over in early October, he faced a seemingly hopeless situation. The formations destroyed at Bryansk and Vyazma had constituted the main line of defense in front of Moscow, and although two further lines were in existence, they were only partially manned. Indeed, as Moscow itself was approached, it was the city's population, hastily mobilized to dig anti-tank ditches and trenches, that made up the bulk of the protecting force. In such circumstances, the only hope for Stalin and Zhukov was to hold the Germans long enough for the weather to break: as in earlier wars, "General Winter" was the last resort, for if the enemy could be denied victory until mud and snow imposed a natural barrier to progress, Moscow might be saved.

Soviet soldiers, motivated by patriotism rather than communism, fought with desperation. Despite further German advances – on 14 October Hoth's Third Panzer Army crossed the River Volga at Kalinin, severing the railway between Moscow and Leningrad, while further south Guderian pushed on as far as Tula by the end of the month – resistance hardened significantly, particularly when Soviet reinforcements began to arrive from the Far East. Between 10 and 30 October, for example, 2nd SS and 10th Panzer Divisions operating in Army Group Center found the going especially hard around Mozhaisk. When they eventually broke through, all momentum had gone. Blitzkrieg was gradually giving way to attrition.

It was at this point that the weather broke. In late October, sunshine gave way to rain, turning roads into quagmires, made worse as tanks, trucks and horse-drawn wagons churned the mud into deep glutinous lakes. The Soviets, more used to such conditions and on the defensive, could cope, but to the Germans it was disastrous. The rate of advance slowed to a crawl as supplies failed to get through and front-line soldiers spent nearly all their time digging their way out of the mud. The situation improved when the first of the winter frosts occurred on 6/7 November, but this raised the additional problem of cold among German armies that had expected the campaign to end much earlier. Even so, as tanks were now able to move across frozen ground, Hitler ordered a final, desperate push for Moscow. It nearly succeeded. On 15 November, Guderian by-passed Tula to threaten Moscow from the south, while other units pressed in from north and west. By the end of the month, German troops were standing in the suburbs of the city – in some cases less than 15 miles from the Kremlin.

They got no further. Soviet reinforcements, including Mongolian soldiers who were well suited to winter conditions, bolstered the defenses and, as the weather deteriorated, the Germans were forced to halt. With temperatures plummeting to –40°F, the oil in tank engines froze, weapons ceased to function and soldiers (some still equipped for summer campaigning) looked to their own survival. By 5 December, it was obvious that the attack on Moscow had failed. The Germans assumed the defensive, defeated by a combination of stubborn Soviet resistance, Hitler's lack of strategic reality, appalling weather and an inadequate logistic system.

An illustration from "Signal", the German Army magazine, shows two officers on the Eastern Front. Confident of a short and successful Russian campaign, the German troops had not been issued with the clothing and equipment which they needed to be able to resist a Russian winter. Steel helmets and hob-nailed boots resulted in severe frostbite.

The crew of a PzKw III attempt to release their vehicle from frozen mud by lighting a fire. By November, 1941, the speed of the German advance had slowed to little over one mile per day – no faster than Napoleon's foot soldiers in 1812.

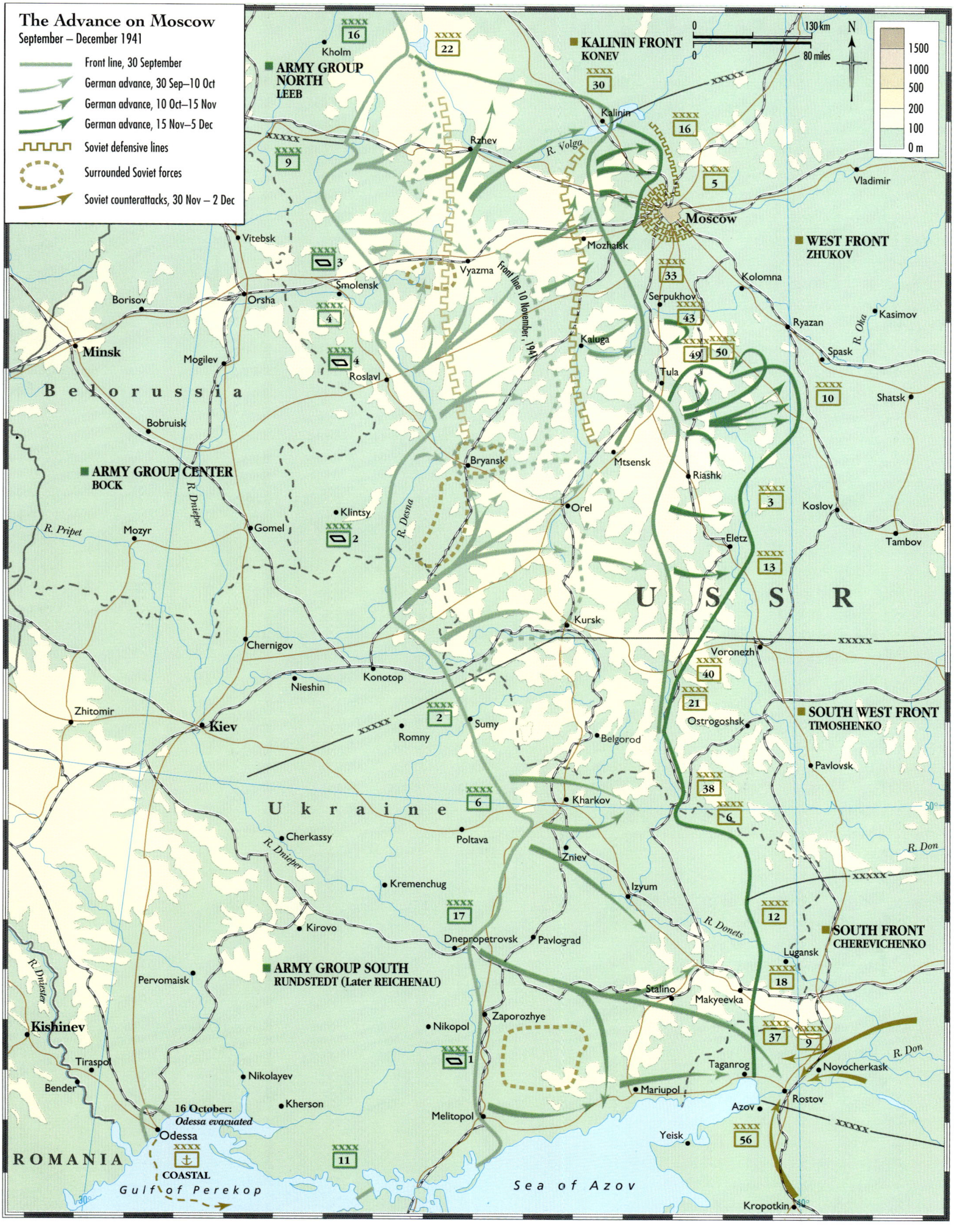
The Advance on Moscow
September – December 1941
Front line, 30 September
German advance, 30 Sep–10 Oct
German advance, 10 Oct–15 Nov
German advance, 15 Nov–5 Dec
Soviet defensive lines
Surrounded Soviet forces
Soviet counterattacks, 30 Nov – 2 Dec
ARMY GROUP NORTH
LEEB
KALININ FRONT
KONEV
WEST FRONT
ZHUKOV
ARMY GROUP CENTER
BOCK
SOUTH WEST FRONT
TIMOSHENKO
SOUTH FRONT
CHEREVICHENKO
ARMY GROUP SOUTH
RUNDSTEDT (Later REICHENAU)
16 October:
Odessa evacuated
COASTAL
Front line 10 November, 1941
Moscow
Kalinin
Rzhev
Vyazma
Mozhaisk
Smolensk
Vitebsk
Orsha
Borisov
Minsk
Mogilev
Roslavl
Bobruisk
Bryansk
Klintsy
Gomel
Mozyr
Kholm
Serpukhov
Kolomna
Ryazan
Kasimov
Spask
Shatsk
Kaluga
Tula
Mtsensk
Riashk
Orel
Koslov
Tambov
Eletz
Kursk
Voronezh
Vladimir
Chernigov
Konotop
Nieshin
Zhitomir
Kiev
Romny
Sumy
Belgorod
Ostrogoshsk
Pavlovsk
Kharkov
Poltava
Cherkassy
Kremenchug
Zniev
Izyum
Kirovo
Dnepropetrovsk
Pavlograd
Lugansk
Pervomaisk
Stalino
Makyeevka
Zaporozhye
Nikopol
Kishinev
Tiraspol
Bender
Nikolayev
Kherson
Melitopol
Mariupol
Taganrog
Novocherkask
Rostov
Azov
Yeisk
Kropotkin
Odessa
Belorussia
Ukraine
USSR
ROMANIA
R. Volga
R. Oka
R. Dnieper
R. Desna
R. Pripet
R. Dniester
R. Donets
R. Don
Sea of Azov
Gulf of Perekop
130 km
80 miles
1500
1000
500
200
100
0 m

The Battle of Moscow DECEMBER 1941 – JUNE 1942

By early December 1941, as the German assault stalled, Zhukov saw an opportunity for a counter-offensive. Despite crippling losses in the battles around the capital, the Soviet armies had been reinforced so that they now numbered nearly 580,000 men. As the German advance ground to a halt, moreover, it did so in two vulnerable salients to the north and south of Moscow, both of which could be "pinched out" prior to a more general offensive to encircle and destroy Army Group Center. The attacks began on 5 and 6 December along a 600-mile front, stretching from Leningrad, in the north, to Kursk, in the south, and achieved immediate success. German units fragmented, forcing Hitler to accept the need for a withdrawal to more secure positions. By the end of the year, Zhukov's forces had pushed the enemy back over 50 miles, saving Moscow.

The offensive had far-reaching effects. On the German side, Hitler blamed his generals for the retreat. As early as 19 December he sacked his commander-in-chief, Field Marshal von Brauchitsch, and assumed direct command himself; five days later he dismissed Guderian, and the commanders of Army Groups North and Center. On the Soviet side, Zhukov found himself under intense pressure to continue the assault, despite heavy losses. On 7 January 1942, Stalin ordered a general attack all along the front, from Lake Ladoga to the Black Sea, with the aim of liberating Demyansk, Rzhev, Vyazma, Bryansk, Orel and Kursk. By then, however, the Germans had recovered sufficiently to transform these cities into fortified "hedgehog" positions that proved impossible to breach. Although the Soviets came close to success in the north, where they trapped the German II Corps around Demyansk, elsewhere they found the going hard. An attempted encirclement of Vyazma, carried out by the Twenty-Ninth and Thirty-Ninth Armies, led to disaster as a German counterattack turned the tables in late January, and the battle quickly degenerated into a slogging match. On 18 February the Soviets even tried to use paratroopers to get behind enemy lines at Vyazma, but few survived. Meanwhile, the Luftwaffe had been flying in supplies to, and flying out the wounded from, the Demyansk pocket, allowing II Corps to survive. It was finally relieved by ground forces in April, leading to a belief that encircled units could be sustained indefinitely by air – something that was to prove disastrous at Stalingrad later in the year.

Nor were the battles confined to the center and north. Army Group South, forced out of Rostov in December 1941 by a localized counterattack, faced a more determined assault around Kharkov in late January 1942. The plan, put forward by Marshal Timoshenko, commander of the South-West Front, was for the Sixth, Ninth and Fifty-Seventh Armies to seize an area around Izyum, on the River Donets south-east of Kharkov, before wheeling north and south to trap substantial German forces. When the attack opened on 18 January, it went well, but the Germans fought with desperation and halted the advance. The Soviets were left holding a vulnerable salient on the west bank of the Donets south of Kharkov.

When the spring thaw began in April 1942, both sides were drawn to the Izyum salient as the most lucrative area for attack. To the Soviets, it offered an opportunity for further advance; to the Germans a chance of pinching out a vulnerable salient. In the event, the attacks virtually coincided. On 12 May, Timoshenko broke through to the north and south of Kharkov, only to encounter, six days later, a German offensive in much the same area. By 23 May the Germans had managed to close the ring around Izyum, trapping the bulk of Timoshenko's forces. Over 70,000 Soviets were killed and 200,000 captured, leaving Hitler free to plan his next move – into the Caucasus.

The defender of Moscow, General Georgi Zhukov. An imaginative and successful strategist, Zhukov was also a charismatic leader who enjoyed the respect of Eisenhower.

"Like mummies we padded along, only our eyes visible, but the cold relentlessly crept into our bodies, our blood, our brains. Even the sun seemed to radiate a steely cold and at night the blood-red skies above the burning villages merely hinted a mockery of warmth."

Heinrich Haape, German Medical Officer

The Battle for Moscow
December 1941 – June 1942
Soviet defense lines:
Abandoned
Active
Front line, December 1941
Soviet attacks
German counterattacks
Front line, end May 1942
0 130 km
0 80 miles
1500
1000
500
200
100
0 m
N
KALININ FRONT
KONEV
WESTERN FRONT
ZHUKOV
BRYANSK FRONT
GOLIKOV
SOUTHWEST FRONT
TIMOSHENKO
SOUTH FRONT
MALINOVSKY
CAUCASUS FRONT
KOSLOV
AZOV FLOTILLA
GORSHKOV
BLACK SEA FLEET
OKTYABRSKY
ARMY GROUP
CENTER
von BOCK
(later von KLUGE)
ARMY GROUP
SOUTH
REICHENAU
(later BOCK)
SEVASTOPOL
(under command
of Caucasus Front)
Soviet evacuation
Partisans
Partisans
Shock
Russia
Belorussia
Ukraine
U S S R
Crimea
Sea of Azov
Black Sea
Gulf of Karkintski
Moscow
Kiev
Kholm
Kalinin
Rzhev
Vitebsk
Vyazma
Orsha
Smolensk
Mogilev
Roslavl
Kaluga
Serpukhov
Tula
Kolomna
Ryazan
Spask
Kasimov
Alexandrow
Kovrov
Vladimir
Gorki
Kineshma
Arsamas
Temnikov
Shatsk
Penza
Kusnetsk
Bryansk
Mtsensk
Riashk
Orel
Klintsy
Gomel
Koslov
Tambov
Eletz
Kursk
Chernigov
Konotop
Nieshin
Voronezh
Atkarsk
Saratov
Balashov
Volsk
Urbach
Engels
Romny
Sumy
Belgorod
Ostrogoshsk
Pavlovsk
Kamishin
Kharkov
Poltava
Cherkassy
Zmiev
Izyum
Kremenchug
Kirovo
Dnepropetrovsk
Pavlograd
Pervomaisk
Zaporozhe
Stalino
Makeyevka
Lugansk
Nikopol
Nikolayev
Kherson
Melitopol
Mariupol
Taganrog
Novo Cherkassk
Rostov
Azov
Yeisk
Tsimlyanskiy
Ust Medviedtsa
Stalingrad
Zarew
Lake Elton
Proletarskaya
Elista
Kropotkin
Vinodyelnoe
Kerch
Taman
Krasnodar
Simferopol
Teodosia
Sevastopol
Novorossilsk
Maikop
Voroshilov
Georgievsk
Mozdok
Tuapse
R. Dnieper
R. Desna
R. Oka
R. Don
R. Donets
R. Donbass
R. Volga
R. Kuma
50°
40°

Pearl Harbor 7 DECEMBER 1941

Just before 8 a.m. on Sunday, 7 December 1941, Japanese aircraft attacked the U.S. Pacific Fleet base at Pearl Harbor, on the Hawaiian island of Oahu. Led by Lieutenant-Commander Mitsuo Fuchida, they had taken off from aircraft carriers, steaming to the north of Oahu, some two hours earlier, achieving complete surprise when they suddenly appeared over the island. American radar operators, warned to expect the arrival of B-17 bombers from California, ignored their screens; in Pearl Harbor, sailors went about their normal Sunday morning business, oblivious to the impending disaster.

The Japanese decision to mount such an audacious assault, nearly 4000 miles from their home base, was the culmination of a number of factors. Continued aggression in China had alienated the Americans, who feared that access to the resources of China would strengthen Japan and undermine U.S. influence in the western Pacific. This was made worse as the Japanese put pressure on the French, for in September 1940 the Vichy authorities agreed to the creation of Japanese bases in northern Indo-China, severing the supply link through Hanoi to Chiang Kai-shek's Nationalist armies in southern China. At much the same time Britain, under threat of invasion at home, had been unable to refuse Japanese demands to close a similar route through Burma. When the Japanese went further in July 1941 by assuming a protectorate over the whole of Indo-China, President Roosevelt felt obliged to act. On 25 July he suspended all trade with Japan and froze Japanese assets in the U.S.A. Britain and the Dutch government-in-exile (still administering the Dutch East Indies) quickly followed suit.

With vital raw materials (particularly oil) no longer available, Japan could not survive, yet to accept American demands that aggression in China should cease before trade resumed was unacceptable to a Tokyo government dependent upon the support of expansionist armed forces. The only solution seemed to be a preemptive strike to weaken the U.S.A. in the Pacific for as long as it took to seize the sources of raw materials in the Philippines, Dutch East Indies, Malaya and Burma. It was recognized that an attack on the U.S.A. would "awaken a sleeping giant", but it was planned that by the time that happened, a ring of air and naval bases would have been established to protect the Japanese gains. The first part of the strategy was the attack on Pearl Harbor, but to ensure secrecy, negotiations with Washington were also pursued. As they continued, the attack fleet of six aircraft carriers, two battleships, two heavy cruisers and 11 destroyers left Japan under the command of Vice Admiral Chuichi Nagumo. He ordered the attack early on 7 December.

When Fuchida's aircraft reached Pearl Harbor, their targets were laid out as if on parade. Seven of the U.S. Pacific Fleet's eight battleships – *California, Maryland, Oklahoma, Tennessee, West Virginia, Arizona* and *Nevada* – were strung out along "Battleship Row", while the eighth – *Pennsylvania* – was in dry dock. With a cry of *Tora!, Tora!, Tora!* ("Tiger!, Tiger!, Tiger!"), Fuchida led the attack against minimal opposition. Within minutes, *California, Oklahoma, West Virginia, Arizona* and *Nevada* had been hit, while simultaneous attacks on U.S. bases at Wheeler Field, Hickam Field and Kaneohe had virtually wiped out American airpower. At 8.40 a.m. a second wave of bombers and fighters swept in, concentrating on the *Nevada* and *Pennsylvania*. By then, the Americans were prepared, and a number of Japanese aircraft were shot down, but enormous damage had been done. Of the eight battleships, five had been lost and the other three damaged; altogether 18 U.S. ships had been sunk or damaged and 347 out of 394 aircraft destroyed.

This was, in fact, less crippling than it seemed: no heavy cruisers, aircraft carriers or submarines had been sunk, and vital base facilities at Pearl Harbor had been spared. The Japanese may have suffered only minor losses (29 aircraft out of 355 committed), but America was forced into war. On 8 December the U.S. Congress officially declared war on Japan; hours earlier the British, under attack in Malaya, had done the same. It was now a global conflict.

The USS Virginia *and USS* Tennessee *photographed shortly after the raid. Despite the devastation wrought, the attack was only partially successful since one of its main objectives – the destruction of the U.S. carrier force – was not achieved.*

"The rise or fall of the empire depends upon this battle; everyone will do his duty with utmost efforts."

Admiral Yamamoto

The wreckage of an American fighter destroyed on the ground during the attack. Afraid of sabotage, Lieutenant General W.C. Short had ordered that all aircraft be parked wing-tip to wing-tip in the center of the airfields, thereby offering the Japanese perfect targets.

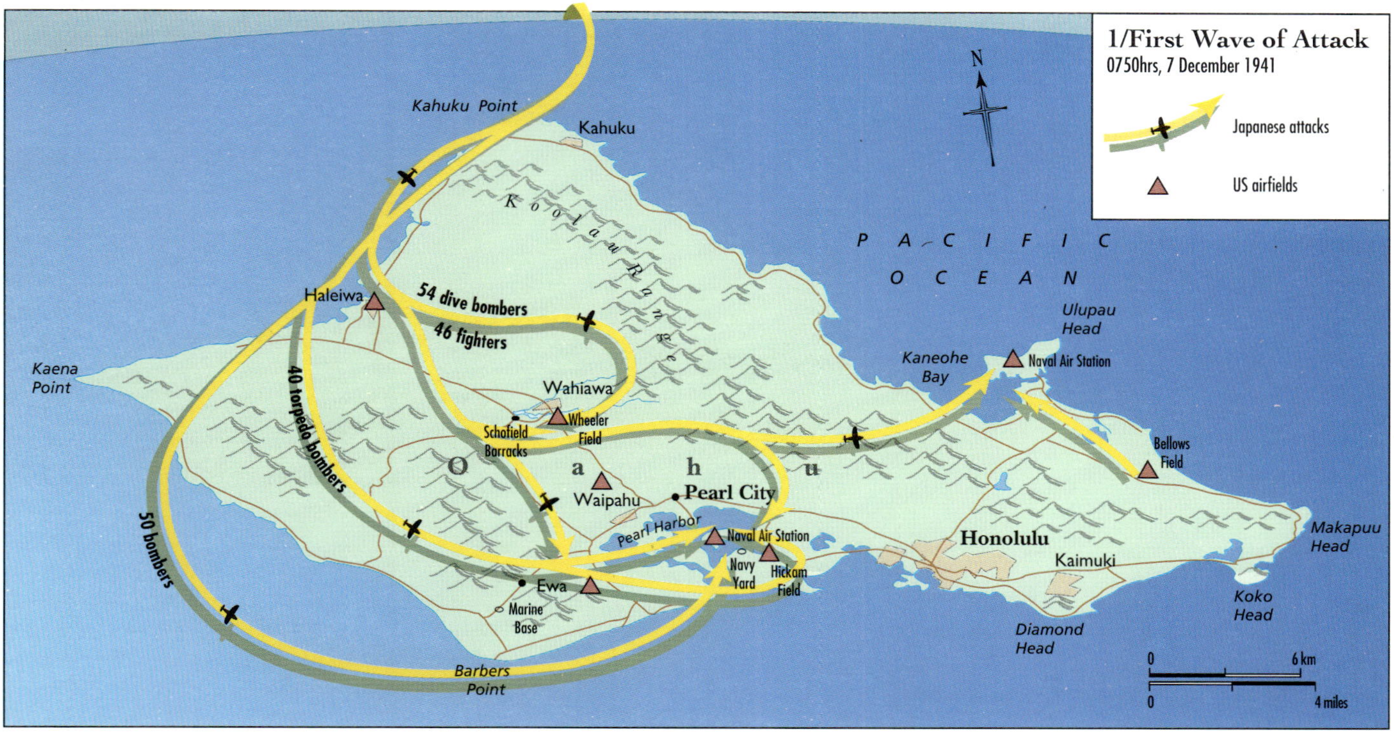

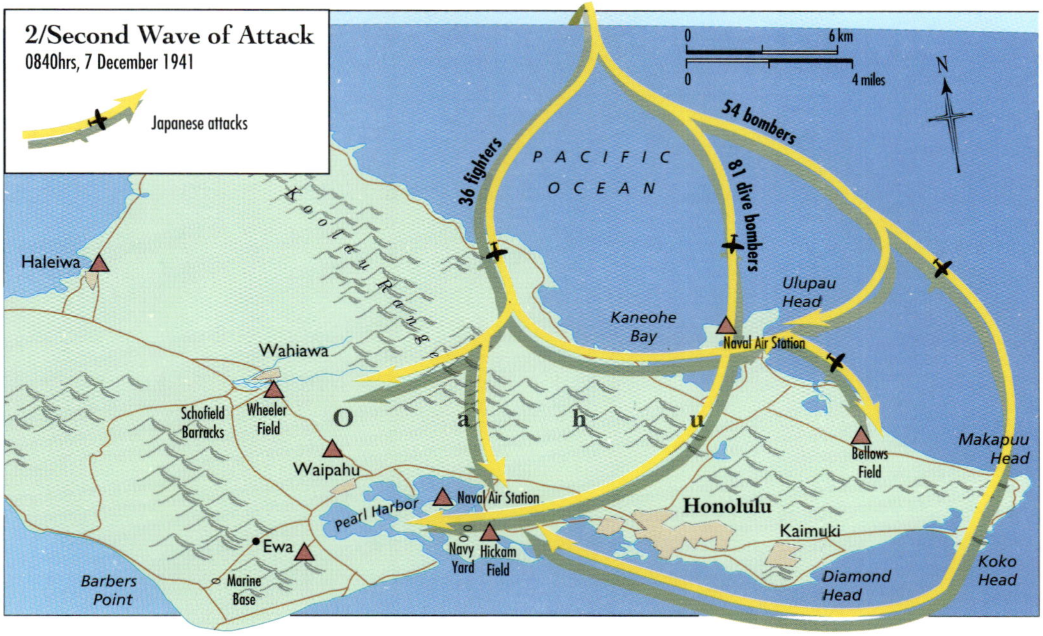

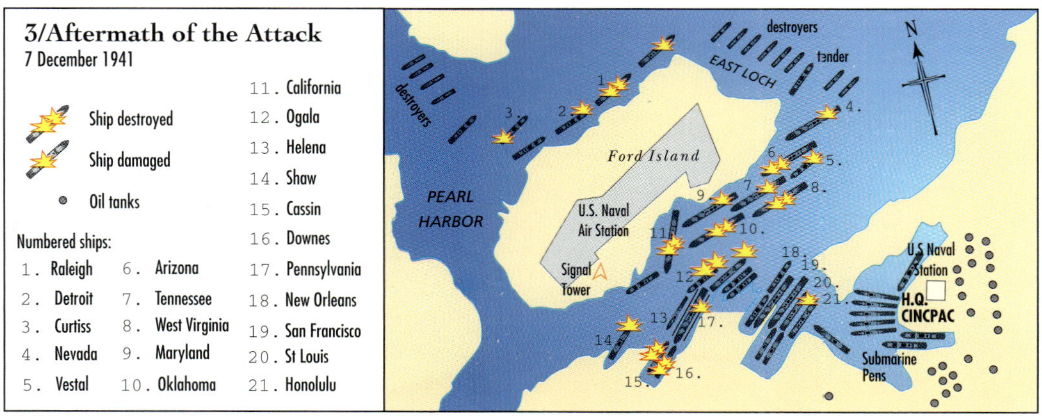

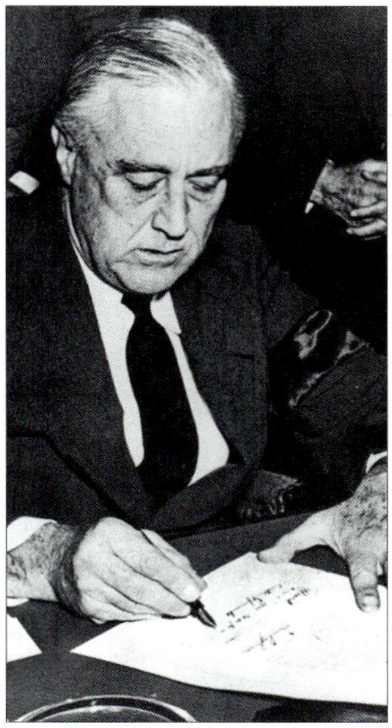

An exhausted and anxious-looking President Roosevelt signs America's declaration of war on Japan, 8 December 1941. The interception of messages between Tokyo and Japan's envoys in Washington had convinced Roosevelt of the inevitability of war by the evening of 6 December, the day before the attack on Pearl Harbor. In his address to the US Congress on the day of the declaration, the President was to call 7 December "a day that will live in infamy."

Malaya and the Philippines DECEMBER 1941 – MAY 1942

At the same time as the attack on Pearl Harbor, but across the International Date Line (so making it 8 December 1941), Japanese forces attacked Malaya, Hong Kong and the Philippines. Their aim in all three cases was to seize territory quickly, exploiting surprise.

The attack on Malaya, carried out by the Twenty-Fifth Army under Lieutenant-General Tomoyuki Yamashita, began in the north, its objective the strategically vital naval base at Singapore. Early on 8 December, troops landed at Singora and Patani, just over the border in Thailand, and at Khota Bahru in Malaya itself. The Thais offered no resistance, allowing Japanese infantry to advance swiftly down the west coast of Malaya; those from Khota Bahru pushed down the east coast, splitting the British defenses. Lieutenant-General Arthur Percival, commanding ground forces in Malaya and Singapore, ordered withdrawal on both axes, allowing the Japanese to make spectacular gains. Jitra fell on 12 December and the island of Penang six days later. By then, most British airpower had been destroyed and the Royal Navy had suffered an humiliating defeat when, on 10 December, the battleship *Prince of Wales* and battlecruiser *Repulse* were sunk by bombers.

Kuala Lumpur fell on 10 January 1942 and little was left to stop the Japanese. On 28 January, Percival ordered his remaining troops back to Singapore. With recently arrived reinforcements, he had at his disposal over 100,000 men against Yamashita's 30,000, but such was the confusion on the British side that this equation meant little. When the Japanese crossed the Johore Strait to land on Singapore on the night of 8/9 February, the defenders were badly deployed and poorly commanded. As they fell back, Yamashita's men seized supply dumps and reservoirs, leaving the British badly weakened. On 15 February, Percival surrendered. The campaign had taken just 70 days. When this was added to the fall of Hong Kong on Christmas Day 1941, after nearly three weeks of fighting, the scale of the British disaster was apparent.

The British were not alone. On 8 December 1941, Japanese aircraft attacked American airbases in the Philippines. Two days later, Guam, in the Mariana Islands, was captured and, on the 23rd, Wake Island, in the central Pacific, surrendered. By then, the Philippines had been invaded. Defended by 140,000 American and

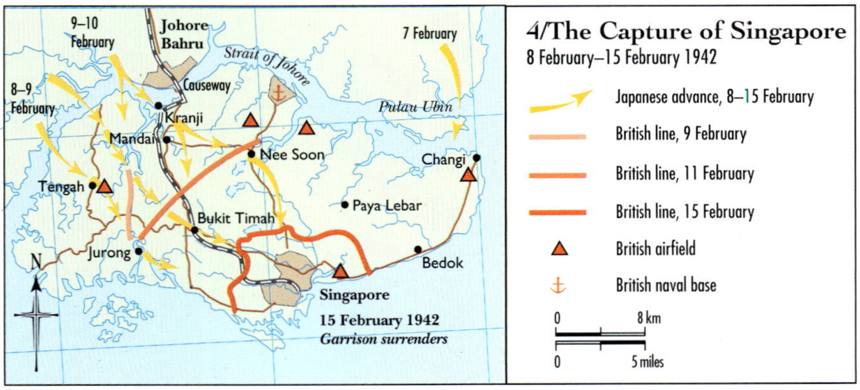

Filipino troops under General Douglas MacArthur, the main island of Luzon should have been strong, but the loss of airpower, coupled with the poor training of the Filipino troops, weakened the garrison. When elements of the Japanese Fourteenth Army under General Masaharu Homma landed at Lingayen Gulf, on 22 December, the defenders were already demoralized, not least by their inability to deal with the smaller landings at Aparri and Vigan, further north, two weeks earlier. As the Japanese advanced, MacArthur withdrew the bulk of his army into the Bataan Peninsula, hoping to hold out until relief arrived.

No relieving force was sent, even though MacArthur's men put up a prolonged fight. The first Japanese attack on Bataan, carried out on 9 January 1942, was held, and it was not until a gap was found in the American lines around Mount Natib on the 22nd that any progress was made. But this was short-lived; as both sides suffered from disease and malnutrition, the campaign bogged down into a stalemate. This was not broken until 3 April, when Japanese troops broke through the last remaining American positions. By then, MacArthur had been ordered by Roosevelt to leave the Philippines; the remains of his army surrendered on 9 April, losing yet more men during the infamous "Bataan Death March" to prisoner of war camps. Only the fortress island of Corregidor, in Manila Bay, remained in American hands. Subjected to artillery bombardment and amphibious assault, it fell on 6 May.

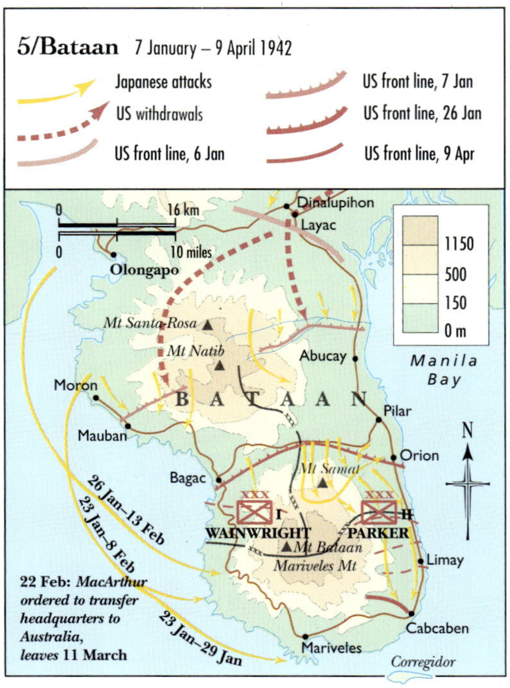

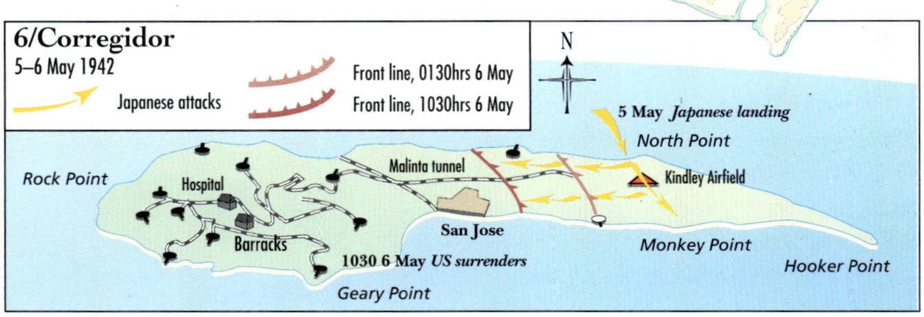

Dutch East Indies JANUARY – MARCH 1942

By early January 1942, with the attacks on Malaya and the Philippines going well, the Japanese felt able to accelerate their plans for the seizure of the Dutch East Indies. Defended by the Royal Netherlands Indies Army, which could expect no reinforcement from a mother country under Nazi occupation,the islands, stretching from the Malay Peninsula almost as far as northern Australia, contained raw materials essential to the Japanese war effort. Attempts were made to co-ordinate an Allied defense – in January 1942, General Sir Archibald Wavell was appointed head of ABDA (American, British, Dutch and Australian) Command, covering the whole of the south-west Pacific – but with few reserves available and an impossibly large area to protect, this was a clear case of too little too late. Two small detachments of Australians, codenamed "Gull Force" and "Sparrow Force", were deployed to Amboina and West Timor respectively, but they could hardly be expected to stand for long against overwhelming Japanese attacks.

The Japanese plan was ambitious. Three Task Forces – the Western from Indo-China, the Central and Eastern from the southern Philippines – were to advance simultaneously, squeezing in on the key objective of Java. Islands were to be taken using a combination of amphibious and airborne forces, protected by strong elements of the Imperial Japanese Navy. The attacks began on 10/11 January, when the Central Task Force captured Tarakan Island, off the east coast of Borneo, coinciding with parachute landings by men of the Eastern Task Force at Manado on Celebes. Opposition was slight in both cases. Central Task Force then moved on to capture the oilfields at Balikpapan, while Eastern Task Force took Kendari and, on 4 February, overran "Gull Force" on Amboina. Action then shifted to the west where, early on 14 February, Japanese transport aircraft dropped 360 paratroopers at Palembang in southern Sumatra, spearheading an amphibious landing at Muntok. Allied aircraft managed to destroy some of the landing ships, but the Dutch defenders onshore did not survive for long. By 17 February, Sumatra had been left to the Japanese.

Elsewhere, a similar story unfolded. Bali was captured without a fight on 19 February (on the same day as Japanese aircraft bombed Darwin in northern Australia, killing 243 people); four days later, after a hard fight against "Sparrow Force", Timor was taken. By then, the Allies had suffered a setback at sea, when a Dutch destroyer was sunk in the Battle of Lombok Strait (19/20 February), leaving Java isolated. Wavell, realizing the hopelessness of the situation, withdrew to India, having officially disbanded ABDA on 25 February; two days later, an Allied fleet clashed with a Japanese naval force in the Battle of the Java Sea. The Allies, unused to operating together and denied air cover, lost five ships but failed to disrupt the Japanese invasion of Java. The next day, 28 February, two of the surviving Allied cruisers, HMAS *Perth* and USS *Houston*, encountered part of the invasion fleet at Bantam Bay. They inflicted heavy damage on the Japanese, only to be sunk by protecting warships. The Allies had nothing left with which to oppose the landings.

Java was invaded on 1 March, when elements of the Western and Eastern Task Forces landed at Eretan Wetan, Bantam and Kragan on the north coast. The units from Kragan encountered no opposition, and took Surabaya with ease; those from Eretan Wetan, aiming for Batavia, were held for a short time by a mixed Australian/British/American force, but when it withdrew into the mountains, intent on fighting a guerrilla campaign, no other defenses remained. Batavia fell on 5 March and three days later all resistance ceased.

U.S. servicemen search the rubble of a bombed house in Darwin, northern Australia. The official death toll was 243 (160 of them sailors) in the sudden attack on 19 February 1942. One journalist remarked that there had never been greater loss of life in a single day in Australia.

An American Hudson bomber lies wrecked in the burned-out skeleton of a hangar at the Royal Australian Air Force aerodrome in Port Darwin. Runways were cratered and within half an hour the airfield was completely destroyed. The harbor was also attacked and eight ships were sunk.

Burma JANUARY – MAY 1942

The Japanese attack on Burma began as early as 16 December 1941, when troops crossed the border from Thailand to capture an important airfield at Victoria Point. Using this as a base, they began to push northwards up Burma's long southern "tail" on 15 January 1942, aiming to link up with more substantial elements of Lieutenant-General Shojiro Iida's Fifteenth Army, the spearheads of which took the Burmese town of Kawkareik on the 20th. The initial objectives were Moulmein and Martaban, at the mouth of the River Salween, from where a railway ran direct to the capital, Rangoon. Once that had been taken, the Japanese could thrust north along the lines of the Rivers Salween, Sittang and Irrawaddy to sever the Burma Road supply route to China, seize Mandalay and threaten the eastern states of India. This would cut British links between India and Malaya, ensure the isolation of Chiang Kai-shek's Nationalist Chinese from the rest of the Allies, and secure Burma's oilfields. In the long-term, it could also create a base for a possible invasion of India.

Burma was defended by two divisions – 1st Burma and 17th Indian – under Lieutenant-General Thomas Hutton, but standards of training and equipment were poor and plans for a strategic withdrawal beyond the Sittang were blocked by Wavell, as head of ABDA, for political reasons. Elements of 17th Indian Division were therefore badly deployed when, on 26 January, Iida's troops opened their attack on Moulmein. Panic broke out, and although some British units fought fiercely, the town fell five days later. An attempt to establish a defense line on the River Bilin failed, allowing the Japanese to push forward toward the Sittang, where a single bridge was carrying the retreating columns.The British commander, Major-General "Jackie" Smyth, ordered the bridge to be demolished, trapping most of his men on the east back. Few escaped. Hutton felt he had little choice but to order an evacuation of Rangoon; a decision that cost him his job. On 1 March, Wavell replaced him with Lieutenant-General Sir Harold Alexander; Smyth, suffering from malaria, was also relieved.

Alexander led the remnants of what was now called Burma Corps (soon to be placed under the command of Lieutenant-General William Slim), northward up the Irrawaddy toward Prome, abandoning Rangoon. The Japanese took the city on 8 March and quickly followed the British. At this point, Chiang Kai-shek's offer to help was accepted and some 6500 men of the Chinese Fifth Army, led by the U.S. Lieutenant-General Joseph ("Vinegar Joe') Stilwell, advanced south to Toungoo, about 150 miles to the east of Prome, on the Sittang. Their arrival, backed by the Sixth and Sixty-Sixth Armies further north, made little difference. On 30 March, after heavy fighting, the Chinese were forced to retreat; three days later, Alexander pulled out of Prome. As the British withdrew to the north-west, across the central plain of Burma, the Japanese seized the opportunity to advance in the east toward Lashio and the Burma Road.

On 16 April, the Japanese took the oilfields at Yenangyaung, north of Prome, hastening the British retreat. The rearguard of Burma Corps crossed the Irrawaddy at Ava on 1 May, blowing the bridge behind them, but this could not prevent a Japanese seizure of Mandalay. By then, Lashio had also fallen and the Chinese were pulling back in the direction of Myitkyina. Burma was effectively in Japanese hands. The British, using railways, roads and rivers, crossed the River Chindwin at Kalewa before struggling up the Kabaw Valley to the Indian border, beyond the reach of the over-stretched Japanese. Burma Corps had by then lost over 13,000 men and had the dubious privilege of having conducted the longest retreat (over 1000 miles) in the history of the British Army. Recovery would take a lot of effort and time.

Japanese troops, entering the British colony of Burma from Thailand in January 1942, had to cross mountains and forests to reach the River Salween, across which lay the strategic city of Martaban. From there ran roads and railway lines to the Burmese capital of Rangoon.

A Japanese soldier guards a pier in Rangoon. The name Rangoon means "end of conflict", but the city was in fact the scene of great conflict during its invasion by the Japanese in 1942 and its recapture by the British in 1945.

1/Invasion of Burma
January – May 1942
Japanese attacks
Chinese withdrawals
(Chinese armies were under the command of US General Stilwell)
British withdrawals
Allied airfields
3500
2000
1000
500
200
0 m
100 km
100 miles
TIBET
BHUTAN
CHINA
INDIA
BURMA
FRENCH INDO-CHINA
(Japanese Occupied)
SIAM
(THAILAND)
Bay of Bengal
Gulf of Martaban
Gulf of Siam
Isthmus of Kra
Burma Road
Sadiya
Fort Hertz
Ledo
Tezpur
Jorhat
Sumprarum
Shingbwiyang
Dimapur
Kohima
Shaduzup
Tali
SIXTY-SIXTH ARMY
Myitkyina
8 May
Tamanthi
Sylhet
Imphal
Bishenpur
Homalin
8 March
Bhamo
Wanting
Kunming
Tongzang
Mawlaik
Katha
Tiddim
Namhkan
Namhpakka
Mien-ning
Dacca
Yazagyo
Kalewa
Comilla
FIFTH ARMY
Lashio
29 April
BURMA ARMY
HUTTON (Later Alexander)
Shwegyin
Mogok
Yeu
Hsipaw
Chittagong
SIXTH ARMY
38
Gangaw
1 March
Mandalay 1 March
Maymo
Tilin
Ava
Pauk
Myinggan
Wundwin
Mong Nawng
Keng Tung
Paletwa
Pagan
Thazi
Taung Gyi
Maungdaw
Yenangyaung
Mong Pawn
Minbu
16 April
Magure
Akyab
Kangan
Tamandu
Minhla
Luang Prabang
Chiang Rai
Loika
Toungoo
Thayetmyo
Cjiengraai
Taungup
Prome
2 April
Sandoway
Kama
Meng Lampun
Pyu
Papun
Sittang
Bilin
Pegu
Rahaeng
Bassein
Rangoon
Pitsanuloke
Kawkareik
Martaban
Moulmein
Meng
Nakawn Sawan
18
56
1
14
7
12
MALAYAN FORCE
OZAWA
4-12 April:
Indian Ocean raid and raid on the Andaman Is.
FIFTEENTH ARMY
IIDA
Early April:
Reinforcements land (see map 2)
Tavoy
Bangkok
Chun-kow
Tonle Sap
Pursat
Mergui
Tenasserim
Phnom Penh
Chum
Victoria Point
16 Dec
Nakawn Sritamarat
R. Chindwin
R. Irrawaddy
R. Sittang
R. Salween
25°
20°
15°
10°
90°
95°
100°
105°
2/Seaborne Reinforcements
April 1941
British movements
Japanese movements
Toungoo
Kerenni States
BURMA
R. Irrawaddy
Bay of Bengal
Gwa
Letpadan
Daiku
Shwegyin
Madauk
Henzada
Tharrawaddy
Sittang
48 Ind
SIAM
(Thailand)
R. Thaungyin
Taikkyi
Pegu
7 Ind
Bilin
Hlegu
Zokali
Kamamaung
Thaton
Paing Kyon
Rangoon
Thongwa
Kunzeik
33
Bassein
Twante
Kyauktan
Paung
Kado
Myawaddy
55
Myaungmya
Kyaikiat
Kungyangon
Martaban
Moulmein
Pyapon
Gulf of Martaban
18
56
1
14
Thanbyuzayat
16°
96°
98°

The Secret War

No country could fight effectively in World War II without access to accurate information about its enemies. At the same time, if it could deny such information about itself to those enemies, the advantage would be doubled. Thus, while overt campaigns were being conducted on land, in the air and at sea around the world, all combatant powers were also conducting a secret war, fought using spies, special agents, Resistance personnel and the technology of communications eavesdropping. Success in undercover operations, invariably unreported, often spelt the difference between victory or defeat.

The human side of the secret war involved men and women of enormous courage, often gathering and reporting information under conditions of hardship and danger. Professional spies also had a role to play. Among the more successful were Leopold Trepper, who ran the pro-Soviet "Red Orchestra" until it was broken up by German counterintelligence agents in 1942, and Elias Basna ("Cicero"), who stole secret documents from the British Embassy in Ankara and sold them to the Germans. But the vast majority of those involved were ordinary people caught up in the drama of the war. Many of those who helped the Allies were members of various Resistance movements that grew up in opposition to Axis occupation. Their activities were coordinated from London by the Special Operations Executive (SOE) – which also had outstations in the Far East – or by the American Office of Strategic Services (OSS), forerunner to the Central Intelligence Agency (CIA).

Resistance movements did not emerge immediately. In those parts of the world occupied by Axis powers between 1939 and 1942, people needed to recover from the shock of defeat before beginning to organize themselves into effective groups. Quite often, resistance was passive, manifested in a general reluctance to cooperate with the occupying authorities, but as time went on it developed in response to repression. The Germans were adept at forming local fascist or pro-fascist organizations to help them administer occupied areas – among the more infamous were the French *Milice* and Danish *Schalburg Korps* – and when they, along with their German allies, began to crack down on dissidence, they alienated some people to the extent of causing them to adopt more active measures of opposition. In France, Belgium and the Netherlands, this might involve offering aid to Allied aircrew shot down over Europe, setting up and running escape lines into neutral countries or back to Britain itself; elsewhere, in the Far East as well as in Europe, it led to the creation of groups dedicated to sabotage and information gathering.

The information that came from such sources was often of vital importance. Members of the French Resistance, for example, provided the Western Allies with plans of German defenses along the coast – the so-called "Atlantic Wall" – and this helped the D-Day planners to choose Normandy in preference to more strongly protected regions further north. By the same token, it was Norwegian and Danish Resistance workers who monitored German experiments with rockets on the Baltic island of Peenemünde, even going so far as to capture substantial parts of a V2 prototype when it wandered off course and crash landed. On a more mundane level, resisters reported on troop movements and troop morale, helping the Allies to build up an accurate picture of enemy strengths and weaknesses.

Taking the process of resistance further, sabotage and disruption could also be effected. Sometimes this involved cooperating with specialist SOE agents parachuted into occupied areas, but at other times it was a responsibility of the local people. One of the crucial roles played by the French Resistance was the mounting of sabotage attacks during the night of 5/6 June 1944, immediately prior to D-Day, when over 1000 raids on rail targets alone helped to disrupt the movement of German reinforcements into the Normandy area. At the same time, most of the French civilian telephone network, upon which the Germans depended for tactical communications, was put out of action. On occasions, this could be taken too far – in June 1944 *maquis* groups in south-eastern France came out in open revolt, using the Vercors Plateau as their base, only to find that the Allies could not provide them with the support they expected – but the diversion of German troops to deal with even the more disastrous uprisings ensured that the front line was denuded. On the Eastern Front, Soviet partisans, co-ordinated from Moscow, followed this as a deliberate (and effective) strategy, while in the Balkans partisans loyal to Tito (in

Yugoslavia) and Enver Hoxha (in Albania) contributed substantially to the liberation of their countries.

But this was only one aspect of the secret war. While spies and resisters were active on the ground, other people were equally involved in the gathering of signals intelligence, scanning the airwaves for information. By far the most dramatic of these operations involved Allied efforts to read German top-secret communications, transmitted via the supposedly unbreakable *Enigma* encryption machine. Patented by a Dutch scientist in 1919 and developed by a German engineer in the early 1920s, *Enigma* operated on the principle that an apparently random mixing of letters, achieved by activating a series of electrically driven rotors on a machine that looked like a typewriter, could produce such a large number of possible computations that they would be impossible to crack. This proved to be incorrect. The weakness of the system lay in the fact that the receiver of a message had to know the password that had set the rotors spinning so that he could reverse the process and read the information. There was also a limit to the number of letters that could be used, meaning that some, reflecting the frequency of their everyday use, would appear more often in any message, regardless of how jumbled it became. Polish mathematicians worked on the *Enigma* problem in the 1930s and, when their country was attacked, passed their findings on to the British and French. When France fell a year later, the problem was passed exclusively to scientists based at the Government Code and Cypher School at Bletchley Park in Buckinghamshire. With the help of crude computers, they gradually cracked the *Enigma* code, although they were never able to read everything and quite often produced information that was out of date by the time it had been deciphered.

What information there was had to be kept secret, for if the Germans ever suspected that *Enigma* had been broken they would either change its nature or stop using it altogether. This meant that any information, known as *Ultra* (from "ultra secret"), could only be passed on to commanders at the highest level, who then had to decide whether its use would jeopardise security. Even then, *Ultra* only dealt with strategic information, such as the movement of a formation from the Eastern to the Western Fronts; it was rarely used once that formation was in the battle area, where radio or telephone would be preferred. In late June 1944, for example, *Ultra* allowed General Sir Bernard Montgomery, as Allied Land Force Commander in Normandy, to know that the II SS Panzer Corps was being moved to the area of Caen – information that caused him to call off the *Epsom* operation despite its apparent success – but it did not tell him how that formation would be used or where it would be stationed once deployed. Nevertheless, *Ultra* had a remarkable impact, giving the Allies an insight into enemy intentions and dispositions that was virtually unique in the history of war. American cryptanalysts enjoyed a similar advantage in the Pacific, where they cracked the Japanese equivalent of *Enigma* (known as *Purple*), distributing its information under the codename *Magic*. This allowed them to preempt Admiral Isoroku Yamamoto's plans for Midway in June 1942; 10 months later *Magic* information led to Yamamoto's death when his aircraft was ambushed and destroyed in the Solomons.

The Allies did not have it all their own way, for although the Axis powers never enjoyed the same sort of insight into enemy decision-making as that provided by *Ultra* or *Magic*, they did have their successes. As early as November 1939, German agents kidnapped two senior members of MI6 at Venio on the German–Dutch border, seriously weakening Britain's offensive intelligence capability, while the swift German advance into France and the Low Countries in May and June 1940 deprived the Allies of most of their existing spy networks. More significantly, in 1941 German agents compromised the Dutch Resistance when they captured an SOE radio operator and forced him to transmit false information back to London. More then 60 Allied agents sent to the Netherlands were arrested before the ruse was discovered. In the Pacific, Japanese spies were in place well before the war began, feeding information back to Tokyo on the state of Allied defenses. One of the most influential had a cover-job in Pearl Harbor and was able to list the ships stationed there prior to the Japanese attack. Taken overall, however, the Allies seem to have held the advantage in the secret war. Their organization, coordination and use of Resistance movements, coupled to their remarkable breaking of enemy codes, gave them an unprecedented degree of valuable information which could be used to pre-empt and trick the Axis powers. It was one more weapon in the "arsenal of democracy".

PART III
Turning the Tide, June 1942 – July 1943

The shift in Allied fortunes between June 1942 and July 1943 was the result of many factors. Growing experience was undoubtedly one of these, for although there were still occasions when the British, Americans and Soviets could (and did) make mistakes, these were becoming rarer and were invariably analyzed to prevent repetition. At the same time, as experience was gained, it was fed back into the training system, helping to produce armed forces that were more professional and effective. Nor was this related just to manpower, for one of the most dramatic changes in this, the middle part of the war, was the Allied realization that better weapons were needed. Some of these, such as new anti-submarine radars, were battle-winners in their own right, while others, such as jet engines and atomic bombs, were still in the early stages of development, but the sudden devotion of resources and technological expertise to the war effort opened up enormous potential, not least in the ability of countries like the U.S.A. to out-produce their enemies. The Allies might still lag behind in some areas, most notably tank design, but what could not be achieved by superior technology could always be overcome by sheer weight of numbers.

But weapons and the men who serve them will only be effective if used correctly, and one of the characteristics of this part of the war was the gradual adoption by the Allies of tactics and techniques designed to counter those employed by the enemy during the earlier period of conflict. This was seen most notably on the Eastern Front where, despite substantial losses, the Soviets not only survived the full force of *blitzkrieg* but also learned from the experience. In 1941, that survival may have been a reflection of nothing more sophisticated than space and weather – the Soviets could trade territory to gain time and use that time to wait for "General Winter", their traditional saviour – but by 1942 this was being developed further. Thus, when Hitler moved south into the Caucasus, the Soviets let him come, then delivered a deliberate counterattack designed to encircle the spearheads in Stalingrad, where they had been enmeshed in urban fighting. By July 1943, this had been refined even more, this time by creating defense in depth around Kursk so that the panzers could not build up momentum, leaving then vulnerable to a massive armored counterstroke. When it is added that the Soviets were also placing emphasis on mobile logistics, mechanization and dedicated close-support airpower, it may be appreciated that they were, in effect, ensuring that they did not repeat the weaknesses to *blitzkrieg* displayed in the German campaigns of 1941 and 1942. It was an expensive way of learning about modern war, and it was probably only the Soviets who could afford to do it that way, but by mid-1943 the foundations had been laid that were to allow Stalin to push his troops all the way to Berlin in less than two years.

Neither the British nor Americans went through quite such a traumatic change, although they, too, were learning new approaches to war. The stategic bombing offensive against Germany was a case in point, where the practical problems involved were being faced and resolved, at least in part. The Americans may still have believed in the "self-defending" bomber by July 1943, but the British had recognized the difficulties inherent in daylight-precision raids and had switched to night-area attacks, achieving some success over Hamburg and lesser cites. On land, it was the British who took on and defeated the *Afrika Korps* at Alamein, responding to the flexibility of desert *blitzkrieg* by reverting to set-piece battles that were dependent on careful planning and superior numbers. When the Americans ignored this, as at Kasserine, they suffered. Nevertheless, it was the Americans who perfected techniques to defeat the Japanese in the Pacific, using a combination of air, naval and amphibious forces (as well as code-breaking) to halt the enemy's advance into the Solomons and turn the tide in a series of naval battles, many of them characterized by the emphasis on carrier-borne airpower. One of the lessons that was emerging in all theaters was the need for all arms and inter-service coordination.

But none of this would have been possible without industrial mobilization on a grand scale, and without the enormous powerhouse of the United States, the other

An heroic portrait of Joseph Stalin, 1930s.

Allied states would have struggled to match their enemies. By the time of Alamein, the British were dependent on American-built Sherman tanks to match the panzers; by the time of Kursk the Soviets were receiving many of the trucks they needed for their logistic effort direct from the United States. In the Battle of the Atlantic – a major strategic Allied victory of the period – it was American-built warships and merchantmen that turned the tide, making it impossible for the Germans to sink more tonnage than was being constructed in American yards. That more than any other single factor marked the difference between Allied victory or defeat.

By July 1943, therefore, the Axis powers were on the defensive – in the Atlantic, Mediterranean and Pacific – and, in retrospect, Allied victory was clearly just a matter of time. But this does not mean that the fighting was any less hard. Some of the war's most difficult and costly battles were fought between June 1942 and July 1943, proving that the Axis still had much to give. Indeed, it would not be unreasonable to argue that if some of those battles, such as Midway, Alamein or Kursk, had gone the other way, the outcome of the war might have been very different; it would certainly have taken the Allies longer to gain the initiative. None of the Axis powers was yet fighting for survival – each was still occupying territory beyond its own national borders – and, on occasions, they could operate in ways that were as stunning as in earlier campaigns. They also remained in possession of vast areas of the globe, from which they had to be evicted before their own countries could be attacked. The fact that during this middle period of the war, at Casablanca in January 1943, the Western Allied leaders adopted their policy of "unconditional surrender" showed that it would be a war to the death. There was still a long way to go.

The RAF raid on the Mohne Dam in 1943. Painted by Frank Wootton.

Battle of the Atlantic JUNE 1942 – MAY 1943

The American entry into the war in December 1941 gave the Allies the potential to win the Battle of the Atlantic, for German U-boats, however successful, would eventually be unable to match the ship-building capacity of American yards. In addition, the provision of American-built escort carriers and long-range patrol aircraft would close the "air gap" in the central Atlantic, while continued improvements to convoy protection, ranging from better radar to more destructive depth-charges, would shatter the "Wolf Packs". But all this would take time and, in 1942, that was not something that seemed to be on the side of the Allies. Sinkings from U-boats continued to cause deep concern – over 1500 merchantmen were lost to submarine attack in 1942 – and German surface raiders were still active.

One of the reasons for Allied problems was the extension of the battle to the Arctic as convoys carrying supplies to a beleaguered Soviet Union struggled through sea-lanes within air range of German bases in Norway. The first Arctic convoy sailed as early as August 1941, but German opposition did not develop until January 1942, when U-boats were used for the first time. In March the battleship *Tirpitz* began to operate in Norwegian waters, threatening Convoy PQ12; later the same month PQ13 came under heavy attack from aircraft, U-boats and destroyers. Air attacks on PQ16 in May proved to be less effective and, as weather conditions improved, the Germans prepared an all-out surface effort to stop the convoys entirely. Four warships – *Tirpitz, Admiral Hipper, Admiral Scheer* and *Lützow* – were moved to Norwegian bases along with their escorting destroyers and torpedo-boats, supported by aircraft and submarines. The British, aware of the danger through decoded German signals, responded by ensuring that the next convoy, PQ17, was well protected, not just by a covering force of cruisers and destroyers but also by elements of the Home Fleet.

PQ17 sailed from Iceland on 27 June. At first, as air attacks were absorbed without heavy loss, all seemed secure, but confusion over the exact whereabouts of the German surface ships led the Admiralty to issue an ill-fated order for the convoy to scatter. *Tirpitz* was, indeed, on the move by 5 July, although she soon returned to Norway when spotted by a Soviet submarine. By then, the ships of PQ17, trying to make their way independently to Murmansk, were under attack from aircraft and U-boats. A total of 24 ships were lost, together with 153 men and over 100,000 tons of supplies. As the Allies redeployed their warships to support the Torch landings in North-West Africa, the Arctic convoys were temporarily suspended. When they were resumed in December, they were better protected, as was shown in the Battle of the Barents Sea when a German force comprising *Admiral Hipper* and *Lützow*, with six destroyers in attendance, was seen off by the British escorts. One result was that Hitler threatened to disband the surface fleet entirely.

Part of his reasoning was that the U-boats were still imposing heavy losses in the Atlantic, and this continued to be the case in the early months of 1943. During March, 120 Allied ships were sunk but by then the Allied advantages were coming together. By April RAF Coastal Command had 30 long-range Liberators available and they, together with the escort carriers, effectively closed the "air gap", while the British and Americans now had enough escort warships to provide special support groups, ready to rush to the protection of any convoy under attack. The show-down came in early May, when Convoy ONS5 was attacked by 42 U-boats; in a running battle that lasted two days, the escorts sank or damaged more than half of the submarines, while only 12 merchant ships went down. On 24 May the Wolf Packs were ordered to break off the Battle of the Atlantic, having lost 32 boats in the previous three weeks. They would return, but never seriously threaten the sea-lanes again. It was a major Allied victory.

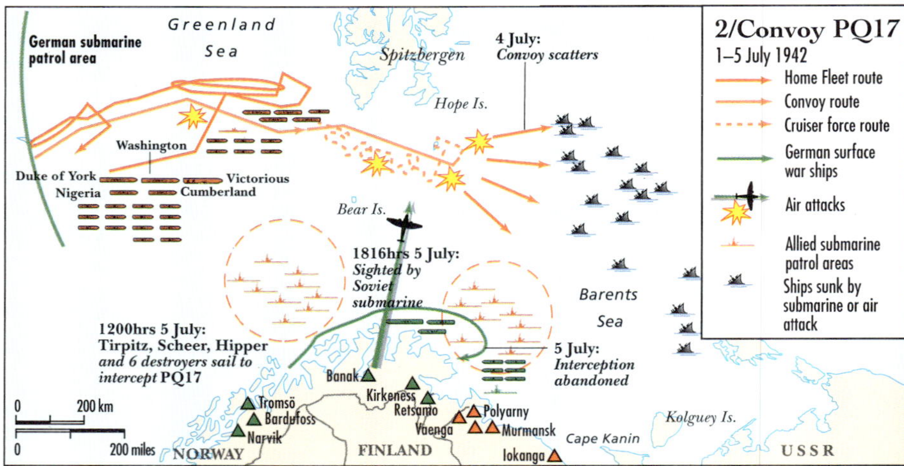

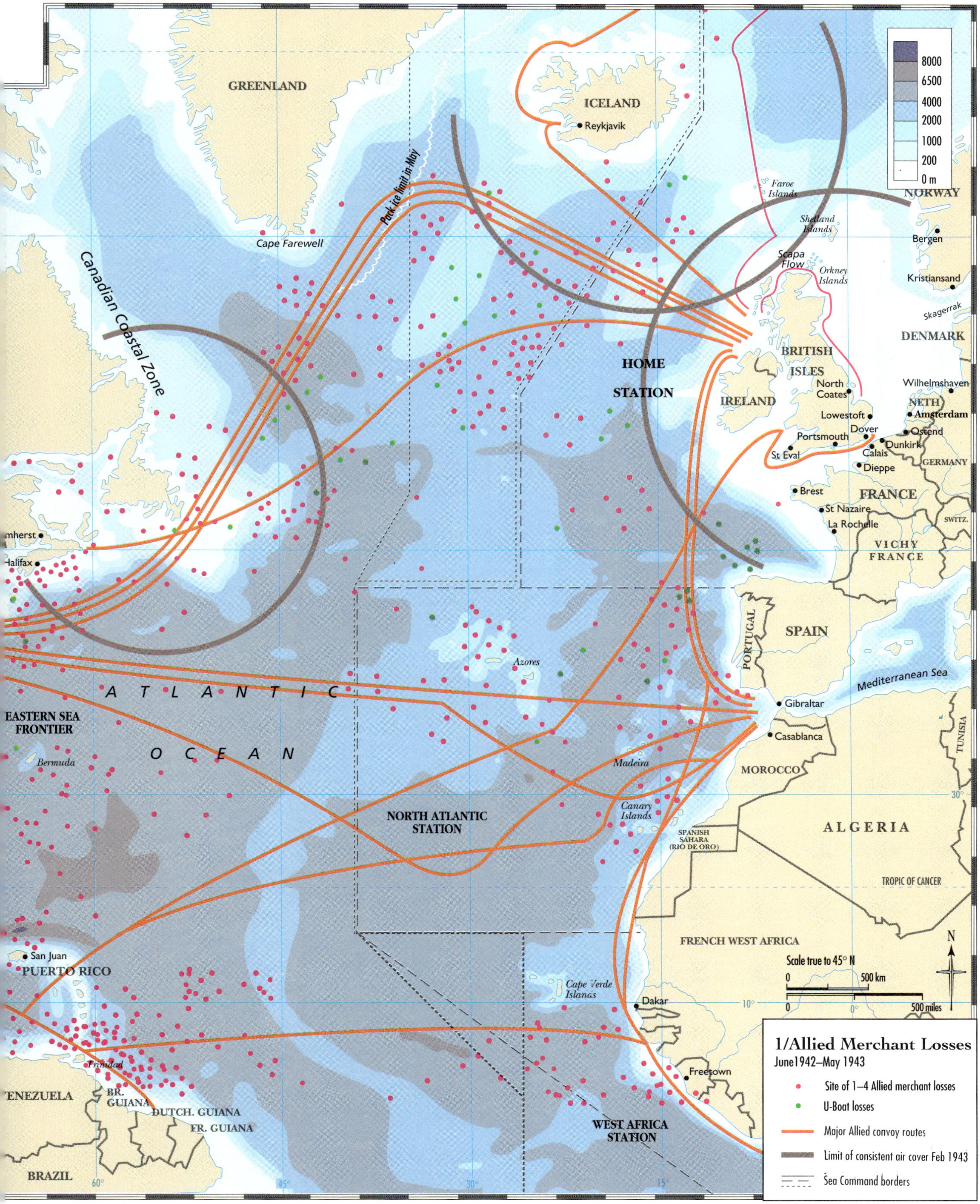

1/Allied Merchant Losses
June 1942–May 1943

- Site of 1–4 Allied merchant losses
- U-Boat losses
- Major Allied convoy routes
- Limit of consistent air cover Feb 1943
- Sea Command borders

Bombing of Germany FEBRUARY 1942 – JULY 1943

The Area Bombing Directive, issued on 14 February 1942, was not easy to carry out. Despite its acceptance that RAF bombers could rarely hit anything smaller than cities from the night-skies over Germany, the destruction of such large targets required the creation of a huge bomber fleet, equipped with navigational and bomb-aiming aids that would ensure effective operations. This would take time and necessitate full political backing, neither of which was readily available. If RAF Bomber Command was to survive, let alone carry out its declared policy of destroying the German war economy, it had to prove itself. That was the job given to Air Marshal Arthur Harris when he was appointed C-in-C Bomber Command on 22 February 1942.

Harris was aware that the means of carrying out the Area Bombing Directive – new radar and bombing aids such as "Oboe" and "H2S" as well as heavier bombers such as the Avro Lancaster – were already in the pipeline, so his first task was to gain time by showing that his command could destroy German cities. He began the process on 28/29 March when 234 bombers, armed with high-explosives and incendiaries, hit Lübeck, concentrating on the medieval timber-framed buildings of the Old Town. Lübeck burned fiercely, as did Rostock when it was selected for attack a month later. But this was only a preliminary. On the night of 30/31 May Harris committed his entire force, including many of his training aircraft, to a "1000-bomber" raid on Cologne. It did little lasting damage and cost Harris 41 of his 1047 bombers, but the raid (closely followed by similar ones against Essen and Bremen) gave his command such publicity that no-one dared to suggest an end to the campaign. Industrial and research priority was afforded to Bomber Command.

This enabled Harris to begin forging the weapon he needed. The task was by no means straightforward. He had to send bombers out over Germany whenever the weather permitted just to guarantee continued support, and losses were never light. By 1942 the Germans had perfected a defense system known as the *Kammhuber Line*, within which individual night-fighters could be guided by radar toward the incoming bombers. If the bombers survived, they still had to face anti-aircraft guns and searchlights over the target itself, then fly back through the *Kammhuber Line* to get home. It was a devastating combination, but worked best against bombers dispatched singly to their targets. Harris quickly realized that if the bombers flew together in a "stream", the defenses would be swamped; if, in addition, the "stream" was guided to its target by more experienced crews using the new radar aids – a task given to the Pathfinder Force – the bombing would be far more concentrated. These techniques were tested between March and July 1943 in what Harris called the "Battle of the Ruhr", when targets in Germany's industrial heart were hit night after night. It was during this battle, on the night of 16/17 May, that 617 Squadron carried out the famous "Dambusters Raid" to breach the Ruhr dams using specially-designed "bouncing bombs". In all cases, damage was inflicted but losses were severe: between March and July, 872 bombers failed to return.

By then, the Americans had become involved. Dedicated to a strategy of daylight precision bombing using well protected B-17 Flying Fortresses and B-24 Liberators of the Eighth Army Air Force, stationed in England, they began operations as early as August 1942, but it took time for them to build up their strength. It was not until July 1943 that a combined offensive against the same target, with the RAF bombing at night and the USAAF bombing during the day, could be contemplated. The target chosen was the city of Hamburg, hit in the early hours of 25 July by the RAF. When daylight came, B-17s flew in, and did so again on the 26th. But the real destruction occurred on the night of 28/29 July when the RAF, protected from German radar by the deployment of "Window" (thin metal strips that "snowed" a radar screen, making it impossible to pinpoint a particular target), achieved such a concentration of bombing that a "firestorm" developed. As hot air from incendiaries rose, colder air rushed in to take its place, acting like a gigantic pair of bellows. The center of the city literally melted and over 30,000 people were killed. Germany was beginning to suffer.

"Oh God, those poor bastards."

British bomber pilot over Hamburg, 25 July 1943

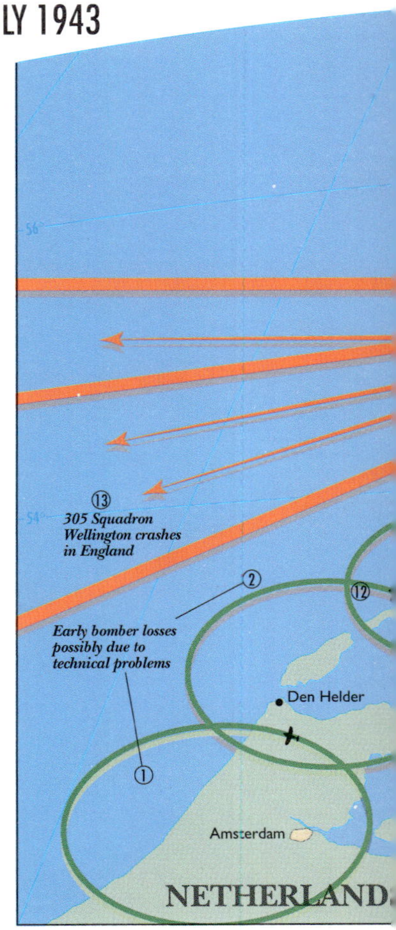

American bomber crews cycle to their widely-scattered aircraft on a base in eastern England. Between August and December 1942 American operations were directed mainly against U-boat pens in occupied France. Not until missions over Germany commenced did losses begin to mount significantly.

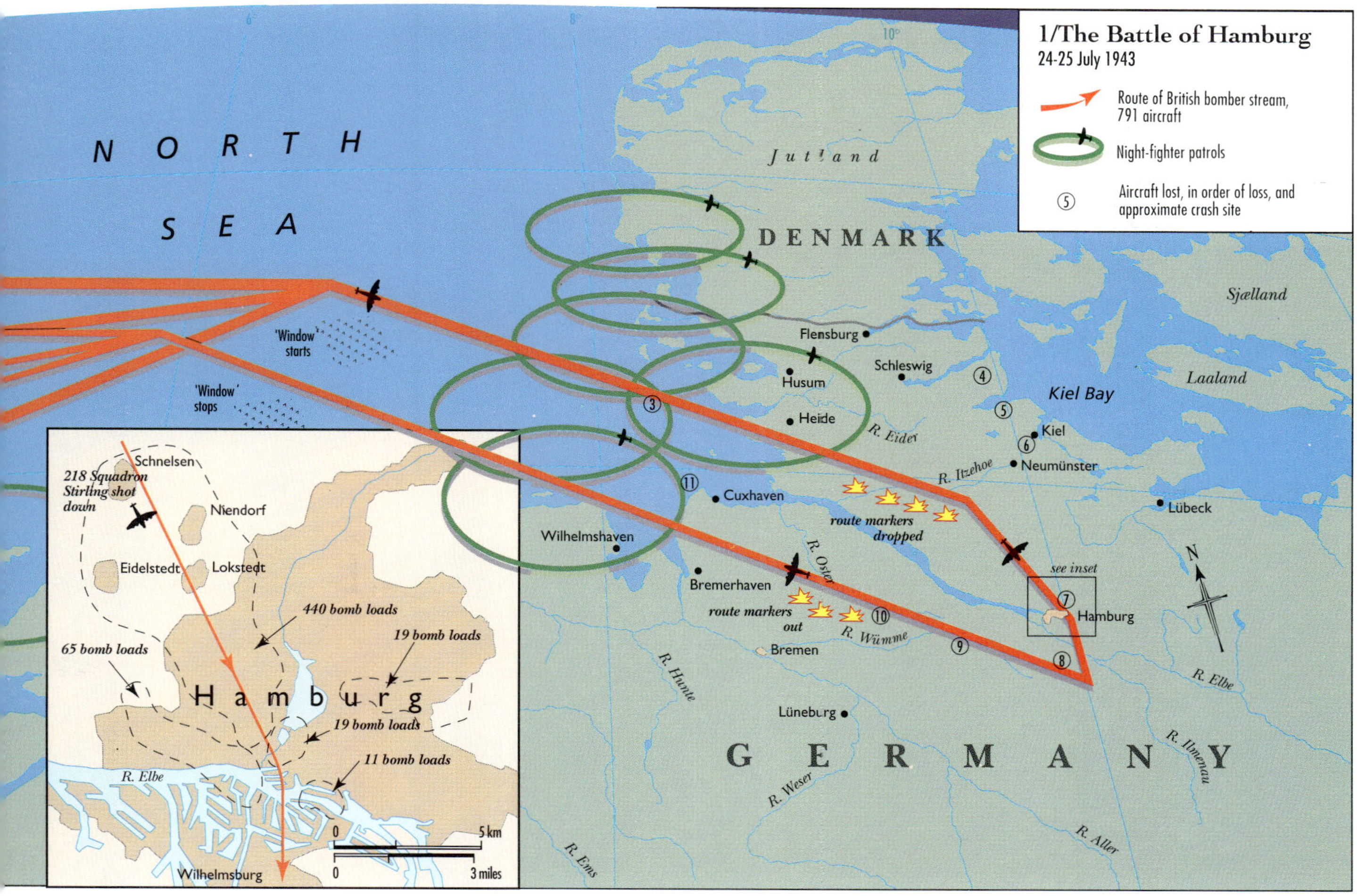
1/The Battle of Hamburg
24-25 July 1943
Route of British bomber stream, 791 aircraft
Night-fighter patrols
Aircraft lost, in order of loss, and approximate crash site
NORTH SEA
Jutland
DENMARK
Sjælland
Laaland
Kiel Bay
'Window' starts
'Window' stops
Flensburg
Schleswig
Husum
Heide
R. Eider
Kiel
Neumünster
R. Itzehoe
Lübeck
Cuxhaven
route markers dropped
Wilhelmshaven
R. Oste
Bremerhaven
route markers out
see inset
Hamburg
R. Wümme
Bremen
R. Hunte
R. Elbe
Lüneburg
R. Ilmenau
GERMANY
R. Weser
R. Aller
R. Ems
Schnelsen
218 Squadron Stirling shot down
Niendorf
Eidelstedt
Lokstedt
440 bomb loads
19 bomb loads
65 bomb loads
Hamburg
19 bomb loads
11 bomb loads
R. Elbe
0 5 km
0 3 miles
Wilhelmsburg

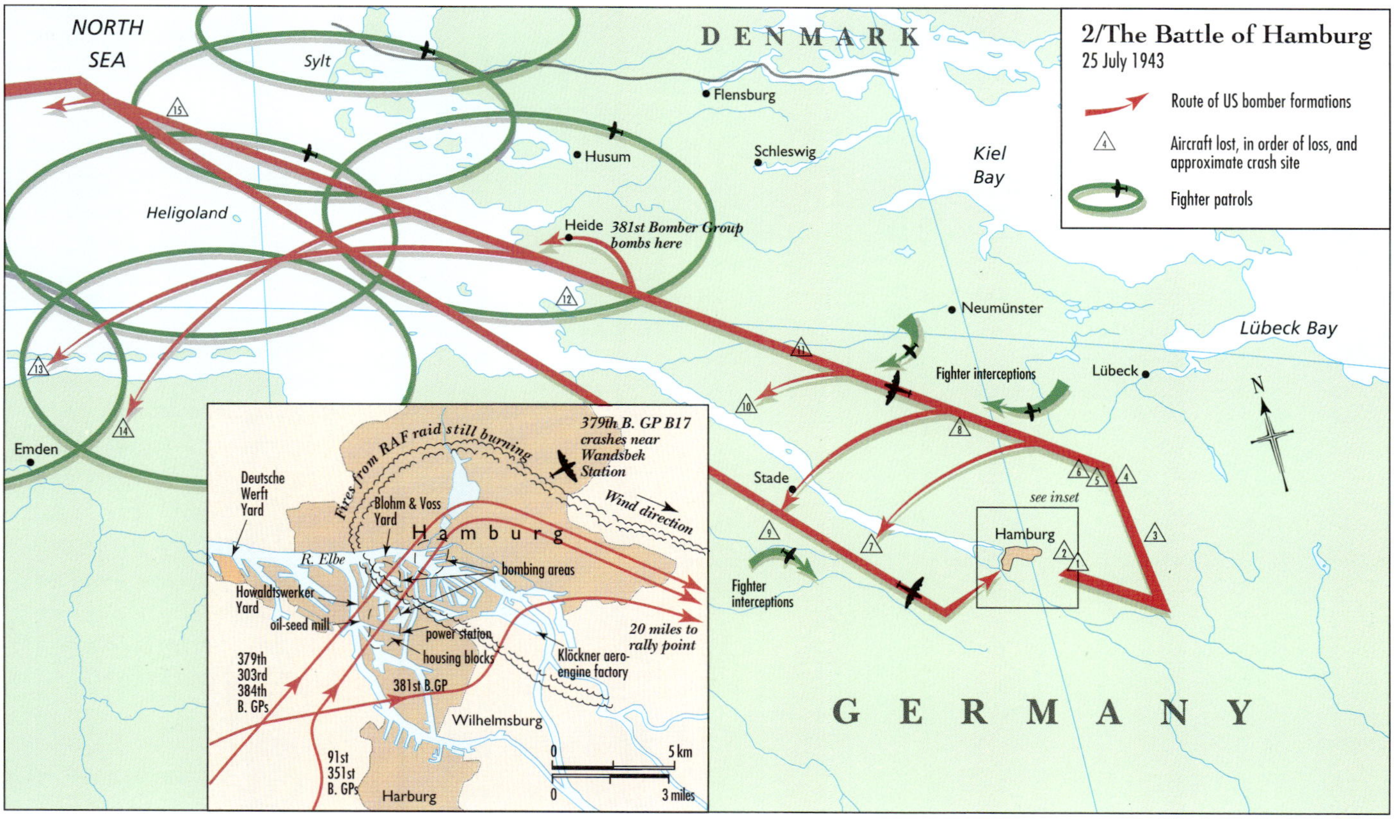
2/The Battle of Hamburg
25 July 1943
Route of US bomber formations
Aircraft lost, in order of loss, and approximate crash site
Fighter patrols
NORTH SEA
Sylt
DENMARK
Flensburg
Husum
Schleswig
Kiel Bay
Heligoland
Heide
381st Bomber Group bombs here
Neumünster
Lübeck Bay
Fighter interceptions
Lübeck
Emden
Stade
see inset
Hamburg
Fighter interceptions
GERMANY
379th B. GP B17 crashes near Wandsbek Station
Fires from RAF raid still burning
Wind direction
Deutsche Werft Yard
Blohm & Voss Yard
Hamburg
R. Elbe
bombing areas
Howaldtswerker Yard
oil-seed mill
power station
housing blocks
20 miles to rally point
Klöckner aero-engine factory
379th 303rd 384th B. GPs
381st B.GP
Wilhelmsburg
91st 351st B. GPs
Harburg
0 5 km
0 3 miles

The Western Desert JUNE – OCTOBER 1942

When the British Eighth Army, commanded by General Auchinleck, retreated into Egypt after its defeat at Gazala in June 1942, it did not stop until it reached the Alamein Line. Rommel followed closely on its heels, determined to reach Cairo and the Suez Canal before an effective defense could be established. On 1 July he sent his panzers to assault British/Imperial positions in the north, between El Alamein and Ruweisat Ridge, aiming to get behind Auchinleck's main line of defense, but the New Zealand and 1st Armored Divisions plugged the gap and by 4 July, the offensive had been blunted.

This gave Auchinleck time in which to regroup and plan his own attack. He had a number of advantages. His lines of supply were short and his forces, although weakened by recent battles, could be reinforced from elsewhere in the Middle East. By the middle of July, for example, he had nearly 400 tanks available. Rommel, by comparison, was operating far from his main supply base at Tripoli and was down to less than 100 running tanks, with no prospect of replacements arriving. In addition, although the Alamein position comprised a series of "boxes" rather than a continuous line, it rested on secure flanks – the Mediterranean in the north and an area of desolate soft sand known as the Qattara Depression in the south. This meant that Rommel's favourite ploy of wide sweeping movements around the enemy was impossible, forcing him to conform to the British preference for a set-piece battle.

Auchinleck opened his attack on 10 July with an artillery bombardment of Italian positions on the coast, followed swiftly by an advance using Australian infantry. The Italians broke and ran; Rommel had to commit his own

Awarded the MC and DSO during World War I, Sir Harold Alexander was one of the British Army's most outstanding generals. A tough field commander, Alexander also possessed great diplomatic skills which enabled him to achieve cooperation between soldiers of different nationalities.

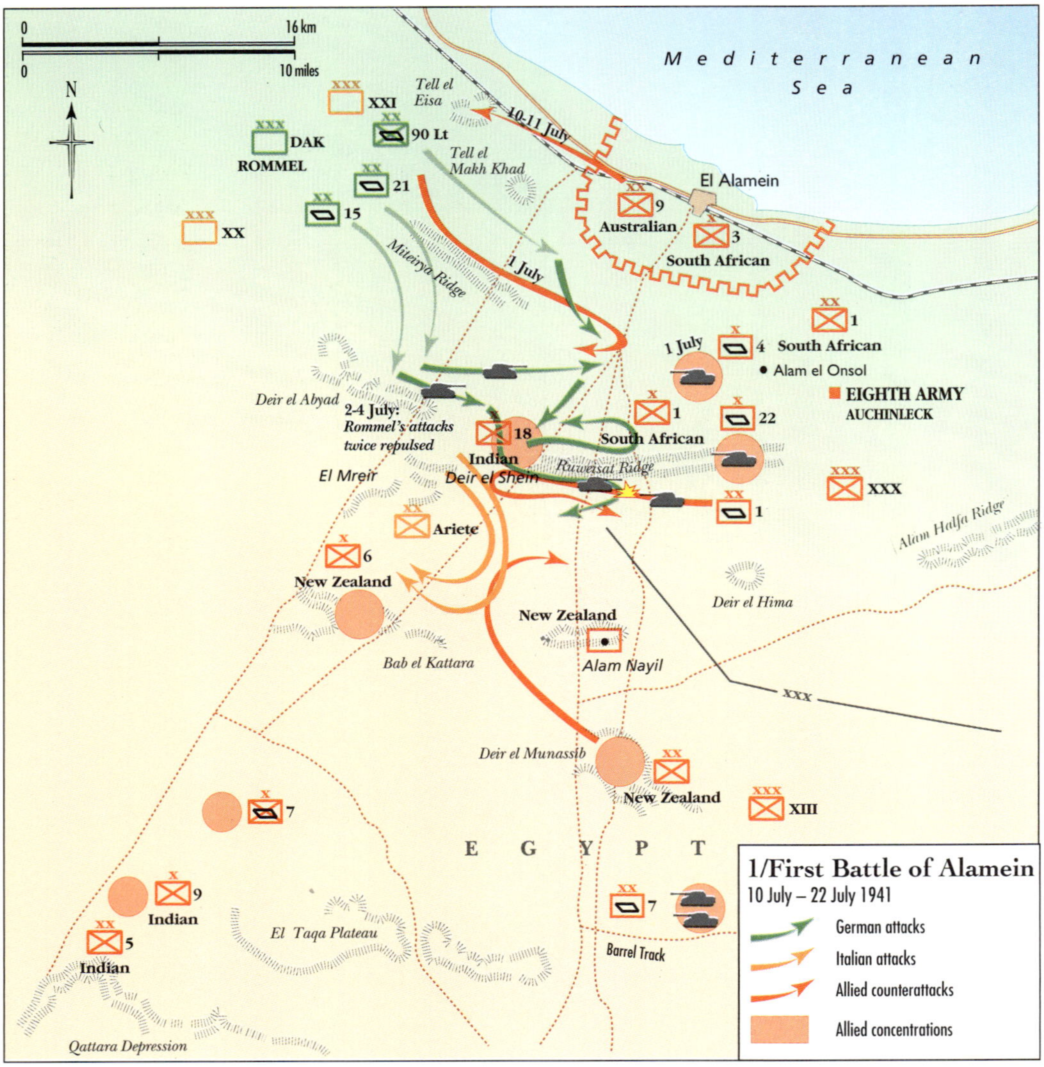

"I thought of what must be going through the minds of so many thousands up there beyond the skyline. I could see them checking things over, brewing up, singing their favorite mournful song, writing their letter home. It took me back twenty-six years to another night and another place where I too had waited in a trench and wondered what it would be like when the whistles blew and the moment came to climb out and take my chance."

Colonel Geoffrey Barkas

German infantry to hold the line. Four days later, Auchinleck ordered the 4th New Zealand Brigade to attack along the Ruweisat Ridge, opening gaps for British armor, but tank-infantry cooperation was still poor. As the 22nd Armored Brigade waited for daylight before advancing, the New Zealanders were overrun. A similar disaster occurred on 21 July, when the 23rd Armored Brigade lost most of its tanks in an unsupported "cavalry charge" against 88 mm anti-tank guns near Deir el Shein. Auchinleck was forced to call off the attack. The First Battle of Alamein may have halted Rommel's advance, but it failed to remove the threat to Cairo and was expensive. Since 1 July, Eighth Army had suffered more than 13,000 casualties.

This was enough to persuade Churchill that Auchinleck had to go. In early August General Sir Harold Alexander was appointed C-in-C Middle East with command of Eighth Army going to Lieutenant-General William Gott. When Gott was killed on 7 August, he was replaced by Lieutenant-General Bernard Montgomery. With reinforcements and fresh stocks of ammunition already arriving, he was in a strong position to respond to Rommel's next offensive, the details of which were known from decoded Enigma messages. True to form, Rommel intended to attack in the north to tie down British/Imperial resources, while sending the bulk of his armor south to infiltrate between less secure "boxes" and aim for the coast, cutting Eighth Army off. Montgomery decided to let him come, tempting the panzers to attack Alam Halfa Ridge, some 12 miles behind the front-line, where the recently arrived 44th Infantry Division would be dug-in behind extensive minefields and supported by the 7th and 10th Armored Divisions of XIII Corps.

Rommel, desperate for fuel, began his attack on the night of 30/31 August and fell straight into the trap. As his tanks and motorized infantry approached Alam Halfa, they became enmeshed in minefields and were subjected to fierce bombardment. Any attempt to advance was stopped by the anti-tank guns of 44th Division and the massed armor of XIII Corps. As casualties mounted, Rommel had no choice but to pull back, leaving about 50 tanks and 400 trucks behind. By 2 September the battle was over. It was Rommel's last chance of victory.

The wreckage of one of the 100 tanks which Rommel was able to field at the First Battle of El Alamein. The British had nearly 400 tanks but they consistently failed to give adequate support to the infantry.

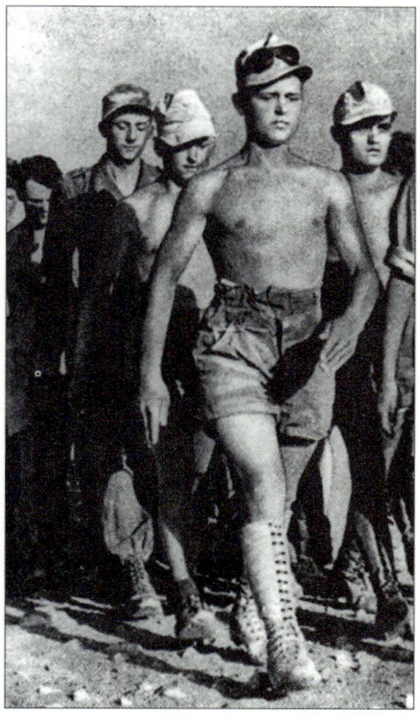

Soldiers of Rommel's Afrika Korps *are marched into captivity. By the time the fighting ended at El Alamein, both sides were suffering from exhaustion, hunger and low morale. Losses had been heavy and no decisive victory had been enjoyed by either army.*

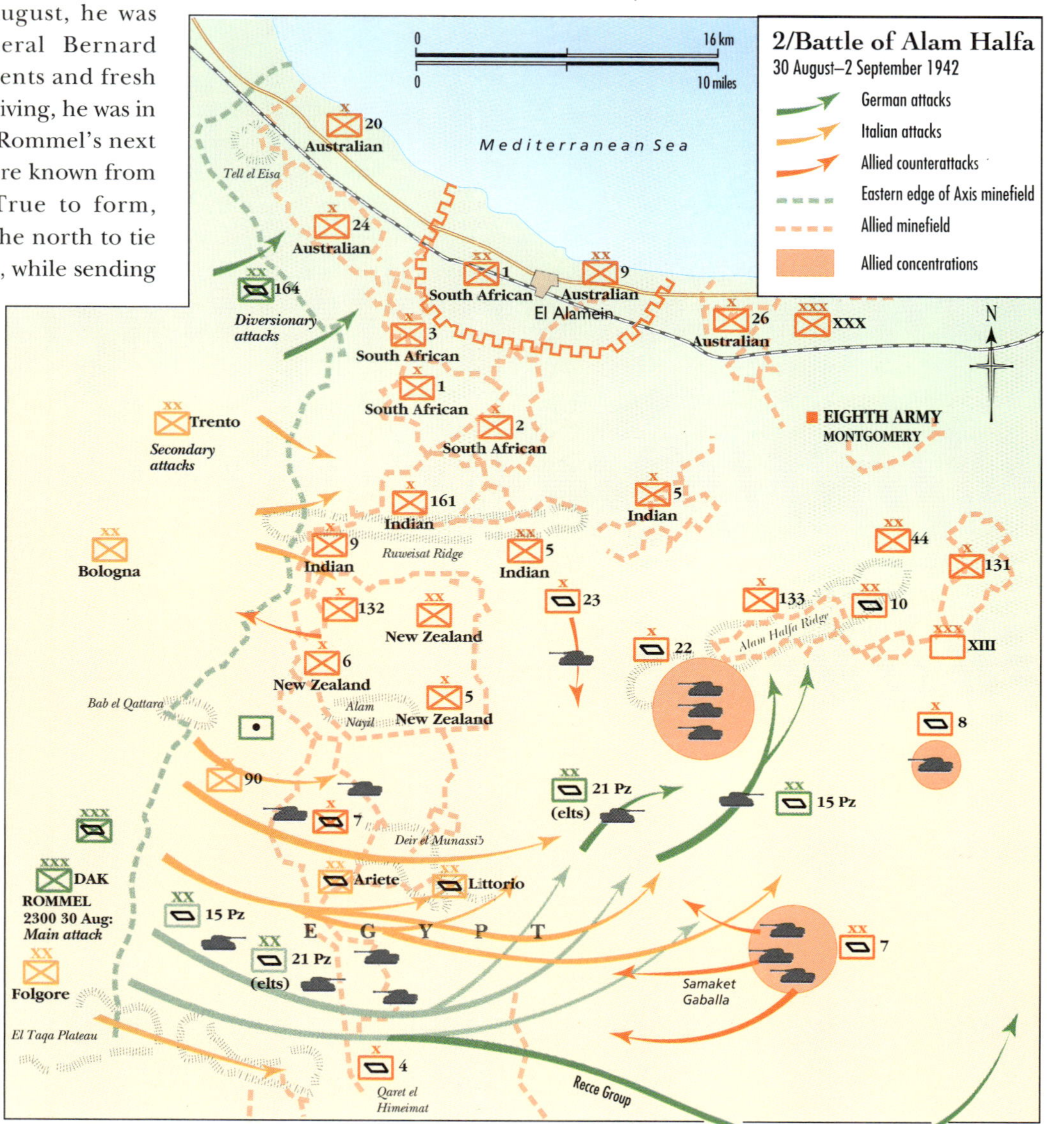

The Western Desert OCTOBER 1942 – JANUARY 1943

After Alam Halfa, Rommel went onto the defensive, shielding his remaining forces behind an elaborate belt of minefields. In the north, facing Tell el Eisa, he stationed his 164th Light Division, with the Italian Trento Division on the Miteirya Ridge, backed by the 15th Panzer and Littorio Divisions. In the center, Ruweisat Ridge and Bab el Qattara were held by the Bologna and Brescia Divisions, with the Folgore and Pavia Divisions to their south; behind them stood the 21st Panzer and Ariete Divisions. The 90th Light Division was kept in reserve at Ghazal, on the coast. Facing Rommel, Montgomery delayed his attack until all was ready.

The Second Battle of El Alamein was planned by 6 October. It was to be a set-piece engagement, concentrated in the north. After an artillery bombardment, Major-General Oliver Leese's XXX Corps would attack between Tell el Eisa and the Miteirya Ridge, opening up corridors through which the armor of Major-General Herbert Lumsden's X Corps would pass. To prevent Rommel rushing forces north, diversionary attacks would take place in the south, using Major-General Brian Horrocks' XIII Corps. The RAF's Desert Air Force would support the ground forces throughout.

Operation *Lightfoot* began at 9.40 p.m. on 23 October 1942 with an artillery bombardment, under which Royal Engineers went forward to clear the minefields. Close behind came the infantry determined to create corridors for the tanks of the 1st and 10th Armored Divisions. Some success was achieved – the New Zealanders, for example, cleared large parts of Miteirya Ridge – but casualties were heavy and the armor was unable to push through quickly enough. It was at this point that Rommel might have made some decisive intervention, but he was on sick leave in Germany and his stand-in, Lieutenant-General Georg Stumme, had died during the British bombardment. Montgomery took the opportunity to urge X Corps on. Even so, without artillery and air support, they would have been hard-pressed to maintain their positions against 15th Panzer Division, which counterattacked throughout 24 and 25 October.

Rushing back, Rommel ordered 21st Panzer Division to move north and, in company with 15th Panzer, to attack Kidney Ridge, to the north-west of Miteirya. They failed to make much headway, suffering heavy casualties on 27 and 28 October. By then Montgomery had halted diversionary attacks and concentrated most of his force for a new offensive, codenamed *Supercharge*, in the north. As the Australians fought toward Tell el Eisa and the coast road, the 1st Armored Division prepared to advance beyond the Miteirya Ridge to take Tel el Akkakir. After the usual artillery bombardment, *Supercharge* began early on 2 November and, despite heavy losses, 1st Armored broke through, closely followed by 7th and 10th Armored Divisions. By late on 4 November, Rommel was in retreat, having lost nearly half his men and well over 400 tanks. Montgomery had lost 13,500 men and about 250 tanks, but was poised for victory.

Rommel skilfully withdrew, but was forced to keep moving by the knowledge that, on 8 November, Allied troops had landed far to his rear, in North-West Africa. Tobruk was retaken by Eighth Army on 13 November and Benghazi five days later. Rommel tried to make a stand at El Agheila, only to be outflanked by the New Zealand Division in mid-December; a similar move at Buerat on 15 January 1943 allowed Montgomery to maintain momentum. At 5 a.m. on 23 January, lead elements of Eighth Army entered Tripoli, having covered 1400 miles in three months.

The crew of a British six-pounder anti tank gun prepare for action in the Second Battle of El Alamein. Montgomery's resources considerably outnumbered those of his opponent but the Germans enjoyed the advantage of a well-prepared system of defenses designed by Rommel.

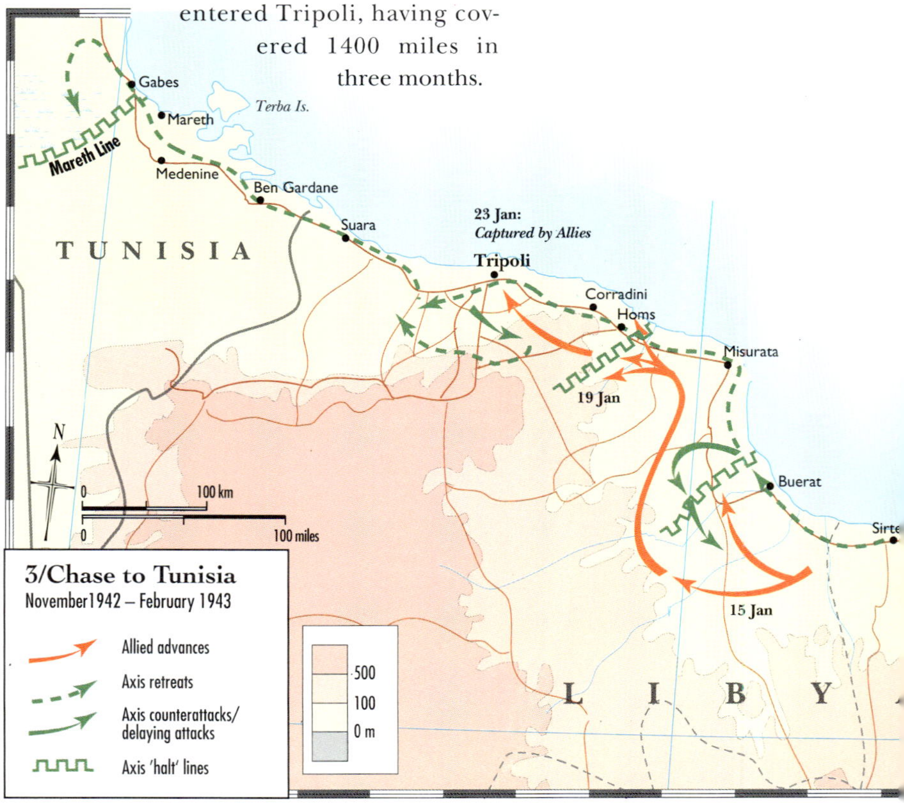

3/Chase to Tunisia
November 1942 – February 1943

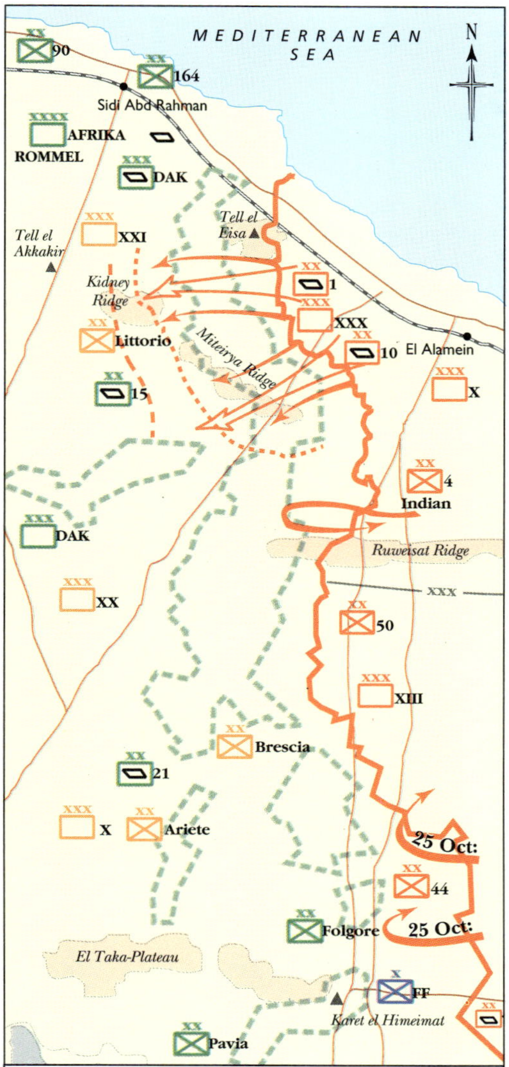

1/Operational plan for "Lightfoot"
23 October 1942

- Initial Allied attacks (mainly in the south)
- 'Corridors' through Axis minefields for armored advances
- "Oslac line" reached 14 Oct
- "Pierson line" original objective
- Axis minefield

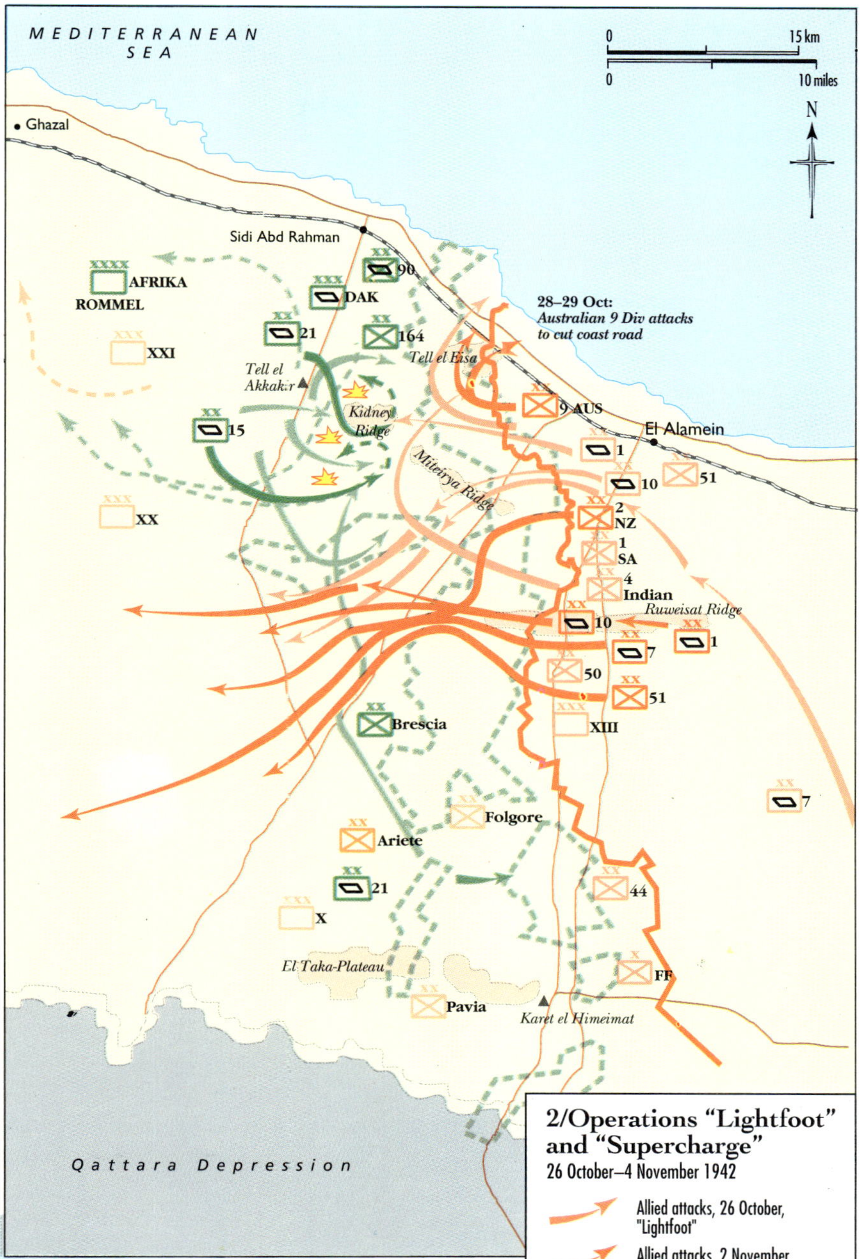

2/Operations "Lightfoot" and "Supercharge"
26 October–4 November 1942

- Allied attacks, 26 October, "Lightfoot"
- Allied attacks, 2 November, "Supercharge"
- Allied airstrikes
- Axis counterattacks
- Axis withdrawals

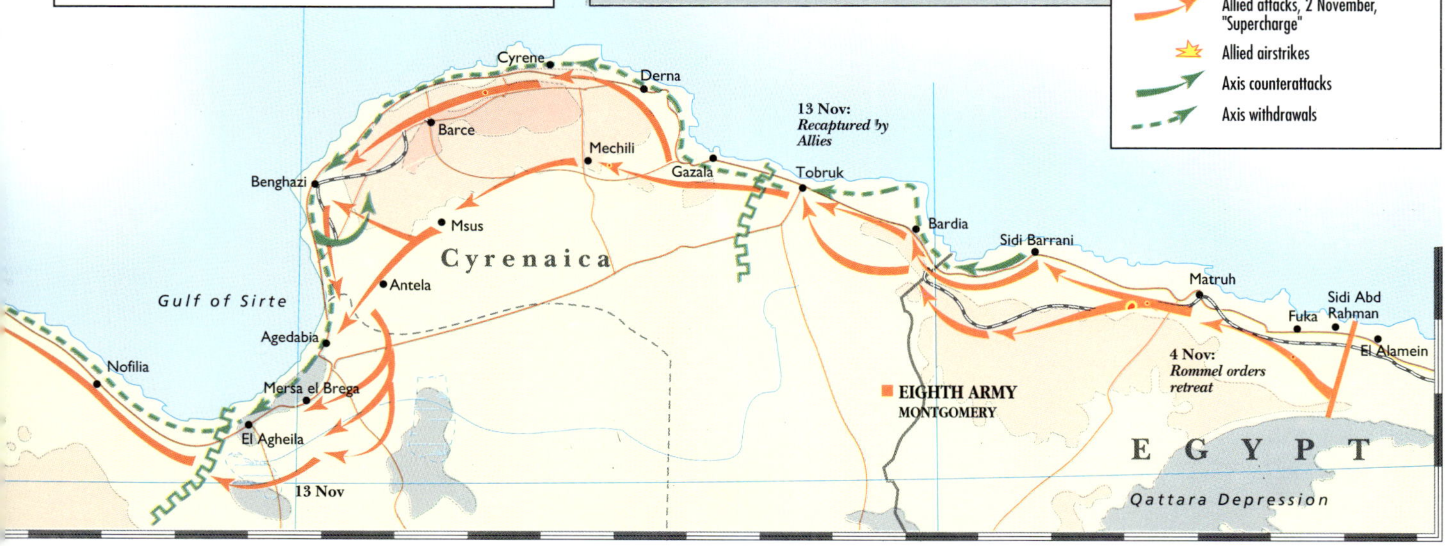

North-West Africa NOVEMBER 1942 – FEBRUARY 1943

Operation *Torch*, the Anglo-American landings in North-West Africa on 8 November 1942, was a gamble. Designed to take Axis forces in Libya in the rear, squeezing them between the invaders and Montgomery's Eighth Army, *Torch* depended for success upon the attitude of the Vichy-French authorities in North-West Africa. If they resisted, the invasion could be costly. In the weeks before the landings, therefore, the Allies negotiated secretly with Admiral Jean Darlan, commander of Vichy forces in North-West Africa, in the hope of gaining his support. But as the invasion fleet gathered, it was still unclear which way the French would turn. Lieutenant-General Dwight D. Eisenhower, the American commander of the Allied force, had to assume that there would be opposition.

He was correct. Though sympathetic, Darlan refused to commit himself to the Allied cause, and the landings were by no means easy. At Casablanca in Morocco, Major-General George S. Patton's Western Task Force of 25,000 men came under attack from the battleship *Jean Bart* and, once ashore, faced chaos on beaches swept by French air and ground fire. In western Algeria, Major-General Lloyd Fredendall's Central Task Force of 39,000 men failed to take the harbor at Oran on 8 November, and had to fight hard to establish their beachheads. Only in Algiers, where Major-General Charles Ryder's Eastern Task Force of 43,000 men landed on three beaches, was immediate success achieved, after some heavy fighting. It was not until 11 November, by which time Oran had fallen and Casablanca was about to be attacked by Allied aircraft, that Darlan surrendered.

The German response was swift. As early as 9 November reinforcements were flown from Sicily to Tunisia, and on the 27th Vichy-France was occupied. Meanwhile, Allied forces around Algiers, renamed British First Army and commanded by Lieutenant-General Kenneth Anderson, had pushed eastward, aiming to prevent Axis consolidation in Tunisia. They nearly succeeded, taking Bougie, Djidjelli, Philippeville and Bône in Algeria before thrusting as far as Souk el Arba, 80 miles from Tunis, by 16 November. But supply lines were over-stretched and, as First Army came under increasing pressure from newly arrived German forces, progress slowed. On 22 December Eisenhower ordered a fresh offensive, sending the British 6th Armored Division along the Medjerda Valley toward Tunis. The key to the valley was Longstop Hill, assaulted by British Guardsmen over Christmas. When they were forced to withdraw, Eisenhower postponed the offensive.

In mid-January 1943, following a meeting between Churchill and Roosevelt at Casablanca, Eisenhower concentrated on planning future Allied landings in Sicily and Italy, leaving the Tunisian battle to General Sir Harold Alexander, appointed to command the newly constituted 18th Army Group, comprising the British First and Eighth Armies as well as the U.S. II Corps. Within a month, Rommel had linked up

"In Africa, for the first time I saw the loneliest and most ominous of all landscapes, a battlefield. And I knew for the first time that strange exhilaration that grips a man when he knows that somewhere out there in the distance hostile eyes are watching him and that any moment a bullet he may never hear, fired by an enemy he cannot see, may strike him."

Major-General Matthew B. Ridgway

1/Operation "Torch"
8 November 1942

- Allied landings, 2 November
- German landings, from 4 November
- Allied front line, mid February 1943

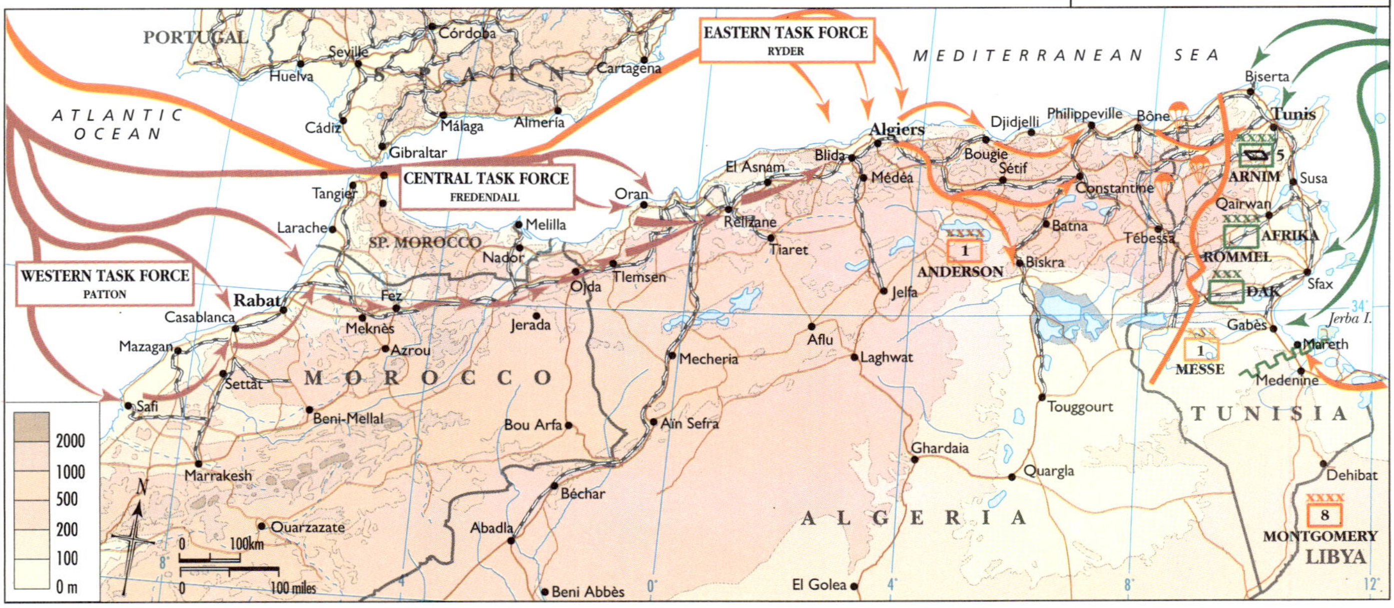

with Axis forces in Tunisia and, as his troops manned a defensive line at Mareth to hold Montgomery at bay, he turned his attention west. On 14 February tanks of 10th Panzer Division attacked U.S. positions at Sidi Bou Zid, at the western end of the Faid Pass in the Eastern Dorsal Mountains; when the American 1st Armored Division mounted a counterattack, it was caught in a trap, losing 46 tanks and over 300 men. The Americans withdrew to the pass at Kasserine, protecting the approaches to Tebessa. They came under ferocious attack on 20 February, falling back in disarray. Fortunately, Rommel did not pursue his advantage immediately; by 22 February, Allied reinforcements had plugged the gap, halting the panzer advance on the roads to Tebessa and Thala. The Americans still had a lot to learn.

American troops are ferried to the North African beaches during Operation Torch. *The plans for* Torch *demanded the assembly of the largest amphibious invasion force ever created. More than 500 ships would transport 107,000 men to Morocco and Algeria.*

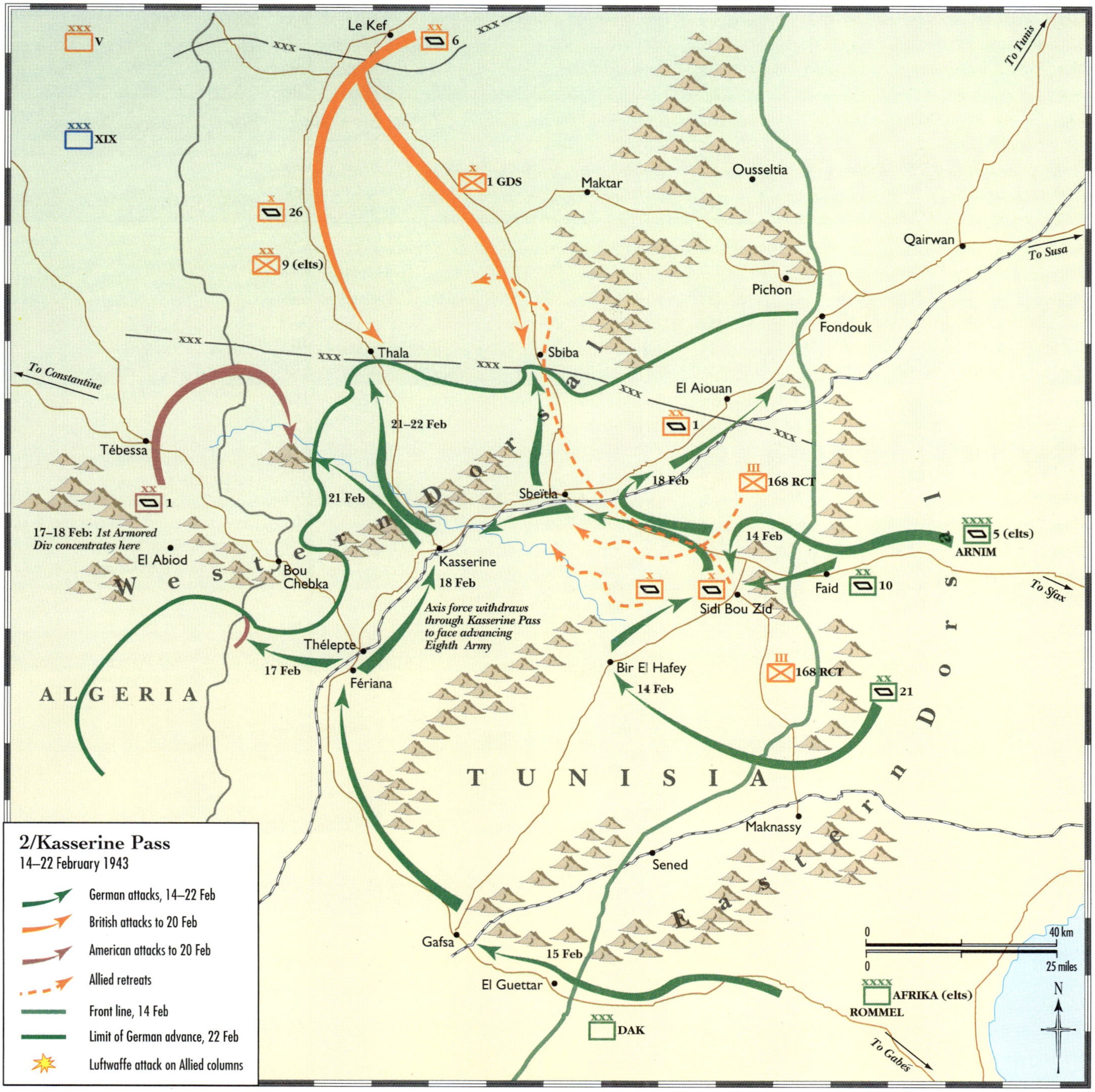

North-West Africa MARCH – MAY 1943

Having failed to break through at Kasserine, Rommel turned back to face Montgomery at Mareth, aiming to attack the town of Medenine. But the Allies, in receipt of decoded German messages, expected the assault, and set up an elaborate anti-tank ambush. When the 10th, 15th and 21st Panzer Divisions advanced on 6 March 1943, therefore, they were met by withering fire from concealed positions, losing 52 tanks and nearly 700 casualties. Three days later, Rommel flew to Germany to plead with Hitler for reinforcements; instead, the Führer sent him on sick leave. He was replaced as commander of Army Group Africa by General Jurgen von Arnim.

Meanwhile, Patton had been given command of the battered U.S. II Corps and was ordered by Alexander to push forward through the mountain passes at El Guettar and Maknassy, at the southern end of the Eastern Dorsal range, threatening the rear of the Mareth Line. Despite heavy fighting, Patton's men could not break through to the coast, although their efforts undoubtedly diverted Axis attention away from the Mareth area. Nevertheless, when Montgomery attacked on 20/21 March, the Battle of Mareth proved not to be easy. His plan, which clearly owed something to his experiences against Rommel, was for a frontal attack to be made on the Mareth Line by the bulk of Eighth Army, while the New Zealand Division looped round to the left, through the Matmata Hills and Tebaga Gap, to seize El Hamma and so outflank the enemy. Heavy rain disrupted the frontal attack, turning the Wadi Zigzaou to mud which effectively halted progress, and Montgomery was forced to rethink. He decided to send the British 1st Armored Division to follow the New Zealanders, while tying down the panzers on the Mareth Line using air and artillery strikes. It worked. Although the British tanks were held off for two days in rock-strewn terrain between Tebaga and El Hamma, by the end of the month the Axis forces were in retreat, aiming to set up a new defensive line along the Wadi Akarit, 40 miles further north. Montgomery did not pause. On 6 April, as Gurkhas captured Djebel Fatnassa, overlooking Wadi Akarit, the 50th and 51st (Highland) Divisions put in a frontal assault that destroyed the Italian defenders. Arnim ordered a withdrawal, abandoning Wadi Akarit and pulling his forces out of El Quettar and Maknassy. Men of Eighth Army linked up with the U.S. II Corps on 7 April.

Arnim decided to make a stand in the north-east corner of Tunisia, from Enfidaville on the east coast, through the Medjerda Valley in the center, to a point some 25 miles from Bizerta on the north coast. It was ideal country for the defenders, comprising mountainous terrain that included the infamous Longstop Hill as well as other, similar, features. On 22 April, the British First Army renewed its attack on Longstop, suffering heavy casualties before finally seizing the summit. To their north, elements of the U.S. II Corps (commanded by Major-General Omar Bradley now that Patton had been moved to planning the Sicily landings) assaulted Hill 609 and once that had been taken, the Axis defenses began to crumble. Arnim, down to 175,000 men and desperately short of petrol for his remaining panzers, was about to be overwhelmed. He was facing Allied armies that totalled some 380,000 soldiers and 1200 tanks, while his supply line to Sicily, already fragile, was being severed by air and naval attack.

The final Allied offensive opened on 6 May. All along the front, the Axis troops fought stubbornly, but there were limits to their capabilities. Bizerta fell to the Americans late on 7 May, just as the armored cars of the British 11th Hussars were entering Tunis. Arnim withdrew to Cape Bon. On 12 May, having nothing left with which to fight, he surrendered, along with the remains of his Army Group. North Africa was in Allied hands.

Backed-up by flamethrowing Churchill Crocodile tanks, the Allies prepare to attack Longstop Hill, closely defended by the Germans because it commanded the entire 25-mile (40-kilometer) stretch of desert to Tunis. The attack on the 800-foot (250-meter) high hill was also hindered by mud and rain.

Allied troops escort prisoners taken during the Tunisian campaign. The French, British and Americans joined forces to defeat Rommel's mighty Panzerarmee Afrika, *but success was hampered by the rough terrain. Mountains, rocks, mud and desert constituted major obstacles to be surmounted in North African operations.*

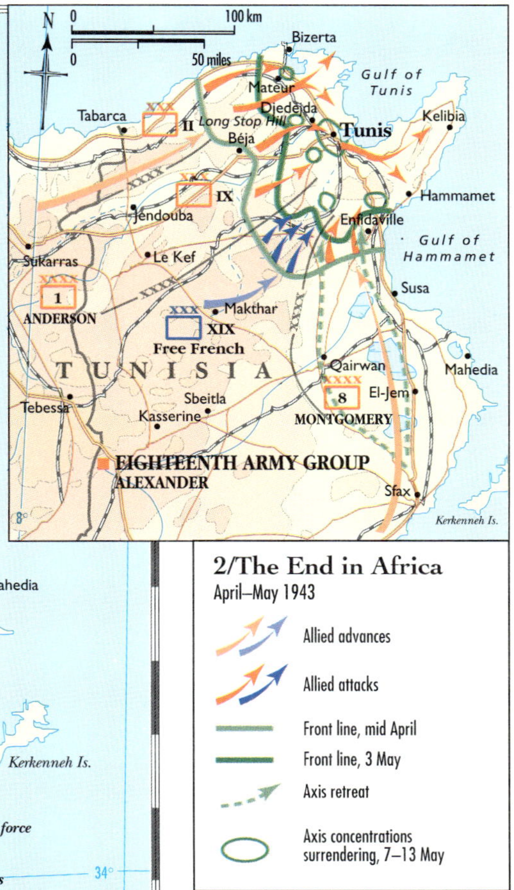

A Free French liaison officer watches a burning lorry abandoned by Rommel and his forces, now in rapid retreat from Montgomery's Eighth Army. The Germans had put up a spirited defense and both sides suffered heavy casualties.

German Advance on the Caucasus

JUNE – NOVEMBER 1942

By the summer of 1942, Hitler was ready to mount a major offensive on the Eastern Front. The destruction of Timoshenko's forces around Izyum in late May had removed a significant threat and prepared the way for an assault designed to capture the oilfields of the Caucasus. With Germany now facing the strategic nightmare of a war on two fronts – in the east against the Soviets and in the west against the British and Americans – all hopes of a short conflict had disappeared, to be replaced by the prospect of a hard slogging match that would require access to raw materials. Without the oil from the Caucasus, Hitler's armed forces would eventually grind to a halt. In addition, if German armies could advance far enough south, their arrival on the Turkish border might just persuade neutral Turkey to commit itself to the Axis cause, opening up the possibility of further advances into the Middle East. With Rommel already deep into Egypt by June 1942, the idea of linking the Eastern Front to that in North Africa was not entirely far-fetched.

But such victories required careful planning, and that was not a feature of Hitler's strategic grasp in 1942. The offensive, codenamed Operation *Blue*, opened on 28 June, when Army Group South advanced from a front between Kursk and Kharkov to take the city of Voronezh, on the River Don. This was worrying to the Soviets, who interpreted it as a move to approach Moscow from the south, and they fought hard to protect the city, which did not fall until 5 July. At the same time, the Germans finally cleared the Crimea, pushing Soviet forces out of the Kerch Peninsula in May and taking Sevastopol on 2 July. However, these were only preliminaries to a far more serious German offensive, presaged by Hitler's decision to reorganize his forces. On 9 July Army Group South was split into Army Group A and B. Each was given precise objectives. As Army Group B, which included those forces already in Voronezh, consolidated its position on the Don and thrust down the Donets Corridor toward Stalingrad, Army Group A was to seize the Donets Basin to the north of Rostov before pushing south into the Caucasus, aiming for Batumi and Baku. Given that these instructions were not issued until July, by which time it was late in the campaigning season, the offensive was dangerously over-ambitious.

Nevertheless, initial progress was good. Once clear of Voronezh, the German Fourth Panzer and Sixth Armies moved easily down the Donets Corridor, sweeping Soviet opposition aside. This led Hitler, on 16 July, to issue the first of a number of confusing counter-orders: because of the lack of opposition in the north, Fourth Panzer Army was to transfer to Army Group A and join First Panzer Army in its advance into the Caucasus. Within days, it was obvious that this was a mistake, slowing Army Group B's advance to the pace of the infantry in General Friedrich Paulus's Sixth Army. In addition, the threat of a Soviet build-up of forces around Stalingrad, where the River Volga jutted out to create a potential base for counterattacks toward Rostov, cutting Army Group A off in the Caucasus, was apparent. On 30 July, therefore, Hitler countermanded his previous orders and moved Fourth Panzer Army back north, with the new objective of spearheading a drive to capture Stalingrad.

The German forces now had two objectives of equal significance – Stalingrad and the Caucasian oilfields – but were not strong enough to take both. Moreover, the confusion over the role of Fourth Panzer Army meant that for the best part of two weeks, it did not contribute effectively to either advance. By the time it resumed its contribution to the northern offensive in early August, momentum had been lost and the Soviets given time in which to prepare the Stalingrad defenses. Although Paulus broke through into the suburbs of the city on 23/24 August, resistance was beginning to stiffen. Meanwhile, in the Caucasus, Army Group A had taken Stavropol on 5 August and Krasnodar on the 9th, but had met serious opposition around Maikop and Piatigorsk. With its supply lines overstretched and tank crews exhausted, Army Group A had reached the limit of its capability and desperately needed reinforcement. Army Group B, about to enter a maelstrom of urban fighting, was in no position to help.

As the German advance on the Caucasus continued, the nature of the fighting changed and troops accustomed to the rapid victories achieved through blitzkrieg *learned the tactics of vicious hand-to-hand street fighting in which submachine guns and hand-grenades were the most effective weapons.*

Hitler's troops advance on Stalingrad. So rapid had been the German advance that the Führer's *dreams of vast conquests for the Reich actually seemed close to realization, but supply lines were being stretched to breaking point, the German army was close to exhaustion and Russian resistance was stiffening.*

"You can no longer retreat across the Volga. There is only one road, the road that leads forward. Stalingrad will be saved by you, or wiped out with you."

Josef Stalin

Operation "Blue"
June – November 1942
German advances to 23 July
German advances to November
Soviet supply routes
Soviet retreats
Soviet air support
Oilfield
2000
1000
500
200
0 m
VORONEZH FRONT
GALIKOV
SOUTHWEST FRONT
VATUTIN
DON FRONT
ROKOSSOVSKY
STALINGRAD FRONT
YEREMENKO
ARMY GROUP B
WEICHS
ARMY GROUP SOUTH
BOCK
ARMY GROUP A
LIST
TRANS-CAUCASUS FRONT
NORTHERN GROUP
TRANS-CAUCASUS FRONT
TYULENEV
BLACK SEA
FLEET
U S S R
HUNGARIAN
(elts)
GUARDS
ITALIAN
ROM
PAULUS
RUOFF
KLEIST
Donets Corridor
R. Don
R. Donets
R. Volga
R. Kuban
R. Kuma
R. Terek
27 July:
River Don
crossed
9 Aug
21 Aug:
Mt Elburus
Kalmyk Steppe
Mouth of the Volga
Caspian Sea
Black Sea
Sea of Azov
Gulf of Taganrog
Caucasus Mountains
Georgia
Azerbaijan
Eletz
Kursk
Voronezh
Svoboda
Ostrogoshsk
Belgorod
Pavlovsk
Kharkov
Smiyev
Izyum
Lugansk
Makyeevka
Stalino
Taganrog
Mariopol
Novo Cherhassk
Rostov
Azov
Yeisk
Tsimlyanskiy
Proletarskaya
Atkarsk
Saratov
Engels
Balashov
Kamishin
Ust Medvieditsa
Kalach
Stalingrad
Zarew
Baskunchak
Astrakhan
Elista
Ulan Erge
Yashkul
Vinodyelnoe
Krapotkin
Kerch
Taman
Krasnodar
Novorossiisk
Armavir
Stavropol
Maikop
Tuapse
Sochi
Pyatigorsk
Georgiyevsk
Mozdok
Kisliar
Grozny
Makhach Kala
Ordzhonikidze
Sukhum
Kutais
Poti
Tiflis
Batumi
45°
40°
N
0
130 km
0
80 miles

Battle for Stalingrad SEPTEMBER 1942 – FEBRUARY 1943

Once committed by Hitler to the capture of Stalingrad in late August 1942, General Friedrich Paulus' Sixth Army, with elements of the Fourth Panzer Army in attendance, faced a nightmare. Although the Russian forces defending the city were in disarray and hampered by the need to bring all supplies and reinforcements across the River Volga under German air and artillery fire, Stalingrad itself offered significant defensive advantages. Buildings ruined by Luftwaffe attack could be transformed into strongpoints, while the Red October, Barrikady and Tractor factories in the north acted as concrete barriers to any advance. After months of maneuver warfare on the steppes of southern Russia, the Germans were about to experience the appalling horrors of urban fighting.

Paulus' first move, beginning on 7 September, was to attack directly into the center of the city, aiming for the west bank of the Volga. Three days later, panzers advanced into the old city further south, splitting the Russian Sixty-Second and Sixty-Fourth Armies apart. On the same day, however, General Vasili Chuikov was appointed to command the Sixty-Second Army, and his arrival breathed new life into the defense. With their backs to the river, the Russian soldiers fought for every inch of territory. Unable to maneuver, the Germans were forced to employ their infantry, with engineer support, to conduct a painstaking and costly advance, fighting from ruin to ruin and from cellar to cellar. By mid-September, Sixth Army occupied most of the old city in the south, but was now in a dangerously exposed salient, the flanks of which were protected by Romanian, Hungarian and Italian troops.

As the German advance became increasingly bogged down, fighting floor to floor in the factories to the north of the city throughout October, the Russians planned a counter-offensive. Codenamed *Uranus*, it envisaged a massive envelopment of Paulus' command. To the north, reserves belonging to the South-West and Don Fronts would push south-eastwards through the Romanian Third Army to link up at Kalach with units of the Stalingrad Front, attacking through the Romanian Fourth Army from the south. When the assault began on 19 November, it achieved instant success. Within four days, the Romanians in the north had been encircled and forced to surrender, and when the Russian Fifth Tank Army reached Kalach on 22 November, it waited less than 24 hours before being joined by elements of the Fifty-First Army from the south. Together, they created a pocket around Stalingrad that contained approximately 250,000 German troops.

Paulus was refused permission to break out by Hitler, who eagerly accepted Reichsmarschall Goering's offer to sustain the Stalingrad pocket by air. It was doomed to failure. Paulus' men needed at least 600 tons of supplies a day just to survive; the most that the Luftwaffe could fly in was 100 tons a day, and that was dependent on the weather, which was beginning to deteriorate. As the Sixth Army and part of the Fourth Panzer Army faced slow starvation, the Russians consolidated their recent gains, creating a solid wedge of territory between Stalingrad and German forces further west. On 12 December, General Erich von Manstein, newly appointed to command a hastily formed Army Group Don, attempted a relief operation, codenamed *Winter Storm*. Spearheaded by LVII Panzer Corps, comprising about 230 tanks, this made some progress, advancing to within 30 miles of Paulus' perimeter by 19 December despite encountering T-34s of the Fifth Tank Army. But by then the Russians had mounted yet another attack, this time against the demoralized Italian Eighth Army on the River Don, and when that enjoyed success, Manstein had no choice but to pull back or face his own encirclement. Once again, Hitler refused to allow Paulus to attempt a breakout.

The Russians concentrated on eliminating the Stalingrad pocket. They were aided by the winter snows and the lack of German supplies, for by Christmas Paulus' command was already disintegrating through exposure and starvation. Wounded men lay unattended in the ruined cellars of the shattered city; others fought among themselves for scraps of food or warmth. To many, Russian offers of surrender terms proved irresistible. On 26 January 1943, men of the Don Front linked up with Chuikov's Sixty-Second Army in the center of Stalingrad, splitting the German defense. On 31 January, Hitler promoted Paulus to Field Marshal. Later that same day a gaunt and dejected Paulus sought terms and ordered his surviving troops – about 90,000 broken men – to lay down their arms. The last of them did so on 2 February.

In October 1942, a German infantry section prepares for battle at the Barrikady factory in Stalingrad. The strain and fatigue of action is beginning to show, and these soldiers' personal weapons – Mauser K98K rifles, an MP38/40 submachine gun and plenty of hand grenades – reflect the nature of the relentless street fighting in the Battle of Stalingrad.

"This man should have shot himself just as the old commanders who threw themselves on their swords when they saw their cause was lost. That goes without saying. Even Varus gave his slave the order: 'Now kill me!'..."

Adolf Hitler commenting on the surrender of Field Marshal Paulus

Battle of Stalingrad
9–29 January 1943
German advances
German retreats
German front line, 9 Jan
Russian attacks
Limit of Russian artillery positions (approximately 200 artillery pieces per km of front line)
Bombardment
1 Grain Elevator
2 Oil Storage Area
3 Red October Factory
4 Barrikady Factory
5 Tractor Factory
200
100
0 m
N
U S S R
R U S S I A
48°30'
49°
44°
44°30'
Kalach
Sovetski
Illarionovski
Platonovski
TWENTY-FIRST ARMY
Marinovka
Voroshilov-Lager
Luftwaffe air lift
Luftwaffe air lift
fighter patrols
SIXTY-FIFTH ARMY
FIFTY-SEVENTH ARMY
Karpovka
Novo-alekseyevski
12 Jan
Baburkin
River Don
Varvarovka
Tsybenko
Gavrilovka
Sovkhov No I
Malaya Rossoshka
XIV Pz
VIII RUM
TWENTY-FOURTH ARMY
fighter patrols
SIXTY-FOURTH ARMY
12 Jan
IV RUM
20 Jan
Kotluban
Yelkhi
Borodkin
Samofalovka
fighter patrols
Straya Otrada
Kuperosnoye
Novaya Nadezhda
Yelshanka
LI RUM
Gumrak
SIXTH ARMY
PAULUS
Koshbavod
Kuzmichi
23 Jan
SIXTY-SIXTH ARMY
XI RUM
28 Jan
Gorodishche
Krasnoarmeisk
29 Jan
Stalingrad
20 Jan
Volga
Krasnaya Sloboda
28 Jan
Orlovka
DON FRONT
ROKOSSOVSKY
fighter patrols
STALINGRAD FRONT
YEREMENKO
SIXTY-SECOND ARMY
Stavenki
Burkauski
Spartakovka
Rynok
Vinnovka
Erzovka
Akatovka

The Siege of Leningrad SEPTEMBER 1941 – JANUARY 1944

The siege of Leningrad began in early September 1941, when Army Group North, advancing from the Baltic States, captured the railway stations at Schlüsselburg and Mga and reached the shores of Lake Ladoga. At the same time, the Finns also attacked the Soviet Union, pushing down the Karelian Isthmus to threaten Leningrad from the north. The city was virtually surrounded, with only a tenuous link with the rest of the country, by boat across Lake Ladoga. Hitler's decision to concentrate on the capture of Moscow, manifested in Operation *Typhoon* in late September, combined with Stalin's decision to send General Georgi Zhukov to organize the Leningrad defenses, undoubtedly saved the latter city, but condemned it to a siege that was to last for nearly 900 days.

During most of that time, Leningrad was under artillery bombardment, and its civilian population suffered unbelievable hardship, not just from the physical destruction but also from the shortage of food. As winter approached in 1941, the city was receiving less than half the rations it needed, and even that figure was cut when German troops captured Tikhvin, a vital railhead through which material was being ferried to Lake Ladoga on 9 November. This left a single, highly vulnerable airfield at Novaya Ladoga as the only link with the outside world. In desperation, the Soviets built a new road through virgin forest from Zaborye to Novaya Ladoga, bypassing Tikhvin to the north, but that took time to complete. When the snows came, Leningrad suffered. A Soviet counterattack managed to recapture Tikhvin on 9 December 1941, and an ice-road was constructed across the frozen Lake Ladoga, but these measures were never enough to prevent starvation.

The spring thaw in 1942 brought some relief, although it also meant that the ice-road over the lake ceased to function. Food became even more scarce, increasing the pressure on the Soviets to raise the siege. The plan, put into effect on 27 August 1942, was for the Leningrad and Volkhov Fronts to attack the German-held corridor between Tosno and Lake Ladoga, opening up a land route to the city. At the same time, Soviet forces caught to the west of Leningrad, in the Oranienbaum "pocket" on the Baltic coast, would attempt to break out, forcing a German withdrawal. Neither offensive succeeded, chiefly because of more pressing crises elsewhere, but also because the Germans had been preparing for their own attack, codenamed *Northern Light*, so had additional forces in the area. In the event, *Northern Light* had to be canceled, although this did nothing to relieve the suffering inside Leningrad. As a second winter set in, starvation and cold seemed set to destroy the surviving population.

The city was saved by a new Soviet offensive in January 1943, at a time when the Germans were understandably obsessed with events around Stalingrad. On 11 January the Leningrad and Volkhov Fronts, by now much strengthened, managed to create a thin corridor along the southern shore of Lake Ladoga and to recapture Schlüsselburg. A railway was hurriedly built through what became known as the "Corridor of Death" and, under constant artillery bombardment, sufficient supplies were pushed through to keep the city alive. This was all that could be achieved in 1943 and it was not until mid-January 1944 that the siege was finally lifted, when three Soviet Fronts (Leningrad, Volkhov and 2nd Baltic) put in a massive attack against Army Group North. By then, it was estimated that over a million people had died in Leningrad. Their sacrifice had succeeded in diverting German resources away from campaigns in other parts of the Soviet Union, while acting as a powerful symbol of Soviet resistance.

Soviet infantry make use of a shattered tank as cover during a patrol of the Leningrad perimeter.

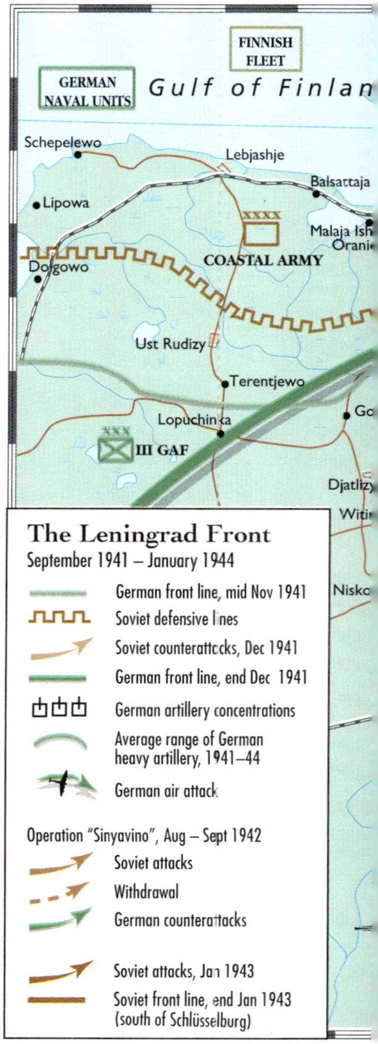

A young German soldier, holder of the Iron Cross, poses with his comrades for Signal, the German propaganda magazine, during the all too brief summer months on the Eastern Front.

Battle for Kharkov JANUARY – MARCH 1943

The German advance deep into the Caucasus, halted to the south of Maikop and Piatigorsk in August 1942, had always been vulnerable to counterattack. At the same time as Soviet forces surrounding Stalingrad thrust westward, the opportunity for a decisive encirclement further south opened up. If the Stalingrad Front (renamed the South Front on 1 January 1943) could take Rostov and reach the Sea of Azov, Army Group A, held in place by attacks from the Trans-Caucasus Front, would be trapped.

As early as 19 November 1942, General Ewald von Kleist's Army Group A came under attack all along its front in the Caucasus, and it was not until 28 December that Hitler reluctantly agreed to a withdrawal. Over 250,000 German troops pulled back into the Taman Peninsula on the north coast of the Black Sea, creating a tenuous link with forces in the Crimea, while to the east of Rostov other units fought desperately to delay the Soviet offensive. They succeeded in doing so until 14 February 1943, when the city was abandoned. By then, Army Group A was reasonably safe.

Meanwhile, the Soviet thrust to the west of Stalingrad was rapidly approaching the major industrial city of Kharkov, identified by Stalin as a key objective. Kursk fell on 8 February to General Filip Golikov's Voronezh Front, creating a salient deep into German lines, but further south Kharkov was developing into a serious battle. Hitler ordered that the city be defended by the elite II SS Corps, commanded by Lieutenant-General Paul Hausser. After only a short time in the city, Hausser realized his position was hopeless. Despite direct orders from Hitler to hold firm, he preferred to save his corps from needless destruction. Amid heavy fighting, Hausser pulled out through the only remaining corridor on 15 February, leaving Kharkov to be liberated by the Soviets.

During a stormy meeting on 17 February Field Marshal Erich von Manstein, commander of the recently reconstituted Army Group

A homeless resident of Kharkov watches the arrival of the liberating Soviets. By February 1943 the once-thriving industrial city had been reduced to rubble.

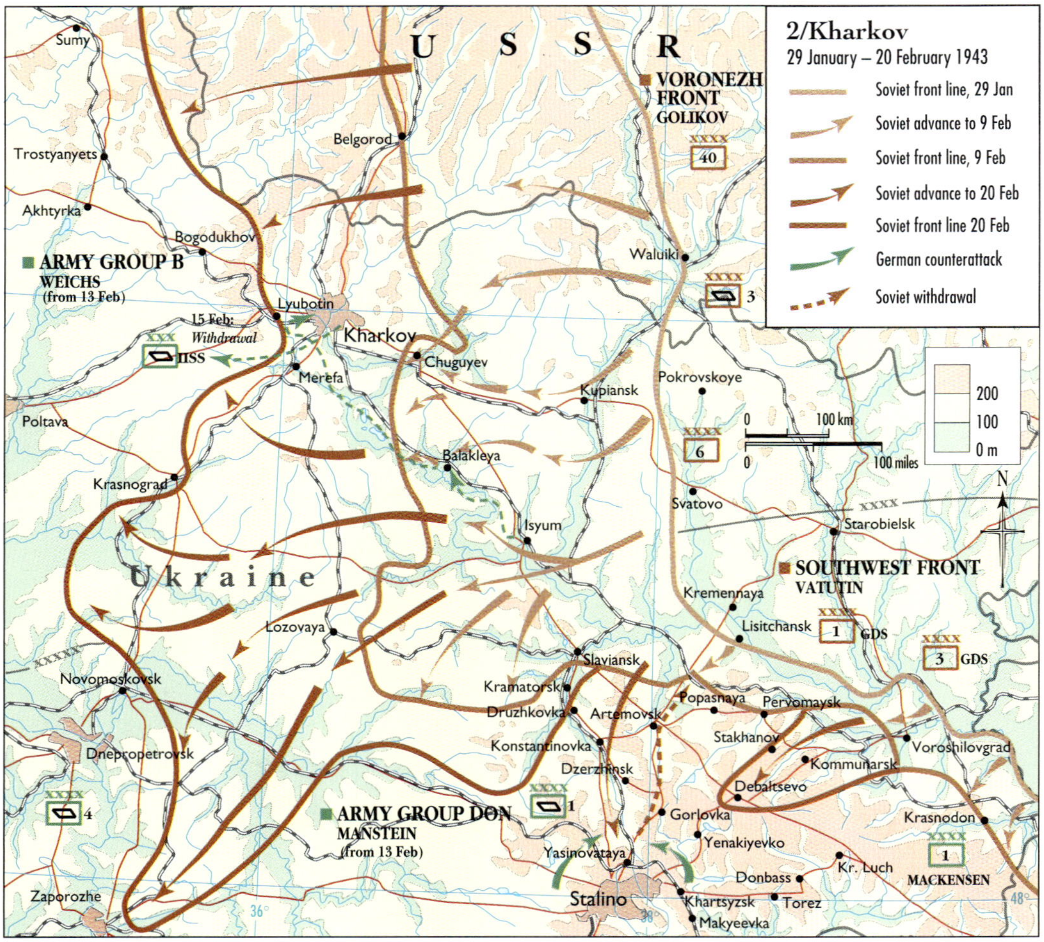

A press photograph shows Soviet troops on the outskirts of Kharkov. The Soviet Union's fourth largest city had become a mere shell, defended by II SS Panzer Korps under the command of Lieutenant-General Paul Hausser. One of the few regular army generals to successfully transfer to the SS, Hausser risked Hitler's wrath by ignoring the order to hold Kharkov to the last man. Instead he conducted an orderly withdrawal and thereby saved his men from certain extinction.

South, managed to persuade Hitler that all was not lost. He was aware that the Soviets were overstretched, while his own troops, although mauled, were regrouping. If they could be used in a counterattack before the spring thaw it was quite possible that the enemy would be forced to withdraw. In the end, Hitler agreed. On 19 February, Hausser halted his retreat near Krasnograd and turned to face the Soviets. Reinforced by General Hermann Hoth's Fourth Panzer Army and supported by the Luftwaffe, this sudden counterattack caught the Soviet Sixth Army by surprise, killing over 23,000 men and capturing nearly 9000. On 15 March, as the Soviets reeled back, German forces entered Kharkov for the third time in 18 months. Manstein's "mobile defense", using armored units to destroy over-extended spearheads, had worked, although a lack of supporting infantry and the beginning of the thaw limited its effect. Some German units managed to thrust northwestwards from Kharkov to seize Belgorod before mud halted all further progress. The front-line now bulged around Kursk, with German forces to north and south. Hitler had already noted the salient as a future objective.

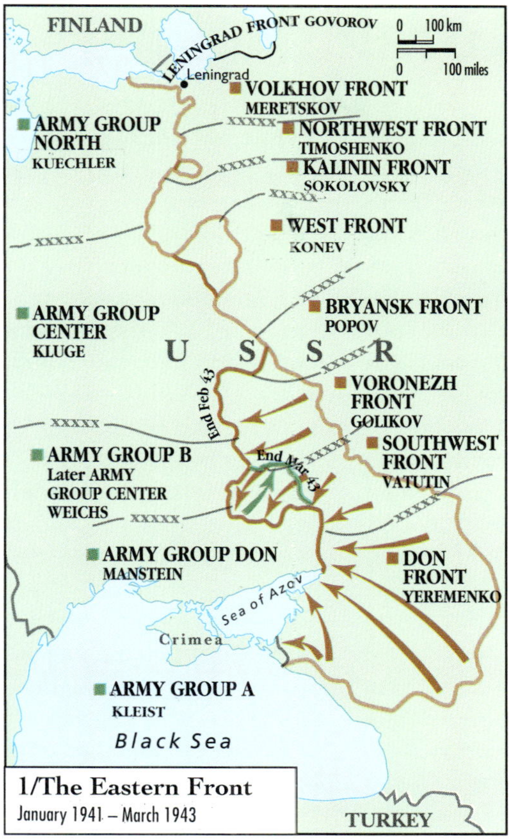

1/The Eastern Front
January 1941 – March 1943

Soviet casualties of the Kharkov battles. Many of the German veterans described the fighting in this region as the worst which they had encountered on the Eastern Front.

"The Russian soldier values his life no more than those of his comrades. To step on walls of dead, composed of the bodies of his former friends and companions makes not the slightest impression on him and does not upset his equanimity at all... Life is not precious to him"

General von Mellenthin

A German soldier surveys the devastation wrought in the outskirts of Kharkov.

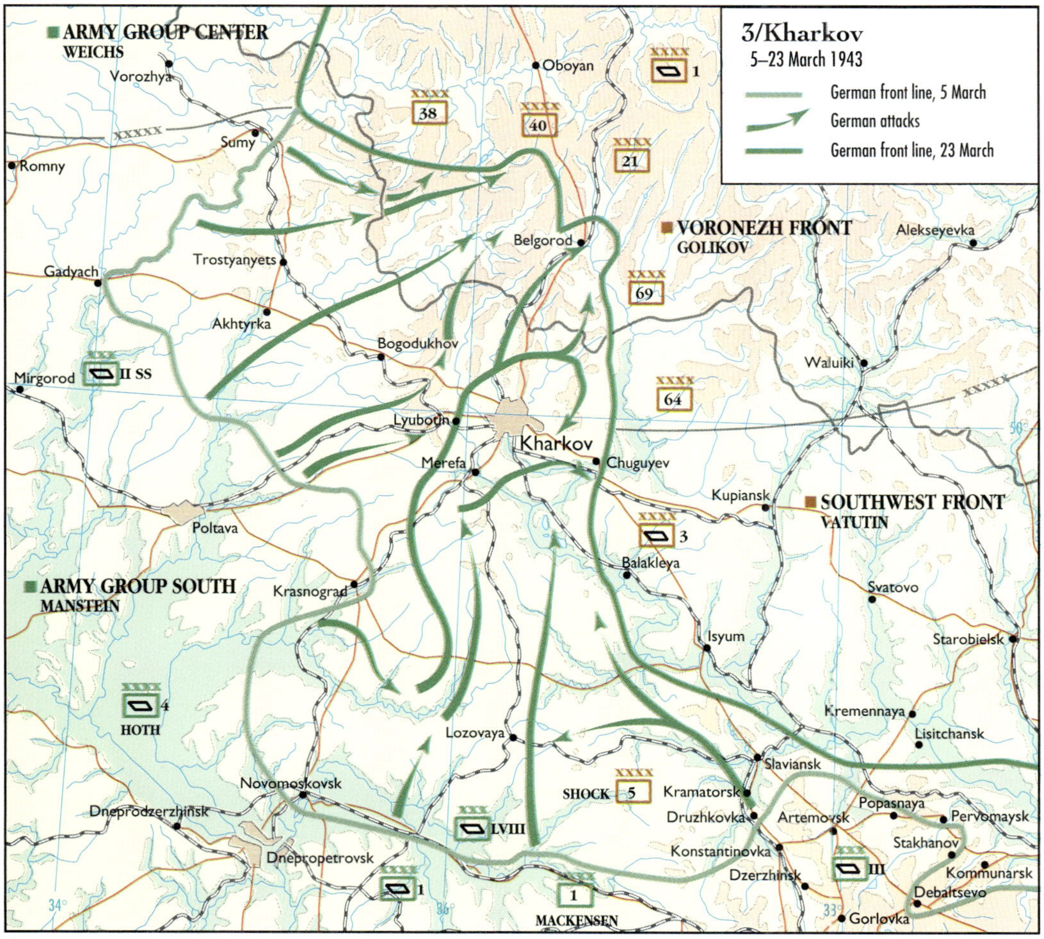

Battle of Kursk JULY 1943

The salient around Kursk, created by Soviet advances in the aftermath of the German defeat at Stalingrad, was guaranteed to attract Hitler's attention. Within it were packed over 1.3 million men, including some of the most experienced units belonging to the Red Army. If they could be destroyed, the initiative recently enjoyed by the Soviets would be reversed. The salient, over 160 miles across, was by no means small, but a pincer assault, using General Walther Model's Ninth Army in the north and General Hermann Hoth's Fourth Panzer Army in the south, advancing at the shoulders of the "bulge" to meet around Kursk, could trap the Soviet forces.

Hitler's first Kursk directive was dated 13 March 1943. If the attack had been mounted then, while the Soviets were still reeling from Manstein's "mobile defense", success might have been likely. But Hitler delayed the offensive, codenamed Operation *Zitadelle*, partly because the spring thaw but more crucially because he demanded the provision of new equipment which German industry was finding difficult to deliver. Thus, although reinforcements were sent to the Fourth Panzer and Ninth Armies, so that by the end of June more than a million men were available, delays in the production of the Panzer Mark V (Panther) led to a succession of postponements. *Zitadelle* was eventually set to begin on 5 July.

This gave the Soviets time in which to prepare their defenses. They also enjoyed the advantage of accurate intelligence about German intentions, gathered from the "Lucy" spy-ring in Switzerland. Under the overall direction of Zhukov, soldiers and civilians alike spent the period between April and late June 1943 ensuring that the salient's natural defenses were enhanced by man-made obstacles designed to channel the attackers into pre-set "killing zones". By 5 July, over 3750 miles of trenches had been dug, with barbed-wire entanglements and minefields to cover any gaps. In some areas, the defenses were 120 miles deep, with artillery (up to 20,000 field guns and multi-barreled mortars) massed in open country between the trench systems. Just behind the defenses, ready to smash any German spearheads that might emerge, were more than 5000 tanks; in reserve was the Steppe Front of 500,000 men. It was a formidable display of strength.

On 2 July, the "Lucy" ring warned that the attack would begin in three days time. Zhukov's response was to order a massive artillery barrage early on 5 July, pre-empting any German bombardment. The psychological impact was significant, but it did not prevent the assault. At 3.30 a.m., men of Fourth Panzer and Ninth Armies moved forward to clear gaps through the minefields, while Stuka dive-bombers screamed above. In the north, Model's soldiers fought hard, but by the end of the day had advanced only four miles. To their south, Hoth's men faced similar problems, and despite penetrating nearly eight miles in places, the pincers remained 140 miles apart.

The battle degenerated into attrition. On 11 July Hoth sent the 1st, 2nd and 3rd SS Divisions east toward the village of Prokhorovka, into a Soviet trap. As the SS panzers emerged from the network of defenses early on the 12th, they were counterattacked by Lieutenant-General Rotmistrov's Fifth Guards Tank Army. It was the greatest armored clash in history, involving an estimated 1000 tanks. By the end of the day, Hoth's overall losses since 5 July had reached 350 tanks and up to 10,000 men; Model had lost 25,000 men and about 200 tanks during the same period. Soviet losses were as high, but, unlike the Germans, they still had uncommitted reserves. Some of these were used on 12 July to mount a counter-offensive at Orel to the north and it was this, plus the news that, two days before, the Western Allies had invaded Sicily, that persuaded Hitler to call off the *Zitadelle* operation. By 20 July, the Germans were in retreat.

2/Eastern Front
July 1943

3/Prokhorovka
12 July 1943

German tank formations
Russian tank formations

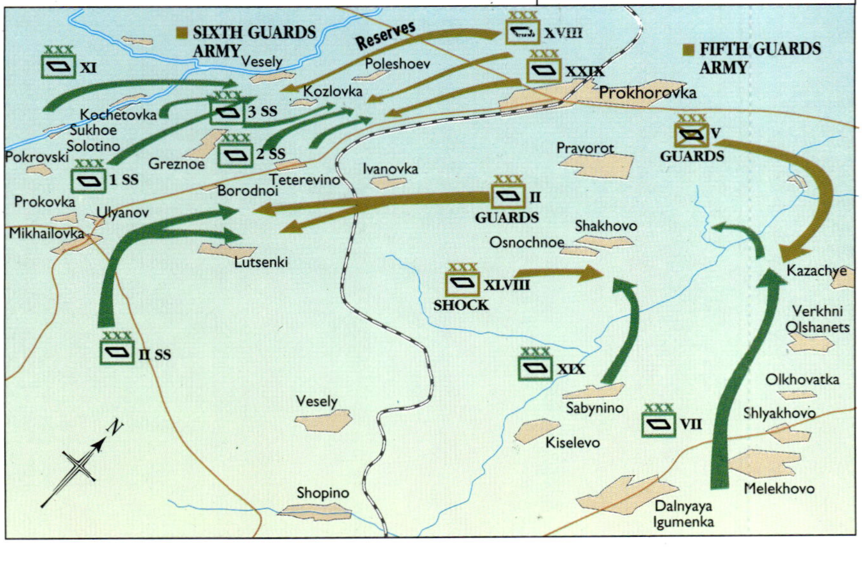

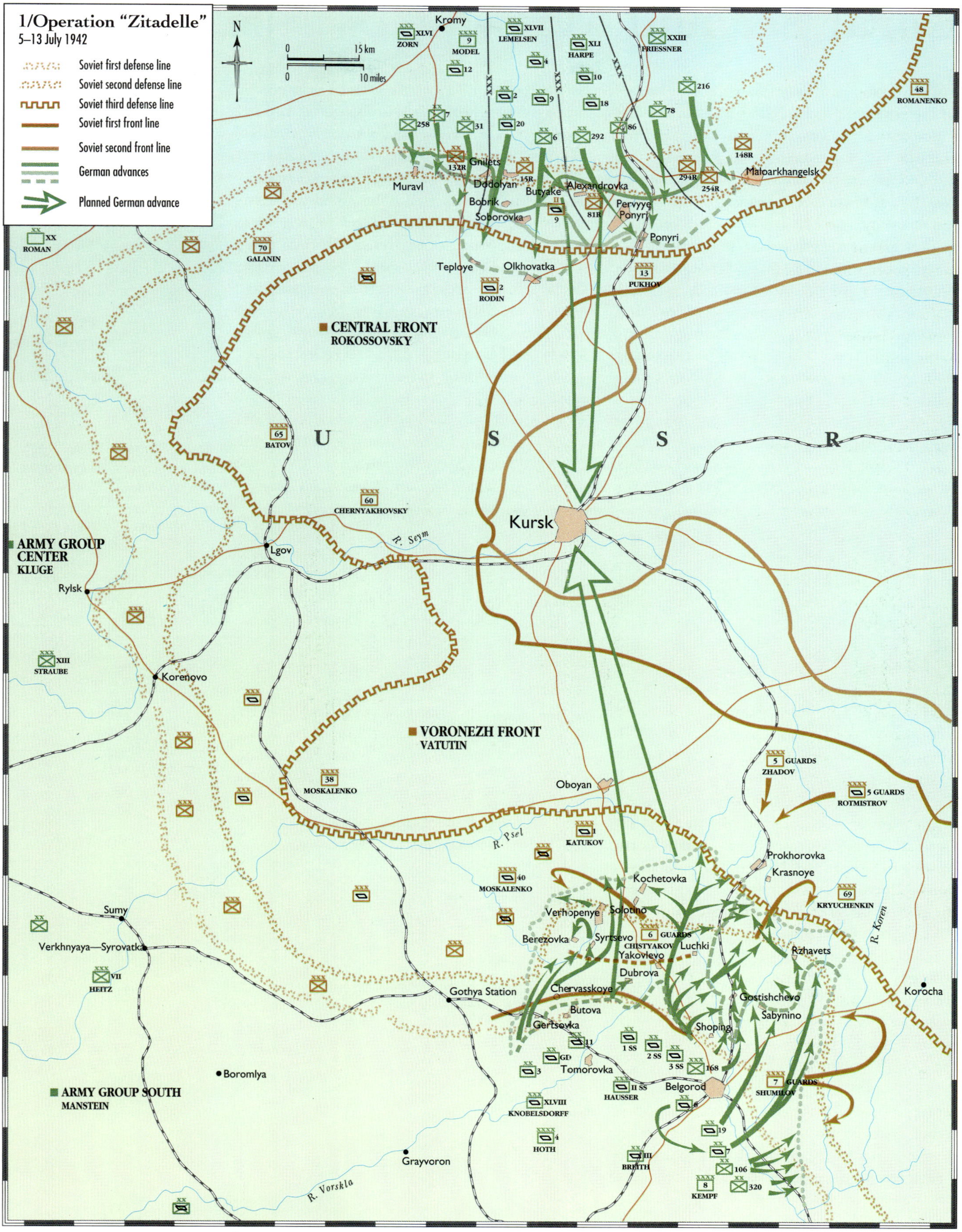
1/Operation "Zitadelle"
5–13 July 1942
Soviet first defense line
Soviet second defense line
Soviet third defense line
Soviet first front line
Soviet second front line
German advances
Planned German advance
0 15 km
0 10 miles
N
Kromy
XLVI ZORN
9 MODEL
XLVII LEMELSEN
XLI HARPE
XXIII FRIESSNER
48 ROMANENKO
12
258
7
31
2
9
20
4
10
18
6
292
86
78
216
137R
15R
294R
254R
148R
81R
Gnilets
Dodolyan
Muravl
Butyrke
Alexandrovka
Maloarkhangelsk
Bobrik
Soborovka
Pervyye Ponyri
Ponyri
Teploye
Olkhovatka
2 RODIN
13 PUKHOV
XX ROMAN
70 GALANIN
CENTRAL FRONT
ROKOSSOVSKY
65 BATOV
U
S
S
R
60 CHERNYAKHOVSKY
Kursk
R. Seym
ARMY GROUP CENTER
KLUGE
Lgov
Rylsk
XIII STRAUBE
Korenovo
VORONEZH FRONT
VATUTIN
38 MOSKALENKO
Oboyan
5 GUARDS ZHADOV
5 GUARDS ROTMISTROV
R. Psel
1 KATUKOV
Prokhorovka
Krasnoye
40 MOSKALENKO
Kochetovka
69 KRYUCHENKIN
R. Koren
Verhopenye
Solotino
Sumy
Berezovka
Syrtsevo
6 GUARDS CHISTYAKOV
Luchki
Yakovlevo
Rzhavets
Verkhnyaya—Syrovatka
VII HEITZ
Dubrova
Chervasskoye
Gothya Station
Gostishchevo
Korocha
Sabynino
Butova
Shoping
Gertsovka
11
1 SS
2 SS
3 SS
168
GD
3
Tomorovka
Boromlya
II SS HAUSSER
Belgorod
7 GUARDS SHUMILOV
ARMY GROUP SOUTH
MANSTEIN
XLVIII KNOBELSDORFF
6
19
4 HOTH
7
III BREITH
106
8 KEMPF
320
Grayvoron
R. Vorskla

Coral Sea and Midway MAY – JUNE 1942

Japanese gains in the aftermath of Pearl Harbor were dramatic but vulnerable. The danger arising from the failure to sink U.S. carriers at Pearl Harbor became apparent in February and March 1942, when Admiral Chester W. Nimitz, U.S. C-in-C Pacific, ordered carrier raids on a number of Japanese-held islands, and the threat to Japan itself was shown on 18 April, when a force of 16 USAAF B-25 Mitchell bombers from the carrier USS *Hornet* hit Tokyo.

The latter incident persuaded Admiral Isoroku Yamamoto, C-in-C of the Japanese Combined Fleet, that the Americans rather than the British posed the greater danger. He had already sent a fleet to engage the British Eastern Fleet based in Ceylon, but soon after the Tokyo Raid the Japanese ships turned back toward the Pacific, where new offensives were being planned. The first of these was in the South-West Pacific, where attacks were to be made on Port Moresby (New Guinea) and in the Solomon Islands to isolate Australia. A striking force of six destroyers, two heavy cruisers and the carriers *Shokaku* and *Zuikaku* was to support the invasion fleets. But the Americans were reading Japanese naval codes and, in response, Nimitz deployed two carrier task forces, centered around the *Yorktown* and *Lexington*, to the Coral Sea and ordered another, comprising cruisers and destroyers, to sail to their support.

Contact between the rival fleets began on 7 May, when Japanese aircraft attacked the tanker USS *Neosho* and sank the destroyer *Sims*. At the same time, U.S. aircraft took off from both *Yorktown* and *Lexington* in response to reconnaissance reports, and subsequently sank the light carrier *Shoho*. This was enough for the Japanese to delay the attack on Port Moresby, preferring

Aircraft line up for takeoff from the deck of USS Enterprise *during the Battle of the Coral Sea.* Enterprise *was the sister ship of* Yorktown.

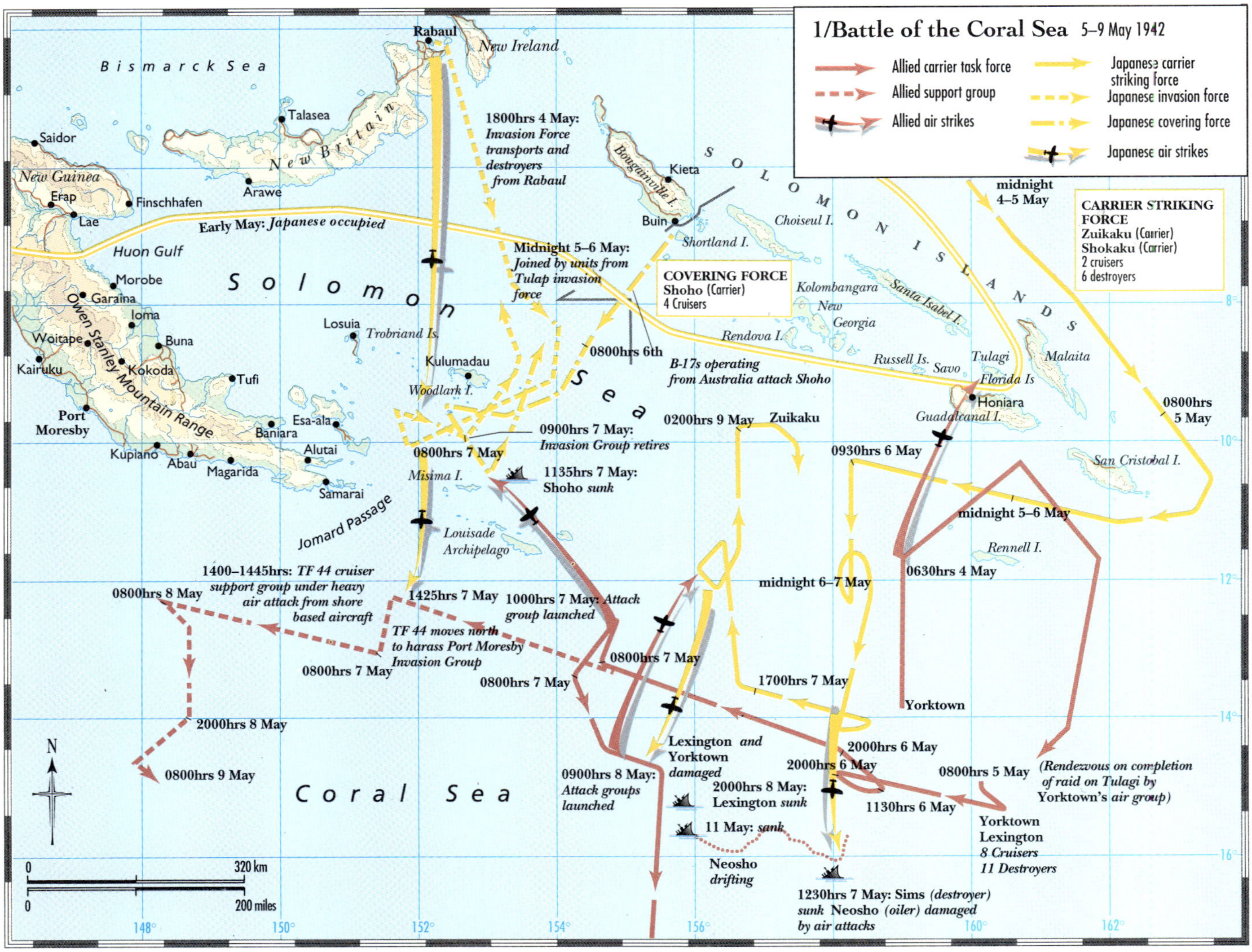

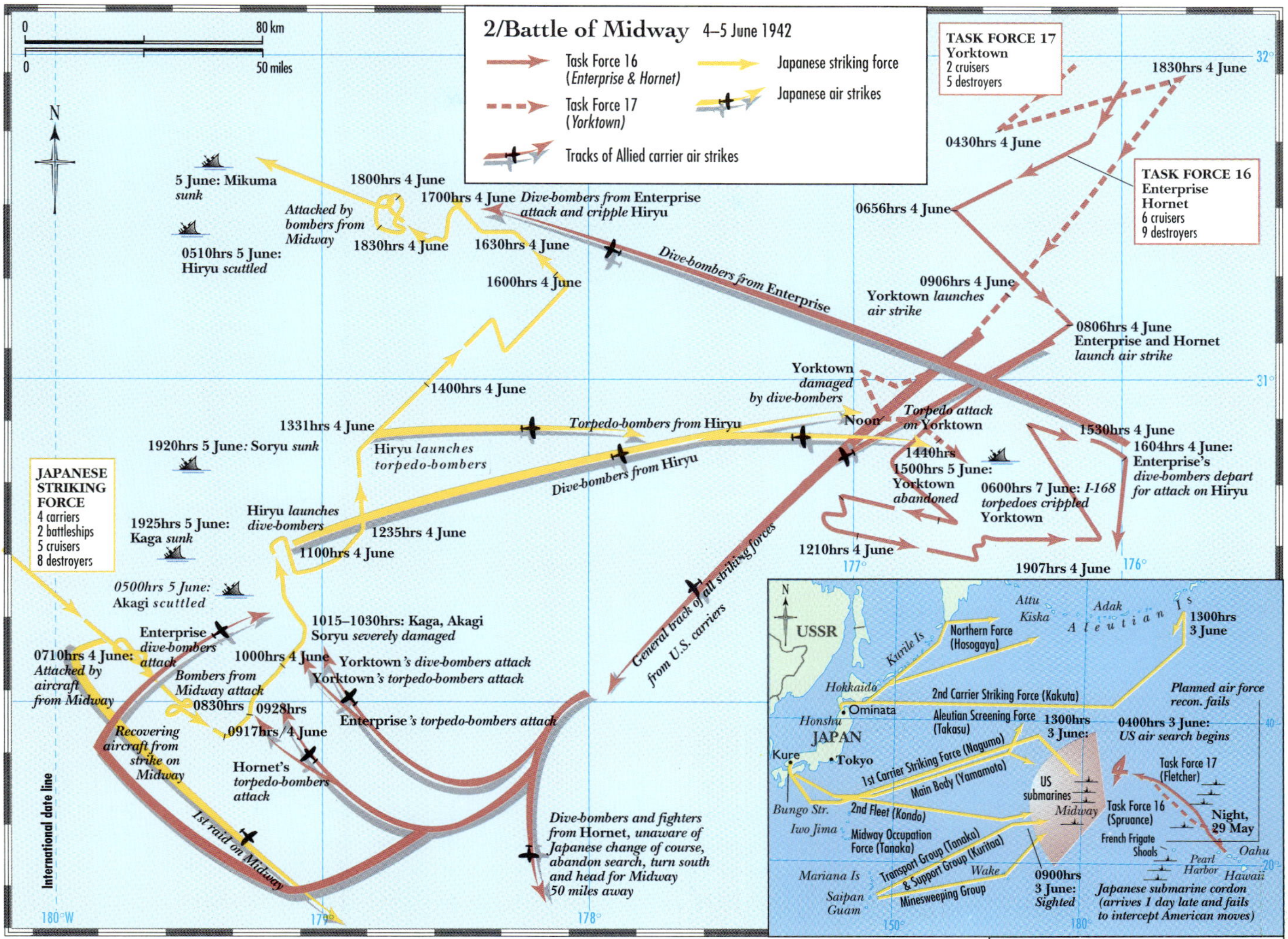

3/Admiral Yamamoto's Operational Plan
25 May–3 June 1942
Allied Task Force 16
Allied Task Force 17
Japanese forces

to seek out and destroy the U.S. carriers. They found them early on 8 May, inflicting damage that was to lead to the loss of *Lexington*, but U.S. aircraft were also active. When they discovered the Japanese carriers, they did enough damage to force *Shokaku* to withdraw and for the Port Moresby invasion to be called off. The Battle of the Coral Sea was by no means a decisive U.S. victory, but it did blunt the Japanese advance.

Yamamoto was already planning the next stage of his offensive, this time with the aim of luring the U.S. Pacific Fleet into a trap. An attack on the Aleutian Islands in the North Pacific would, it was argued, split the U.S. force, leaving the main target – Midway Atoll in the Central Pacific – inadequately protected. Once the atoll had been taken, the Americans would be forced to react, pitting themselves against a superior Japanese fleet, centered around Vice Admiral Chuichi Nagumo's First Carrier Striking Force, comprising the carriers *Akagi*, *Kaga*, *Hiryu* and *Soryu*. However, support groups of battleships, cruisers and destroyers were badly deployed and, as at Coral Sea, Nimitz was aware of the plan. He chose to ignore the attacks on the Aleutians on 3 June, and sent his carrier task forces, comprising *Hornet*, *Enterprise* and *Yorktown*, to protect Midway.

The battle began on 4 June, when Nagumo launched an air-strike on Midway. It did little damage and, as the aircraft landed back on the carriers, U.S. torpedo-bombers from *Hornet*, *Enterprise* and *Yorktown* arrived. They were greeted by a hail of anti-aircraft fire and swarms of Zero fighters that together virtually wiped out the attackers, but as Nagumo prepared to make a counterstrike, U.S. dive-bombers appeared. In the ensuing engagement, three Japanese carriers (*Akagi*, *Kaga*, and *Soryu*) were destroyed. *Hiryu* escaped and was able to launch an airstrike that led to the loss of *Yorktown*, but *Hiryu* was caught later in the day and set on fire. She sank early on 5 June. Nagumo withdrew, losing the cruiser *Mikuma* to air attacks. Altogether, the Japanese lost four carriers, a cruiser and 332 aircraft they could ill afford; by comparison, U.S. losses of a carrier and 137 aircraft could be easily replaced. It was a decisive moment.

The 20,000-ton carrier USS Yorktown, *was damaged in the Coral Sea and again in the Battle of Midway, when the carrier had to be abandoned.*

Guadalcanal AUGUST 1942 – FEBRUARY 1943

Despite defeat in the Coral Sea in May 1942, the Japanese did manage to take New Britain, Bougainville, Choiseul, New Georgia and the small islet of Tulagi in the Solomons. They also landed troops on Guadalcanal, aiming to construct an airfield near Tenaru to disrupt communications between the U.S.A. and Australia. Reports of the Japanese move prompted the Americans to commit the 1st Marine Division to an invasion of the island. The Marines landed early on 7 August 1942, catching the Japanese defenders by surprise. The airstrip was captured late on 8 August. Landings on Tulagi, Tanambogo and Gavutu were equally successful.

The Japanese responded promptly. On the night of 8/9 August, seven cruisers and a destroyer arrived off Savo Island and sank three U.S. cruisers, badly damaged a fourth and left the Australian cruiser *Canberra* ablaze. This allowed the Japanese to land reinforcements on Guadalcanal in the first of a series of runs known to the Americans as the "Tokyo Express". On 21 August, an attack was mounted on the airstrip, christened Henderson Field by the Americans. In a battle along the River Ilu, to the west of the Tenaru, over 800 Japanese were killed for the loss of 35 Americans.

A second "Tokyo Express" was planned in late August, this time backed by a powerful fleet. The plan was to send the carrier *Ryujo* to act as a decoy, drawing the Americans into a trap. It did not work. On 24 August aircraft from *Enterprise* and *Saratoga* sank *Ryujo*, then protected their carriers when a Japanese airstrike followed. *Enterprise* was damaged, but enough U.S. aircraft survived to wreak havoc on 25 August, sinking a transport vessel and a destroyer, so persuading the Japanese to switch the "Tokyo Express" to the hours of darkness.

Even so, Japanese reinforcements continued to arrive, and fighting was bitter. On 12 September over 600 Japanese died in an unsuccessful attack on "Bloody Ridge", about a mile south-west of Henderson Field. Two days later the American 7th Marine Regiment was landed as reinforcements, and two weeks later elements of the U.S. Army's American Division also arrived. The carrier *Wasp* was sunk during the former operation, but on the night of 11/12 October a Japanese cruiser and destroyer were sunk off Cape Esperance.

In late October, the Japanese were slaughtered in renewed attacks on Henderson Field. On the 26th, aircraft from *Enterprise* and *Hornet* damaged *Shokaku* and *Zuiho* off the Santa Cruz Islands, but could not prevent simultaneous Japanese strikes hitting their own ships. *Hornet* was abandoned. Two weeks later the Americans lost two cruisers and seven destroyers but sank two Japanese battleships, four destroyers and 10 transports. It enabled the Americans to isolate the enemy forces and the Japanese were gradually pushed back from Henderson Field. Between 14 January and 8 February 1943, the Japanese evacuated the island. It had been an expensive but decisive campaign.

Japanese prisoners were taken in the land fighting during the Battle of Guadalcanal in the Solomon Islands. Hunger and disease drove other Japanese soldiers to loot local villages, and incensed natives responded mercilessly: Japanese heads adorned many houses for years to come.

1/The Approach to Guadalcanal and New Guinea
August 1942

Main line of Japanese advance
Main lines of Allied advance and supplies

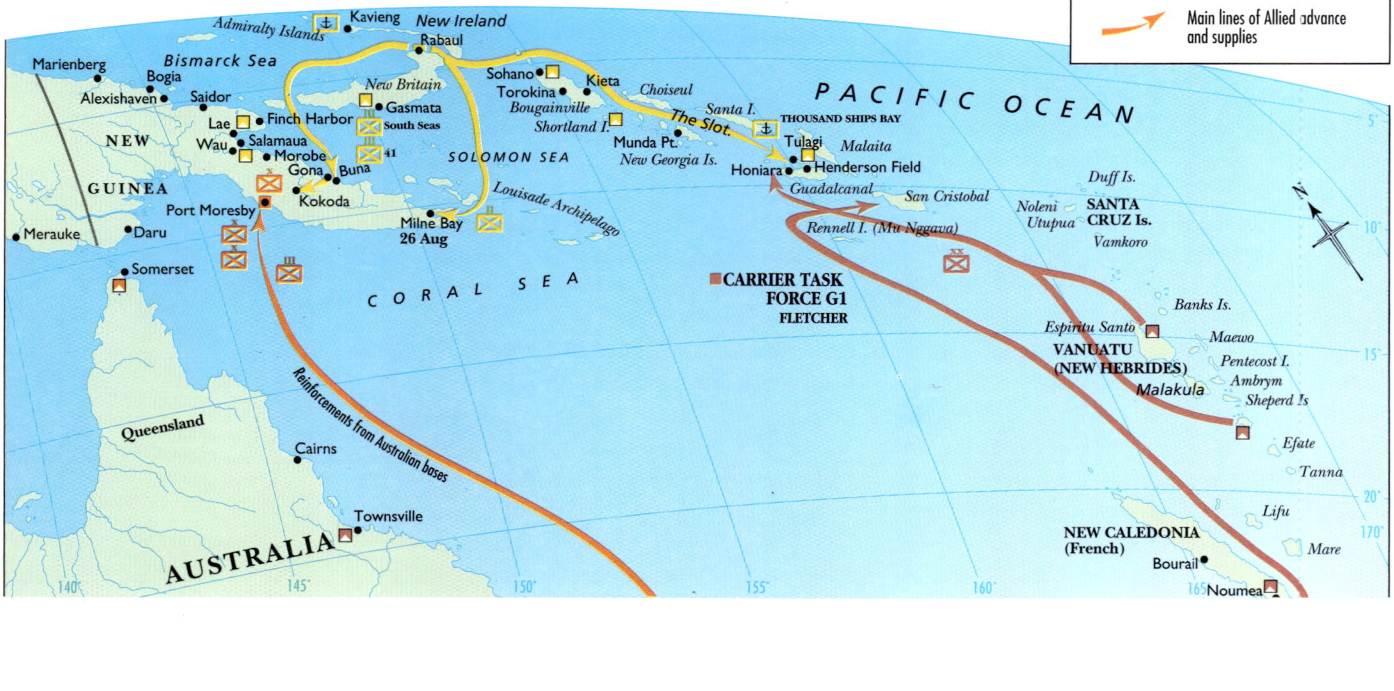

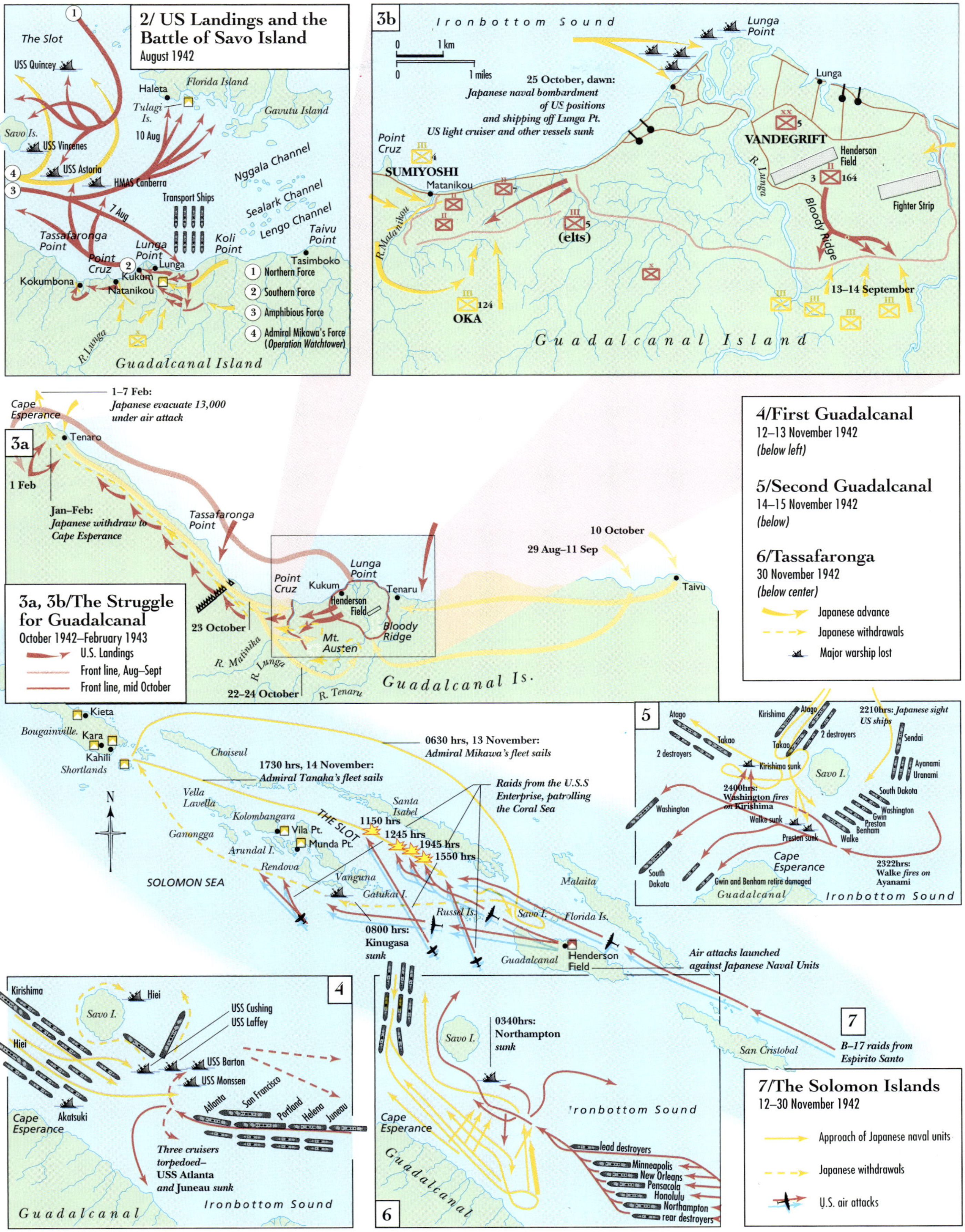
2/ US Landings and the Battle of Savo Island
August 1942
The Slot
USS Quincey
Savo Is.
USS Vincennes
USS Astoria
HMAS Canberra
Haleta
Tulagi Is.
10 Aug
Florida Island
Gavutu Island
Nggala Channel
Sealark Channel
Lengo Channel
Transport Ships
7 Aug
Tassafaronga Point
Lunga Point
Point Cruz
Koli Point
Taivu Point
Tasimboko
Lunga
Kukum
Kokumbona
Matanikou
R. Lunga
Guadalcanal Island
1 Northern Force
2 Southern Force
3 Amphibious Force
4 Admiral Mikawa's Force (Operation Watchtower)
3b
Ironbottom Sound
0 1 km
0 1 miles
Lunga Point
Lunga
25 October, dawn:
Japanese naval bombardment of US positions and shipping off Lunga Pt.
US light cruiser and other vessels sunk
Point Cruz
SUMIYOSHI
Matanikou
R. Matanikou
VANDEGRIFT
Henderson Field
R. Lunga
164
Bloody Ridge
Fighter Strip
(elts)
OKA
124
13–14 September
Guadalcanal Island
1–7 Feb:
Japanese evacuate 13,000 under air attack
Cape Esperance
Tenaro
3a
1 Feb
Jan–Feb:
Japanese withdraw to Cape Esperance
Tassafaronga Point
10 October
29 Aug–11 Sep
Taivu
Point Cruz
Kukum
Lunga Point
Tenaru
Henderson Field
Bloody Ridge
Mt. Austen
23 October
R. Matinika
R. Lunga
22–24 October
R. Tenaru
Guadalcanal Is.
3a, 3b/The Struggle for Guadalcanal
October 1942–February 1943
U.S. Landings
Front line, Aug–Sept
Front line, mid October
4/First Guadalcanal
12–13 November 1942
(below left)
5/Second Guadalcanal
14–15 November 1942
(below)
6/Tassafaronga
30 November 1942
(below center)
Japanese advance
Japanese withdrawals
Major warship lost
Kieta
Bougainville.
Kara
Kahili
Shortlands
Choiseul
0630 hrs, 13 November:
Admiral Mikawa's fleet sails
1730 hrs, 14 November:
Admiral Tanaka's fleet sails
Vella Lavella
Kolombangara
Ganongga
Vila Pt.
Munda Pt.
Arundel I.
Rendova
THE SLOT
Santa Isabel
1150 hrs
1245 hrs
1945 hrs
1550 hrs
Raids from the U.S.S Enterprise, patrolling the Coral Sea
SOLOMON SEA
Vangunu
Gatukai I.
Russel Is.
Savo I.
Florida Is.
Malaita
0800 hrs:
Kinugasa sunk
Guadalcanal
Henderson Field
Air attacks launched against Japanese Naval Units
San Cristobal
7
B–17 raids from Espirito Santo
5
Atago
Kirishima
Takao
2 destroyers
2210hrs: Japanese sight US ships
Sendai
Ayanami
Uranami
Kirishima sunk
Savo I.
2400hrs:
Washington fires on Kirishima
Washington
South Dakota
Walke sunk
Preston sunk
Gwin
Preston
Benham
Walke
Cape Esperance
Gwin and Benham retire damaged
Guadalcanal
2322hrs:
Walke fires on Ayanami
Ironbottom Sound
4
Kirishima
Hiei
Savo I.
USS Cushing
USS Laffey
USS Barton
USS Monssen
Atlanta
San Francisco
Portland
Helena
Juneau
Akatsuki
Cape Esperance
Three cruisers torpedoed–
USS Atlanta and Juneau sunk
Guadalcanal
Ironbottom Sound
Savo I.
0340hrs:
Northampton sunk
Ironbottom Sound
Cape Esperance
Guadalcanal
lead destroyers
Minneapolis
New Orleans
Pensacola
Honolulu
Northampton
rear destroyers
6
7/The Solomon Islands
12–30 November 1942
Approach of Japanese naval units
Japanese withdrawals
U.S. air attacks

New Guinea / New Georgia JULY 1942 – AUGUST 1943

On 22 July 1942 Japanese troops under Major-General Tomitaro Horii landed at Buna on the northern coast of Papua in south-eastern New Guinea. Their task was to cross to Port Moresby on the southern coast, using the Kokoda Trail through the Owen Stanley Mountains. The first 20 miles of the trail from Buna to the River Kumusi, were relatively straightforward, but once across the river it degenerated into little more than a muddy track along razor-edged ridges before culminating in a precipitous descent known as the "Golden Staircase", about 40 miles from Port Moresby.

Horii's men had advanced to Imita Ridge by 16 September, having fought continuously with the defending Australians. Both sides were wracked by fever and exhaustion, but the Australians had their backs to their supply dumps. Reinforcements arrived at Port Moresby, while elements of the U.S. 32nd Infantry Division landed at Pongani on Papua's north coast, to threaten the Japanese rear. On 26 September Horii began to withdraw back along the trail toward Buna. The Australians followed, catching the Japanese rearguard at Templeton's Crossing, Oivi and Gorari before pushing on to the Kumusi. Japanese survivors fell back into Buna, Sananda and Gona, where elaborate bunker defenses had been constructed. The Australians and Americans closed in. Gona fell on 9 December, Buna on 2 January 1943 and Sanananda was overwhelmed on 24 January. The direct threat to northern Australia had been turned back and a major land defeat inflicted on the enemy.

In January 1943 the Japanese sent troops from Salamaua, in North East New Guinea, to seize a small Australian garrison at Wau, about 30 miles inland. But on 29 January, with the Japanese close to the airstrip, the Australians airlifted reinforcements into Wau and pushed the enemy back. A month later the Japanese tried to reinforce garrisons at Salamaua and Lae by sending a convoy through the Bismarck Sea. Caught by Allied aircraft on 3 March, four destroyers and all the transports were sunk, isolating the Japanese remaining in New Guinea.

To exploit the recent victories, the Americans decided to mount a two-pronged assault on the Japanese Empire. While Admiral Nimitz in the Central Pacific Area prepared amphibious forces for a campaign through the Marshall and Mariana Islands, General MacArthur was to maintain the offensive in the South-West Pacific Area, concentrating on the Solomons and New Guinea. The two advances would converge on Formosa, cutting Japan off from resource areas further south. By May 1943, MacArthur had planned Operation *Cartwheel*, which aimed to destroy the Japanese base at Rabaul on the island of New Britain. As MacArthur swept west along the northern coast of New Guinea, Admiral William Halsey, commanding U.S. Third Fleet, would island-hop along the Solomons chain. Halsey's first objective was Rendova Island, taken on 30 June, but this was only a preliminary to the main assault, on New Georgia. As U.S. naval forces destroyed enemy troop convoys in the Kula Gulf, a series of landings were made, the most important of which concentrated on Japanese positions around Munda, on the south-western coast of the island. Munda fell on 4 August; two days later, in Vella Gulf, another Japanese convoy was destroyed.

Cartwheel still had a long way to go, but momentum was beginning to build.

Disconsolate Japanese prisoners are searched for concealed weapons by their American captors. The Japanese soldiers' code of honor stigmatized surrender as the lowest degradation and encouraged suicide as an alternative.

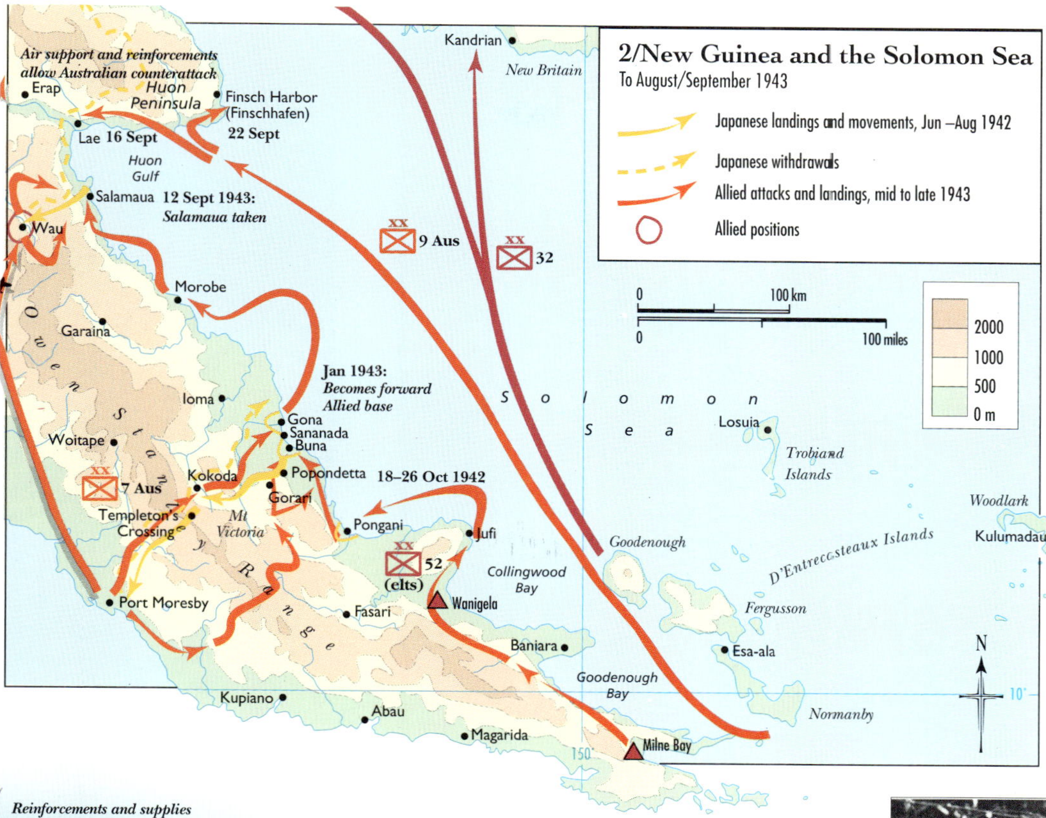

Wounded members of an American infantry unit are attended by a Medical Corps officer while they await the arrival of a stretcher-bearer to evacuate them from the island of New Guinea.

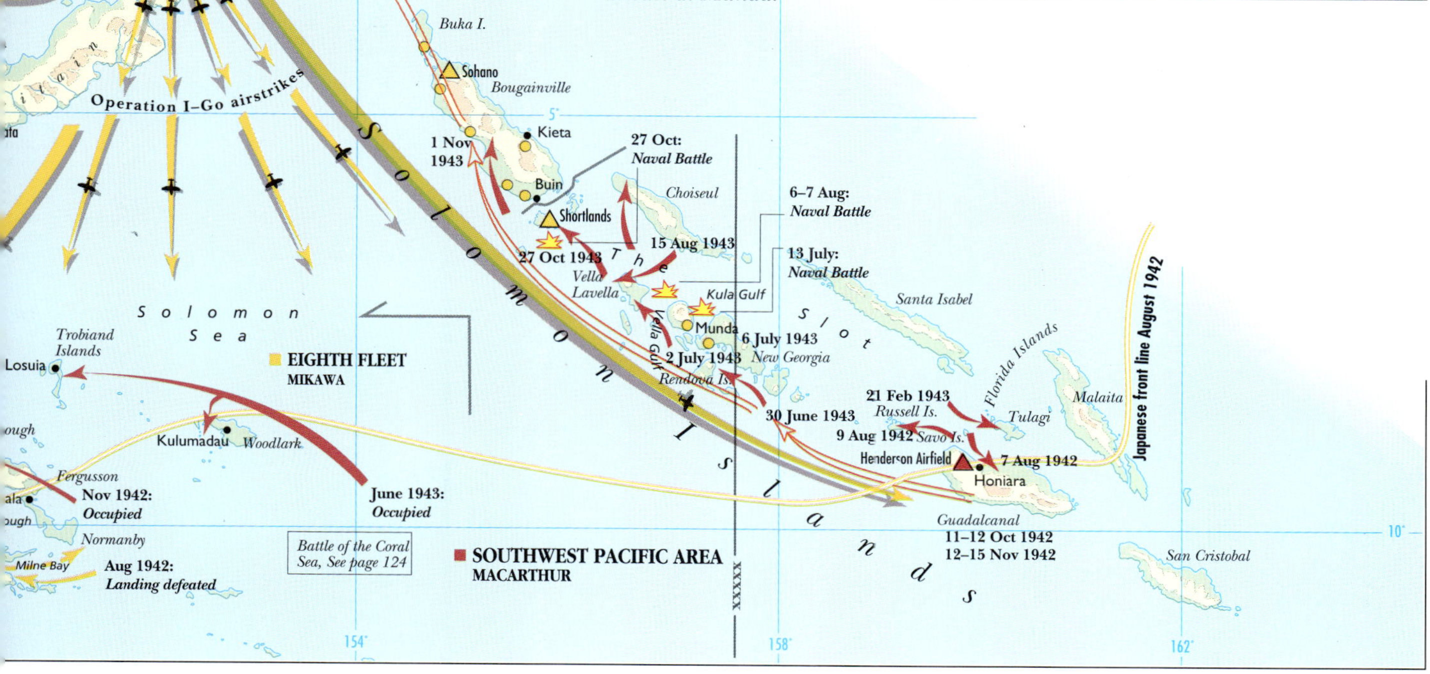

American soldiers taking part in Operation Cartwheel *follow the Munda Trail, which takes them through waist-high streams and over ridges and ravines covered by dense jungle. Their mission, to stage an attack on the Japanese airbase at Munda.*

Burma SEPTEMBER 1942 – AUGUST 1943

The British retreat through Burma to Assam in eastern India in early 1942 left the Japanese overstretched and incapable of advancing further, at least for the moment. This gave General Sir Archibald Wavell, C-in-C in India, a vital breathing space in which to regroup his shattered forces. His task was not easy. What remained of Burma Corps was weak and reinforcements were not immediately available. In addition, the front-line in Assam was isolated – supplies had to travel down a single railway track from Calcutta to Dimapur, and from there by road across mountains to Kohima and Imphal – and the soldiers were subject to a range of debilitating diseases, particularly malaria and dysentery. Morale among the troops, who called themselves the "Forgotten Army", was not high.

Wavell's first priority, once the retreat was over, was to convince his men that they could take on the Japanese and defeat them. However, his natural desire to wait until conditions had improved was curbed by demands from Prime Minister Winston Churchill to take the offensive as early as possible. The result was an ill-fated campaign in Arakan, on the north-west coast of Burma, that was characterized by confusion and defeat. In September 1942, the 14th Indian Division left Chittagong and moved forward by sea and land to Cox's Bazar, aiming to attack south into the Mayu Peninsula to prepare the way for a seaborne landing on Akyab Island by 29th Independent Brigade.

The advance was far too slow – lead elements of 14th Division did not reach Donbaik, 10 miles from the tip of the peninsula, until early January 1943 – and 29th Independent Brigade did not arrive, having been sent instead to South Africa. Meanwhile, the two Japanese brigades in the Mayu Peninsula had constructed elaborate defenses around Donbaik, aware that reinforcements were on their way from Toungoo. When 14th Division encountered the defenses, they stalled, enabling the Japanese 55th Division to loop round to the east, crossing the "impassable" Arakan Yoma Mountains and catching the British in the flank. On 5 April the headquarters of the British–Indian 6th Brigade was overrun, precipitating a retreat which, by 14 May, saw the survivors of 14th Division back where they had started eight months before, having suffered more than 5000 casualties.

Within weeks, command arrangements in India were changed. Wavell was made Viceroy and replaced as C-in-C by General Sir Claude Auchinleck. At the same time, the British–Indian Army was reorganized and trained more specifically for operations in Burma, while attempts were made to improve road communications in Assam. By then, and coinciding with the failure in Arakan, Brigadier Orde Wingate had completed a "long-range penetration operation" behind Japanese lines, using the 77th Indian Infantry Brigade, more usually known as the "Chindits". On 14/15 February 1943, seven columns, each of 400–500 men, crossed the River Chindwin with the intention of cutting the Mandalay–Myitkyina railway in the area between Indaw and Kyaikthin. Some success was achieved, although Japanese responses soon made further progress impossible. In addition, many of the Chindits – British,

Brigadier Orde Wingate, seen here in discussion with an American liaison officer. Consisting of British, Gurkha and Burmese troops, his force was officially known as the 77th Indian Infantry Brigade, but the men were named Chindits after the Burmese word chinthé, meaning "mythical lion".

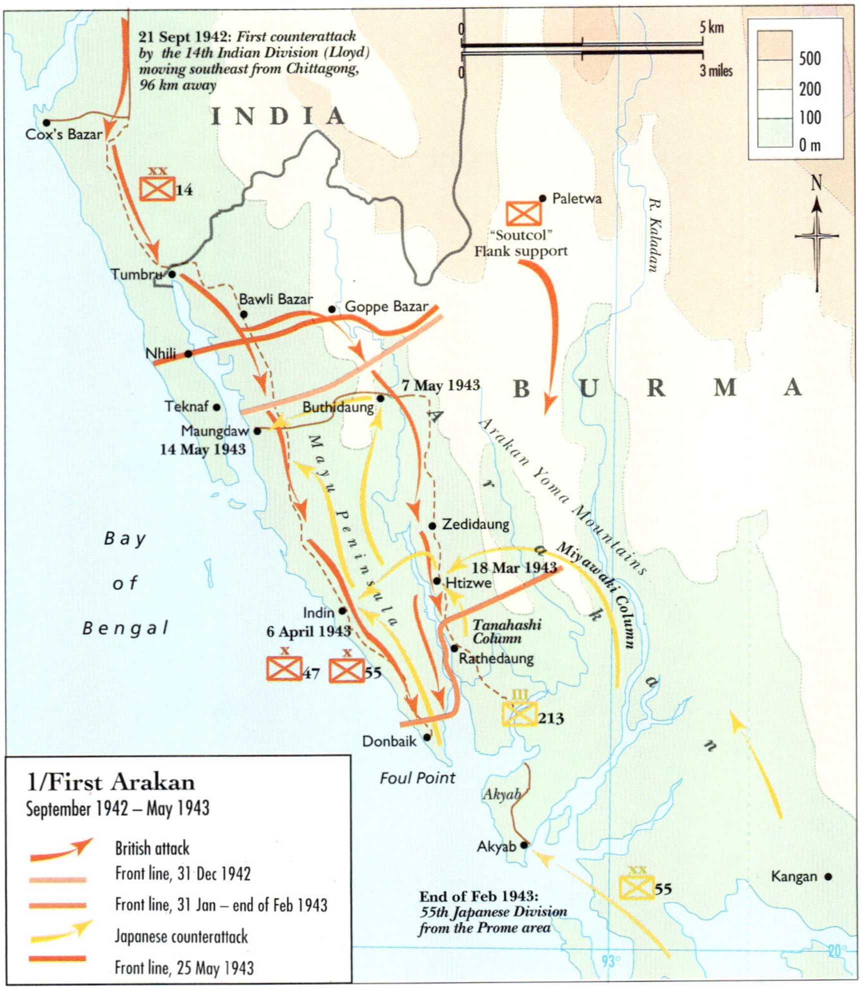

Gurkha and Indian – suffered badly from disease and malnutrition. The columns were ordered back to India in late March, the last survivors recrossing the Chindwin a month later. By then, of the original 3000, over 800 had been lost and many of the others were too sick to continue. It was an expensive operation, but one that did much to improve morale, showing that it was possible to fight the Japanese in jungle conditions.

Yet more command changes occurred in August 1943. At the "Quadrant" Conference of the Anglo-American Combined Chiefs of Staff, a new South-East Asia Command was established, covering an area from Ceylon to Thailand, with Vice Admiral Lord Louis Mountbatten in charge. His deputy was the American Lieutenant-General Joseph Stilwell, whose experiences of cooperating with the Nationalist Chinese promised their future involvement in northern Burma. In Assam, meanwhile, Lieutenant-General William Slim was given command of a new Fourteenth Army and preparations began for another Allied counter-offensive.

The task of the Chindits was to kill and demoralize Japanese troops, and generally to hamper Japanese operations in Burma by destroying railway lines and bridges and by attacking Japanese outposts. Wingate's brigade suffered heavy losses, but was successful in shattering the myth of Japanese invincibility.

> *"Success did not inflate him, nor misfortune depress him."*
>
> **Field Marshal Sir Claude Auchinleck on General Slim**

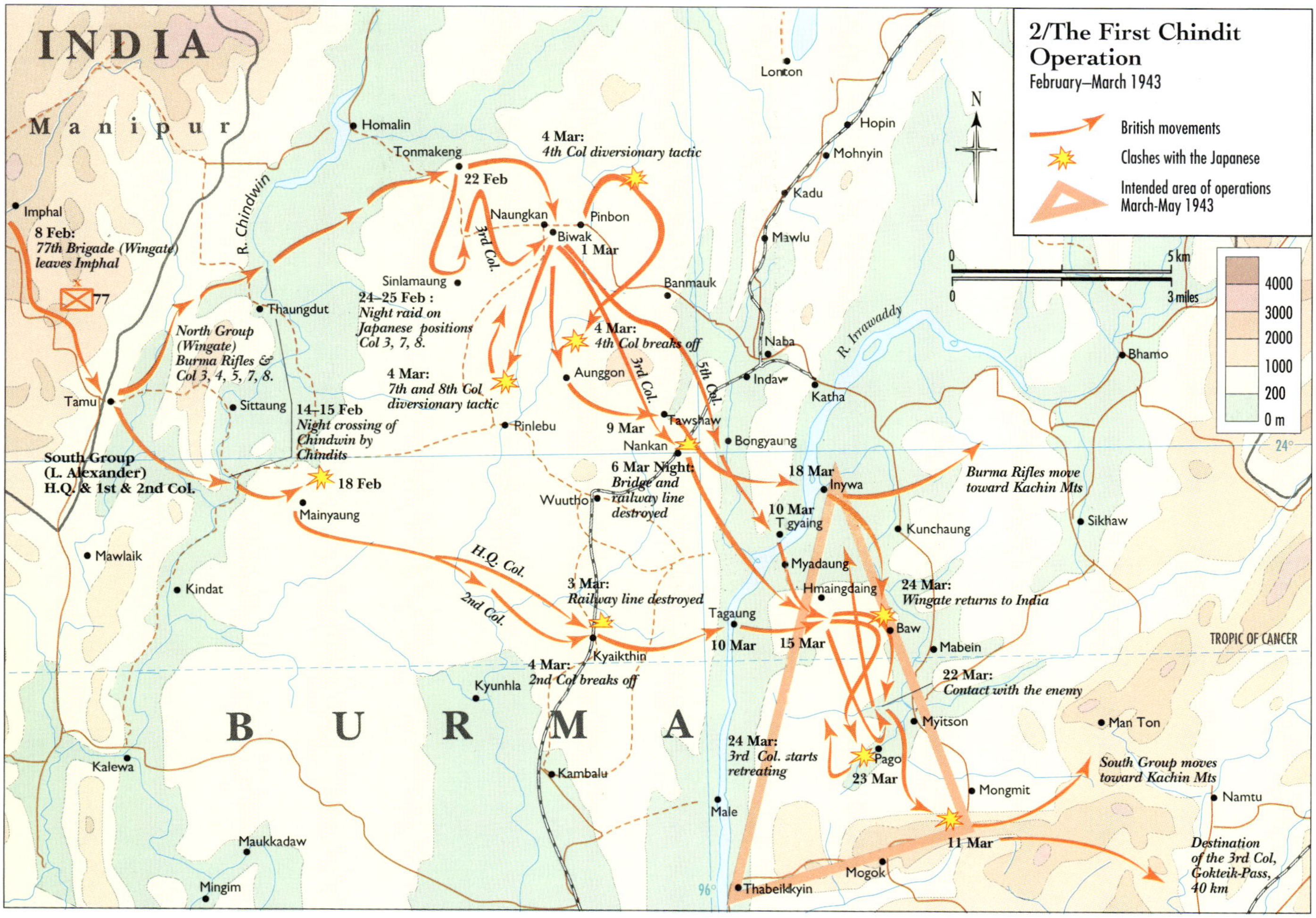

War Economies of the Major Powers

Total war requires total commitment. If a state is fighting for its survival or the survival of its political ideology, it has no choice but to use everything at its disposal, in both human and economic terms, to counter the threat. In World War II this meant an ability not just to field large armed forces, capable of taking on the enemy wherever necessary around the world, but also an ability to feed, clothe and equip those forces for sustained and costly operations. In order to win, a state had to mobilize its people and its economy to the full, while undermining the enemy's capability to do the same. Although it is always dangerous to talk in terms of single factors leading to victory or defeat, the outcome of World War II may be seen quite clearly in the demographic and economic balance between the two sides. The Allied powers still needed to fight effectively, but once their manpower was fully tapped and their economies fully mobilized, they were in a position of enormous strength, from which they could outnumber and outproduce the Axis.

In 1939, this was not the case. The German economy, geared towards the possibility of war for a number of years and based on an ideology that enjoyed substantial public backing, was far stronger than that of its Anglo-French rivals, who had only begun to rearm seriously a year before. In addition, the Soviet Union, with its enormous agricultural and mineral potential, was allied to Germany and able to supply raw materials along routes that the Allies could not interdict. By comparison, although the British and French had access to the resources of their combined empires in Africa, the Middle East, Australia and the Far East – areas that between them produced the bulk of the world's raw materials – they needed to keep sea-lanes open and merchant ships operating in order to guarantee the necessary imports. German submarine and surface-warship offensives in 1939 were designed to stop such imports, and came close to success. Moreover, once Poland had been defeated and Norway, Denmark, France and the Low Countries occupied, the British were left in a much weaker situation, made worse once the Italians threatened the route through the Mediterranean. By early 1941 President Franklin D. Roosevelt's decision to offer "Lend Lease", whereby U.S. weapons and resources were supplied to Britain on the understanding that they did not need to be paid for until the war was over, had redressed the balance a little, but the goods had still to be shipped across the North Atlantic, braving the U-boat "Wolf Packs".

Just to survive, the British had to adopt a full war economy. This meant conscription into the armed forces and government direction of labor into war factories or agriculture. It also involved strict rationing of food and a strong emphasis on self-sufficiency in order to cut down on agricultural imports, freeing merchant ships to carry more raw materials. By 1943, more than 70% of Britain's population between the ages of 16 and 65 was actively involved in the war effort, the vast majority of those not actually serving in the armed forces being committed to the manufacture of weapons, food or clothing. It was a massive undertaking.

By then, however, the balance had shifted. Hitler's decision to attack the Soviet Union in June 1941, followed six months later by America's entry into the war, suddenly gave the Allied powers enormous economic and manpower strength. In simple numerical terms, the Axis states – Germany, Italy and Japan were outnumbered, for they could call on a combined population of less than 200 million compared to the Allies' 360 million. But there was more to it than that. Germany may have gained access to the resources of western Russia in 1941 and 1942, but Hitler failed to prevent a Soviet withdrawal of industrial potential to areas of safety beyond the Ural Mountains and did not manage to capture a key asset – the oilfields of the Caucasus. Once attacked, Stalin made the decision to move more than 1500 factories to the east – something that involved nearly five million railway movements – and to destroy anything that was left. In addition, what the Germans did capture tended to be wasted. Local people were alienated by repressive anti-Slav policies and many joined the partisans, intent on sabotage, while the problems experienced by the German army in getting supplies forward in Russia had just the same impact in the opposite direction. Finally, the destruction wrought by the fighting often denied the Germans any economic gain; altogether by 1945 more than 1700 Soviet towns and 70,000 villages had been virtually wiped from the map along with their productive capacity.

The Japanese suffered very similar problems in the Far East. Their offensive in late 1941/early 1942 may have been triggered in large measure by their need to capture resource areas so that they could continue to fight, but they never enjoyed the full advantages of their "Great East Asia Co-Prosperity Sphere". Allied forces adopted a deliberate policy of destruction as they retreated – oilfields in Burma and Borneo, for example, went up in flames in early 1942 – and Japanese policies of occupation alienated many local people. The latter problem could be overcome by forced labor (which included the illegal use of prisoners of war), but output was never as high as it might have been if the workers had been willing volunteers. Furthermore, whatever was produced in the Philippines, Malaya or Dutch East Indies had to be shipped to Japan, creating the same sort of problem as that faced by the British – the need to secure sea-lanes. Allied submarine, air and mining operations in the Pacific proved to be far more effective than those of the Germans in the Atlantic; by late 1944 Japan was effectively cut off from her resource areas, facing the threat of imminent starvation. Rice imports alone had been reduced to about a tenth of pre-war levels and there was not the spare agricultural land in the Home Islands to make up the shortfall.

The United States faced none of these problems. Once mobilized – and many commentators have pointed out that even at the height of World War II the U.S. economy was nowhere near full capacity – the potential was enormous. Access to war materials was virtually guaranteed, either within the U.S.A. itself or within easy reach in Latin America, agricultural land was available in large quantities, and the population of 132 million was large. These advantages allowed the American economy to grow at a remarkable rate – the Gross National Product, measured in 1939 terms, rose from $88.6 billion in 1939 to $135 billion in 1944 – until, by the end of the fighting, it was reckoned that the Americans were manufacturing more than 40% of the world's armaments. This was enough to equip most of the Allied armed forces and to lead the way in the development and production of new weapons. The Manhattan Project alone cost over half a billion dollars to produce just three atomic devices.

American manufacturing statistics during the war years are sobering. By late 1943 it has been estimated that U.S. factories were producing an aircraft every 4 minutes 53 seconds and a rifle a minute, often in locations which before the war had no tradition of arms manufacture. New factories were built from scratch and existing ones expanded. When the Boeing Aircraft Company received the contract to produce the first 250 B-29s, for example, they opened an immense new factory at Wichita, Kansas, and once the order had been increased to 500, turned to other companies such as General Motors and North American Aviation to help out. Even more impressive was American ship-building capacity. As early as May 1941, as part of Lend Lease, Roosevelt ordered the construction of two million tons of merchant shipping. The only way to meet such a target was for the constructors to standardize their designs, producing what was known as the Liberty Ship, a 70,000-ton capacity merchantman built largely of prefabricated parts. The first Liberty Ship took 244 days to complete, but this was later cut to 42 days and, on one occasion, the process of keel-to-launch took a staggering 80.5 hours. In 1942 alone a total of 597 Liberty Ships was constructed, giving the Allies an unrivaled capability to carry bulk cargoes worldwide. No amount of U-boat activity could sink more tonnage than was coming off the slipways.

These manufacturing feats were reflected in the balance of production between Allied and Axis powers during the war as a whole. In 1942, for example, the Allies produced over 100,000 aircraft to the Axis 26,000; in the same year the Allies produced 58,000 tanks while the Axis could manage only 11,000. By 1945, the United States was devoting about 40% of its economy to war production and had built, since 1941, more than 250,000 aircraft, almost 90,000 tanks, 350 destroyers and 200 submarines. The Axis powers could do nothing to match such achievements.

But the effects were far-reaching. Although the U.S.A. could sustain such mobilization, other countries could not. By 1945 the economies of the Axis countries were in ruins, having been deliberately destroyed by Allied actions, but some of the Allied powers were also suffering. Britain – the only major power to fight non-stop from September 1939 until September 1945 – was virtually bankrupt, having expended an estimated 25% of its national assets, and France was in no better position. In the aftermath of the war, such countries had to turn to the Americans for aid, further boosting an economy that had already grown by 50% during the war years.

寫眞週報
情報局編輯
十二月二日・第二百四十九號・廿セン
大東亞戰争一周年

PART IV
Allied Offensives, July 1943 – December 1944

The Allied breakthrough began in September 1943, when the first of the Axis powers – Italy – surrendered. In a purely practical sense, this did not alter the scale of the fighting, for the Germans soon occupied most of Italy and imposed on the Allied armies one of the most difficult campaigns of the war, but as a symbol of Allied strength and capability it was immensely powerful. As it also involved the projection of Western Allied forces onto the continent of Europe for the first time since 1940, it began the steady process of squeezing in on Germany that was not to end until Berlin was occupied.

But the Western Allies were not in complete agreement over how this process was to be best achieved, and although the period between July 1943 and December 1944 was to see significant Allied victories, it also witnessed deep strategic debates, not just in Europe but also in the Pacific. To the Americans, intent on finishing the war in Europe as quickly as possible so that forces could be transferred to face the Japanese, the attack on Sicily and Italy in 1943 was peripheral, made more so by a feeling that the British were using it as a means of securing imperial influence in the Mediterranean. American planners were far more interested in mounting a cross-Channel invasion that would project force much closer to Germany and so shorten the conflict, and the debate over this issue dominated most of the meetings between Western Allied leaders. Practical problems, not least in terms of building up the necessary forces in Britain, intervened to delay the D-Day assault until June 1944, but even then the disagreements did not go away. Despite the undoubted success of the landings in Normandy, controversy reigned over the best way to break out from the beachheads and, once that had been achieved, how best to approach the frontiers of Germany. The role of General Dwight D. Eisenhower, as Supreme Allied Commander, was crucial in preventing this from developing into something more dramatic, but his preference for a "broad-front" advance to the border, reinforced by the failure of the "single thrust" to Arnhem in September 1944 as well as by his desire to see American forces play a major part in the destruction of Germany, brought him into confrontation with the British.

Nor were such debates confined to the ground campaigns. The controversy over the aims and methods of strategic bombing continued during this period, made worse by the failure of American daylight bombers over Schweinfurt in August and October 1943 and the heavy losses suffered by the RAF night bombers, not least against Nuremburg in late March 1944. To the air leaders, the decision to divert bombers to support of the D-Day landings denied them the opportunity to prove that bombing could end the war without the need for land campaigns, but to the men on the ground, any denial of the heavy fire support that could be provided by such bombers was little short of stupidity. Problems could still arise – the bombing of the monastery at Cassino in February 1944 and the destruction of Caen five months later had the appearance of taking a sledge-hammer to crack a nut – but no-one could doubt the enormous impact that airpower was having on the conduct of war.

This was true at sea as much as on the ground, for it was carrier-borne airpower that was winning battles in the vastness of the Pacific in 1944. That campaign was also controversial. The fighting in the South-West Pacific, conducted by American and Australian troops under General Douglas MacArthur, was among the most arduous of the war, but once the campaigns in the Solomons and New Guinea were over, MacArthur had every intention of moving on to liberate the Philippines. Unfortunately, that was not the strategy favored by the commander in the Central Pacific, Admiral Chester Nimitz, and his preference for a two-pronged thrust that would meet at Formosa had the backing of influential people in Washington. In the end, the liberation of the Philippines took precedence, but the debates engendered showed how difficult it was to conduct a global war.

The Soviets had none of these problems, chiefly because their aim – the total destruction of Germany – was clear and unequivocal. They also had only one way to achieve it: by advancing steadily west until they reached

General Hideki Tojo, Prime Minister of Japan, 1941–1944.

Berlin. The fact that they were able to do this so quickly was down to superior numbers – by 1944 it was not unknown for Stalin to concentrate over 2.5 million men for a single campaign – as well as superior techniques, many of them perfected during the difficult campaigns of 1941–43. It was also a result of Germany's strategic dilemma: the nightmare of having to face active enemies on more than one front at a time. By mid-1944, that nightmare had become reality. The war at sea had been lost, German cities were under air attack, British and American forces were in Italy and France, and the Soviets were advancing into Poland and East Prussia. However effective the German armed forces might still be – and the sudden counterattack through the Ardennes in December 1944 implies that they retained some of their previous capabilities – they were staring defeat in the face by the end of the fifth year of the war. Italy, Romania and Bulgaria had all been defeated, Finland had dropped out of the war against the Soviet Union and Hungary was under attack. The only ally left was Japan and she was in no position to offer practical help. Hitler's insistence that his "wonder weapons", the V1 pilotless plane and V2 rocket, would gain the victory his armed orces were incapable of achieving, shows just how desperate he had become.

Japan was also being squeezed, Her campaigns in Burma and China were not going well, while in the Pacific the American landings in the Marshalls, Gilberts, Marianas and Philippines all brought the end of the war that much closer. What was already becoming apparent, however, was the fanaticism with which the Japanese fought the closer the Americans came to the Home Islands; a trend that had worrying implications for the future. Indeed, one of the characteristics of total war – that it was a fight literally to the death – was becoming more and more obvious despite (or because of) the desperate situation that affected the remaining Axis powers.

U.S. forces enter the town of St. Lô, 17 July 1944. Painted by Ogden Pleissner.

Sicily JULY – AUGUST 1943

Even before the victory in North-West Africa, the Western Allies had been locked in debate about the next strategic move. The Americans pressed for an immediate cross-Channel invasion to liberate France and the Low Countries, before thrusting for Berlin. Churchill opposed this, partly because more time was needed before Allied troops would be ready for a campaign in North-West Europe, but also because he hoped for further gains in the Mediterranean, particularly against the weakened Italians. If Italy could be knocked out of the war, not only would this deal a blow to the Axis cause but it would also secure sea-lanes to the Suez Canal, while opening up invasion routes into the Balkans. Against their better judgement, the Americans agreed to delay the cross-Channel attack and to take part in an offensive against the Italians, starting in Sicily, although they did insist that this should not divert resources from other operations. The Sicily attack, codenamed Operation *Husky*, was to involve Lieutenant-General George S. Patton's U.S. Seventh and General Sir Bernard Montgomery's British Eighth Armies from North-West Africa.

Air and naval bombardments neutralized the outlying islands of Pantelleria and Lampedusa in June 1943 and, on the night of 9/10 July an enormous invasion fleet, comprising more than 2500 ships and landing craft carrying over 180,000 men, approached the south-eastern coast of Sicily. The soldiers were to land early on the 10th along a stretch of coast that ran from Syracuse in the east to Licata in the west, within range of fighter aircraft from Malta and North Africa, and were to be preceded by U.S. and British airborne drops inland, designed to seize key bridges and terrain. Allied intelligence had accurately predicted the main dispositions of the 315,000 Italian and 50,000 German troops on the island, although no-one could say how well they would fight.

When the airborne forces arrived, they faced unforeseen problems. Winds were higher than expected and many of the transport pilots, new to this type of operation, soon became disorientated. The British contingent – 1200 men in 144 gliders – was scattered far and wide. Over 200 of them landed in the sea and were drowned, while only 73 managed to reach their main target, a bridge at Ponte Grande, south of

Residents of the Sicilian town of St Agata look on as a member of the U.S. Medical Corps battles to save the life of a wounded compatriot. Powdered blood plasma, supplied by American blood banks, was carried to the front line in jeeps and greatly reduced American fatalities during the campaign.

Syracuse. Nor did the Americans – 2781 paratroopers carried in 226 C-47 transports – fare much better: they too were scattered and less than 200 arrived on their objective close to the main U.S. landing beach at Licata. The seaborne landing went more smoothly. At Licata, the Italians fled, while the British landings at Pachino and Avola were virtually unopposed. Only at Gela, in the American sector, were problems encountered, when German troops of the Hermann Goering Division, equipped with Tiger tanks, counterattacked on 11 July. This led Patton to call in airborne reinforcements, who arrived during the night of 11/12 July to be greeted by intense anti-aircraft fire from their own side. More than 220 paratroopers died.

Nevertheless, the main invasion had been a success and the Allies quickly pushed inland. Montgomery, on the right, linked up with the troops at Ponte Grande and took Syracuse, before advancing north towards Catania. Commando and airborne operations on 13 July secured more bridges, but the terrain proved difficult, preventing a breakout onto the Catania Plain. The 1st Canadian Division was sent west to loop round Mount Etna, crossing into the American sector. Patton was furious, but used the incident to gain permission to shift his advance north-eastwards. The campaign soon became a race for Messina, while Axis forces withdrew in the same direction. Patton beat his British rival to the town by two hours, arriving on the steps of the town hall at 10.15 a.m. on 17 August. By then, the enemy had conducted an orderly retreat across the Strait of Messina to the toe of Italy. By 17 August Sicily was in Allied hands after a campaign lasting 38 days. It cost 31,000 casualties but opened the way to an invasion of the Italian mainland.

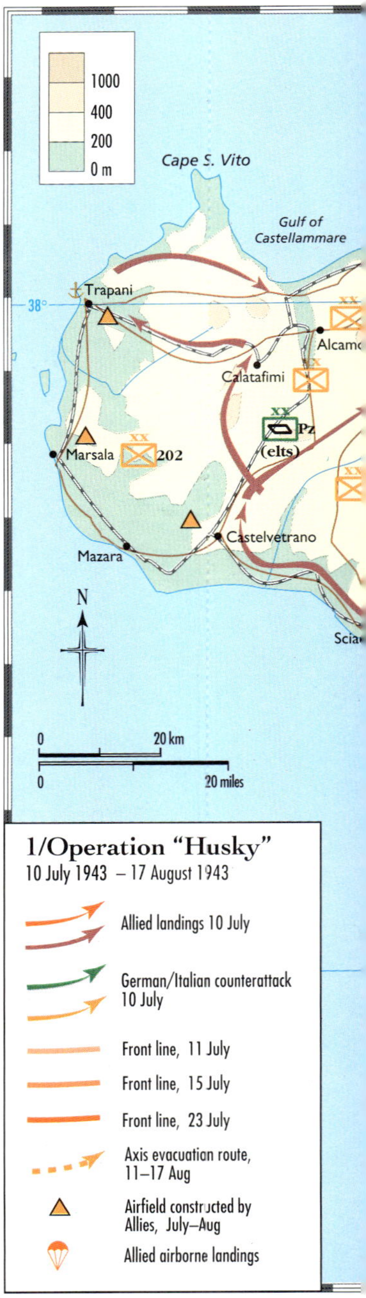

Convoys of Italian prisoners block northern coast roads, as Allied troops race to Messina on the heels of the fast-retreating Germans. Once the defenders had fled, crowds of Sicilians gathered on the streets to offer the Allies gifts of food and wine.

2/Operational Plans
1942 – 1943

1. Operation Avalanche US 5th Army
2. Operation Baytown British 8th Army
3. Operation Slapstick British 8th Army
4. Other projected moves

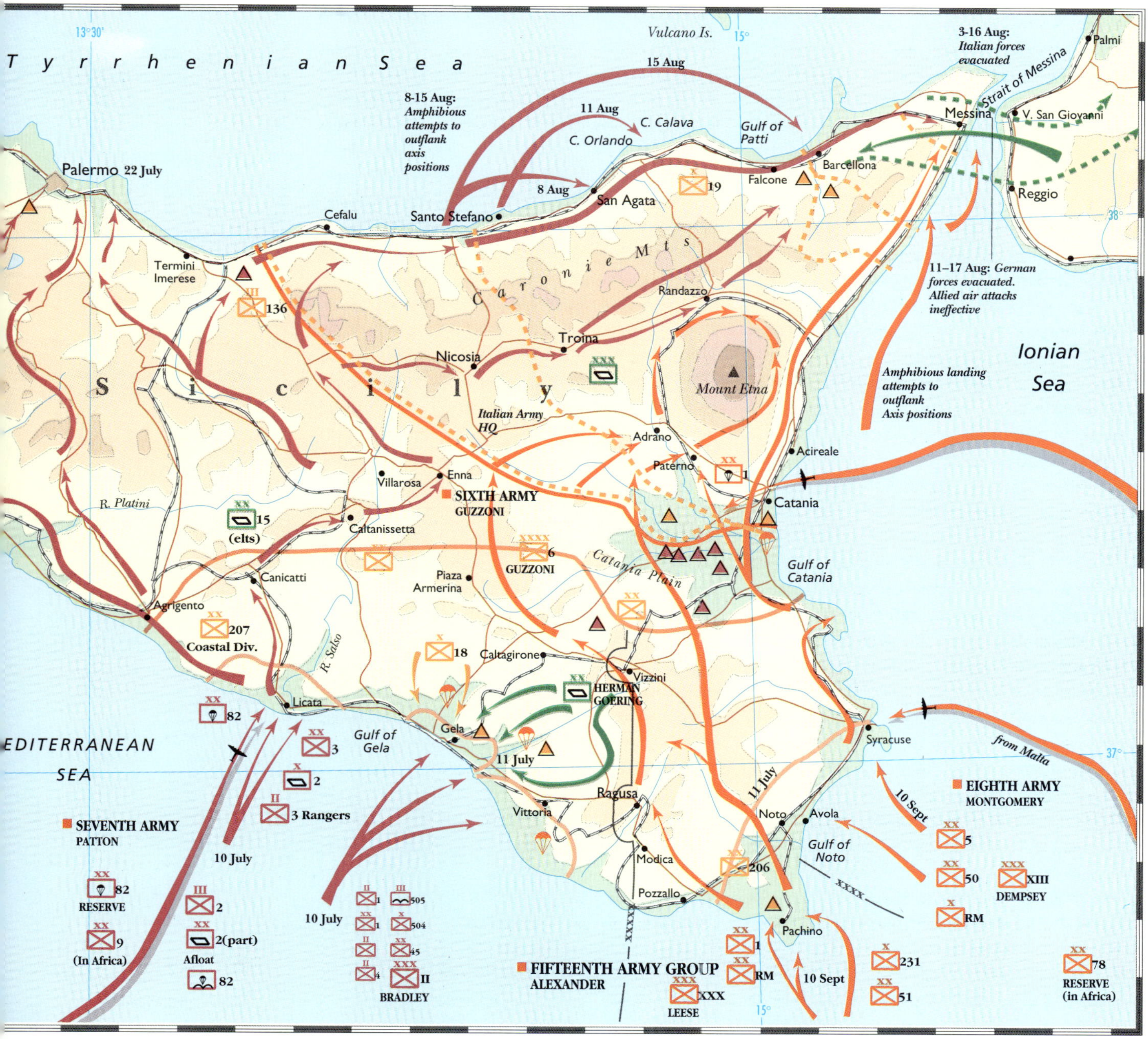

Invasion of Italy SEPTEMBER – DECEMBER 1943

The Allied invasion of Sicily had dramatic consequences on the Italian mainland. On 25 July, after a meeting of the Fascist Grand Council, Benito Mussolini was forced to resign. He was replaced by Marshal Pietro Badoglio, who immediately began to negotiate with the Allies. On 3 September 1943, Italy surrendered.

By then, the Allies had already decided to invade the mainland. Indeed, on 3 September, elements of the British Eighth Army crossed the Strait of Messina in Operation *Baytown*, landing unopposed on the Calabrian coast. But once it was known that Mussolini had gone, the Allies became more ambitious, aiming to establish beachheads at Salerno, just to the south of Naples. Lieutenant-General Mark Clark's U.S. Fifth Army, comprising the U.S. VI Corps and the British X Corps would land as soon as the Italian surrender became official, hoping to occupy large areas of Italy before the Germans reacted. Salerno was not ideal as a landing site – exits from the beaches were narrow and the two corps would be divided by a corridor created by the River Sele – but a successful landing there would secure most of southern Italy and open the road to Rome. It was a gamble worth taking.

Any hopes that the Allied invasion would be unopposed were soon dashed as the Germans responded forcibly to the collapse of their ally. Rommel disarmed Italian divisions and occupied the northern provinces, while Field Marshal Albrecht Kesselring did the same to the Naples area. Thus when the first of the Allied units landed at Salerno early on 9 September in Operation *Avalanche*, they were opposed by elements of General Heinrich von Vietinghoff's Tenth Army, which could call in reinforcements easily. The U.S. VI Corps found the going hard, and established only a tenuous foothold. The British to their left fared better, chiefly because they had insisted on a heavy naval bombardment, even so they could not seize one of their objectives, Montecorvino airfield. The only good news was that the British 1st Airborne Division had landed at Taranto and Brindisi, and was advancing up the coast toward Bari.

On 10 September, the troops at Salerno came under intense pressure. Neither the British nor Americans could take the hills that dominated the Sele corridor and the Luftwaffe began attacks on the invasion fleet, using remote-controlled "glide-bombs". By 12 September, Vietinghoff had decided to concentrate his panzers against the Americans, who were forced to pull back and by the 13th the beachhead had been reduced to a depth of less than two miles. Fortunately, the Germans then shifted to the British sector, which was better defended, not least by warships offshore. As the panzers suffered, the Allies managed to push reinforcements across the beaches and, by 18 September, the crisis was over. On 20 September, Montgomery's Eighth Army from Calabria made contact with the Salerno forces. Naples fell on 5 October, by which time Foggia on the east coast was also in Allied hands.

The Germans pulled back carefully, disputing every line of defense and drawing the Allies north into mountainous terrain, made worse by successive rivers. As early as 13 October, both corps in Fifth Army had to fight hard to cross the Volturno, only to find another river, the Garigliano, in their path. After heavy fighting in appalling weather, Clark called a temporary halt to the offensive on 15 November. Further east, in Eighth Army's sector, similar problems became apparent as Montgomery's men struggled to cross the Rivers Trigno and Sangro. By the end of December, the Allied advance had stalled completely. What they had encountered was the Gustav Line, stretching from coast to coast through seemingly impassable mountains. The campaign now became a hard slog.

U.S. infantrymen, welcomed by local people, patrol the northern Italian town of Caiazzo after the German surrender.

"I'd never known real terror until that moment... Cadavers of men from previous attacks lay scattered all over the hill. It was a horrible experience for us to see these countless dead men, many of them purpled and blackened by the intense heat."

Paratroop Sergeant Ross Carter, at Salerno

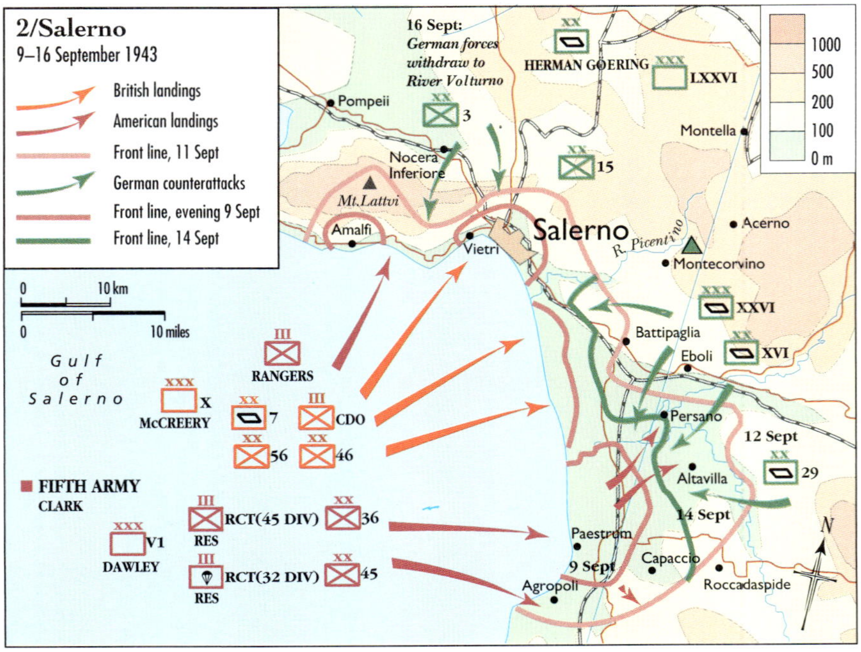

1/Southern Italy
September – December 1943
Allied landings, attacks and advances 3 Sep–15 Dec
German withdrawal
Front line, 14 September
Front line, 25 September
0 50 km
0 50 miles
1500
1000
500
200
100
0 m
TENTH ARMY
VIETINGHOFF
FIFTH ARMY
CLARK
EIGHTH ARMY
MONTGOMERY
Main Gustav Line
1st Gustav Line
Barbara Line
Victor Line
Adriatic Sea
Tyrrhenian Sea
Ionian Sea
Gulf of Manfredonia
Gulf of Salerno
Gulf of Taranto
ITALY
German units withdraw destroying communications
3 Sept: Italian fleet escapes to Malta
Pescara
Ortona
Vasto
Tivoli
Sulmona
Sora
Frosinone
Cassino
Terracina
Gaeta
Guglionesi
Campobasso
S. Severo
Monte S. Angelo
Manfredonia
Foggia
27 Sept
Caserta
Benevento
Aversa
Naples
Avellino
Mt. Vesuvius
Ventotene
Ischia
Capri
Sorrento
Amafi
Salerno
Battipaglia
19 Sept
9 Sept
Agropoli
Castellabate
Pisciotta
Avigliano
Potenza
Auletta
Cerignola
Canosa
Barletto
25 Sept
Trani
Andria
Minervino
Corato
Molfetta
Bari
Bitonto
14 Sept
Altamura
Matera
Monopoli
Martina
Metaponto
Taranto
11 Sept
Brindisi
Manduria
Lecce
Nardo
Maglie
Gallipoli
Lagonegro
S. Arcangelo
Roca Imperiale
Amendola
Castrovillari
Belvedere Marittimo
Cetraro
Paola
Acri
Rossano
Cosenza
Strongoli
Crotone
Nicastro
Cantanzaro
13 Sept
15 Sept
Valentia
Nicotera
Palmi
Canloma
Messina
V. San Giovanni
Reggio
Locri
Bianco
Patti
Barcellona
Randazzo
0430hrs 3 Sept
Stromboli
Salina
Lipari
Vulcano
R. Sangro
R. Trigno
R. Garigliano
R. Volturno
R. Sele
R. Bradano
R. Neta
RANGERS
RES
COMMANDOS
McCREERY
DAWLEY
CAN
IND
LXXVI
XIV
VIII
VI
X
II
V
2N2
42°
41°
40°
39°
15°
16°30′
18°

Monte Cassino and Anzio JANUARY – MAY 1944

The Gustav Line was strongest in the west, covering the Liri Valley and the approaches to Rome. Its key defensive feature was Monte Cassino, towering 1700 feet above the town of Cassino and topped by a Benedictine monastery, but this was only one of a series of mountain strongholds that barred the Allied advance in the winter of 1943–44. When General Mark Clark's U.S. Fifth Army approached from the south, with the British Eighth Army (now commanded by General Sir Oliver Leese) on its right, the weather was poor and the troops were close to exhaustion. Waiting for them in Cassino town and the surrounding mountains (but not, at this stage, in the monastery) were men of Lieutenant-General Fridolin von Senger und Etterlin's XIV Panzer Corps.

Clark decided to begin with a frontal assault, knowing that the U.S. VI Corps, now commanded by Major-General John P. Lucas, was scheduled to land behind German lines at Anzio on 22 January 1944. On 17 January, therefore, the British X Corps fought to establish bridgeheads across the River Garigliano while, to their right, the U.S. 34th and 36th Divisions tried to cross the Rapido. Neither assault achieved the anticipated breakthrough, for although crossings over both rivers were gained, casualties were high: by 11 February, when the First Battle of Cassino was called off, over 4000 British and 10,000 Americans had been lost.

Meanwhile, the landings at Anzio, codenamed Operation *Shingle*, had gone ahead, achieving an unexpected measure of surprise. Early on 22 January men of the British 1st and U.S. 3rd Divisions, with commando and tank support, had stormed ashore onto undefended beaches. Rome appeared to be unprotected, but the over-cautious Lucas delayed any exploitation, preferring to consolidate the beachhead. It was a missed opportunity. By the end of the day the Germans had hastily transferred units from northern Italy to block the Allied advance. When Lucas finally decided to move on 30 January, putting in a two-pronged attack through Cisterna and Campoleone, the Allies were opposed by panzers which inflicted heavy casualties. The fighting degenerated into attrition, with the Allies gradually losing ground. On 16 February, a German assault drove a wedge between the British and American sectors, and it took air and naval support to save the day. By the 19th, the situation had improved, but not enough to save Lucas, who was relieved of command. Major-General Lucien K. Truscott took over, although there was little he could do to prevent deadlock. The Anzio forces were going nowhere.

By then, Clark had ordered a second assault on Cassino, using the New Zealand Corps against Cassino town while French troops tried to bypass to the north around Monte Belvedere.

Founded by St. Benedict in AD 529, Monte Cassino was of great architectural importance. The monastery's spectacular setting was its downfall and the Allied attack was the fifth in its turbulent history. This time it was reduced to ruins and could not be rebuilt. Most of the monks and the priceless art treasures had been evacuated long before the assault began.

German paratroop reinforcements were rushed in to defend the bombed monastery, and it was transformed into an impenetrable fortress. Here they hide in ruined houses and among the debris of St. Benedict's, ready to ambush Allied infantrymen.

As a preliminary, on 15 February, the monastery on top of Monte Cassino was bombed in one of the most controversial decisions of the war. Enormous damage was inflicted, but von Senger sent paratroopers to occupy the rubble. Nor did the bombing help the New Zealanders, who penetrated Cassino town only to be thrown back by a panzer counterattack. By the 20th, the second battle was over.

A month later, Clark tried again. On 15 March a massive air and artillery bombardment destroyed Cassino town preparatory to another assault by the New Zealanders, while in the hills above the ruins other British/Imperial troops fought hand-to-hand with the enemy in driving rain. By 23 March, it was apparent that no real progress was being made and the third battle was brought to a close. The only option now seemed to be to swamp the entire area with artillery and air attacks before advancing with overwhelming numbers. This approach was tried on 11 May, although the breakthrough came from a more traditional assault by French troops in the Aurunci Mountains, to the south-west of Cassino. This threatened to turn the Gustav Line and, on 17 May, the Germans began to withdraw. On the 18th, Polish troops finally seized the monastery after five days of bitter fighting. As the Germans pulled back, the forces at Anzio were able to break out, linking up with other elements of Fifth Army on 26 May. The road to Rome was open, but the costs had been high: since January casualties on both sides together had exceeded 45,000 men.

Advance to the Gothic Line JUNE – DECEMBER 1944

Once a link had been created between the Allied forces from Cassino and those at Anzio, General Mark Clark, commanding the U.S. Fifth Army, had an opportunity to trap substantial enemy formations. If the U.S. VI Corps, breaking out from the Anzio beachhead after months of deadlock, could reach the Valmontone Gap, to the east of the Alban Hills, before the Germans around Cassino had fully disengaged, large parts of General Heinrich von Vietinghoff's Tenth Army would be encircled. But Clark had other priorities, Aware that the Allied invasion of North-West Europe was imminent, he was determined to liberate Rome before Italy became a secondary theater in the eyes of the press. He therefore restricted the advance toward Valmontone to one division and diverted the rest of VI Corps to a direct attack on the Italian capital. On 30 May, a breakthrough was made at Velletri and, on 4 June, Clark marched into Rome. It was a major public relations victory only two days before D-Day in Normandy, but it did mean that most of the German Tenth Army was able to avoid confrontation and withdraw to the north, ready to fight another day.

The German retreat was orderly and effective. As Tenth Army, with General Eberhard von Mackensen's Fourteenth to its right, pulled back, bridges were demolished and roads mined. Field Marshal Albrecht Kesselring, overall commander in Italy, had already made preparations to stand firm on the Gothic Line, a series of defenses that stretched some 200 miles from just south of La Spezia on the west coast to Pesaro on the east. Construction of the Line had begun the previous year, although the more the Allies could be delayed the better, for German reinforcements were arriving from the Eastern Front. If the Allies could be slowed down enough, the rains and mud of the coming fall would clearly help the German defenders.

As soon as Rome was in Allied hands, the decision was taken for Clark's Fifth Army to advance along the west coast, while General Sir Oliver Leese's British Eighth Army (which included substantial Canadian and Polish contingents) thrust along the Adriatic coast and through the hills in the center. At first, all went well – by 16 June the Allies had advanced about 90 miles, following the German rearguard – but as they approached the Gothic Line, enemy resistance stiffened. Although Perugia, Siena, Leghorn and Ancona were liberated in the next three weeks, Kesselring's troops did all they could to deny the Allies any momentum. They were aided by an Allied decision to extract seven divisions from Italy for the invasion of Southern France on 15 August, although General Sir Harold Alexander, overall Allied commander in Italy, was aware through Ultra information of German dispositions. This enabled him to conduct a series of offensives in August and September 1944 that made significant inroads into the Gothic Line defenses before the weather turned.

Alexander's campaign was based on a degree of deception, designed to trick the enemy and force him to concentrate resources in the wrong areas. On 25 August, an attack was made by Eighth Army on the Adriatic coast which crossed the River Metauro and pushed the Germans into the Gothic Line. There was then a pause, persuading Kesselring that the British had shot their bolt, a perception reinforced on 2 September when Clark's Fifth Army took Pisa. German reserves were rushed over to the west coast in response, only to find that the Eighth Army was on the move again. On 12 September eight divisions attacked along a 30-mile front to take San Fortunato and enter Rimini, breaching the Gothic Line. The pressure was maintained by Clark in the west, whose forces reached the Apennine passes at Futa and Giogo on 16 September, aiming for the Po Valley. By then, however, the Germans had realized what was happening and were able to respond more effectively. They blocked further progress in early October, by which time the rains had turned the ground to mud. Clark had to suspend all operations in late October, and although a further advance was made by Eighth Army in December to reach Ravenna, the campaign ground to a halt. Nothing more could be done until the spring.

"The soldiers came marching in the moonlight. They were silent, very tired, marching almost like robots. The people came out of the houses to cheer them but they only smiled, waved and kept on going."

Vera Cacciatore, resident of Rome

German troops prepare to evacuate Rimini in the face of the continued Allied advance. When the town fell, Kesselring noted in his diary, "I have the terrible feeling that the whole thing is beginning to slide."

Soldiers of the British Eighth Army search houses in Ravenna, the last town to be captured in 1944 before the onset of winter. In the high mountain passes rain had already begun to turn into sleet and snow, hampering the Allied advance.

The Liberation of Rome and Advance to Ravenna
June–December 1944
Front line, 30 May
Front line, 4 June
Front line, 17 June
Allied attacks
Allied attacks
Allied attacks
German attack, late December
Front line, end December
2000
1000
500
100
0 m
N
0
20 km
0
20 miles
ARMY GROUP SOUTHWEST
KESSELRING
10
VIETINGHOFF
14
VON MACKENSEN
8 German divisions, 4 arriving from Eastern Front to reinforce Gothic Line
Futa Pass
Giogo Pass
Gothic Line
Apennines
FIFTH ARMY
TRUSCOTT
EIGHTH ARMY
McCREERY
FIFTEENTH ARMY GROUP
CLARK
French Expeditionary Corps
EIGHTH ARMY
LEESE (Later McCREERY)
FIFTH ARMY
CLARK (Later TRUSCOTT)
FIFTEENTH ARMY GROUP
ALEXANDER (Later CLARK)
4 June: U.S. Forces enter Rome, first Axis capital to fall
Trasimere or Albert Line
Viterbo Line
Front Line, 30 May
Gulf of Venice
ADRIATIC SEA
Ligurian Sea
TYRRHENIAN SEA
ITALY
SAN MARINO
Vatican City
Rome
Alban Hills
Bologna
Florence
Cremona
Piacenza
Mantova
Padova
Chioggia
Parma
Ferrara
Codigoro
Reggio
Modena
Imola
Lugo
Ravenna
Forli
Rimini
Pesaro
Fano
La Spezia
Carrara
Pistoia
Prato
Viareggio
Lucca
Pisa
Leghorn
Volterra
Siena
Arezzo
Citta di Castello
Urbino
Ancona
Iesi
Fabriano
Gubbio
Corona
Perugia
Macerata
Fermo
Piombino
Elba Is.
Portoferraio
Grosseto
Orvieto
Foligno
Ascoli
Teramo
Terni
Viterbo
Rieti
L'Aquila
Pescara
Montecristo Is.
Civitavecchia
Sulmona
Tivoli
Valmontone
Velletri
Frosinone
Sora
Latina
Anzio
Cassino
Terracina
Gaeta
Novigrad
Motovun
Fiume
Parenzo
Rovigno
Labin
Rasa
Pola
Cherso
R. Po
R. Tiber
R. Metauro
POL
CAN
II
IV
X
I
V
XIII
VI
10°
12°
13°
42°
43°
44°
45°

Russian Counter-offensives JULY – DECEMBER 1943

Soviet victory in the Battle of Kursk, combined with attacks on the Orel salient to the north, forced the troops of Field Marshal Gunther von Kluge's Army Group Center onto the defensive. Under attack from partisans in their rear, where guerrilla raids were disrupting supply lines and absorbing forces that would otherwise have been facing the main Soviet armies, the Germans soon found themselves under overwhelming pressure. Although General Konstantin Rokossovsky's Central (Belorussian) Front was slowed in its advance, nothing could be done to prevent the fall of Orel on 5 August 1943. By then, General Nikolai Vatutin's Voronezh Front, supported to its south by General Ivan Konev's Steppe Front, had opened another offensive, designed to straighten the line to the south of the Kursk salient. Using massed armor and mechanized formations, the Soviets took Belgorod on 5 August, threatening the German hold on Kharkov.

Hitler's response to these crises was a familiar one: he ordered his troops to stand fast and refused any requests to withdraw. Field Marshal Erich von Manstein, commander of Army Group South, responsible for the defense of Kharkov, tried desperately to stem the Soviet advance by switching tank units from one trouble-spot to another, but even he could achieve little. By mid-August, Kharkov was under attack from three sides simultaneously and it began to look as if General Erhard Raus' II Corps would be trapped. On 22 August Hitler was forced to face reality and authorize a withdrawal; Kharkov was liberated on the following day.

Soviet intentions were quite clear. Having built up enormous forces – over 2.6 million men and 2400 tanks in the area between Smolensk and Rostov, with access to further reinforcements if needed – they could afford to mount a series of simultaneous offensives all along that part of the front, designed to overstretch their enemy and force his withdrawal. Stalin's plan was to take full advantage of the recent victories to push the Germans back to the River Dnieper, straightening the front line from Smolensk to the Sea of Azov before the end of the year. In the process, he aimed to outflank and isolate the German Seventeenth Army in the Crimea, liberate the Ukraine and thrust deep into Belorussia, removing once and for all any threat to the capital. It was an ambitious

"There is no doubt that at this stage of the war the Russians collared for their ordinary infantry divisions anyone, regardless of training, age or health – and sometimes of sex – and pushed them ruthlessly into battle."

General von Mellenthin

Immediately prior to the commencement of the Soviet counter-offensive, Russian tank crews are addressed by their commanding officer.

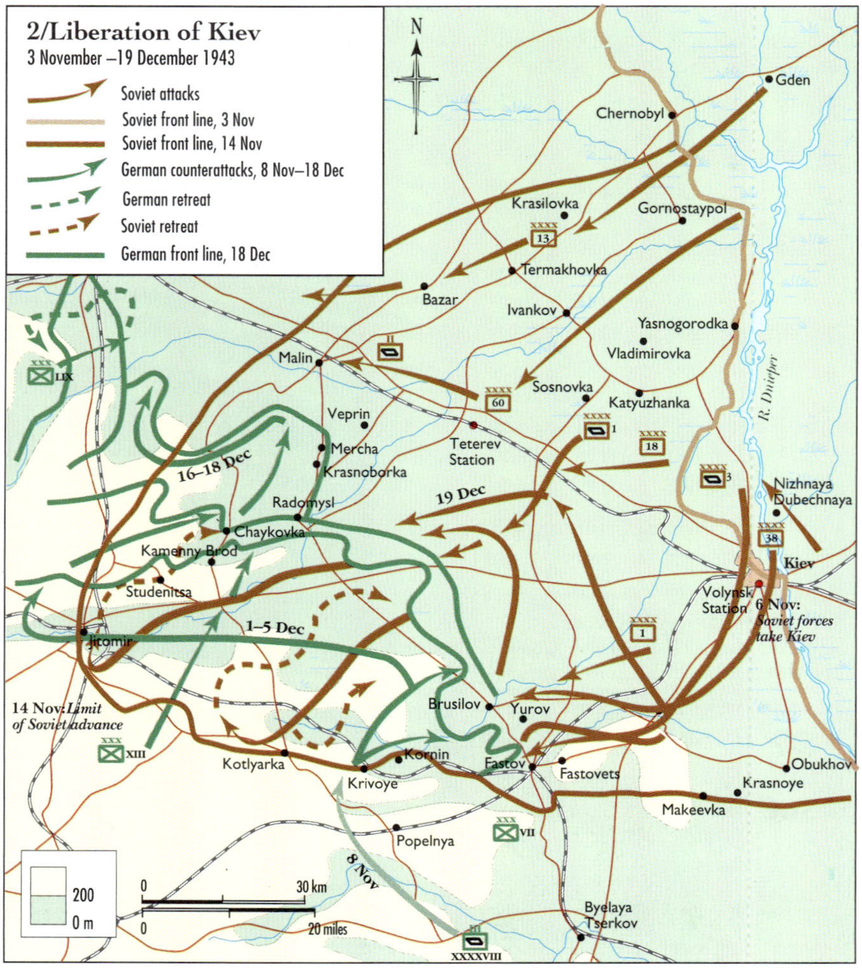

strategy, but one that succeeded in virtually all respects.

Manstein had foreseen the danger, although any plans he had for defending areas to the east of the Dnieper were disrupted by Hitler's insistence that Kharkov should be held. By the time permission had been granted for a withdrawal, the Soviets were already threatening Manstein's flanks. His retreat was, therefore, chaotic as nearly 750,000 Axis troops tried to pull back to the apparent safety of the Dnieper before the enemy beat them in the race for the river. Their situation was not helped by a further Führer order that nothing of value should be left for the advancing Soviets. Agricultural produce was confiscated and moved back to Germany, clogging the roads, while factories and bridges were destroyed. Army Group South was lucky to survive at all. On 21 September, as the last of its coherent units crossed the Dnieper at Kanev, Soviet spearheads were hot on their heels.

The Soviets did not pause. Pushing groups of men across the river on rafts, they seized a small bridgehead on the west bank at Bukrin, reinforcing it with airborne troops. Early in October, other Soviet forces reached Zaporozhye, to the south of Kanev, and crossed the river on abandoned barges; in mid-October another bridgehead was established to the north, around Lyutezh. Kiev was captured on 6 November. By then, Smolensk had been liberated – it fell to overwhelming Soviet formations as early as 25 September – and, in the far south, a massive build-up of forces was threatening Field Marshal Ewald von Kleist's Army Group A. In December 1943, the Soviets attacked from the Zaporozhye bridgehead and along the northern shore of the Sea of Azov, toward the mouth of the Dnieper at Kherson, trapping over 650,000 German troops in the Crimea. Hitler was facing disaster.

Captured by the Russians, shivering German PoWs anxiously await the determination of their fate.

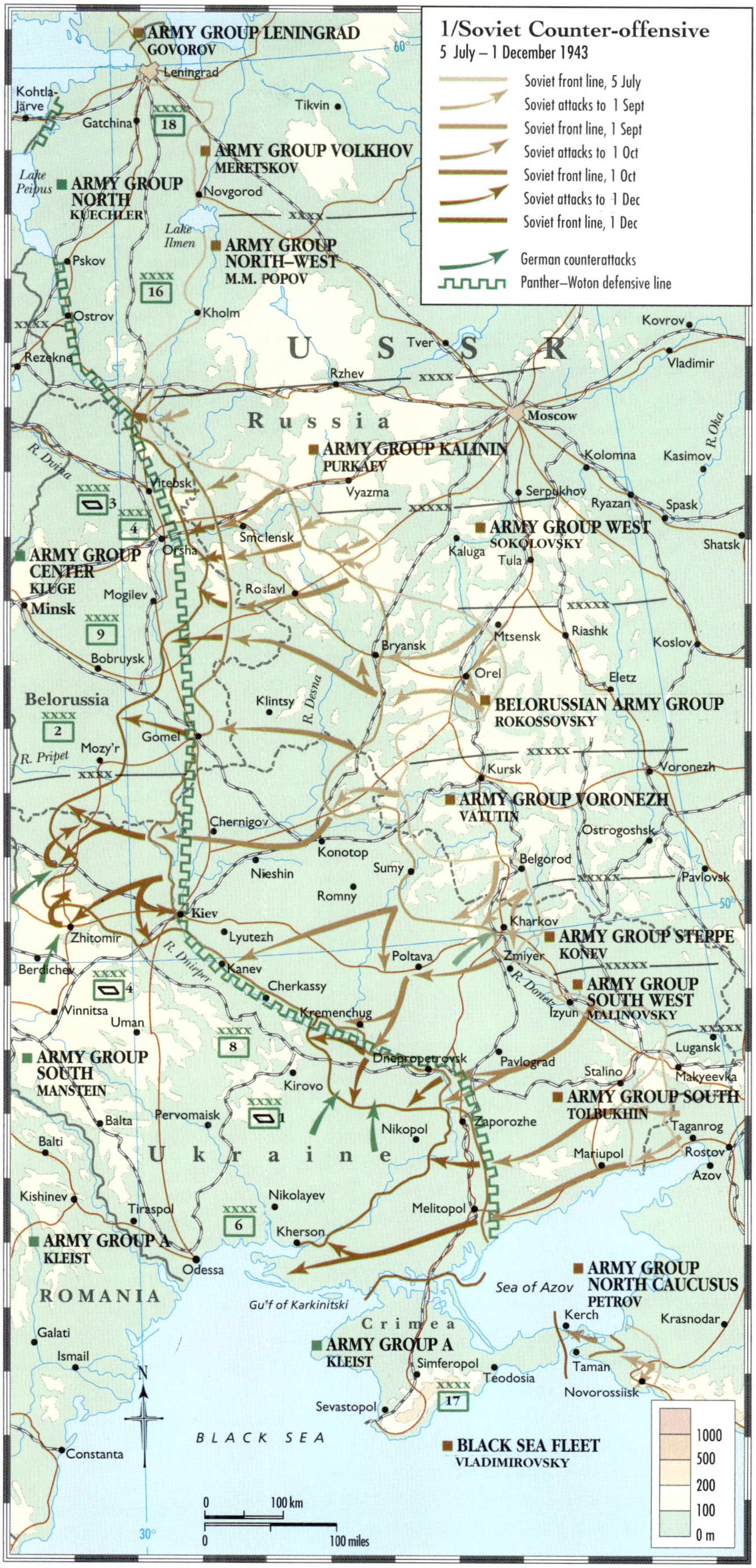

Leningrad and the Baltic States JAN – OCT 1944

While the Soviets were fighting in the center and south to reach, and then cross, the River Dnieper liberating Kharkov, Smolensk and Kiev, they were also preparing for an offensive in the north to raise the siege of Leningrad. General Leonid Govorov, commander of the Leningrad Front, was ordered to start his planning in September 1943, although it was to take until the end of the year to complete the preparations. As elsewhere on the Eastern Front, the main Soviet advantage lay in overwhelming numbers, not just of men but also of equipment and ammunition; by January 1944 the German Eighteenth Army around Leningrad was facing three Soviet armies. One of these, the Second Shock Army, had been moved into the Oranienbaum "pocket" to the west of Leningrad in great secrecy during November and December 1943. It was to attack south-eastwards toward Krasnoye Selo, where it would link up with the Forty-Second Army, scheduled to advance south from the Pulkovo Heights, within the Leningrad perimeter. At the same time, the Sixty-Seventh Army would push down from Schlüsselburg to protect the flank of the Forty-Second. To the south, armies of General Kiril Meretskov's Volkhov and General Markian Popov's 2nd Baltic Fronts would attack along the River Volkhov and around Lake Ilmen, threatening Novgorod. The overall aim was to push the Germans back as far as Lake Peipus, Pskov and Ostrov, removing the danger from Leningrad entirely.

Govorov's offensive began on 14 January 1944 when, after a massive artillery bombardment, the Second Shock Army caught the Germans by surprise. Twenty-four hours later another artillery barrage heralded the attack from the Pulkovo Heights, and although some German units fought desperately to prevent a breakthrough to Krasnoye Selo, it was soon apparent that their numbers were insufficient. Their plight was not aided by the opening of Meretskov's offensive along the Volkhov. By 17 January the commander of Army Group North, Field Marshal Georg von Kuechler, was concerned enough to approach Hitler for permission to withdraw to the so-called Panther Line along the River Narva, and when, unsurprisingly, this was refused, many of his units faced destruction. On 19 January Novgorod fell to the Soviets and Kuechler had no choice but to order a withdrawal. He was immediately sacked by Hitler, who sent Field Marshal Walther Model to replace him, although there was little that he could do to reverse the situation. In mid-January, the siege of Leningrad was officially lifted and, as the German retreat began, Soviet forces made significant territorial gains. On 1 February, Second Shock Army took Kingisepp on the River Luga and approached the city of Narva; 12 days later Luga was liberated. Model ordered the remains of his Sixteenth and Eighteenth Armies back to the Panther Line.

One of the results of Soviet victory around Leningrad was that the Finns, threatening the city from the north-west, were isolated from their German ally. As early as March 1944, Finnish leaders sent a delegation to Moscow to ask for peace terms, but Stalin's demands were unacceptable. The Soviets were more interested in mounting an offensive to defeat the Finns. Their plan was for the Karelian Front, commanded by Meretskov from February 1944, to attack all along the frontier, from Petsamo in the north to Lake Ladoga in the south, while elements of Govorov's Leningrad Front advanced into the Karelian Isthmus. The offensive opened on 10 June, forcing the Finns in Karelia to withdraw toward Viipuri. Ten days later, Meretskov attacked between Lakes Ladoga and Onega, shattering the Finnish II Corps. As the Finns manned a succession of new defensive lines, the momentum of the Soviet thrusts was lost, enabling the newly appointed Finnish President, Field Marshal Carl von Mannerheim, to negotiate his country's withdrawal from the war on 19 September. However, this did not prevent further Soviet attacks in the far north in October, seizing Petsamo and Kirkenes (the latter over the border in Norway).

By then, Soviet offensives in Belorussia had threatened the flanks of Army Group North in Estonia, forcing it to withdraw toward the Baltic coast. Riga fell on 15 October 1944 and Army Group North was surrounded with its back to the sea. The Soviets were able to take Estonia, Latvia and Lithuania against minimal opposition, even crossing the border into East Prussia before the end of the year.

"They were just a bunch of men overcome by desperate fear and utter physical exhaustion. Their attitude was infectious. I suddenly felt the whole force of this misery and never-ending wretchedness; it gripped me like an iron fist and pressed on my head, until for next to nothing I would have dropped my machine-pistol and howled like a dog."

A German soldier witnesses an attempted mutiny in Finland

Russian infantry advance under cover of a T-34 tank. Declared by Heinz Guderian to be "the best tank in the world", the T-34 was armed with a 76.2 mm cannon and two machine-guns.

The Relief of Leningrad and the Liberation of the Baltic States
January–October 1944
Front line, mid January
Soviet attacks to 1 Mar
Front line, 1 March
Soviet attacks to end Aug
Front line, end August
Soviet attacks to end Oct
Front line, end October
German counterattacks
German pockets
2000
1000
500
200
0 m
NORWAY
FINLAND
USSR
Ribachi Peninsula
25 October
7 October
10 September
Neiden
Kirkenes
Petsamo
Salmijarvi
Nautsi
Murmansk
20 MTN
14
19
KARELIAN FRONT
MERETSKOV
Turku
Kandalaksha
Kuolojarvi
Markajarvi
Salla
Kuhm
Repola
Ilomantsi
Joensuu
32
20 June: Attacks launched
Finns force Soviet armies back to the "U defense line"
Suojarvi
Karelian Isthmus
FINLAND
Petrozavodsk
Lake Onega
Salmi
Lake Ladoga
Olonets
Viipuri
Porvoo
Helsinki
LENINGRAD FRONT
GOVOROV
Gulf of Finland
7
7 June: 7th Army attacks
2 SA
42
21
23
Oranienbaum
Krasnoyeselo
Schlüsselburg
Leningrad
67
8
Tallinn
Narva
Kingisepp
18
Gatchina
ARMY GROUP NARVA
FRIESSNER
R. Luga
R. Volkhov
Hijumaa
Baltic Sea
Saaremaa
ESTONIA
Pärnu
Lake Peipus
ARMY GROUP NORTH
KUECHLER
(later Model)
Luga
54
Tikvin
VOLKHOV FRONT
MERETSKOV
Tartu
Novgorod
Lake Ilmen
59
16
Gulf of Riga
ARMY GROUP NORTH
LINDEMANN
(later Friessner)
Ventspils
ARMY GROUP NORTH
FRIESSNER
(later Schörner)
Riga
LATVIA
Pskov
1 SH
SECOND BALTIC FRONT
M.M. POPOV
(later Yeremenko)
Ostrov
22
Jelgava
Kholm
Siauliai
Rezekne
Memel
LITHUANIA
Daugavpils
USSR
Tver
16
Rzhev
4 SH
3Pz
R. Dvina
East Prussia
Kaunas
13 July
Vilna
6 GDS
ARMY GROUP CENTER
REINHARDT
(later Bush)
Vitebsk
43
FIRST BALTIC FRONT
BAGRAMYAN
Vyazma
Belorussia
Borisov
Orsha
Smolensk
Grodno
31
Russia
Bialystok
R. Niemen
Minsk
11th July
Mogilev
Kaluga
WEST FRONT
SOKOLOVSKY
Roslavl
POLAND
Baranowicze
Bobruisk
West
SOKOLOVSKY
Siedlce
28 July
Pinsk
11 GDS
Bryansk
Brest-Litovsk
R. Dnieper
13
Klintsy
Orel
130 km
80 miles
N

The Ukraine DECEMBER 1943 – MAY 1944

By the end of 1943 the Soviet forces in the southern sector of the Eastern Front, facing Field Marshal Erich von Manstein's Army Group South and Field Marshal Ewald von Kleist's Army Group A, were poised for further advances. Any German hopes that the winter weather and enemy exhaustion would create a pause were soon dashed. On 24 December General Nikolai Vatutin's 1st Ukrainian Front launched attacks to liberate Korosten and Zhitomir; on 5 January 1944, General Ivan Konev's 2nd Ukrainian Front took Kirovograd further south. These advances threatened the German First Panzer and Eighth Armies, occupying an area around Korsun, but Hitler, refused to allow withdrawal. On 24 January Konev began the process of encirclement by moving forces north-west from Kirovograd; four days later he linked up with Vatutin at Zvenigorodka, trapping more than 60,000 German troops.

Manstein ordered an immediate counterattack to relieve the Korsun "pocket", sending XLVII Panzer Corps to assault the south-eastern perimeter and III Panzer Corps to strike from the west. An early thaw turned the ground to mud, but by 11 February lead elements of III Panzer Corps had managed to reach Lysyanka, close to their beleaguered comrades. On the night of 16/17 February, the troops inside the pocket tried to break out, only to be caught in a Soviet trap. According to the Germans, about 30,000 men of the First Panzer and Eighth Armies escaped, but Soviet sources disagree, claiming that few were spared. Army Group South had suffered a stunning blow, made worse on 4 March when, despite the mud, 1st Ukrainian Front (now commanded by Marshal Georgi Zhukov) suddenly renewed its advance westward. Konev joined the offensive on 5 March and, 24 hours later, Marshal Radion Malinovsky's 3rd Ukrainian Front began its offensive further south. There was little that either Manstein or Kleist could do. By 10 March, Konev and Zhukov looked set to link up to the west of Vinnitsa, threatening the remains of First Panzer Army with another encirclement, this time around Kamenets Podolsky. Other elements of 2nd Ukrainian Front, thrusting south into Moldavia, threatened the rear of Army Group A, itself under growing pressure from Malinovsky. Kleist had no choice but to pull back to the River Bug, although even that was not enough to ensure his escape.

The steep cliffs and mountainous backdrop of Sevastopol, home to the Soviet Black Sea Fleet, made it a natural fortress. When Soviet troops returned to reclaim their city in 1944, Hitler ordered his troops to "defend to the last man". But bitter street fighting claimed thousands of German lives and the Führer finally gave his men permission to evacuate.

Manstein flew to Hitler's headquarters in late March to plead for reinforcements and for permission to relieve First Panzer Army. For once, he got his way – II Panzer Corps was moved from France to mount a relieving attack, linking up with First Panzer Army around Tarnopol on 10 April – but it cost him his command. By the end of April Army Group South had been renamed Army Group North Ukraine and given to Field Marshal Walther Model, while Army Group A had been transformed into Army Group South Ukraine under General Ferdinand Schörner. By then, the defenses on the River Bug had been breached and Odessa had fallen to Malinovsky's spearheads. Soviet troops entered Romania on 10 April.

Further east, the Soviets had begun to clear the Crimean Peninsula, still held by the German Seventeenth Army. Cut off by Soviet advances in late 1943, which had created bridgeheads on the Perekop Isthmus and around Kerch, the Seventeenth Army could have been withdrawn by sea but, as usual, Hitler refused to countenance such a move. Instead, he insisted on reinforcements being sent in, so that by April 1944 the peninsula contained some 76,000 German and 46,000 Romanian troops. They were faced by three Soviet armies, totaling nearly half a million men and 600 tanks, backed by aircraft which ruled the skies. The Soviet attack began on 8 April, and within less than three weeks, the Axis defenders had been pushed back to the fortress city of Sevastopol. This was assaulted on 5 May and fell quickly. On 9 May about 30,000 Axis survivors struggled down to beaches on Cape Kherson, but fewer than 1000 men were rescued by German and Romanian ships. By 12 May the Crimea was back in Soviet hands.

"I cannot remember a human gaze ever conveying such willpower. In his otherwise coarse face, the eyes were probably the only attractive and certainly the most expressive feature, and now they were boring into me as if to force me to my knees. At the same moment the notion of an Indian snake-charmer flashed through my mind, and I realized that those eyes must have intimidated many a man before me."

Field Marshal Erich von Manstein, describing an interview with Hitler

---

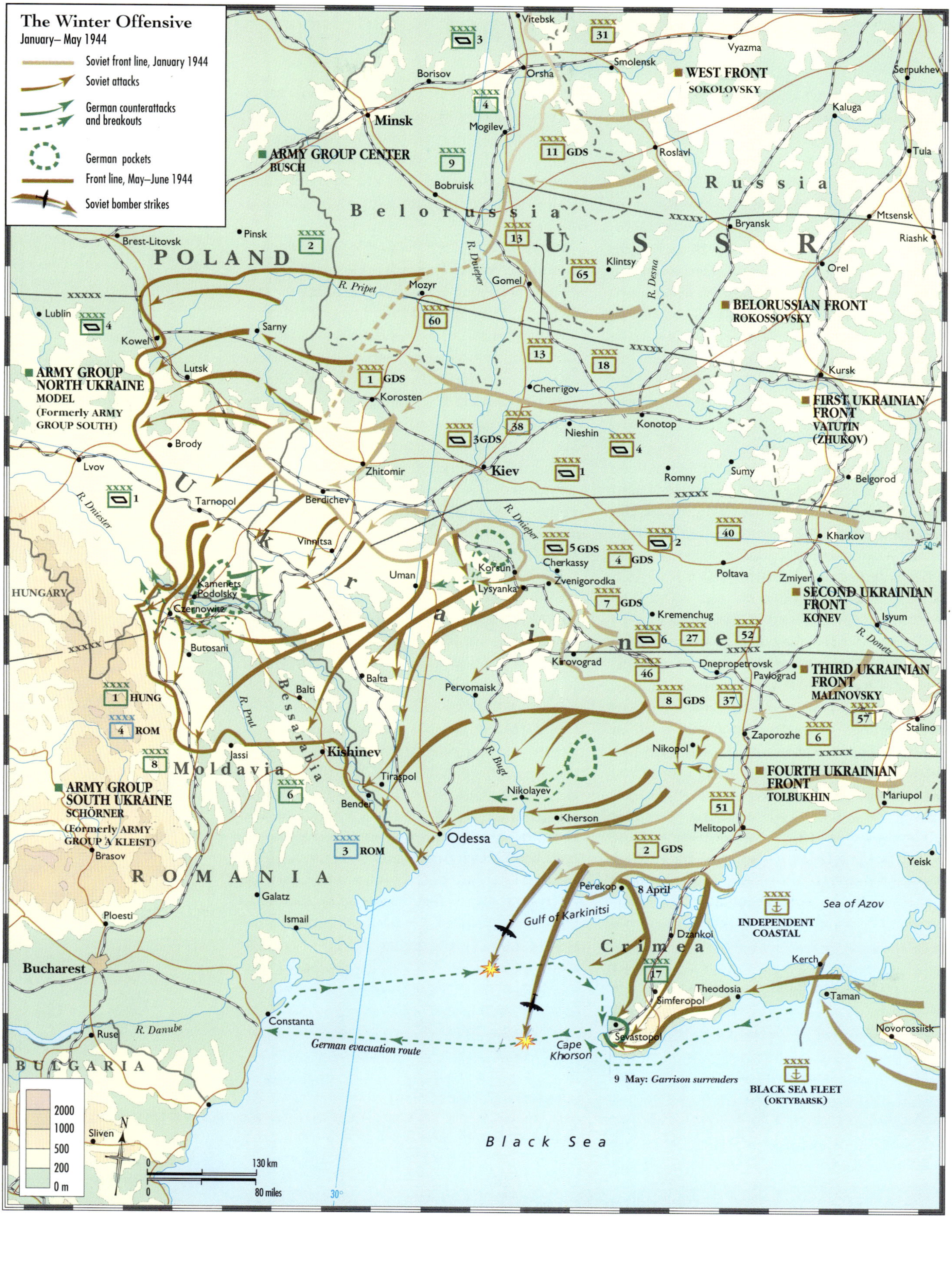
The Winter Offensive
January– May 1944
Soviet front line, January 1944
Soviet attacks
German counterattacks and breakouts
German pockets
Front line, May–June 1944
Soviet bomber strikes
Vitebsk
Vyazma
Smolensk
Borisov
Orsha
Serpukhev
WEST FRONT
SOKOLOVSKY
Kaluga
Minsk
Mogilev
ARMY GROUP CENTER
BUSCH
Roslavl
Tula
Bobruisk
Russia
Belorussia
Bryansk
Mtsensk
Riashk
Pinsk
Brest-Litovsk
POLAND
USSR
Klintsy
Orel
R. Pripet
Mozyr
Gomel
R. Dnieper
R. Desna
Lublin
Kowel
Sarny
BELORUSSIAN FRONT
ROKOSSOVSKY
Lutsk
ARMY GROUP NORTH UKRAINE
MODEL
(Formerly ARMY GROUP SOUTH)
Korosten
Cherrigov
Kursk
FIRST UKRAINIAN FRONT
VATUTIN
(ZHUKOV)
Brody
Nieshin
Konotop
Lvov
Zhitomir
Kiev
Romny
Sumy
Belgorod
R. Dniester
Tarnopol
Berdichev
Ukraine
Kharkov
Vinnitsa
Cherkassy
Poltava
Uman
Korsun
Zvenigorodka
HUNGARY
Kamenets Podolsky
Lysyanka
Zmiyer
SECOND UKRAINIAN FRONT
KONEV
Czernowitz
Kremenchug
Isyum
R. Donets
Butosani
Kirovograd
Dnepropetrovsk
Pavlograd
THIRD UKRAINIAN FRONT
MALINOVSKY
Balta
Pervomaisk
Balti
Bessarabia
R. Prut
Stalino
Zaporozhe
Kishinev
Jassi
Nikopol
Moldavia
R. Bug
FOURTH UKRAINIAN FRONT
TOLBUKHIN
Tiraspol
Nikolayev
ARMY GROUP SOUTH UKRAINE
SCHÖRNER
(Formerly ARMY GROUP A KLEIST)
Bender
Mariupol
Kherson
Melitopol
Odessa
Brasov
ROMANIA
Yeisk
Perekop
8 April
Galatz
Sea of Azov
Gulf of Karkinitsi
INDEPENDENT COASTAL
Ploesti
Ismail
Dzankoi
Crimea
Kerch
Bucharest
Theodosia
Simferopol
Taman
Constanta
Novorossiisk
Ruse
R. Danube
Sevastopol
Cape Khorson
German evacuation route
BULGARIA
9 May: Garrison surrenders
BLACK SEA FLEET
(OKTYBARSK)
Sliven
Black Sea
2000
1000
500
200
0 m
N
130 km
80 miles
30°

Resistance in the East JUNE – AUGUST 1944

By June 1944, Soviet advances in the south and around Leningrad left the German Army Group Center, commanded by General Ernst von Busch, occupying an enormous salient to the west of Smolensk. Centered on four key locations – Vitebsk, Orsha, Mogilev and Bobruysk – the salient was clearly vulnerable, yet Hitler remained obsessed with a growing threat to the Hungarian and Romanian oil-fields. Despite the Western Allies' invasion of North-West Europe on 6 June 1944, the Führer insisted on sending reinforcements to Army Groups North and South Ukraine, leaving Busch to hold a 650-mile front with only 500,000 men. Against him the Soviets built up overwhelming forces – the 1st, 2nd and 3rd Belorussian and 1st Baltic Fronts together totaled about 1.2 million men, 4000 armored fighting vehicles and 6000 aircraft – and planned a crushing blow that would push the Germans out of the Soviet Union and into Poland. Codenamed Operation *Bagration* (after a Russian general who fought against Napoleon in 1812), it was scheduled to begin on 22 June 1944, the third anniversary of Barbarossa.

By then, Soviet operational methods had improved. Gone were the days of general advances on a broad front; instead, tanks, infantry and aircraft were concentrated in key "breakthrough sectors" and breaches made in German defenses using massive artillery bombardments, sometimes involving nearly 300 guns per mile of front line. Deception measures (known to the Soviets as *maskirovka*) prevented the defenders from concentrating their resources, while constant air-strikes and partisan attacks disrupted enemy supply lines and delayed the movement of reserves. Thus, when *Bagration* opened at 5 a.m. on 22 June, the Germans were spread out and surprised, allowing the Soviets to make spectacular gains. In the north, General Ivan Bagramyan's 1st Baltic and General Ivan Chernyakovsky's 3rd Belorussian Fronts fought to encircle Vitebsk, and although Hitler agreed to a withdrawal on 24 June, it was too late to save the bulk of LIII Corps. Vitebsk fell on 27 June, for a loss of about 30,000 German troops. Meanwhile, further south, elements of Chernyakovsky's armies took Orsha, while Lieutenant-General M.V. Zakharov's 2nd Belorussian Front crossed the River Dnieper and threatened Mogilev. To complete the German overstretch, Marshal Konstantin Rokossovsky's 1st Belorussian Front encircled Bobruysk, trapping another 40,000 German troops. Hitler, true to form, ordered Army Group Center to stand form and sacked its commander, replacing him with Field Marshal Walther Model.

Mogilev fell on 28 June and Bobruysk the following day. As 2nd Belorussian Fronts initiated an enormous pincer movement, aiming to trap the Germans in Minsk. When that city fell on 3 July, substantial numbers of the German Fourth and Ninth Armies were forced to surrender, leaving a gap which Chernyakovsky was able to exploit. Entering Vilnius on 13 July, he then swept northward toward Riga, eventually cutting off Army Group North. This secured the northern flank of the thrust into Poland, while Ivan Konev's 1st Ukrainian Front covered the southern flank by attacking to the east of Lvov on 13 July. Army Group North Ukraine fell back to the River Bug (the 1939 border between Germany and the USSR), but not before its XIII Corps had been encircled at Brody, losing some 25,000 men. Lvov fell on 27 July.

The main attack into Poland had already begun. On 18 July Rokossovsky moved to encircle Brest-Litovsk, reaching the River Vistula at Pulawy and Magnuszew a week later. As his troops crossed the river and thrust to within 8 miles of the outskirts of Warsaw, resistance fighters of the Polish Home Army in the city rose against the German occupiers, confident that liberation was at hand. On 1 August about 40,000 fighters, led by Major-General Tadeusz Bor-Komorowski, seized key points throughout the city, only to find that the Soviets had stopped in their tracks. The reason given was that they had run out of supplies, but there is little doubt that it suited Stalin to see the Polish Home Army, containing anti-communist elements, destroyed. The Germans duly obliged, razing Warsaw in two months of bitter repression. The Soviet armies did not move beyond their bridgeheads at Pulawy, Magnuszew and, further south, around Sandomierz, until January 1944.

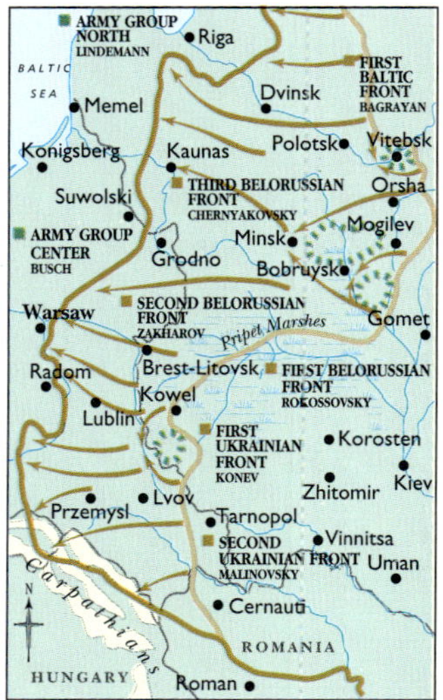

1/Operation "Bagration"
22 June –late July 1944

Russian attacks
Front line, late July
German resistance pockets

"In the village, by a house that had served the Nazis as a field hospital, she showed us a pit that had been covered over by soil. The pit was full of the bodies of little boys and girls between ten and twelve years. We learned that the Nazi butchers had used them to give blood transfusions to their wounded officers."

Russian soldier

Hands raised, units of the Polish Home Army surrender to the German occupiers. Although the western Allies had succeeded in flying supplies to the partisans, all hopes of lasting success were dashed by the failure of the Red Army to succor the insurgents.

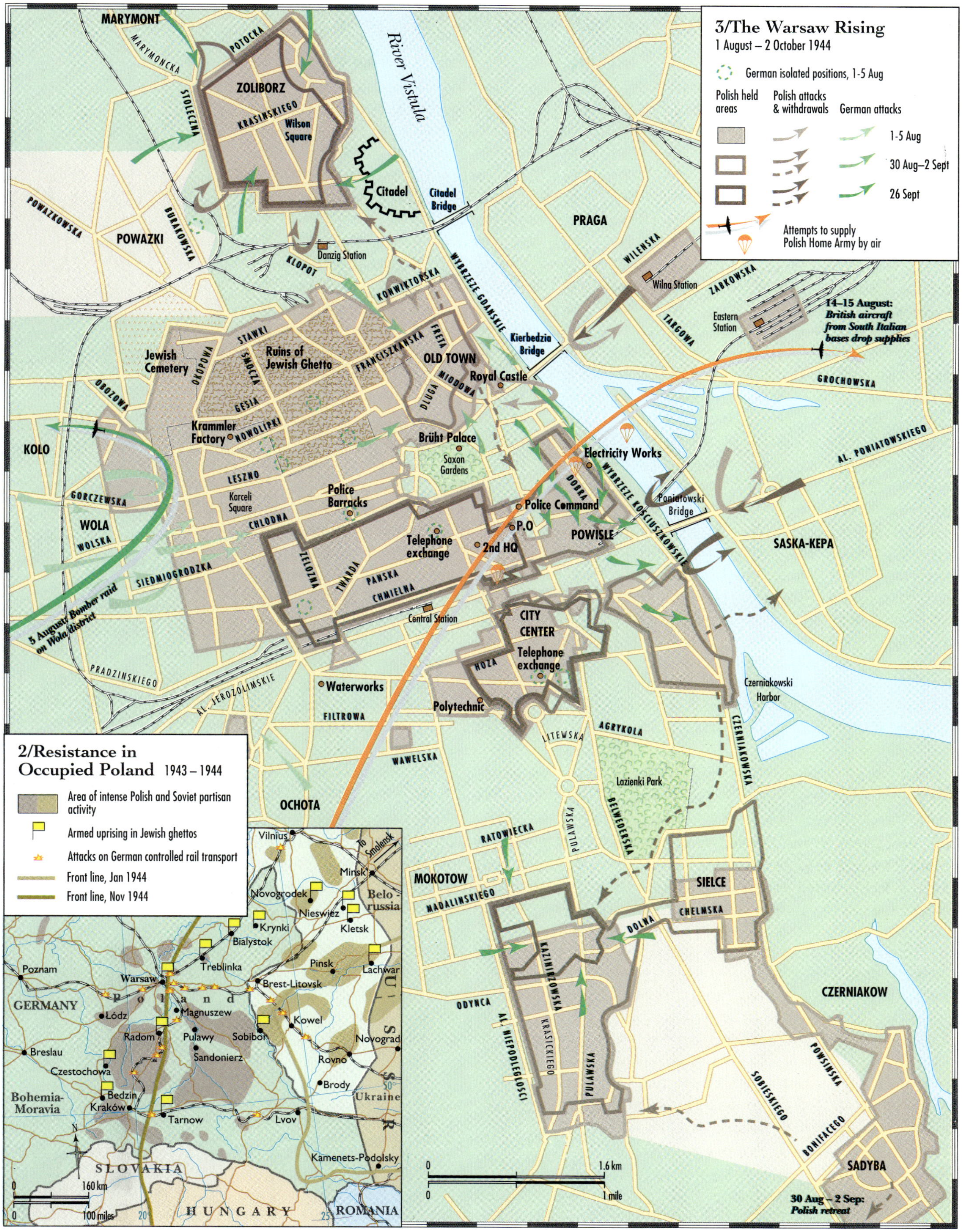
3/The Warsaw Rising
1 August – 2 October 1944
German isolated positions, 1-5 Aug
Polish held areas
Polish attacks & withdrawals
German attacks
1-5 Aug
30 Aug–2 Sept
26 Sept
Attempts to supply Polish Home Army by air
River Vistula
MARYMONT
MARYMONCKA
POTOCKA
ZOLIBORZ
STOLECZNA
KRASINSKIEGO
Wilson Square
Citadel
Citadel Bridge
PRAGA
POWAZKOWSKA
POWAZKI
BURAKOWSKA
Danzig Station
KLOPOT
KONWIKTORSKA
WYBRZEZE GDANSKIE
WILENSKA
Wilno Station
ZABKOWSKA
TARGOWA
Eastern Station
14–15 August: British aircraft from South Italian bases drop supplies
Kierbedzia Bridge
STAWKI
Jewish Cemetery
OKOPOWA
SMOCZA
Ruins of Jewish Ghetto
FRANCISZKANSKA
FRETA
OLD TOWN
MIODOWA
DLUGA
Royal Castle
GROCHOWSKA
OBOZOWA
GESIA
Krammler Factory
NOWOLIPKI
Brühl Palace
Saxon Gardens
Electricity Works
AL. PONIATOWSKIEGO
KOLO
LESZNO
Karceli Square
Police Barracks
DOBRA
WYBRZEZE KOSCIUSZKOWSKIE
Poniatowski Bridge
GORCZEWSKA
Police Command
P.O
WOLA
WOLSKA
CHLODNA
Telephone exchange
2nd HQ
POWISLE
SASKA-KEPA
ZELAZNA
TWARDA
PANSKA
CHMIELNA
SIEDMIOGRODZKA
5 August: Bomber raid on Wola district
Central Station
CITY CENTER
Telephone exchange
HOZA
PRADZINSKIEGO
AL. JEROZOLIMSKIE
Waterworks
Polytechnic
Czerniakowski Harbor
FILTROWA
LITEWSKA
AGRYKOLA
CZERNIAKOWSKA
WAWELSKA
Lazienki Park
OCHOTA
BELWEDERSKA
PULAWSKA
RATOWIECKA
MOKOTOW
SIELCE
MADALINSKIEGO
CHELMSKA
DOLNA
KAZIMIERZOWSKA
KRASICKIEGO
ODYNCA
AL. NIEPODLEGLOSCI
PULAWSKA
CZERNIAKOW
POWSINSKA
SOBIESKIEGO
BONIFACEGO
SADYBA
30 Aug – 2 Sep: Polish retreat
0 1.6 km
0 1 mile
2/Resistance in Occupied Poland 1943 – 1944
Area of intense Polish and Soviet partisan activity
Armed uprising in Jewish ghettos
Attacks on German controlled rail transport
Front line, Jan 1944
Front line, Nov 1944
Vilnius
To Smolensk
Minsk
Novogrodek
Belo-russia
Nieswiez
Kletsk
Krynki
Bialystok
Treblinka
Pinsk
Lachwar
Poznam
Warsaw
Brest-Litovsk
GERMANY
Lódz
Magnuszew
Kowel
Radom
Pulawy
Sobibor
Novograd
Breslau
Sandonierz
Rovno
Czestochowa
Brody
Bedzin
Bohemia-Moravia
Kraków
Tarnow
Lvov
Ukraine
Kamenets-Podolsky
SLOVAKIA
HUNGARY
ROMANIA
0 160 km
0 100 miles

The Balkans AUGUST – DECEMBER 1944

Soviet advances through the Ukraine in the early months of 1944 took the armies of Marshal Rodion Malinovsky's 2nd and Marshal Feodor Tolbukhin's 3rd Ukrainian Fronts to the borders of Romania. On 20 August both Fronts resumed their advance, concentrating their attentions against the Romanian Third and Fourth Armies, located at Tiraspol and Jassy respectively, on either flank of the German Sixth Army. Romanian resistance was weak, allowing the Soviets to surround the Sixth Army, inflicting enormous casualties. It was enough to trigger political change in Romania. On 23 August King Michael ordered the arrest of the pro-fascist dictator, Marshal Ion Antonescu, and tried to negotiate terms with the Allied powers. Hitler promptly sent nearly 6000 German reinforcements into Romania to force the reinstatement of Antonescu, even ordering the bombing of Bucharest, but this merely stiffened King Michael's resolve. On 26 August, he declared war on Germany and sent representatives to talk to the Allies in Cairo. They were directed instead to Moscow, Stalin and Churchill having already agreed to "carve up" the Balkans into spheres of influence, Romania being firmly within that assigned to the Soviets. King Michael's emissaries had no choice but to sign an armistice in Moscow, an action that effectively made their country a satellite of the Soviet Union.

Once this happened, Bulgaria was isolated. Ruled by a regency council on behalf of the underage king, Simon II, Bulgaria had never declared war on the Soviets, and on 26 August an attempt was made to exploit this by withdrawing from the war. Unfortunately, Stalin refused to accept such niceties and, in order to ensure Soviet occupation of Bulgaria, resolved the issue by declaring war on 5 September. This allowed Tolbukhin to send troops into Bulgaria, where they met no resistance. Three days later, the regency council (soon to be replaced by a communist government) declared war on Germany, although this did not avoid the need for an armistice with the Soviets, signed in Moscow on 28 October. With the south-eastern Balkans clear, the Soviets were now in a position to thrust west into Hungary, threatening to cut off Axis troops in Yugoslavia and Albania. Greece was to be left to the British.

But the Soviet advance into Hungary was not easy. The Regent of Hungary, Admiral Miklos Horthy, tried to pre-empt events by opening negotiations with the Soviets in October, but when Hitler heard about this he had the admiral arrested, replacing him with the fascist leader Ferenc Szalasi. He also bolstered the German defenses in Hungary, with particular emphasis on the approaches to Budapest. Thus, when Malinovsky's troops pushed into Hungary in early October, they were met by strong German forces, which fought well around Debrecen and Nyiregyhaza, defeating the armored spearheads of 2nd Ukrainian Front in a series of tank battles. Even when the Soviets brought forward reinforcements and penetrated as far as the suburbs of Budapest in early November, the defenses held. The city, effectively surrounded in December, did not fall until February 1945.

Meanwhile, Tolbukhin had advanced from Bulgaria into northern Yugoslavia, approaching Belgrade in early October. There his forces were joined by communist partisans led by Josip Broz ("Tito"), who had been fighting a ruthless guerrilla war against Axis occupiers of Yugoslavia since 1941, aided in recent months by the British-run Special Operations Executive (SOE). Belgrade fell on 20 October, by which time large tracts of southern Yugoslavia were already in Tito's hands. These events threatened to isolate General Alexander Löhr's German Army Group E in Greece and Albania, which now began to withdraw in a desperate race to escape the closing trap. Large elements were left behind on the Aegean Islands (including Crete) and others were harried mercilessly by Albanian communists under Enver Hoxha, but by mid-November Löhr had managed to make contact with Army Group F to the north of Sarajevo. As the Germans moved out of Greece in October, British troops replaced them, only to become involved in a bitter civil war, fought between communists and royalists, that was to outlast the main, global conflict.

Members of an elite Black Sea commando unit prepare for a raid behind German lines. Such highly-trained special strike units were developed by both sides during the war for use in raiding operations.

"There is an iron discipline in the Russian Army; punishment meted out by officers and political commissars is of a draconian character and unquestioned obedience to orders has become a feature of their military system."

General von Mellenthin

A Romanian soldier surrenders to sailors of the Soviet Black Sea Fleet. Romanian resistance was, at best, half-hearted since many Romanians had long been disenchanted with the alliance with Nazi Germany. Soon the Germans found themselves fighting, not only the Russians, but their erstwhile allies as well.

The Drive into the Balkans
8 August – 15 December 1944

- Soviet attacks to mid September
- Front line, mid September
- Soviet attacks to mid December
- Front line, mid December
- Romanian and Bulgarian advances (after both countries change allegiance)
- German counterattacks
- German withdrawls
- Remaining pockets of German resistance

Bombing of Germany AUGUST 1943 – APRIL 1944

Despite the fact that Hamburg was hit by RAF and USAAF bombers, by night and day respectively, in late July 1943, co-operation between the two air forces was the exception rather than the norm. As early as January 1943, at the Casablanca Conference of Allied leaders, a common aim was laid down for the bomber offensive, stressing the "progressive destruction and dislocation of the German military, industrial and economic system and the undermining of the morale of the German people", but British and American views about how to achieve this differed radically. Air Marshal Arthur Harris, C-in-C of RAF Bomber Command, believed that night area bombing was the only way to ensure success, while his counterparts in the USAAF favored daylight precision raids to guarantee the destruction of worthwhile targets. In June 1943 the Combined Chiefs of Staff acknowledged this dichotomy when they issued the "Pointblank Directive": henceforth, the RAF was to continue bombing cities while the USAAF concentrated on more precise targets such as aircraft factories and oil installations. Both found the going hard.

The Americans began their "Pointblank" offensive on 1 August 1943, when 178 B-24 Liberators of the Ninth USAAF flew from Benghazi in North Africa to attack oilfields at Ploesti in Romania. It was an ambitious move, involving a round trip of more than 2700 miles, much of it over Axis-occupied territory. A sobering total of 53 bombers failed to return, having experienced a combination of bad weather, fighters and anti-aircraft guns. The oil refineries at Ploesti suffered little damage.

A similar disaster occurred on 17 August, when 376 B-17 Flying Fortresses of the Eighth USAAF tried to destroy an aircraft assembly works at Regensburg and ball-bearing factories at Schweinfurt, in Bavaria. The plan was to attack in two waves, the first of which, comprising 146 B17s, would hit Regensburg and then fly on to Allied bases in North Africa, after which the second, comprising 230 bombers, would take advantage of disruption to enemy defenses and concentrate on Schweinfurt before returning to England. Timing was the key – the second wave had to arrive as German fighters were on the ground refueling – but poor weather over England delayed the Schweinfurt force and allowed the enemy to recover. The Regensburg force lost 24 bombers, but failed to divert German attention. Thus, when the Schweinfurt force eventually arrived over occupied Europe, it met enemy fighters head-on; in a series of running battles, 36 Flying Fortresses were shot down. A second raid, on 14 October 1943 – this time just against Schweinfurt – fared little better: 291 B-17s took off, of which 60 failed to return. Neither raid stopped the production of ball-bearings.

Such crippling losses convinced the Americans that the "self-defending" bomber was a myth. What was needed if daylight raids were to continue was fighter escort all the way to the target, and this was not provided until late 1943, when the P-51D Mustang, fitted with a Rolls-Royce Merlin engine, became available. Even then, the problem of poor weather could not be solved, and although more successful raids were mounted in early 1944, not least against Berlin, it was obvious that the Americans were still struggling to achieve success.

The same was true of the British. In fall 1943, Harris tried to persuade his American allies that a combined offensive against Berlin, with night raids being followed by daylight attacks, would cripple Germany. They remained unconvinced, forcing Harris to go it alone. On 18 November the first of 16 major raids on the German capital was mounted, but casualties were heavy. Between November 1943 and March 1944 Bomber Command lost 1047 aircraft over Germany, 95 of them in a single raid on Nuremberg on 30/31 March. German defenses were still effective and the impact on German industry and morale was not decisive. Despite vehement opposition from the commanders of both the British and American bomber fleets, it was decided to divert the bulk of the heavy bombers to support of the D-Day landings. On 1 April 1944, the pressure on Germany was eased. It would not be renewed until August.

> *"I'm afraid these air raids are now such a mix-up of attack and counterattack that one can never fix the blame fairly and squarely. This is now a total war, and woe to the one who loses it. It will be total destruction."*
>
> Else Wendel, German housewife

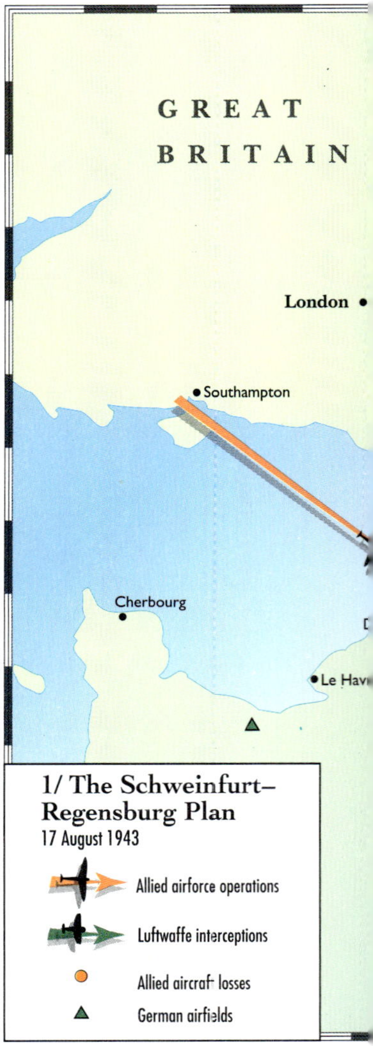

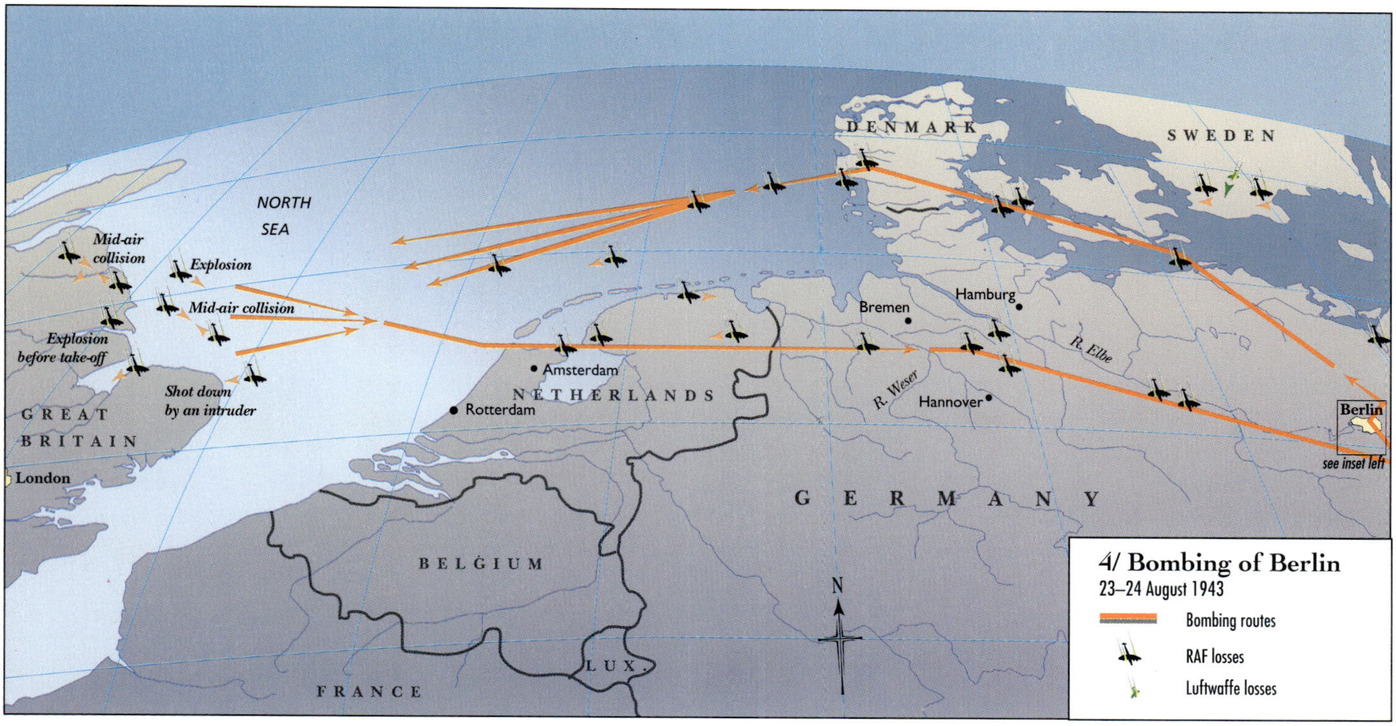
4/ Bombing of Berlin
23–24 August 1943
Bombing routes
RAF losses
Luftwaffe losses
NORTH SEA
Mid-air collision
Explosion
Mid-air collision
Explosion before take-off
Shot down by an intruder
GREAT BRITAIN
London
DENMARK
SWEDEN
Hamburg
Bremen
R. Elbe
R. Weser
Hannover
Amsterdam
Rotterdam
NETHERLANDS
Berlin
see inset left
GERMANY
BELGIUM
LUX.
FRANCE
N

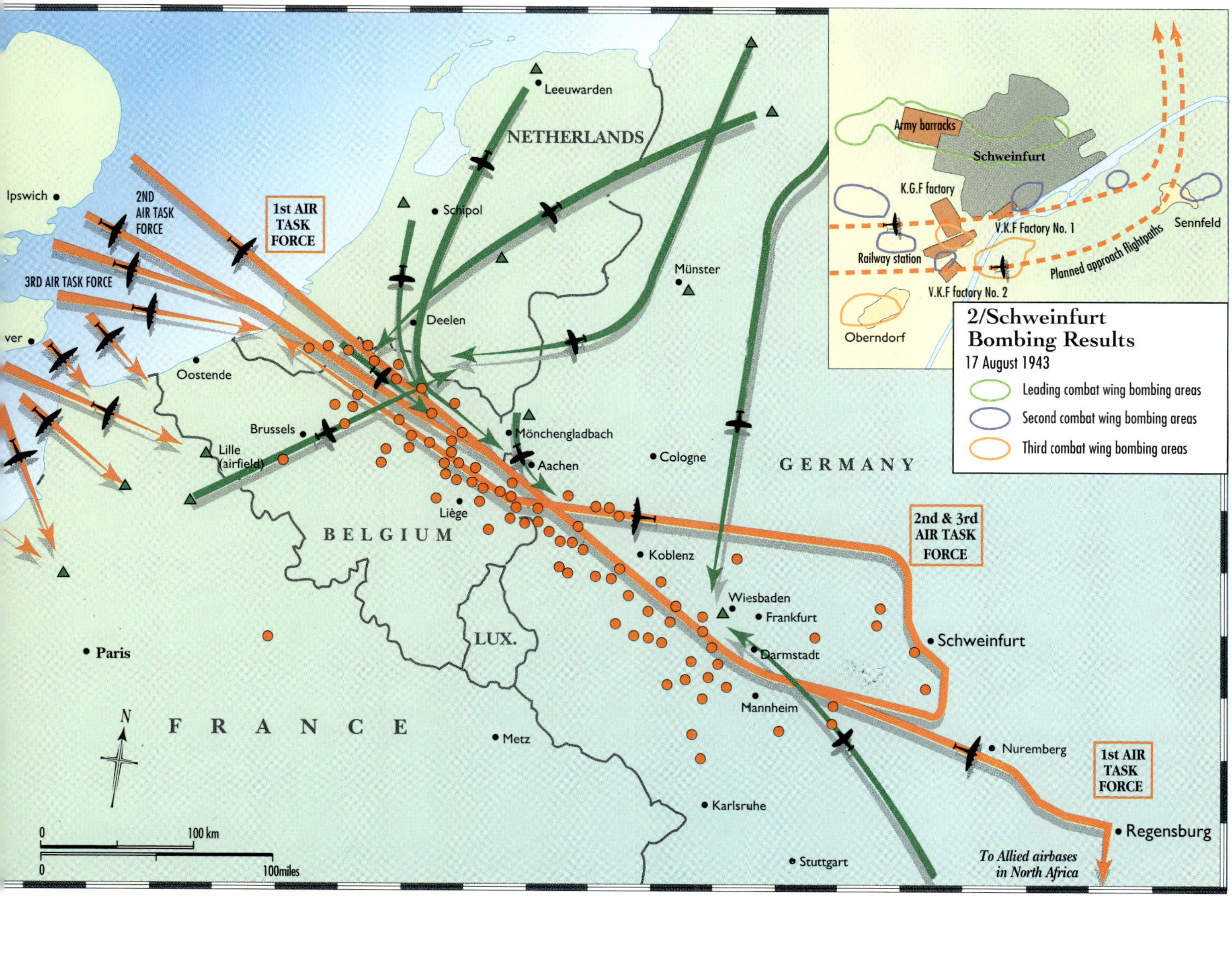
2/Schweinfurt Bombing Results
17 August 1943
Leading combat wing bombing areas
Second combat wing bombing areas
Third combat wing bombing areas
Army barracks
Schweinfurt
K.G.F factory
V.K.F Factory No. 1
Railway station
V.K.F factory No. 2
Planned approach flightpaths
Sennfeld
Oberndorf
Ipswich
2ND AIR TASK FORCE
3RD AIR TASK FORCE
1st AIR TASK FORCE
Leeuwarden
NETHERLANDS
Schipol
Deelen
Münster
Oostende
Brussels
Lille (airfield)
Mönchengladbach
Aachen
Cologne
GERMANY
Liège
BELGIUM
Koblenz
2nd & 3rd AIR TASK FORCE
Wiesbaden
Frankfurt
Darmstadt
Schweinfurt
Paris
LUX.
Mannheim
FRANCE
Metz
Nuremberg
1st AIR TASK FORCE
Karlsruhe
Regensburg
Stuttgart
To Allied airbases in North Africa
N
0
100 km
0
100miles

Planning Overlord MARCH 1941 – MAY 1944

As early as June 1940 Prime Minister Winston Churchill displayed his intention to resume the offensive against the Germans, when he called for the creation of "specially trained troops of the hunter class" whose job it would be to raid the enemy-occupied coast of Europe. Known as the Special Service Brigade, these troops were organized into 500-strong "commandos" under Admiral of the Fleet Sir Roger Keyes. At the same time, parachute forces were raised, with much the same intention.

Commando raids began immediately, although their impact was small. Techniques took time to perfect and it was not until 4 March 1941, when 500 men landed on the Lofoten Islands off Norway's north-western coast to destroy fuel stores, that success was achieved. The appointment of Lord Louis Montbatten as Chief of Combined Operations in October 1941, replacing Keyes, gave extra impetus to the raiding groups; on 27 December, commandos landed on Vaagso and Maalo in Norway, and on the night of 27/28 February 1942 paratroopers captured a German radar set at Bruneval, on the northern coast of France, bringing it back to England for investigation. On 26 March, commandos accompanied the destroyer HMS *Campbeltown* to St Nazaire to destroy the only dry-dock close to the Atlantic that was capable of accommodating German battleships. Each raid was valuable in terms of experience, although casualties were not always light: out of 611 commandos and sailors committed to St Nazaire, for example, 397 failed to return.

At least St Nazaire was a success. On 19 August 1942 the most ambitious raid so far attempted – an Anglo-Canadian amphibious assault on the French port of Dieppe, designed to test techniques and gather intelligence about German defenses – ended in disaster. Commandos ordered to destroy a gun battery to the east of Dieppe encountered an enemy convoy before they landed, alerting German sentries, and although another gun battery in the west was seized, the main assault on Dieppe failed. Canadian troops met stubborn reistance as they landed at Puys and Pourville, from where they were supposed to capture headlands overlooking the port, and when the landings directly in front of Dieppe went in, the attackers came under terrifying fire. A small number of Churchill tanks got ashore, but the Germans had blocked all roads leading from the beaches. After less than six hours the commander of the raiding force, the Canadian Major-General John Hamilton Roberts, ordered the survivors to withdraw. Some 300 Canadians were picked up but the rest were either killed or captured. Altogether, the Dieppe operation cost 1027 dead and 2340 captured out of a force of 6100 men. The raid proved how foolish it was to attack a defended port head-on.

This lesson was important as the Allies planned for a more permanent return to the continent, an operation (codenamed *Overlord*) that was essential if the Germans were to be defeated. In March 1943 the British Major-General Frederick Morgan was appointed COSSAC (Chief of Staff to the Supreme Allied Commander), and directed to put together pre-

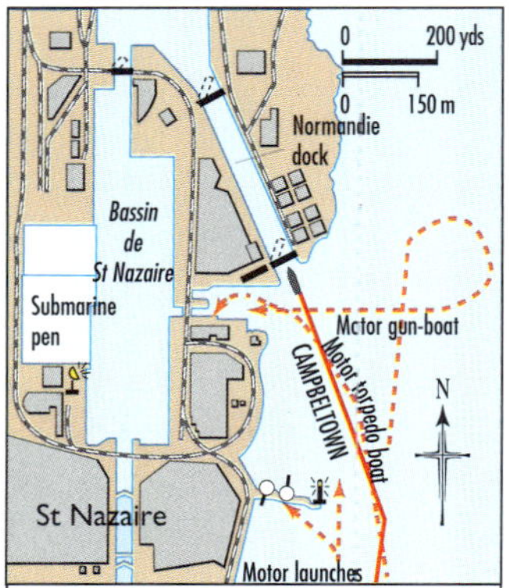

1/Raid on St Nazaire
28 March 1942
Track of HMS Campbeltown
Track of assault teams

"This operation will be the primary United States-British ground and air effort against the Axis in Europe."

Report of the Chiefs of Staff, First Quebec Conference, August 1943

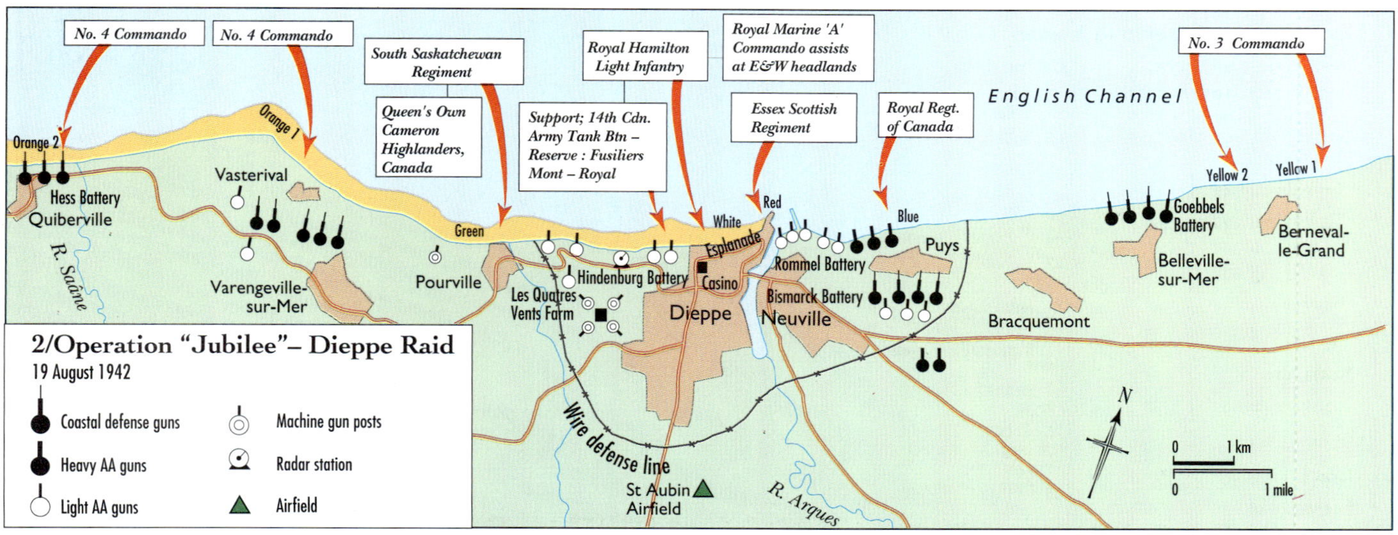

2/Operation "Jubilee"– Dieppe Raid
19 August 1942
Coastal defense guns
Heavy AA guns
Light AA guns
Machine gun posts
Radar station
Airfield

liminary plans, with a provisional launch-date of 1 May 1944. Using intelligence gathered from the French Resistance and from air reconnaissance, he finally chose the coast of Normandy as the site for the invasion – other areas, such as the Pas de Calais, were known to be too well defended – and, by June 1943, he had sketched out a plan that would involve assault landings by three infantry divisions with airborne flank support. In December, General Dwight D. Eisenhower was appointed Supreme Allied Commander, with General Sir Bernard Montgomery in charge of the actual landings, and they insisted on increasing the size of the assault to five divisions, each landing on a specific beach – Americans in the west (Utah and Omaha) and Anglo-Canadians in the east (Gold, Juno and Sword) – still with airborne support. A massive naval fleet, including over 200 warships, was made available and, from 1 April 1944, Allied heavy bombers were diverted to operations related to *Overlord*. At the same time, nearly two million soldiers, with all their supplies and equipment, were gathered in southern England and special training exercises carried out. As the Germans, confused by deception operations codenamed *Fortitude*, waited, the date was put back to 5 June 1944. All that was needed was Eisenhower's decision to go ahead.

British commandos train in the Scottish countryside prior to the commencement of their operations against German installations.

D-Day 6 JUNE 1944

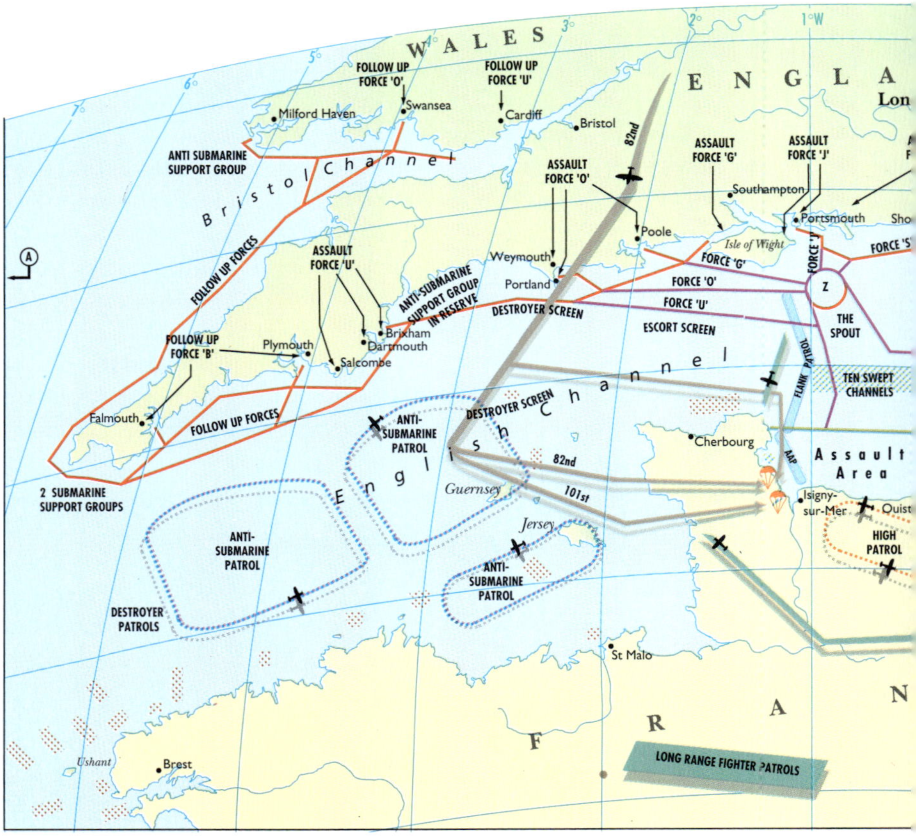

By 1 June 1944, Allied forces tasked with mounting an invasion of the Normandy coast were ready to go. The Supreme Commander, General Dwight D. Eisenhower, had done all he could to prepare his men, but he could not control the weather. On 4 June, meteorologists reported heavy seas and rain, and the landings, scheduled for 5 June, were postponed for 24 hours. On 5 June, after reports that there was a brief period of better weather on the way, Eisenhower reluctantly ordered the assault to begin the following day. It was a huge gamble.

As the invasion fleet, carrying men of Lieutenant-General Omar Bradley's U.S. First and Lieutenant-General Miles Dempsey's Anglo-Canadian Second Armies, left ports in England, the *Overlord* plan swung into action. During the night of 5/6 June the French Resistance sabotaged German communications, while Anglo-American airborne troops prepared to secure the flanks of the assault area. The first to land, at 12.16 a.m. on 6 June, were British glider troops, who seized key bridges over the River Orne and Caen Canal, in the east. They were followed by paratroopers – men of the U.S. 82nd and 101st Airborne Divisions in the west and of the British 6th Airborne Division in the east – under orders to destroy German defensive positions and prevent troop movements. Although dispersed by high winds, the airborne soldiers confused the enemy, who were convinced that any invasion would take place in the Pas de Calais. As dawn approached and glider-borne reinforcements arrived, US paratroopers secured Ste Mère-Église, to the rear of Utah beach, and British paratroopers destroyed a gun battery at Merville, overlooking Sword.

By then, the invasion fleet was offshore. At 5.30 a.m., over 2000 Allied warships began a bombardment of the coast, while aircraft closed in to hit more precise targets. An hour later, troops of the U.S. 4th Infantry Division left their landing ships to secure Utah beach, at the base of the Cotentin Peninsula, on the extreme right of the assault area. They landed in the wrong place because of strong currents offshore, but this turned out to be an advantage. German resistance was weak, enabling the Americans to push inland to link up with parachutists in Ste Mère-Église. To their east, however, landing craft containing men of the U.S. 1st Infantry Division, tasked with securing Omaha beach, were disrupted by heavy seas and, when the troops landed at just before 7 a.m. they encountered stiff opposition from the German 352nd Division. Casualties mounted alarmingly and it looked as if Omaha might have to be abandoned. The tide of battle only began to turn when destroyers were brought close inshore to bombard enemy positions and small groups of determined Americans fought their way beyond the sea-wall. By 10 a.m. routes inland had been secured, at the cost of nearly 3000 Americans killed or wounded on "Bloody Omaha".

Meanwhile, Anglo-Canadians had landed further east. On Gold beach, men of the 50th (Northumbrian) Division landed at 7.25 a.m., encountering heavy opposition in Le Hamel before pushing through to the outskirts of Bayeux. To their left, Canadians and British Commandos on Juno beach had to fight to establish a foothold, although by the afternoon of D-Day lead elements had broken through toward Caen. Finally, on the extreme left, men of the British 3rd Infantry Division, with Commando support, took Sword beach and linked up with airborne troops on the Caen Canal. By nightfall, the Allies had over 150,000 troops ashore. The Germans, caught by surprise, had killed less than 2500 of the invaders. It was a major Allied success.

Airborne troops file into transport aircraft and gliders late on 5 June. In the early hours of the next morning, before the seaborne attack, they were to destroy batteries and bridges along a 60-mile (100-kilometer) stretch of the Normandy coast.

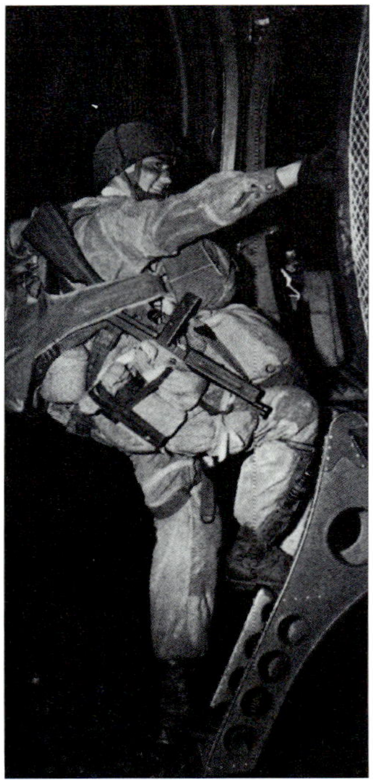

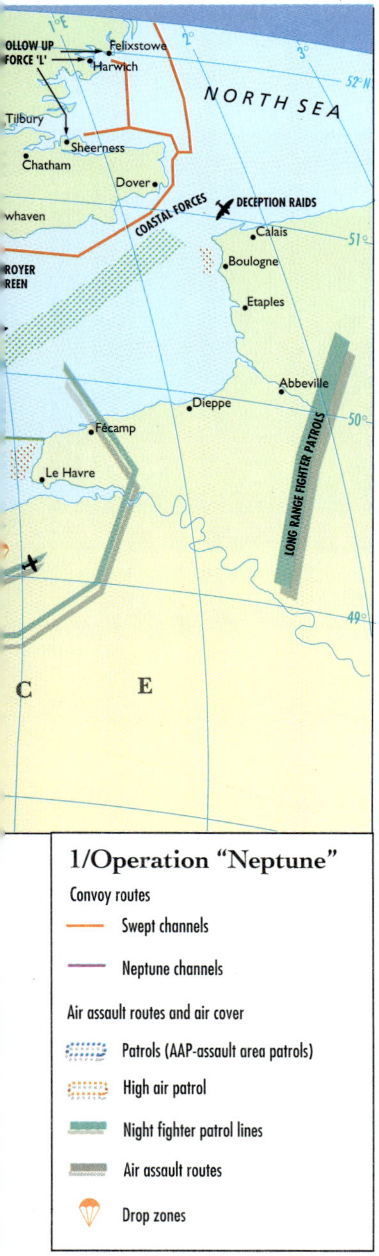

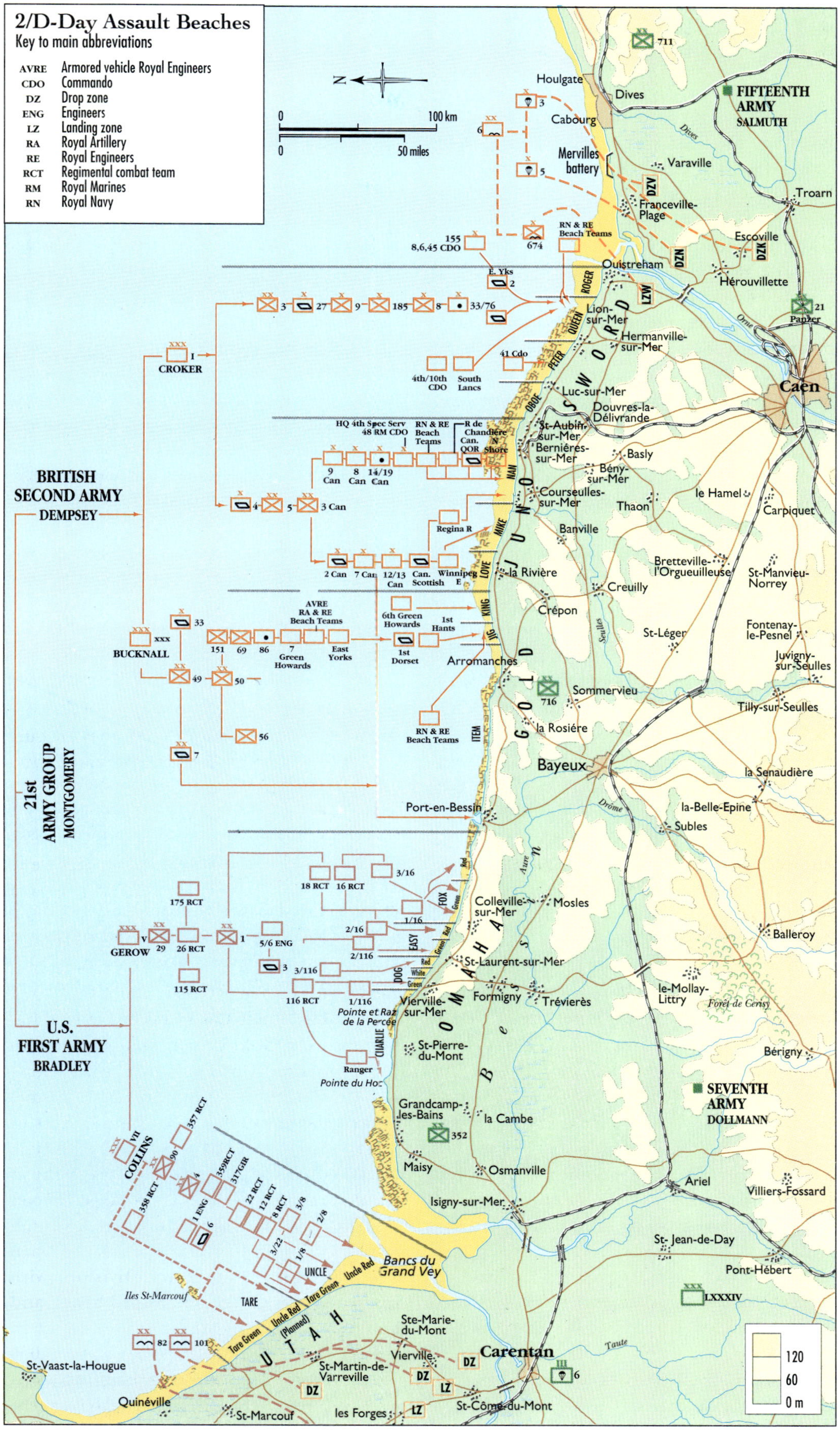

"As we moved in toward the land in the gray early light, the 36 ft coffin-shaped steel boat took solid green sheets of water that fell on the helmeted heads of the troops packed shoulder to shoulder in the stiff, awkward, uncomfortable, lonely companionship of men going to battle."

Ernest Hemingway,
American reporter and novelist

Battle for Normandy JUNE – JULY 1944

Despite success on 6 June, some D-Day objectives had not been taken. Chief among these was the town of Caen, vital as a center of communications. British troops had approached it late on 6 June but German defenses had proved too strong. On the opposition flank, the Americans needed to take the port of Cherbourg. If the Allies were to win they must secure a port which would enable them to build up their forces faster than the Germans. Two prefabicated "Mulberry" harbors were already being put together, one off the American beaches and one off the British, but they were regarded as temporary measures only.

As efforts were made to link the D-Day beaches together (something that took until 12 June), German reinforcements concentrated their efforts against the British and Canadians. This allowed the Americans from Omaha to move inland and those from Utah to push west, across the Cotentin Peninsula. They reached the west coast at Barneville on 18 June, after which VII Corps advanced towards Cherbourg. A break-in was achieved by 25 June, and the last enemy fortress fell four days later. By then, the Germans had demolished the port facilities and a storm on 18 June had destroyed the American Mulberry. To cap it all, as U.S. forces moved south they entered difficult "hedgerow" country (bocage) and became bogged down.

Meanwhile, battles raged around Caen. On 13 June a British attempt to exploit a gap in German defenses along the River Aure, was stopped at Villers-Bocage. As more German reinforcements arrived, General Montgomery, commanding all land forces in Normandy, ordered a concerted effort (codenamed Operation *Epsom*) into the Odon River valley, to the south-west of Caen. The assault, by men of Lieutenant-General Sir Richard O'Connor's VIII Corps, began on 26 June after a massive artillery bombardment. Despite stiff opposition, British units managed to cross the River Odon on 28 June and seize Hill 112. Two days later, however, O'Connor was ordered to pull back. Intercepted German signals had indicated that overwhelming enemy reinforcements were on their way.

Montgomery decided to shift emphasis to a direct attack on Caen. On 7 July heavy bombers pounded the town as a preliminary to Operation *Charnwood*. Canadian and British troops moved forward on 8 July, but losses were heavy. *Charnwood* was called off after 48 hours, with only the northern part of the town in Allied hands. This left the area to the east of Caen as the only remaining avenue of advance, using the bridgehead to the east of the River Orne, seized by British paratroopers on 6 June, as the concentration area. Montgomery, under increasing pressure to escape an attritional campaign, ordered O'Connor's corps, comprising three armored divisions, to attack from Ranville to take the Bourguébus Ridge (Operation *Goodwood*), opening the route to Falaise. At the same time, U.S. forces in the west mounted a major attack toward Avranches (Operation *Cobra*).

Major-General Karl-Wilhelm von Schlieben, commander of the 16,000-strong garrison at Cherbourg, arrives at U.S. Army headquarters to surrender to Lieutenant-General "Lightnin' Joe" Collins.

"They wish to hell they were someplace else, and they wish to hell they would get relief. They wish to hell the mud was dry and they wish to hell their coffee was hot. They want to go home. But they stay in their wet holes and fight, and then they climb out and crawl through minefields and fight some more."

Bill Mauldin, war artist

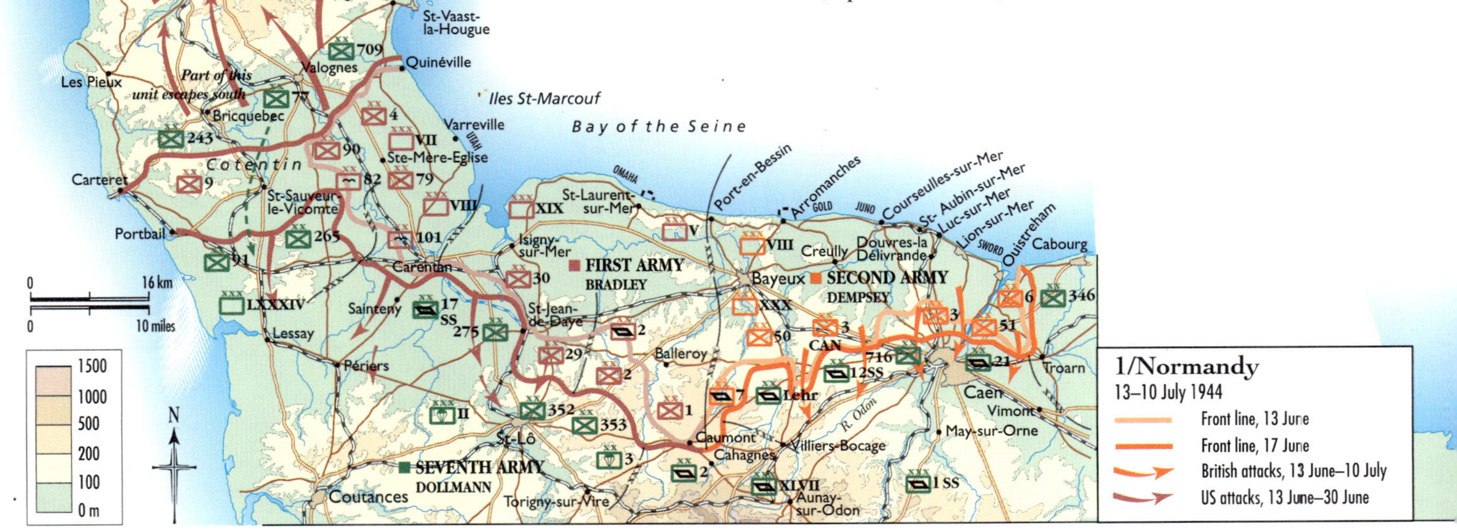

Goodwood was not a success. After air and artillery bombardments, the lead armored units advanced early on 18 July into an area heavily defended by the Germans. The armor, denied infantry support, was massacred by Tiger tanks and 88mm anti-tank guns. By the time the offensive was called off on the 20th, the British had lost over 400 tanks. The only consolation was that German attention had been diverted away from *Cobra* in the west.

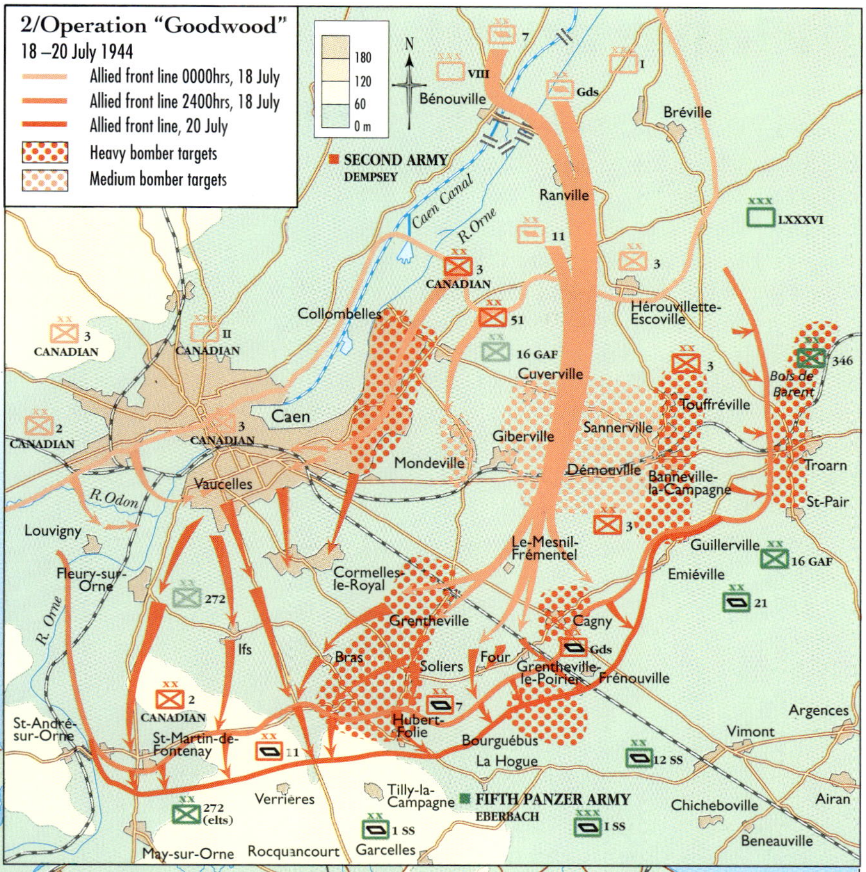

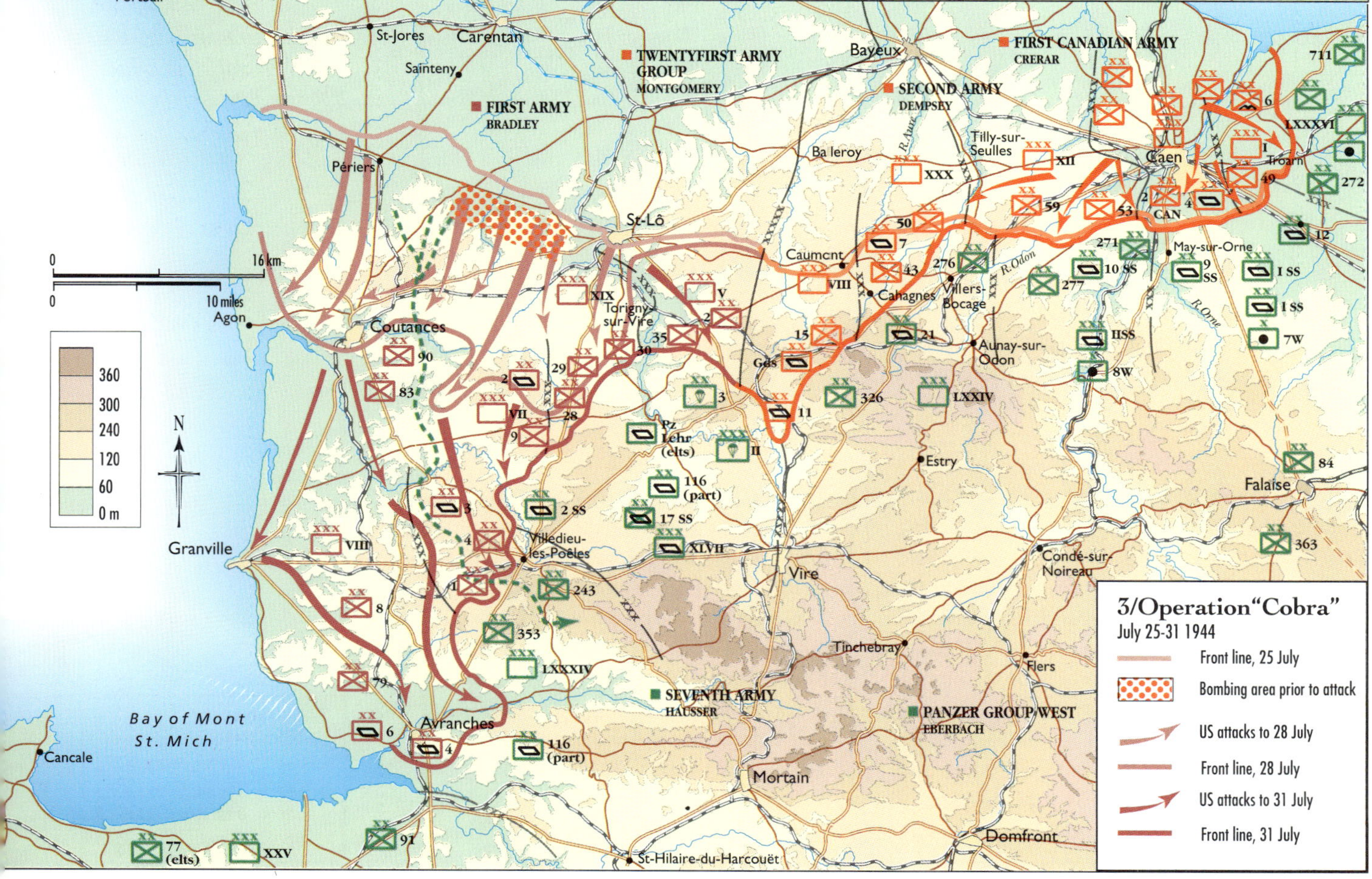

Falaise and Liberation of Paris AUGUST 1944

Lieutenant-General Omar Bradley, commanding the U.S. First Army, had been preparing for Operation *Cobra* – a breakout to the south through Avranches – since early July. His plan was for a general advance toward a line running from Coutances to St Lô and Caumont, after which a concentrated drive for Avranches would begin. It proved to be a difficult business. Although Anglo-Canadian efforts around Caen diverted German forces away from the American sector, Bradley's men found themselves fighting through a nightmare of sunken lanes and thick hedges. By 14 July, having suffered nearly 10,000 casualties in 12 days, the American advance had stalled. St Lô was not taken until 18 July, and by the 24th – projected date for *Cobra* – Coutances was still in enemy hands and the weather was deteriorating. Bradley postponed the operation until the 25th.

When *Cobra* finally began, it did not enjoy initial success. However, the enemy was beginning to crack. Command changes, occasioned when Hitler sacked Rundstedt as C-in-C West on 1 July, had been exacerbated on the 17th when Rommel, commanding Army Group B, was badly injured in an Allied air attack. The attempted assassination of the Führer on 20 July did nothing to help, leading to widespread "purges" of officers suspected of involvement. In addition, Rundstedt's replacement, Field Marshal Hans von Kluge, was convinced that the Allied breakout would come in the east, around Caen, and refused to send reinforcements to face the Americans. Thus, although the early stages of *Cobra* were hard, a breakthrough did occur. As U.S. forces pushed toward Coutances from the north, others came in from the north-east and threatened encirclement. The town fell on 28 July, opening a route onto more open ground.

Avranches was taken on 30 July, allowing Bradley to release Patton's newly arrived Third Army for a drive into the Brittany Peninsula. Almost immediately, as it became apparent that Patton was advancing away from the main German armies, Bradley (now commanding the U.S. 12th Army Group) refined his strategy. On 3 August he ordered Patton to send part of his army east from Rennes, aiming for Orléans and the River Seine, south of Paris. Hitler's insistence that Kluge mount an ill-fated counterattack at Mortain, to the east of Avranches, on 6 August meant that Patton encountered little opposition. German armies in Normandy faced a massive encirclement.

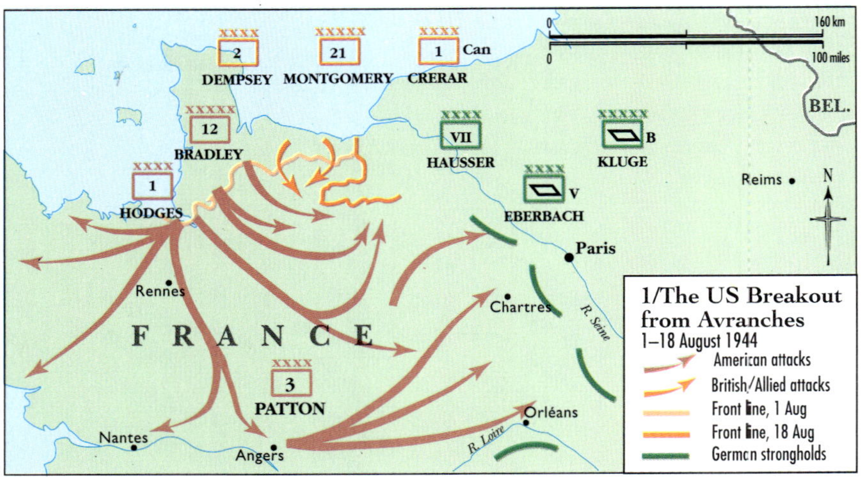

1/The US Breakout from Avranches
1–18 August 1944

Meanwhile, as the Anglo-Canadians south of Caen pushed toward Falaise, the possibility arose of a smaller – but potentially decisive – encirclement. On 8 August Patton was ordered to send troops north from Le Mans to seize Argentan before linking up with Montgomery's newly activated 21st Army Group (comprising the British Second and Canadian First Armies). Argentan fell on 12 August, but Montgomery's men failed to break through. On the 14th Polish and Canadian tanks charged German positions to approach Falaise. The town eventually fell on the 16th. By then the Germans were aware of the pocket that was emerging around Falaise and were pulling back. The neck of the pocket was not closed until 20 August, trapping about 60,000 enemy troops. Hit by air attack and artillery barrages, over 10,000 Germans died. The rest surrendered, leaving the Allies free to advance beyond the Normandy area.

The Supreme Allied Commander, General Eisenhower, ordered his forces to cross the Seine, bypassing Paris. Free French units, part of Bradley's command, refused to accept this, particularly when news came through of a rising in Paris which had begun on 19 August. Under orders from General Charles de Gaulle, Major-General Jacques Philippe Leclerc's 2nd Armored Division set off for the capital, defying the Americans and forcing them to follow. Late on 24 August the first of Leclerc's tanks arrived in the center of Paris. Less than 24 hours later, the German garrison surrendered. There was little left to halt the Allied advance.

2/The Falaise Pocket
13–20 August 1944

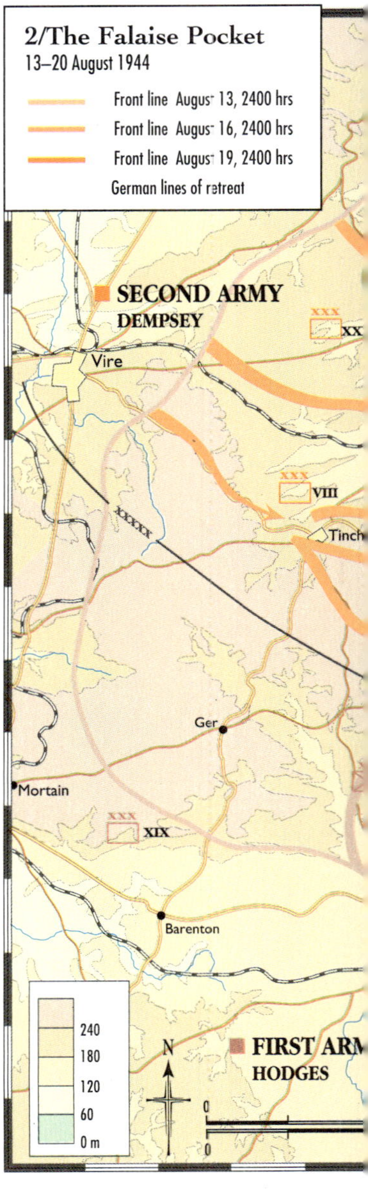

3/The Liberation of Paris and Advance into Belgium
25 August–15 September 1944
American attacks
British/Allied attacks
160 km
100 miles
N
U K
Southampton
Portsmouth
Brighton
English Channel
Dover
Dunkirk
Calais
Boulogne sur Mer
Ostend
Ghent
Antwerp
Brussels
BELGIUM
Liège
Aachen
BRANDENBERGER
OB WEST
RUNDSTEDT
GERMANY
Lille
Tournai
Douai
Arras
Valenciennes
Charleroi
Cambrai
Abbeville
St Quentin
Dieppe
Amiens
CRERAR (Can)
Charleville Mézières
LUX.
Luxembourg
BLASKOWITZ
Siegfried Line
Laon
Thionville
Metz
Cherbourg
Jersey
Le Havre
Rouen
Caen
DEMPSEY
Beauvais
Soissons
Reims
R. Meuse
Caumont
Coutances
St Lô
Lisieux
R. Seine
Evreux
Paris
Château Thierry
Châlons-sur-Marne
KNOBELSDORFF
Brest
Morlaix
St Malo
St Brieuc
Avranches
MONTGOMERY
Dreux
Nancy
Strasbourg
R. Marne
ATLANTIC OCEAN
Quimper
SIMPSON
Alençon
Chartres
Fontainebleau
R. Moselle
MANTEUFEL
R. Rhine
Rennes
Laval
FRANCE
HODGES
Troyes
Chaumont
Colmar
SHAEF
EISENHOWER
le Mans
Orléans
Auxerre
WIESE
Lorient
Vannes
Blois
R. Loire
Belfort
Basel
St Nazaire
Angers
Tours
Belle Ile
Nantes
Cholet
BRADLEY
Vierzon
PATTON
Dijon
Besançon
Bourges
Berne

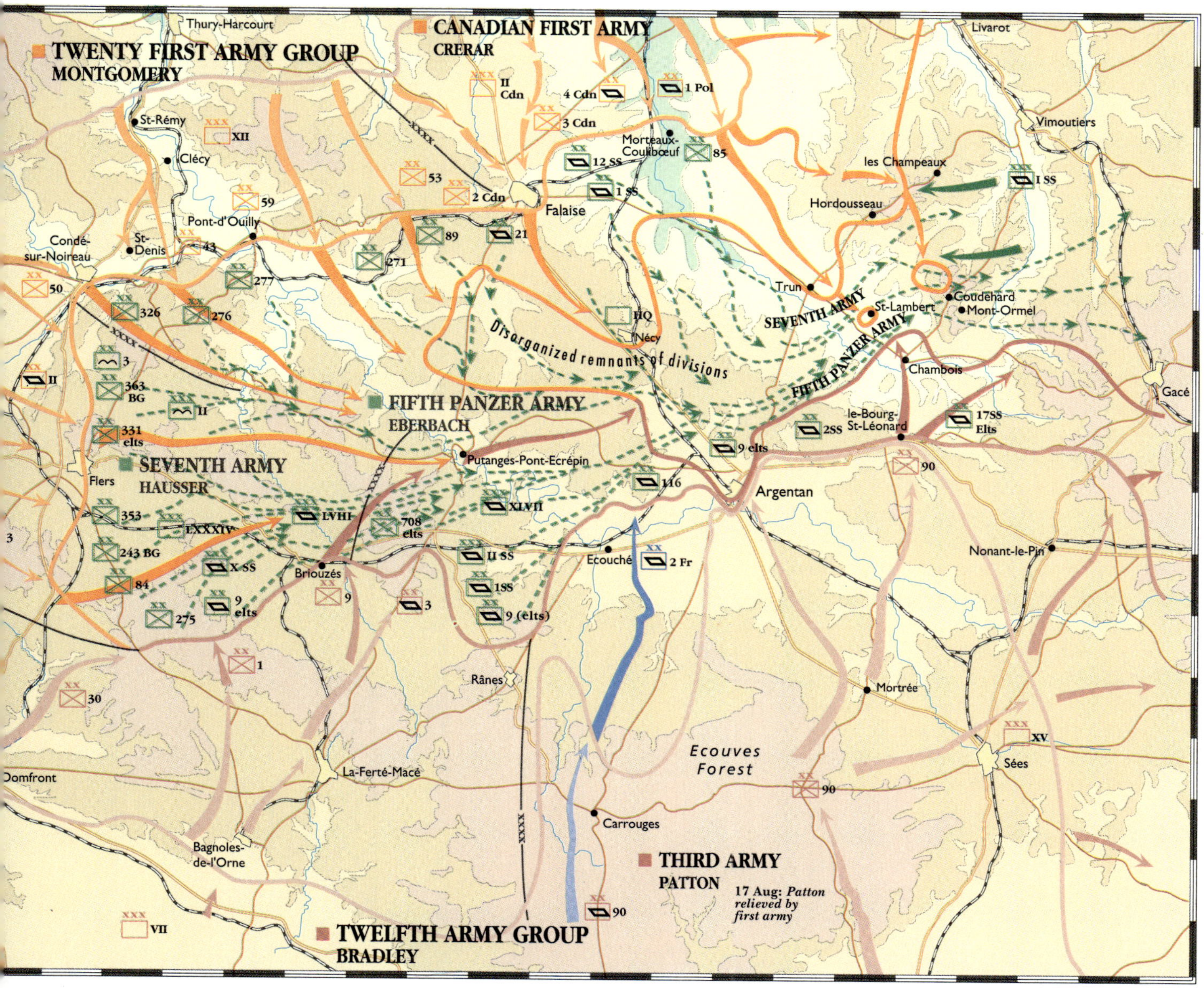
Thury-Harcourt
TWENTY FIRST ARMY GROUP
MONTGOMERY
CANADIAN FIRST ARMY
CRERAR
Livarot
II Cdn
4 Cdn
1 Pol
St-Rémy
XII
3 Cdn
Clécy
Morteaux-Coulibœuf
85
12 SS
Vimoutiers
les Champeaux
I SS
53
2 Cdn
Falaise
1 SS
59
Pont-d'Ouilly
Hordousseau
Condé-sur-Noireau
St-Denis
43
89
21
271
277
Trun
50
326
276
HQ
Nécy
SEVENTH ARMY
St-Lambert
Coudehard
Mont-Ormel
Disorganized remnants of divisions
FIFTH PANZER ARMY
Chambois
363 BG
II
FIFTH PANZER ARMY
EBERBACH
Gacé
le-Bourg-St-Léonard
17SS Elts
331 elts
2SS
9 elts
Putanges-Pont-Ecrépin
SEVENTH ARMY
HAUSSER
90
Flers
116
Argentan
353
LXXXIV
LVIII
XLVII
708 elts
243 BG
X SS
II SS
Ecouché
2 Fr
Nonant-le-Pin
84
Briouzés
9 elts
275
1SS
9 (elts)
Rânes
Mortrée
30
XV
Ecouves Forest
Sées
Domfront
La-Ferté-Macé
90
Carrouges
Bagnoles-de-l'Orne
THIRD ARMY
PATTON
17 Aug: Patton relieved by first army
VII
TWELFTH ARMY GROUP
BRADLEY

Operation Dragoon AUGUST – SEPTEMBER 1944

When Allied planners first looked at the problem of liberating France in early 1943, they recognized that if more than one invasion took place, German defenses would be split. The original plan therefore envisaged the main assault in northern France (*Overlord*) taking place at the same time as a subsidiary attack in the south, along the Mediterranean coast. The latter was codenamed Operation *Anvil*.

But the British, aware that an advance in Italy would open up routes into Austria and the Balkans, saw *Anvil* as an unnecessary diversion of resources. By comparison, the Americans were enthusiastic, largely because *Anvil* promised large territorial gains for little cost. As it was the Americans who dominated the alliance, Prime Minister Winston Churchill had no choice but to agree. His reluctance was reflected in a new codename: *Anvil* was dropped and replaced by *Dragoon*, chiefly because Churchill felt he had been "dragooned" into it.

Even then, the practicalities of mounting two simultaneous amphibious operations proved too much. A shortage of landing craft forced a postponement of *Dragoon* until after *Overlord* had begun. In addition, there was a shortage of available Allied reserves and three experienced U.S. infantry divisions (the 3rd, 36th and 45th) were withdrawn from Italy to carry out the attack. Together with a mixed Anglo-American airborne division and elements of the Free French, they would land on beaches between Cannes and Cavalaire before thrusting west toward Toulon and Marseilles. Once the latter had been taken, a more general advance north would be made, following the valley of the River Rhône toward Dijon and Belfort, where links would be forged with U.S. troops pushing south-east from the Normandy area.

The invasion fleet, comprising 880 ships, gathered in Naples in early August 1944, by which time Allied air forces had begun to soften up German defenses, manned by units of Lieutenant-General Friedrich Wiese's Nineteenth Army, along the Riviera. Just after 4 a.m. on 15 August, Allied airborne troops dropped through fog to take the village of Le Muy, 25 miles west of Cannes, while French commandos seized the offshore islands of Port Cros and Levant. A naval bombardment paved the way for the main assault, carried out by the U.S. divisions against minimal opposition. By the end of the day, 94,000 men and 11,000 vehicles were ashore, the parachutists at Le Muy had been relieved and the first of the Free French formations were in the process of landing. The Germans had already begun to pull back.

The Allies made spectacular gains. By 28 August the Free French had liberated Toulon and Marseilles and were approaching Avignon. To the east, men of the U.S. 36th Division (of Patch's Seventh Army) had taken Gap and were pushing west towards Montélimar, hoping to trap the retreating Germans. They did not succeed, but their actions did hasten the German withdrawal, allowing the French, with the U.S. 3rd and 45th Divisions, to advance quickly along the Rhône. Meanwhile, Allied airborne troops on the right flank had approached the Italian frontier, taking Nice on 30 August.

Patch attempted a second trap, sending the 36th Division to Grenoble and then to the north of Lyons, but Wiese was too quick for him. Joined by troops retreating from western France, Wiese pulled back to the Belfort Gap between the Vosges and Jura Mountains, reaching comparative safety by early September. By then, Patton's U.S. Third Army was approaching the same area and, on 12 September, he and Patch linked up. *Dragoon* had achieved much, destroying the bulk of the German Nineteenth Army and helping to create a solid Allied line close to the German border.

Nurses of the French Medical Corps land with U.S. forces during Operation Dragoon.

"You know … where you are going. We are going to hold there 'til hell freezes over or we are all relieved, whichever comes first."

Lt. Colonel William P. Yarborough

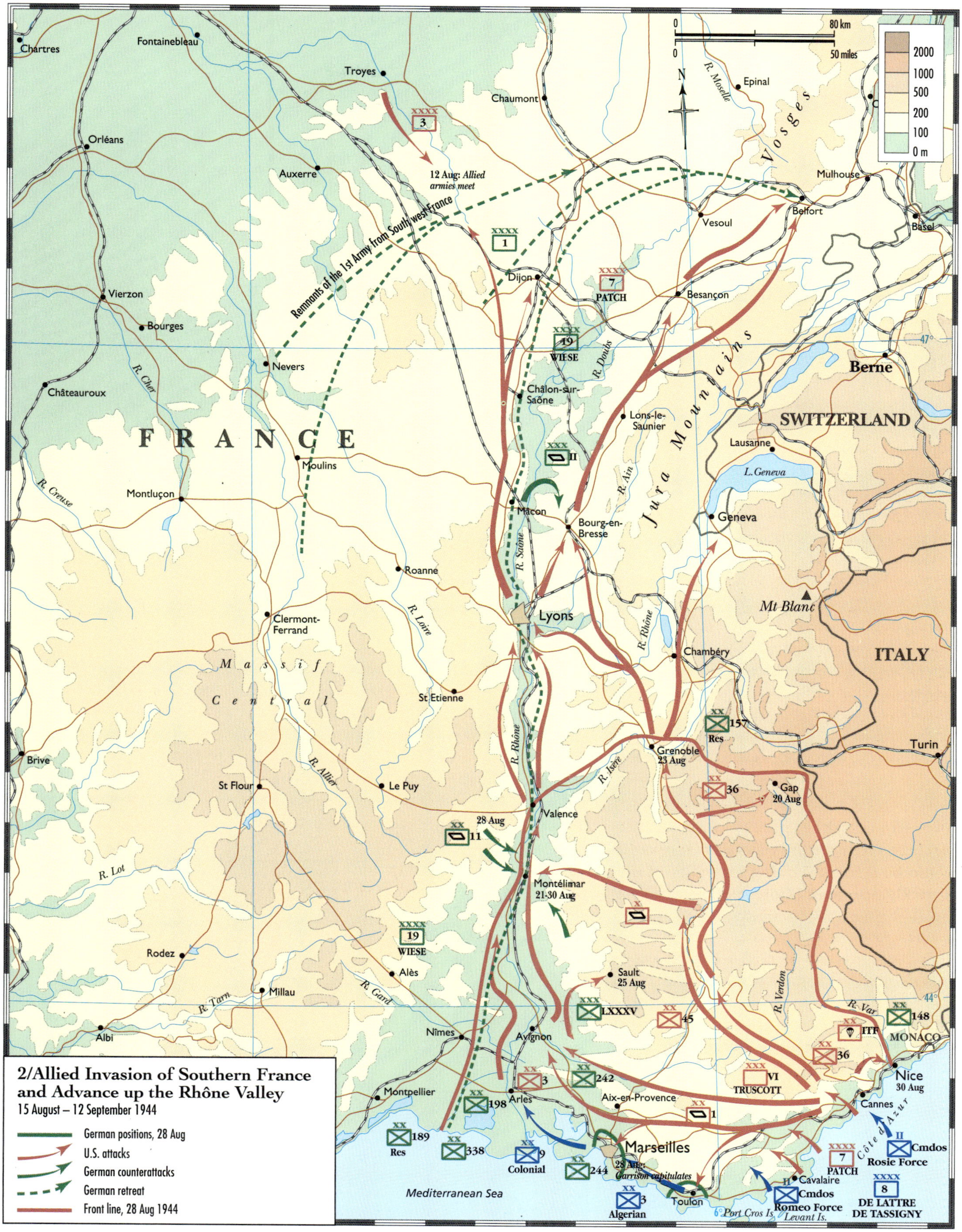

2/Allied Invasion of Southern France and Advance up the Rhône Valley
15 August – 12 September 1944

Stalemate in the Fall SEPTEMBER – NOVEMBER 1944

On 1 September 1944, Eisenhower took personal command of Allied forces in Europe. He had every reason to feel confident. Once his troops had broken out from Normandy and crossed the River Seine, a spectacular advance had liberated most of northern France. But problems emerged. Although Allied troops had liberated Brussels and Antwerp, approached the Ardennes and advanced towards Metz by mid-September, their supply chain was close to collapse. Moreover, German resistance was hardening. It was at this point that the newly promoted Field Marshal Montgomery, commanding 21st Army Group, suggested an audacious plan. If airborne troops could seize bridges across waterways in southern Holland, including the Lower Rhine at Arnhem, ground forces could link up with them and threaten the German industrial heartland of the Ruhr. Despite opposition from some American commanders, Eisenhower gave the go-ahead on 10 September.

Codenamed *Market Garden*, the plan was for the U.S. 82nd and 101st Airborne Divisions to capture bridges across the Wilhelmina Canal north of Eindhoven and the Rivers Maas and Waal at Grave and Nijmegen, while the British 1st Airborne Division seized crossings on the Lower Rhine at Arnhem. The airborne troops would then be relieved by British armored units advancing north, which would spearhead an assault on the Ruhr. The operation was scheduled to begin on 17 September. The British, under Major-General Robert Urquhart, accepted a flawed plan which involved dropping them about eight miles to the west of Arnhem instead of directly onto their objectives, and in the rush to ensure that all was ready on time, reports that the II SS Panzer Corps was recuperating in the Arnhem sector were ignored.

At first, the attack seemed to go well. American troops were dropped on 17 September and their objectives quickly taken. At Arnhem, lead elements of 1st Airborne Division seized their landing zones and began to march into the town against minimal opposition. But the ground offensive was delayed and, as the Germans recovered from their initial shock, Arnhem proved difficult to capture. Although men of the 2nd Parachute Battalion, commanded by Lieutenant-Colonel John Frost, reached the main road bridge, they quickly became isolated. Reinforcements, dropped on 18 September, were sucked into a battle to the west of the bridge against German armor and infantry.

Frost's men held out until 21 September, when they were forced to surrender. By then, Urquhart had pulled the rest of his division back to occupy a perimeter around the Hartenstein Hotel, hoping for relief. But the ground advance had been slow and despite American successes at Eindhoven and Nijmegen, it was not until 25 September that firm contact was made with Urquhart. That night, the remnants of 1st Airborne Division withdrew back across the river, having suffered 7842 casualties. The Rhine had not been breached.

Eisenhower shifted to a broad advance by all the armies under his command. While Montgomery concentrated on clearing the Scheldt Estuary to open up the port of Antwerp – something that was to take until November to complete – American armies pushed east on a front between Aachen and the Swiss border. As they approached Germany, they encountered heavy opposition. Aachen did not fall until 21 October, by which time other troops of Lieutenant-General Courtney H. Hodges' U.S. First Army had entered a nightmare battle in the Hürtgen Forest that was to continue, in appalling weather, until 1 December. On their right, Patton's U.S. Third Army could not take Metz until 25 November, and although U.S. and French troops further south managed to break through to Strasbourg, their lines of communication were threatened by a German pocket around Colmar. The Allied advance stalled.

Celebrated as liberators upon their arrival in the Dutch town of Arnhem, exhausted survivors of the 72-hour battle to take the Arnhem road bridge are taken prisoner by the Germans.

"This was war on such a concentrated scale that it made you feel terribly small, frightened and insignificant: something like an ant menaced by a steam roller."

Louis Hagen, Glider pilot

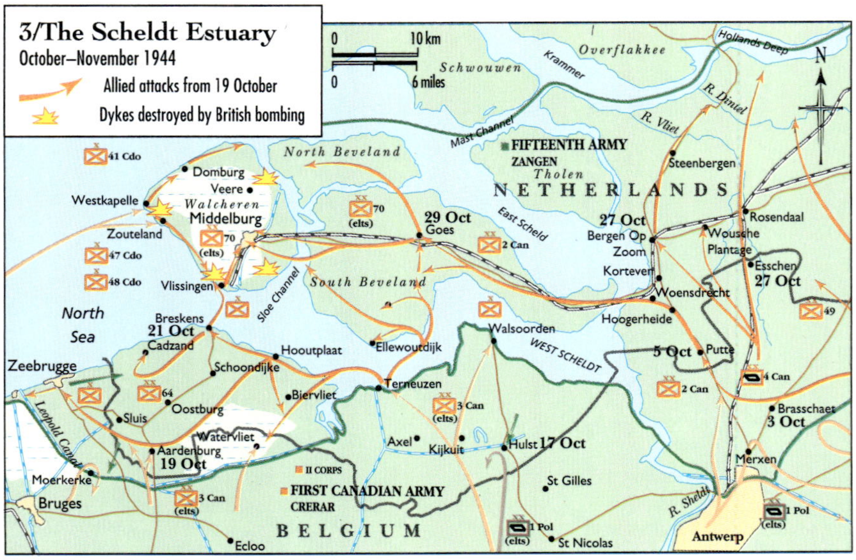

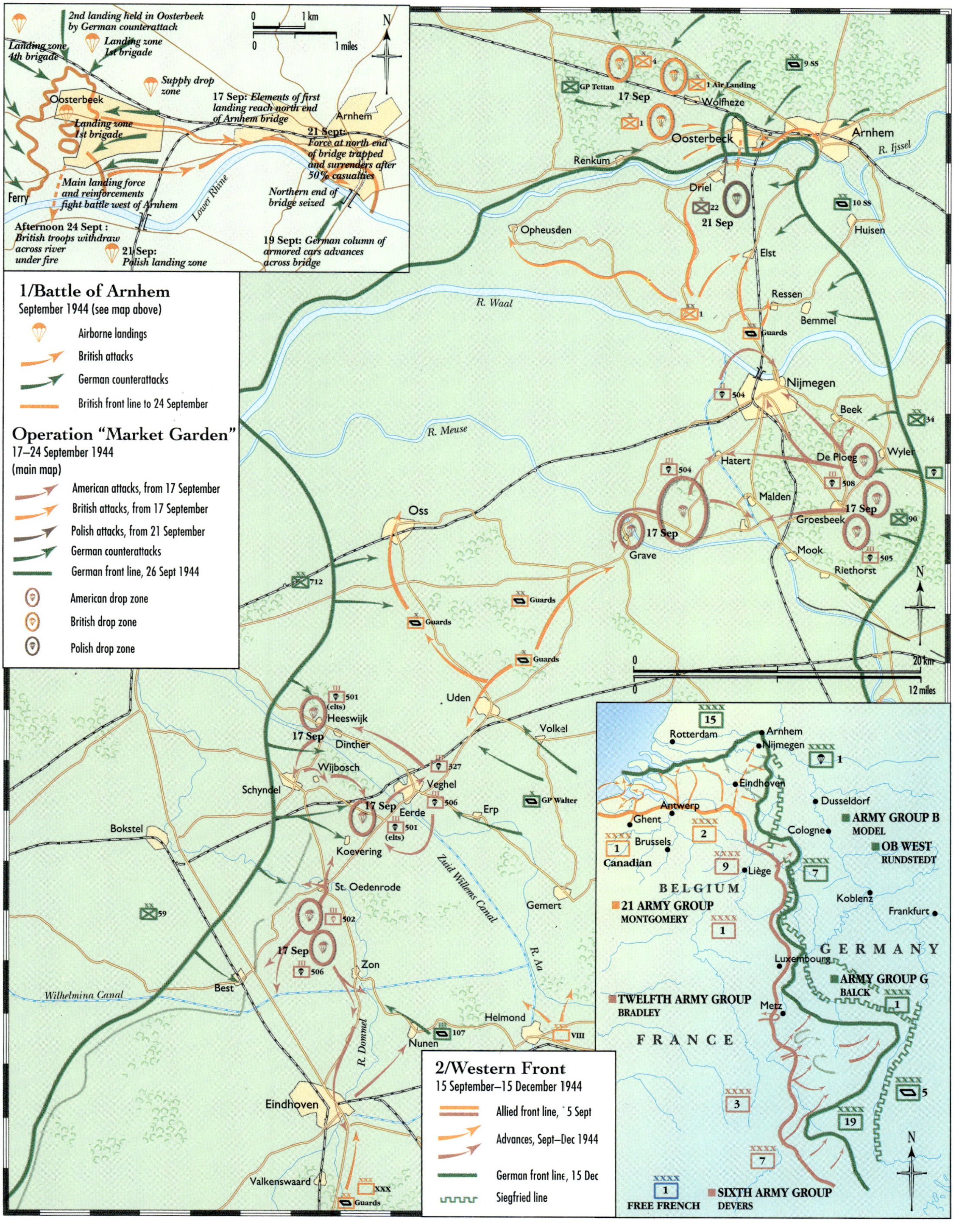
2nd landing held in Oosterbeek by German counterattack
Landing zone 4th brigade
Landing zone 1st brigade
Supply drop zone
0 1 km
0 1 miles
N
Oosterbeek
Landing zone 1st brigade
17 Sep: Elements of first landing reach north end of Arnhem bridge
Arnhem
21 Sept: Force at north end of bridge trapped and surrenders after 50% casualties
Main landing force and reinforcements fight battle west of Arnhem
Ferry
Lower Rhine
Northern end of bridge seized
Afternoon 24 Sept : British troops withdraw across river under fire
21 Sep: Polish landing zone
19 Sept: German column of armored cars advances across bridge
1/Battle of Arnhem
September 1944 (see map above)
Airborne landings
British attacks
German counterattacks
British front line to 24 September
Operation "Market Garden"
17–24 September 1944
(main map)
American attacks, from 17 September
British attacks, from 17 September
Polish attacks, from 21 September
German counterattacks
German front line, 26 Sept 1944
American drop zone
British drop zone
Polish drop zone
GP Tettau
1 Air Landing
9 SS
17 Sep
Wolfheze
Oosterbeck
Arnhem
R. Ijssel
Renkum
Driel
21 Sep
10 SS
Huisen
Opheusden
Elst
R. Waal
Ressen
Bemmel
Guards
Nijmegen
504
Beek
34
R. Meuse
Hatert
De Ploeg
Wyler
504
508
Malden
17 Sep
Groesbeek
90
Oss
17 Sep
Grave
Mook
505
Riethorst
712
Guards
Guards
Guards
0 20 km
0 12 miles
501 (elts)
Heeswijk
17 Sep
Uden
Volkel
Dinther
Wijbosch
327
Veghel
Schyndel
17 Sep
Eerde
506
Erp
GP Walter
Bokstel
501 (elts)
Koevering
Zuid Willems Canal
St. Oedenrode
59
502
Gemert
17 Sep
506
Zon
R. Aa
Best
Wilhelmina Canal
Helmond
107
Nunen
VIII
R. Dommel
Eindhoven
Valkenswaard
XXX
Guards
15
Rotterdam
Arnhem
Nijmegen
1
Eindhoven
Antwerp
Dusseldorf
Ghent
2
ARMY GROUP B
MODEL
Brussels
1
Canadian
Cologne
OB WEST
RUNDSTEDT
9
Liège
7
BELGIUM
21 ARMY GROUP
MONTGOMERY
Koblenz
Frankfurt
1
GERMANY
Luxembourg
ARMY GROUP G
BALCK
TWELFTH ARMY GROUP
BRADLEY
Metz
1
FRANCE
2/Western Front
15 September–15 December 1944
Allied front line, 15 Sept
Advances, Sept–Dec 1944
German front line, 15 Dec
Siegfried line
3
5
19
7
N
1
FREE FRENCH
SIXTH ARMY GROUP
DEVERS

Gilberts and Marshalls NOVEMBER 1943 – FEBRUARY 1944

Operation *Cartwheel*, General Douglas MacArthur's offensive in the South-West Pacific, continued to put pressure on the Japanese in the Solomons and New Guinea during the final months of 1943. As U.S. forces, joined by the 3rd New Zealand Division, moved forward from New Georgia and Vella Lavella, landing on Mono and Choiseul on 27 October and at Empress Bay in Bougainville on 1 November, the Japanese base at Rabaul came within bombing range. Meanwhile, Australian troops in New Guinea had closed in on Salamaua in July and August. The Japanese moved reinforcements down from their base at Lae, only to find that the Australians had outwitted them: on 4 September an amphibious landing secured Lae and forced the enemy to pull back into the Finisterre Mountains. On 22 September another landing took Finschhafen, on the tip of the Huon Peninsula, after which the Australians moved north to seize Nuzam on 1 January 1944. By then, the Americans had assaulted New Britain, landing at the western end of the island, far distant from Rabaul. The Japanese, caught by surprise, maintained their defenses around Rabaul, but MacArthur was content merely to isolate the base, hitting it with carrier-borne airpower. Further operations against the Green Islands and the Admiralty Group in February 1944 completed the encirclement of Rabaul, which was left to "wither on the vine".

While MacArthur's men struggled to secure their objectives, Admiral Chester W. Nimitz prepared to attack key islands and atolls in the Central Pacific. His first operation, codenamed *Galvanic*, targeted the atolls of Tarawa and Makin in the Gilbert Islands. Naval and air bombardments began on 13 November 1943 and continued for a week, although the Japanese – 4836 men on Tarawa and about 800 on Makin – were well dug in and their casualties were low. As the 2nd Marine Division prepared to assault the small island of Betio, on the southern extremity of Tarawa, and Butaritari on Makin, they had no knowledge of Japanese strength.

In the event, the Makin assault, initiated early on 20 November, proved to be relatively straightforward. Despite some Japanese counterattacks, the atoll was cleared by the morning of the 23rd. But the same was not true on Betio. As the first waves of Marines approached the shore on 20 November, they were greeted by withering Japanese fire from hidden positions and the heavily laden Marines found that they could not advance beyond the beach. A second landing on the 21st fared no better, and it took two more days to secure Betio. By then the Americans had lost nearly 1000 dead. It was a portent of things to come.

Nimitz's next objective was the Marshall Islands. Rather than risk getting bogged down in fighting for small atolls in the east, he decided to go straight for the main Japanese base on Kwajalein. In December 1943 and January 1944 Rear Admiral Marc A. Mitscher's Task Force 58 battered enemy defenses. On 1 February, men of the U.S. 7th Infantry Division landed on Kwajalein while troops of the 4th Marine Division assaulted the outlying islands of Roi and Namur. Fighting was fierce but all objectives had been secured by the 4th. Exploiting Japanese confusion, Nimitz immediately ordered a further assault, this time against Eniwetok, an atoll 350 miles to the north-west. Assaulted by the 22nd Marine Regiment and 106th Infantry Regiment, Eniwetok was taken between 17 and 23 February, by which time air attacks were already hitting the Japanese naval base at Truk in the Caroline Islands. Like Rabaul in New Britain, Truk was bypassed. Nimitz was looking beyond, to the Mariana Islands.

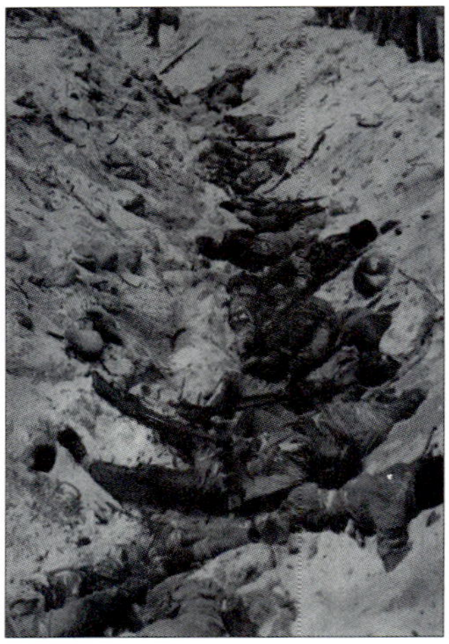

A trench on Namur, one of the main islands of Kwajalein atoll, is lined with the corpses of Japanese troops.

7/Strategic situation in Pacific, after the taking of the Gilbert and Marshall Islands
February 1944

"During the day I saw the first five of many Japs I saw who committed suicide rather than fight to the end. In one hole, under a pile of rubble, supported by a tin roof, four of them had removed the split-toed, rubber-soled jungle shoes from their right feet, had placed the barrels of their .303 rifles against their foreheads, then had pulled the triggers with their big toes. The other had chosen the same method some five hundred Japs chose on Attu: holding a hand grenade against his chest, thus blowing out the chest and blowing off the right hand."

Robert Sherrod, war correspondent

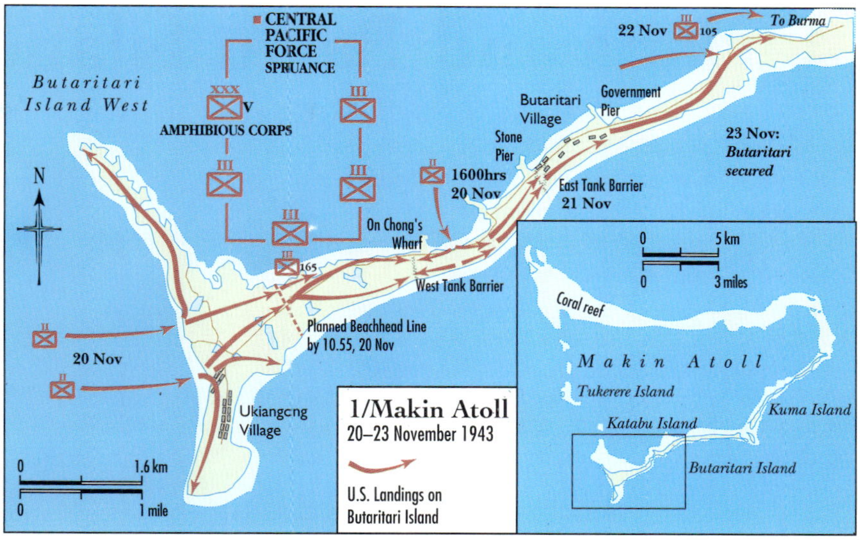

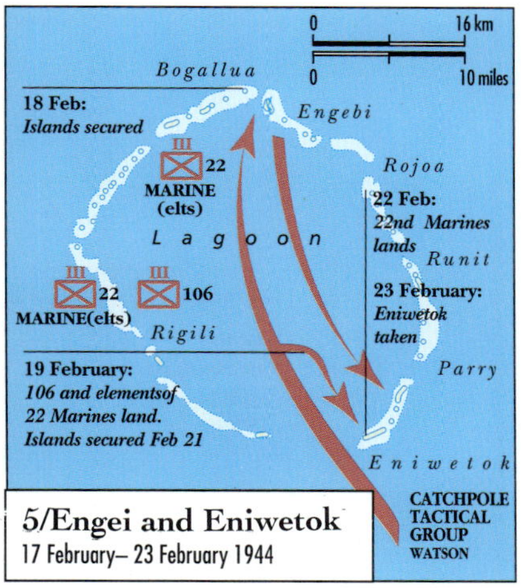

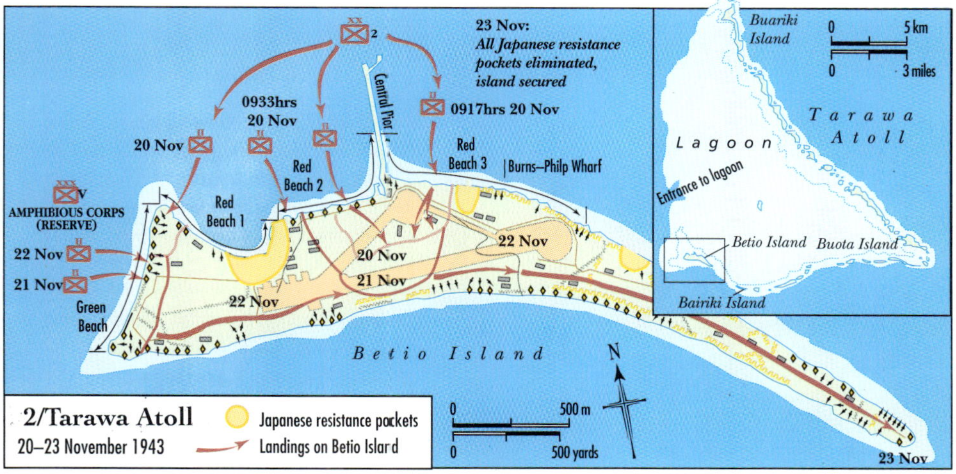

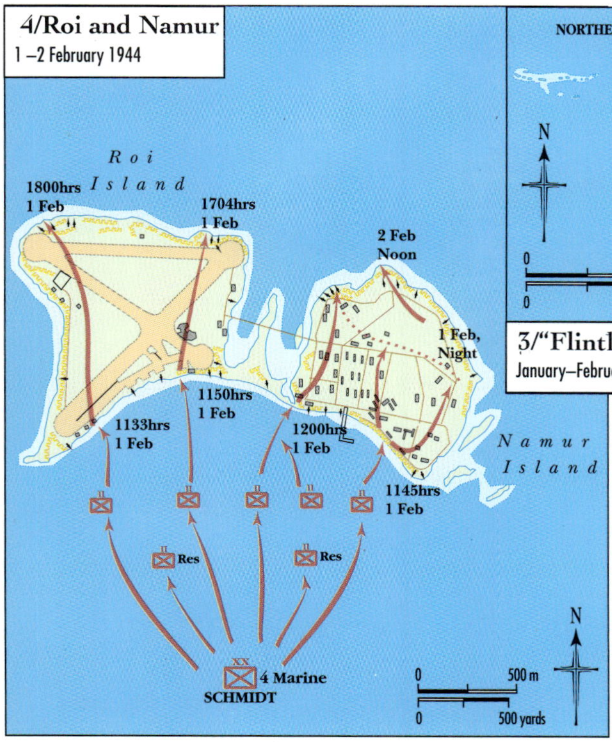

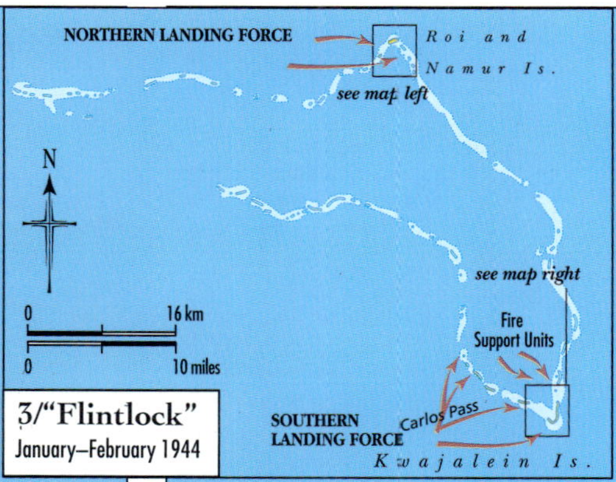

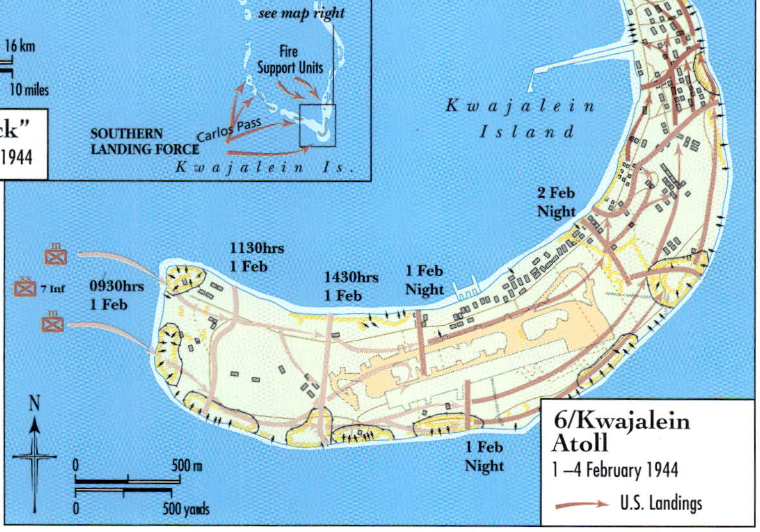

Mariana and Palau Islands JUNE – AUGUST 1944

The Marianas, comprising the islands of Saipan, Guam and Tinian, were of vital importance in American plans to defeat the Japanese. Lying less than 1500 miles from the Japanese Home Islands, their capture would not only breach the inner ring of enemy defenses, but would also give the Americans airbases from which to mount bombing attacks on Japan itself. Admiral Chester W. Nimitz, U.S. commander of the Central Pacific Area, decided to prepare for amphibious assaults on the Marianas while his troops were still securing the Marshalls. Air attacks on Japanese defenses began in February 1944, and four months later Vice Admiral Raymond A. Spruance's Fifth Fleet, more than 530 ships strong, concentrated its fire against Saipan, the first objective. In response, the Japanese Combined Fleet sailed to confront the Americans in the Philippine Sea.

On 15 June, 700 amphibious vehicles carrying men of the 2nd and 4th Marine Divisions approached the south-west coast of Saipan. They met heavy resistance – the island was defended by 32,000 men, commanded by Lieutenant-General Yoshitsugu Saito – and by nightfall the Americans had suffered some 2000 casualties. But reinforcements poured ashore, enabling the Marines to fight off counterattacks and then push eastward to seize an airfield at Aslito. Within seven days the southern half of the island was secure, upon which the invaders turned north into more difficult terrain. By the beginning of July the remnants of Saito's force had been pushed back into Marpi Point. Many Japanese committed suicide rather than face capture, although about 2000 prisoners were taken. By 9 July the battle was over, having cost the Americans nearly 3500 dead.

Guam, situated 150 miles to the south-west of Saipan, was the next objective. On 21 July, men of the 3rd Marine Division and 1st Provisional Marine Brigade landed on beaches to the north and south respectively of the Orote Peninsula on the west coast. Japanese defenders – 5500 naval personnel under Captain Yutaka Sugimoto and 13,000 army troops under Lieutenant-General Takeshi Takashina – imposed some casualties, but the toughest fighting was yet to come. As the Americans moved inland, they encountered dug-in positions amid rugged terrain, particularly around Mount Alifan in the south, taken after bitter hand-to-

American Marines, landing on the beaches of Saipan and the other Mariana Islands, fought off determined counterattacks. Hundreds of Japanese infantrymen were killed, and 31 of the Emperor's tanks were destroyed. Rather than face the ignominy of imprisonment, their commander, Lieutenant-General Saito, committed hara-kiri *with a ritual sword.*

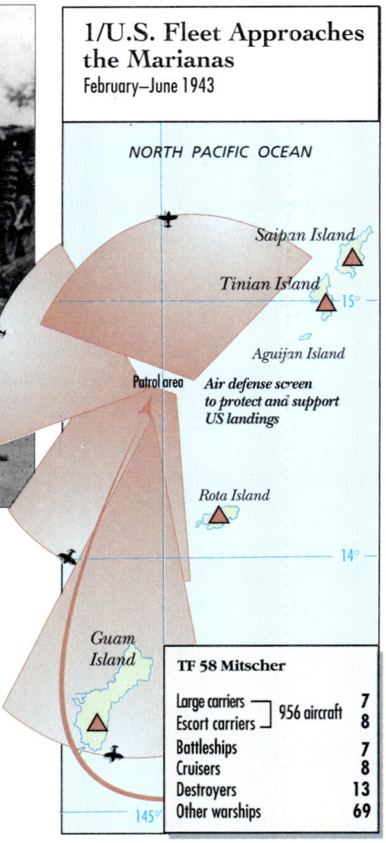

hand engagements. Further north, the 3rd Marine Division struggled to seize a series of mountain ridges on the way to Agana. Japanese resistance became more fanatical as the advance continued, manifested in suicidal *banzai* charges that imposed heavy casualties. The northern coast of Guam was not secured until 10 August, by which time the Americans had lost 1744 dead. The Japanese garrison was destroyed, with only a few survivors withdrawing into the jungle. The last surrendered in 1972.

That left Tinian, less than three miles to the south of Saipan. A decoy landing by the 2nd Marine Division on 24 July ensured that the Japanese commander, Colonel Keishi Ogata, concentrated the bulk of the garrison of 9000 men in Tinian town, while the main American assault went in further north. By nightfall, over 15,000 men of the 4th Marine Division had landed close to Ushi Point. Joined by the 2nd Marines on the 25th, the invaders moved down the east coast and across the island toward Tinian town. Despite counterattacks, the Americans had secured the island by 1 August, having lost nearly 400 dead. While the fighting continued, American Construction Battalions (CBs or SeeBees) began to build airfields for the B-29s that would bomb Japan.

By then the decision had been made to liberate the Philippines rather than attack Formosa. In response, Nimitz ordered an assault on the Palau Islands, 800 miles south-west of Guam, which he argued were essential as bases for the Philippine operation. On 15 September, III Amphibious Corps landed on Peleliu, expecting an easy assault. They did not get it. The Japanese defenders fell back into prepared positions, forcing the Americans to fight for every yard. The island was not declared secure until 30 September, having cost the invaders 1950 killed. A similar assault on Angaur on 17 September, carried out by the 81st Infantry Division, suffered fewer casualties but took until late October to complete. In both cases, the Japanese were wiped out.

"We must utilize this opportunity to exalt true Japanese manhood. I will advance with those who remain to deliver still another blow to the American Devils and leave my bones on Saipan as a bulwark of the Pacific."

Lieutenant-General Yoshitsugu Saito

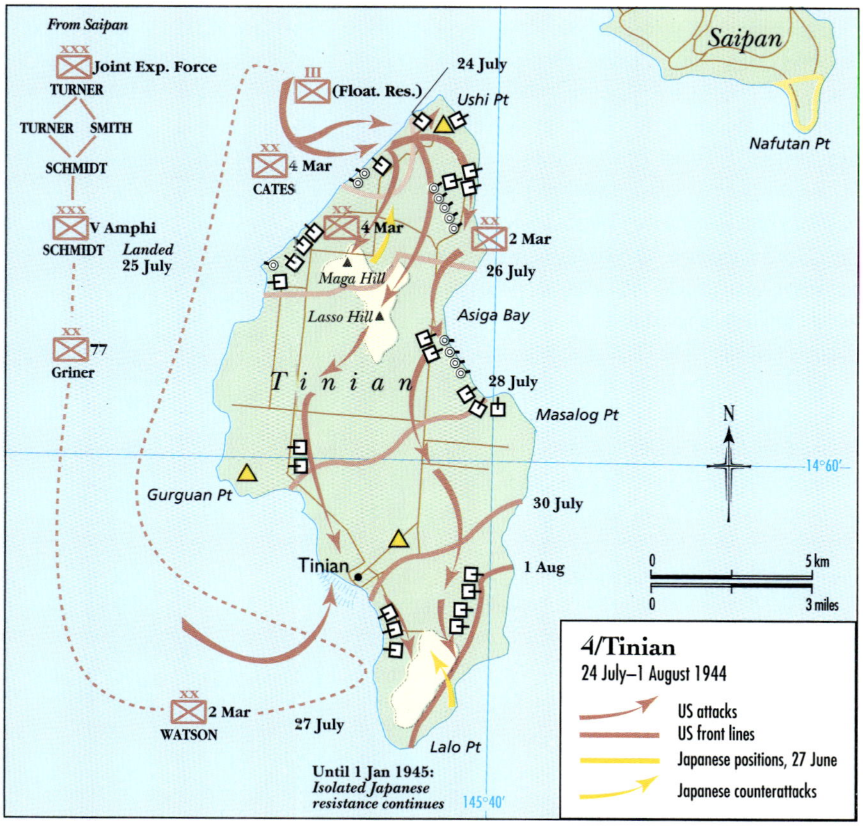

Battle of the Philippine Sea JUNE 1944

The American decision to invade the Mariana Islands in June 1944 inevitably elicited a Japanese response. As soon as it was obvious to them that Admiral Chester W. Nimitz intended to attack Saipan, Tinian and Guam, they initiated Operation *A-Go*, a pre-planned naval offensive. On 15 June, as American troops fought to secure Saipan, the First Mobile Fleet under Vice Admiral Jisaburo Ozawa was ordered to sail into the Philippine Sea, where it would be joined by Vice Admiral Matome Ugaki's Southern Force. Altogether, Ozawa would have nine carriers (with 473 aircraft), five battleships, 11 heavy cruisers, two light cruisers and 28 destroyers with which to engage and destroy the U.S. Task Force 58 (TF58), protecting the Marianas' landing force.

Vice-Admiral Marc A. Mitscher, commander of TF58, had a total of 15 carriers (with 902 aircraft), seven battleships, 21 cruisers and 69 destroyers at his disposal. Moreover, he was aware of Operation *A-Go* through intercepted Japanese naval messages. By mid-June, the Americans had 43 submarines in the Western Pacific, and it was one of these that reported the rendezvous of the two Japanese forces to the east of the Philippines late on 16 June. Mitscher already knew what to do: after his aircraft had knocked out the enemy carriers and slowed down the rest of the Japanese fleet, his battleships and cruisers would close in for the kill. Meanwhile, Ozawa too had finalized his plan. After detaching a decoy group some 125 miles ahead of this main fleet, aiming to force Mitscher to commit the bulk of his air capability, planes from the rest of his carriers would attack TF58 and destroy it.

The Battle of the Philippine Sea began early on 19 June, when Japanese reconnaissance aircraft located TF58. Ozawa immediately ordered air attacks, but they were disastrous. By the end of the morning, in what U.S. pilots dubbed the "Great Marianas' Turkey Shoot", Ozawa had lost 243 aircraft to the Americans' 30. Little damage was inflicted on TF58, although while the attacks were taking place the Japanese flagship *Taiho* was damaged by a torpedo from the U.S. submarine *Albacore*, forcing Ozawa to transfer his command to a destroyer. Just after noon he faced further loss when the carrier *Shokaku* was torpedoed; three hours later, *Taiho* exploded and sank. At this stage, Ozawa was unaware of the scale of his air losses – he thought that most of the planes had landed on Guam after attacking the American fleet – and was unwisely preparing to re-engage.

Mitscher spent most of 20 June searching for the enemy, and it was not until late afternoon that reconnaissance aircraft reported Ozawa's position some 275 miles to the north-west of TF58. Although this was at the extreme range of U.S. carrier aircraft, Mitscher ordered an attack, and this was not cancelled even when it was realized that the Japanese were steaming away from the Americans, increasing the range by the minute. The attackers found their prey at 6.25 p.m., catching the Japanese by surprise. The first waves badly damaged the carriers *Zuikaku* and *Chiyoda*, before switching their attention to the battleship *Haruna* and the heavy cruiser *Maya*; subsequent attacks sank the carrier *Hiyo* and damaged both the *Ryuho* and *Junyo*. Only 17 U.S. aircraft were lost over the target, but a further 82 either ran out of fuel or crash-landed when they returned, in the dark, to TF58.

Ozawa was keen to continue the battle, but his masters in Tokyo ordered him to withdraw late on 20 June. By then, he had not sunk a single U.S. ship, yet had lost 426 aircraft as well as substantial parts of his fleet. The Americans may not have been able to close in for the kill, but they had achieved a decisive victory.

The U.S. Fifth Fleet patrols the Philippine Sea. Critics of Admiral Spruance have maintained that the opportunity for a major victory over the Japanese was lost through over-caution but the naval war in the Pacific was, in fact, all but over.

1/The Philippine Sea
1000hrs 13 June – 0300hrs 19 June 1944

U.S. air patrols
Approach of U.S. fleet
Approach of Japanese fleet

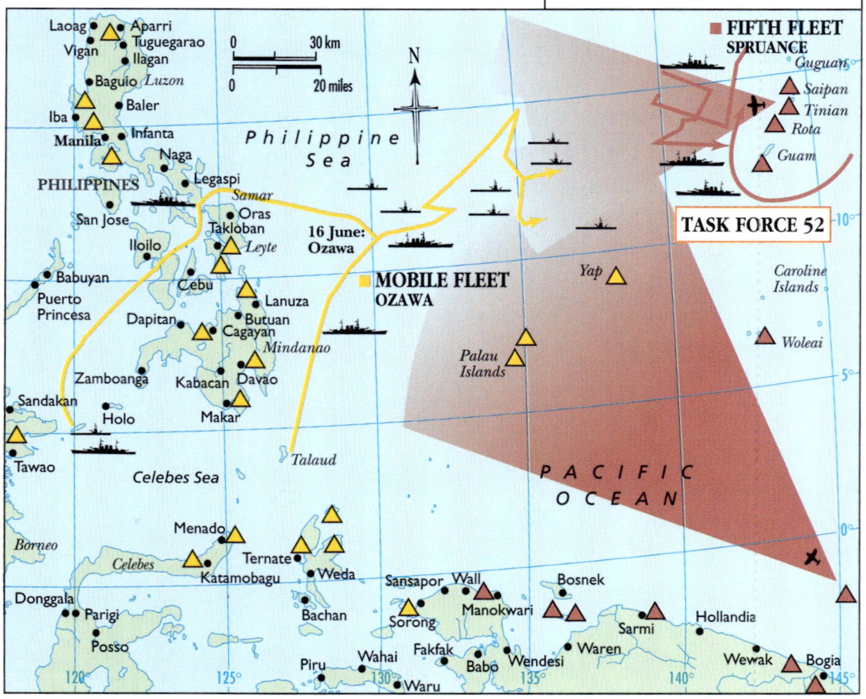

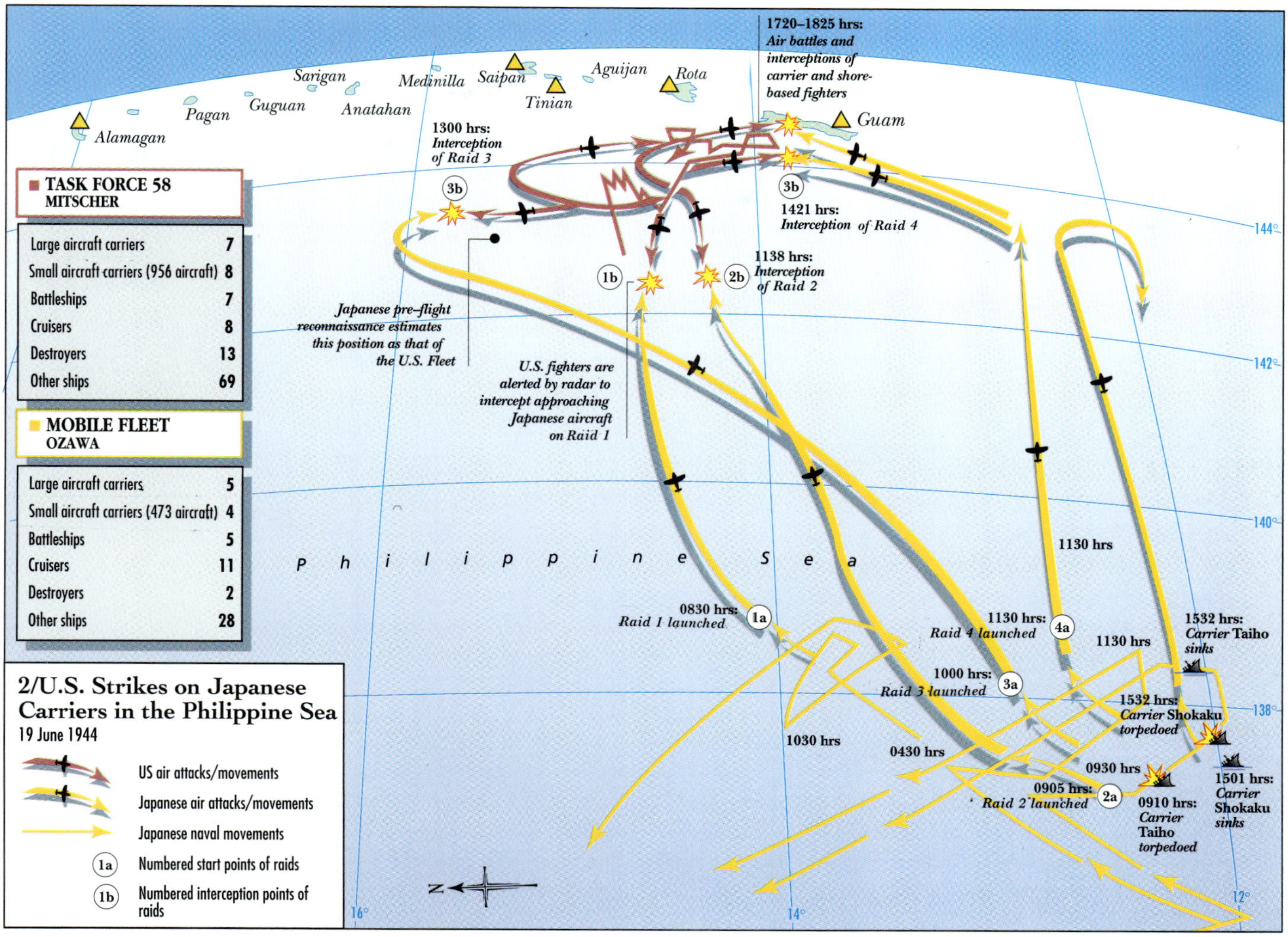

2/U.S. Strikes on Japanese Carriers in the Philippine Sea
19 June 1944

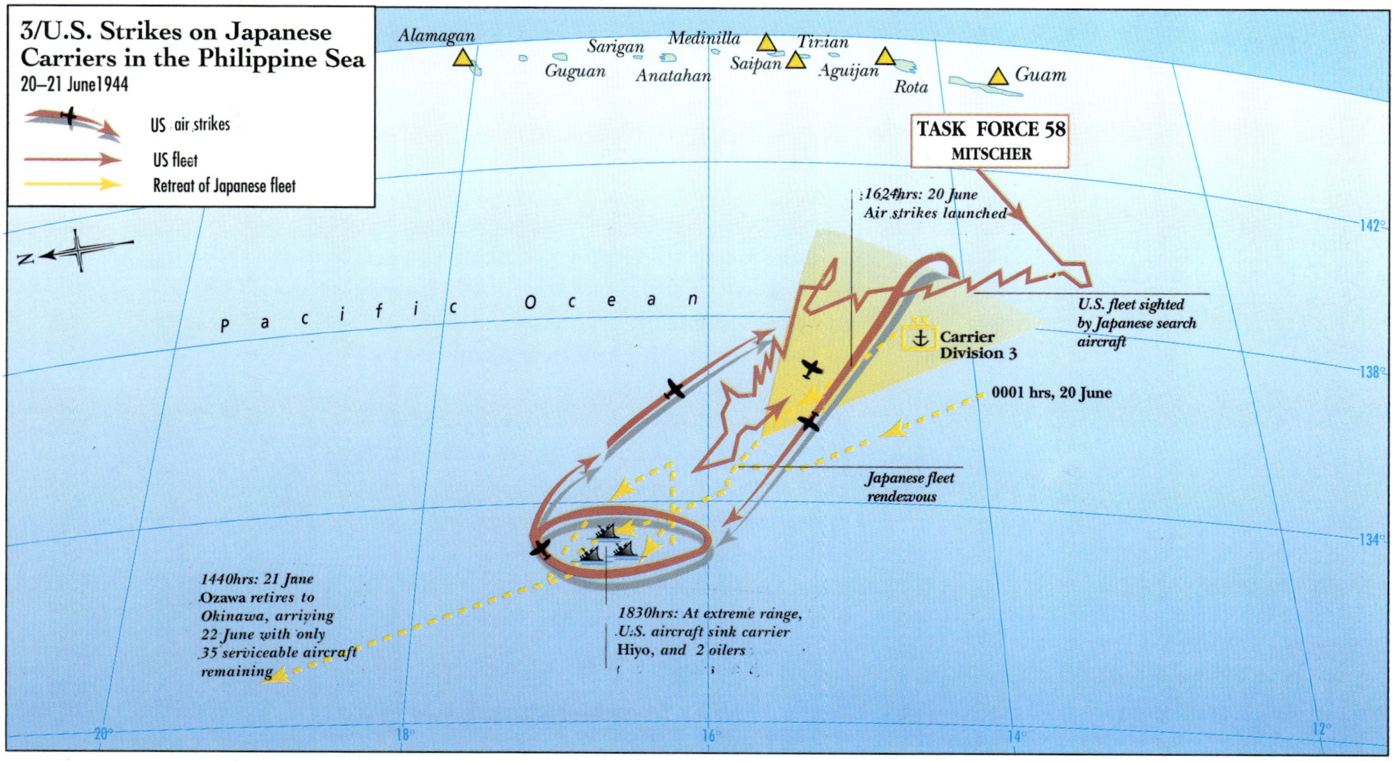

3/U.S. Strikes on Japanese Carriers in the Philippine Sea
20–21 June 1944

Leyte and Leyte Gulf OCTOBER – DECEMBER 1944

While American forces were engaged in the Marianas, Allied troops further south under MacArthur slowly cleared New Guinea. On 13 April 1944 Australian units captured Bogadjim, at the base of the Huon Peninsula, but the Japanese had already withdrawn to Wewak, nearly 200 miles away. Expecting a respite, they were caught by surprise when, on 22 April, MacArthur mounted amphibious landings at Aitape and Hallandia, further along the coast. Wewak was left isolated, enabling the Allies to assault the island of Wakde on 18 May and Biak 11 days later. In September, MacArthur went beyond New Guinea to attack Morotai, less than 400 miles from the Philippines.

MacArthur saw the Philippines as his next objective, but planners in Washington were still directing him to bypass the islands to link up with Admiral Nimitz's Central Pacific Forces in Formosa. Not until September 1944, when U.S. air raids met little opposition over the Philippines, was the go-ahead given for an amphibious landing on the island of Leyte. On 20 October, protected by over 800 ships of the Third and Seventh Fleets, men of Lieutenant-General Walter Krueger's U.S. Sixth Army carved out beachheads on the east coast of Leyte, to the south of Tacloban. The Japanese pulled back to prepared positions inland.

The Japanese plan for the defense of the Philippines, codenamed *Sho-1*, included a massive naval commitment to engage the American fleet and destroy the landing force. A decoy fleet of carriers, cruisers and destroyers, commanded by Vice Admiral Jisaburo Ozawa, would approach Leyte from the north-west to draw the main American force away from the landing area, which would then be attacked in a pincer movement. Vice-Admiral Takeo Kurita's First Striking Force would sail from Borneo through the Sibuyan Sea, then swing south through the San Bernardino Strait to approach Leyte from the north, while Vice Admiral Shoji Nishimura's Southern Force, backed by Vice-Admiral Kiyohide Shima's Second Striking Force from Japan, would enter Leyte Gulf from the south through the Surigao Strait.

The plan went wrong from the start. Early on 23 October, as Kurita's ships moved through the Palawan Passage, north of Borneo, they were intercepted by American submarines which sank two cruisers and badly damaged a third. Alerted to the Japanese move Admiral William F. Halsey, commander of the Third Fleet, sent out carrier aircraft on 24 October which damaged Kurita's flagship *Yamato* and pulverized its sister-ship *Musashi*. A Japanese air attack to the east of Luzon led to the loss of the carrier *Princeton*, but the balance was clearly in favor of the Americans. Kurita withdrew to the west of the San Bernardino Strait, hoping that the Americans would take Ozawa's bait.

This is exactly what Halsey did late on the 24th. As he moved north, away from Vice Admiral Thomas C. Kinkaid's Seventh Fleet, the San Bernardino Strait was left unprotected, enabling Kurita to make his way through. Meanwhile, further south, Nishimura's Southern Force was weaving through the Surigao Strait, where he suddenly found his passage blocked by a force of American warships under Rear-Admiral Jesse B. Oldendorf. Nishimura's fleet was hit by over 4000 shells in 18 minutes and effectively destroyed. Shima, following in his wake, immediately withdrew. The southern prong of the Japanese plan had been blunted.

Early on 25 October, Kurita emerged from the San Bernardino Strait and moved towards the American landing area. Opposed by nothing more than escort carriers, he seemed set to inflict telling damage, particularly as Kinkaid presumed that Halsey had left a covering force to protect the landing fleet. When it was obvious that he had not, Halsey had no choice but to disengage from battle with Ozawa off Cape Engano and rush back south. As he did so, Kurita realized that a trap was about to be sprung. He withdrew through the San Bernardino Strait, ending the Battle of Leyte Gulf. It had cost the Japanese four carriers, three battleships and 19 cruisers and destroyers. By comparison, the Americans had lost one light carrier and five other vessels and had secured naval supremacy around the Philippines. The ground fighting on Leyte was to continue until late December, but its outcome was never seriously in doubt.

"The devastating accuracy of this gunfire was the most beautiful sight I have ever witnessed."

U.S. naval observer at Surigao Strait

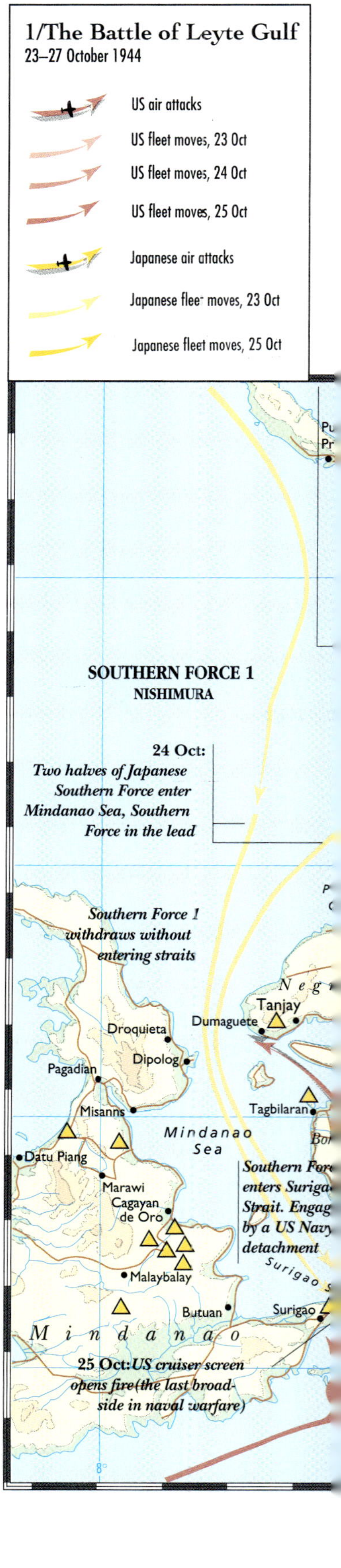

A Japanese destroyer is attacked and sunk during the Battle of Leyte Gulf. During the three-day clash the Imperial Japanese Navy, the most recently formed fleet of all the great powers, was annihilated. Unopposed, the American victors were in a position to take complete control of the Philippine Sea.

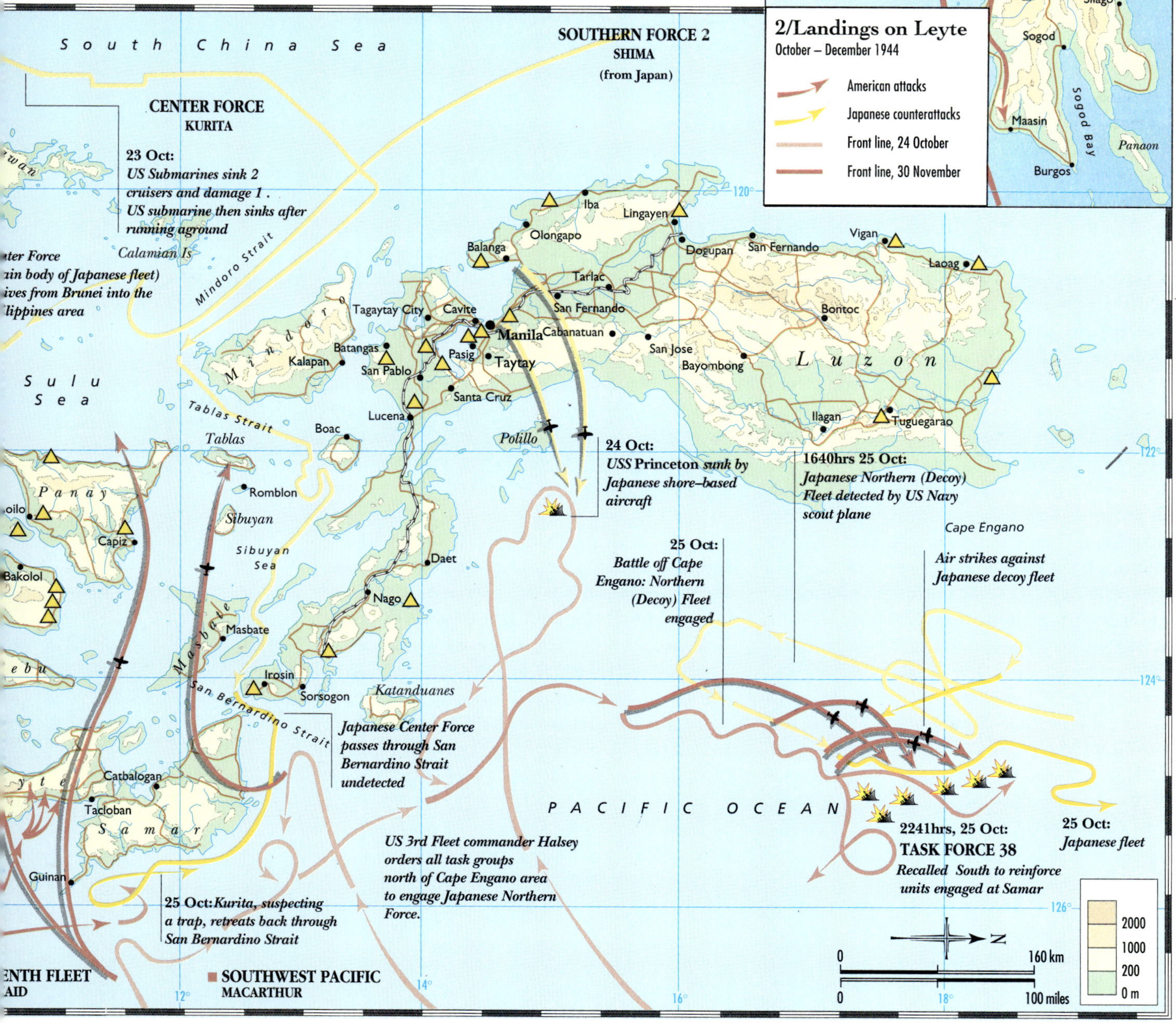

War in China APRIL – DECEMBER 1944

By 1944 China and Japan had been at war for nearly seven years. The Japanese offensives of 1937–39 had left them in possession of most of north-eastern China, from Peking to Shanghai, while the offensives of 1941–42 had added a number of south-eastern ports such as Hong Kong and Wenchow. Nationalist Chinese forces under Chiang Kai-shek had withdrawn westward to Chungking, from where they tried unsuccessfully to intervene in Burma in 1942. They were poorly equipped and morale was low; Chiang seemed to be more concerned about the threat from Mao Tse-tung's communists than about the Japanese. The only Chinese success, in early 1944, was an attack into northern Burma, commanded by Chiang's American adviser, Lieutenant-General Joseph Stilwell, and involving both U.S. and British forces.

Indeed, it was pressure from the Americans, who needed to keep the Japanese army in China tied down, that ensured Chiang's continued commitment to the war. As early as December 1941 Colonel Claire L. Chennault's "Flying Tigers" – U.S. pilots who fought initially as mercenaries but later became part of the Fourteenth Air Force – began to operate in China. In 1942 U.S. transport planes began to fly supply missions over the Himalayas from Assam to Kunming – an airlift known as "Flying the Hump". By 1944, Fourteenth Air Force bombers were hitting Japanese supply lines in north-eastern China and plans were being finalized for the deployment of B-29 Superfortress bombers, capable of reaching Japan itself, to airfields around Chengtu.

American air activity in China triggered a series of Japanese offensives, known collectively as *Ichi-go*, between April and December 1944. The overall aim was to clear the railway from Peking, through Hankow, to Canton and Indo-China, but an integral part of the plan was to seize the U.S. airbases around Chungking on the River Yangtze. The offensives began in mid-April, when 150,000 Japanese advanced toward Chengchow from the east and south. The city fell on 22 April, allowing the advance to continue westward to take Loyang in May and Lingpau in June. At much the same time, other Japanese units moved south from Chengchow, aiming to link up with an offensive north from Hsinyang. By mid-June, the Japanese held the railroad from Peking to Hankow and the Chinese were in retreat.

Meanwhile, an attack south from Hankow had approached the city of Changsha, although here the Chinese fought more effectively. Despite losing Changsha on 5 June and Hengchow (where the railroad branched off toward Indo-China) two months later, Chiang's men, supported by Fourteenth Air Force, inflicted heavy casualties and gained valuable time. Even so, when yet another Japanese offensive began in late August, aiming to clear the railroad down to Canton, vast tracts of territory had to be abandoned. By November, Kweilin, Liuchow and Nanning, together with nearby airfields, were in Japanese hands and Chiang's base at Chungking was under threat. In December a small force of Japanese advanced out of northern Indo-China to make contact with units around Lungchow. The railroad was now clear along its full length from Peking to Hanoi.

But the Japanese were at full stretch. Their supply lines were extremely tenuous and, having suffered enormous casualties during *Ichi-go*, they had problems holding on to their new territory. The link between Indo-China and Hengchow could not be maintained for long, particularly after Chiang's forces began to recover (with American aid) from their recent setbacks. By November 1944 Chiang was actively involved in a massive campaign of re-equipment and training, co-ordinated by his new American adviser, Major-General Albert Wedemeyer (Stilwell having been removed at Chiang's request). Altogether, a total of 39 new divisions were planned, and although they were by no means fully effective by the end of the war nine months later, their appearance on the battlefield ensured that the Japanese kept more than half a million men in China. If they had been available to garrison the Philippines or any of the Pacific islands assaulted by the Americans, the campaigns of 1944–45 in those areas would have been substantially more costly.

Brigadier-General Arms, head of the U.S. training school in Kwangsi province, shows an American rifle to Chiang Kai-shek, Generalissimo of the Chinese Army. The Americans provided China with money, arms, equipment and military advice, as the Chinese force was badly-organized, poorly-trained and ill-equipped, and had lost their Burma Road link to India, which was vital for supplies.

"... the idea of building up a great American-led Chinese army to march to the sea vanished with Stilwell."

General Slim

"Flying Tigers" make ready to launch an attack on Japanese aircraft over China. Painted to resemble sharks, their Curtiss P-40B fighters were difficult to maneuver and had a limited range and poor gunsights, yet succeeded in destroying over 300 enemy planes between December 1941 and July 1942. This was largely thanks to the tactics devised by their founder, Colonel Chennault.

War in China
July 1937 – December 1944
Territory seized to July 1937
Territory held by end 1941
Territory held by December 1944, after Ichi-go Operations
Major lines of Japanese advance 1937–41
Supply road from India
Ichi-go Operation lines of advance
Communist controlled from 1935
Japanese conflict with USSR
U S S R
MONGOLIA
Inner Mongolia
Manchuria (Manchukuo)
KOREA
JAPAN
JAPANESE EMPIRE
FRENCH INDO-CHINA
PHILIPPINES
Sea of Okhotsk
Sea of Japan
Yellow Sea
East China Sea
South China Sea
PACIFIC OCEAN
Gulf of Tongking
La Perouse Strait
Korea Strait
Formosa Strait
Bashi Channel
Batintang Channel
1939: Japanese forces defeated by Red Army under Zhukov
1939
Irkutsk
Chita
Nerchinsk
Novyi Selenginsk
Yero Mine
Urga (Ulan Bator)
Barskotu
Manchouli
Nomonhan
Tsitsihar
Harbin
Toanan
Hsinking
Kirin
Blagovyenshchensk
Alexandrovsk
Konstantinovsk
Khabarovsk
Vladivostok
Changkufeng
Seishin
Numkiangsien
Heilungkiang
Jehol
Feugtien
Moukden
Lohning
Dolon Nor
Chahar
Chengteh
Honan
Peking
Yungping
Tientsin
Port Arthur
Tinnampo
Genzan
Seoul
Chemulpo
Masan
Fusan
Tatung
Ningsia
Chihli (later Hopeh)
Shensi
Chengting
Taiyuan
Fenchow
Yenan
Kansu
Lanchow
Kungchang
Lungchow
Lingpau
Sian
Loyang
Kaifeng
Chengchow
Tsinan
Shunteh
Shantung
Kiachow
Tsingtao
Haichow
Kiangsu
Hwaian
Honan
Yingchow
Hsinyang
Nanking
Chingkiang
Soochow
Shanghai
Siangyang
Hupeh
Anhwei
Hankow
Wuchang
Anking
Hangchow
Shaohing
Ningpo
Chekiang
Wenchow
Szechwan
Kweichow
Chengtu
Kiating
Chungking Emergency Nationalist capital
Burma Road
Changteh
Changsha
Hunan
Nanchang
Kiangsi
Yenping
Loyang
Foochow
Fukien
Hengchow
Chaotung
Kweiyang
Kweichow
Kweilin
Shiuchow
Kwangtung
Amoy
Swatow
Kunming
Yunnan
Mengtsz
Liuchow
Kwangsi
Wuchow
Canton
Shiuhing
Sunchow
Nanning
Lungchow
HONG KONG (British)
MACAO (Portuguese)
Hanoi
Haiphong
Kiungchow
Hainan
Vinh
Taihoku
Formosa
Sakhalin
Hokkaido
Abasiri
Sapporo
Hakodate
Aomori
Akita
Sendai
Niigata
Utsunomiya
Tokyo
Yokohama
Honshu
Nagoya
Kyoto
Osaka
Kobe
Hiroshima
Kochi
Shikoku
Moji
Fukuoka
Kyushu
Kumamoto
Nagasaki
Kagoshima
R. Angara
Lake Baikal
R. Selenga
R. Kerulen
R. Amur
R. Ussuri
R. Liao Ho
R. Hwang Ho
R. Yangtze
0 500 km
0 300 miles
40°
140°
30°
130°
20°
110°
120°

Burma NOVEMBER 1943 – DECEMBER 1944

Allied plans for operations in Burma, finalized in late 1943, involved two campaigns. In the west, British/Indian XV Corps would advance into Arakan while in the north American Lieutenant-General Joseph Stilwell would lead Chinese divisions, backed by U.S. and British units, to take Myitkyina. Both achieved some success before being disrupted in March 1944 by a major Japanese offensive into eastern India, the defeat of which took precedence. By the end of 1944, the Japanese were in retreat.

Fifteen Corps advanced into Arakan along two axes: in the west, the 5th Indian Division entered Maungdaw on 8/9 January 1944, while to their east, the 7th Indian Division battled towards Buthidaung. The divisions were linked through the Ngakyedauk Pass, close to which the commander of 7th Indian Division, Major-General Frank Messervy, established his headquarters (the "Admin Box"). On 4 February, the Japanese counterattacked. As part of their 55th Division slipped round Messervy's left flank, aiming to cut westwards to sever British supply lines, a direct attack was made on the Admin Box. Messervy held out until relieved on 24 February; he then resumed the offensive, seizing Buthidaung on 11 March and Razabil 24 hours later. Further advances were delayed because of events in eastern India.

Meanwhile, Stilwell's offensive in northern Burma had begun. Chinese advances to the south of Ledo in late 1943 had stalled, but when Stilwell brought in American troops – about 3000 men of "Merrill's Marauders" – new impetus was found. In March 1944 the Chinese drove down the Hukawng Valley, while Merrill's Marauders operated further east, aiming for Myitkyina. The advance was supported by the Chindits, whose orders were to attack Myitkyina from the south-west. On 5 February, Brigadier Bernard Fergusson's 16th Long Range Penetration (LRP) Brigade set out from Ledo to create a base to the north of Indaw known as "Aberdeen"; in March, the 77th and 111th LRP Brigades were airlifted in to establish similar positions to the east at "White City" and "Broadway". An attack on Indaw, carried out by Fergusson's men on 26 March, failed, although Japanese assaults on Broadway and White City were repulsed in April. Coming under Stilwell's command in May, the Chindits were ordered to seize Mogaung, to the west of Myitkyina. They did so on 26 June, but by then they were exhausted and it was left to the Americans and Chinese to take Myitkyina on 3 August.

But these successes would have been meaningless if Lieutenant-General William Slim's Fourteenth Army had not held firm in eastern India. On 7/8 March 1944 Lieutenant-General Renya Mutaguchi, commander of the Japanese Fifteenth Army, crossed the River Chindwin with 100,000 men, intent on taking Imphal and Kohima before driving north-east for Dimapur. The advance involved three divisions. In the south, the 33rd tried to surround two Indian divisions before thrusting north toward Imphal; in the center the 15th attempted to move through Sangshak to sever the road between Imphal and Kohima; in the north the 31st advanced on Kohima. All three came close to success and by late March both Imphal and Kohima were besieged. Slim airlifted 5th Indian Division into Imphal from Arakan, while ordering the British 2nd Infantry Division to relieve Kohima from the north.

As Japanese attacks on Imphal were repulsed, a major battle developed for possession of Kohima. The village witnessed some of the toughest fighting of the Burma campaign but by late May the Japanese were running desperately short of supplies and, as British and Indian troops seized key defenses on Jail Hill and around the Deputy Commissioner's bungalow, a withdrawal was ordered. By early June this had developed into a general retreat. Slim's pursuing forces reached the Chindwin in November, poised for an advance into central Burma. The Japanese had suffered over 60,000 casualties.

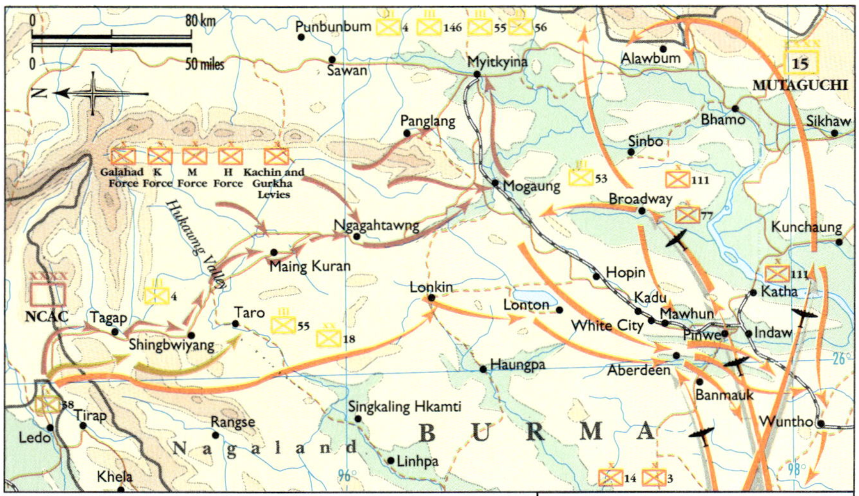

1/Northern Burma
February–August 1943

British movements
U.S. movements
Chinese movements

"We had no ammunition, no food, no clothes, no guns ... the men were barefoot and ragged and threw away everything except canes to help them walk ... At Kohima we were starved and then crushed."

Shizuo Maruyama, Japanese war correspondent

In their slow and exhausting advance toward Myitkyina the Chindits made use of inflatable rubber dinghies which were light and easily transported through the jungle terrain.

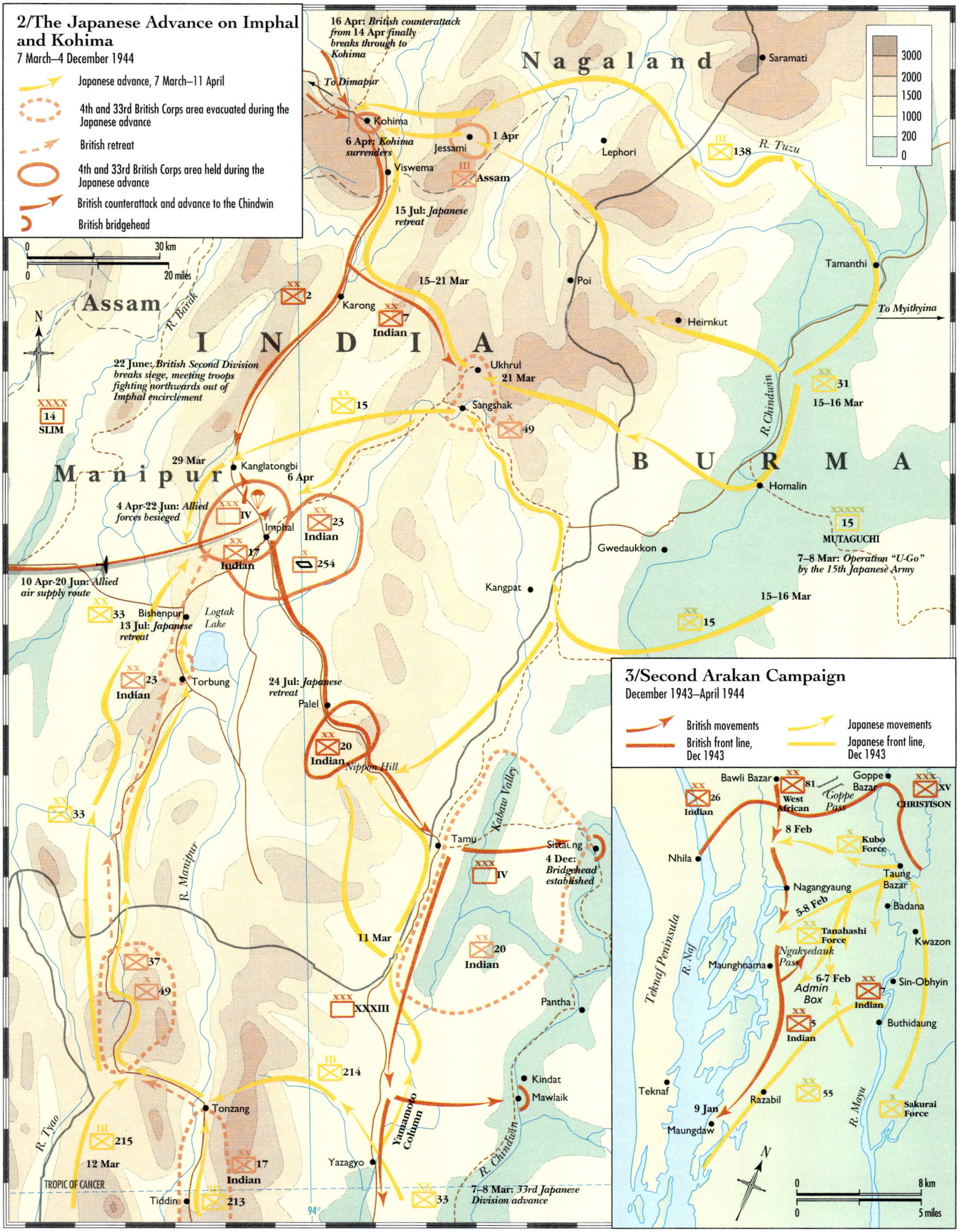

2/The Japanese Advance on Imphal and Kohima
7 March–4 December 1944

3/Second Arakan Campaign
December 1943–April 1944

The Weapons of War

World War II acted as a forging-house for new technology. As countries mobilized their human and economic assets to fight a global war, they released enormous resources that could be devoted to the development and manufacture of new or refined weapons. Between 1939 and 1945 the technology of war went through a revolution, culminating in the manufacture and use of weapons of instantaneous mass destruction, the like of which had not been seen before.

But the atomic bombs were only part of the picture. Armies, navies and air forces all benefited from the technological revolution, increasing their firepower and mobility to a significant extent. This was particularly true of armies, reflecting the preferred doctrine of most combatant powers in favor of battles of maneuver rather than attrition, trying to avoid a repetition of the heavy losses of World War I. The German doctrine of *blitzkrieg*, for example, required the provision of tanks, artillery and infantry carriers that could move quickly over difficult terrain, supported by airpower. This led, even before the war began, to the manufacture of light, fast-moving panzers, tracked artillery tractors and half-tracks, with motor-cycles and armored cars for reconnaissance and Junkers Ju-87 Stuka dive-bombers for support. The Allies had nothing similar at the time, having diverted many of their tanks to the support of infantry, which necessitated the manufacture of heavier, slower armored vehicles and soft-skinned trucks.

Changes occurred as the war progressed. Although German mobility led to the seizure of vast tracts of land in the period 1939–42, Allied technology was already catching up, forcing the Germans to alter their tactics and weapons. As early as 1941, for example, panzer units of Army Group South in Russia encountered the Soviet T-34 tank, with its sloped armor and 76mm main armament, leading Hitler to insist that his manufacturers produce something similar. This emerged as the PzKpfw V Panther – virtually a copy of the T-34 in certain respects – and coincided with the production of the PzKpfw VI Tiger. These were formidable machines – the Tiger, with its 88mm gun, was almost unstoppable – but they were heavier and much closer than earlier models. Indeed, by the end of the war the Tiger had been developed further into the Royal or King Tiger, complete with 150mm of armor and infra-red night-sights, but at nearly 68 tons it proved to be far too heavy to execute *blitzkrieg*-style advances and needed so much petrol that its radius of action was seriously curtailed. By comparison, the Allies concentrated on mass-producing tanks such as the American M-4 Sherman, which combined firepower and speed. This was fine so long as the Sherman did not come up against a Tiger or King Tiger: by 1944 the Americans had nicknamed their tank the "Ronson" because it "lit first time", just as the popular cigarette lighter was supposed to do. By 1945 the British had begun to produce the Centurion and the Americans were field-testing the M-26 Pershing, both designed to counter the Tiger by mounting 17-pounder and 90mm main guns respectively, although by then it was a bit late.

Similar trends may be seen in the development of artillery, the most striking being that towards self-propelled guns capable of keeping up with an armored advance. In most cases, this involved nothing more than mounting an ordinary field gun on an armored chassis, although if this happened to be a German 88mm, the Allies were in trouble. Their usual mount was a 25-pounder or 105mm field gun, capable of inflicting damage but not of taking our enemy armor. For that, special anti-tank guns had to be developed, some of which could also be mounted on a tracked chassis. At infantry level, anti-tank capability included the introduction of hand-held weapons such as the German *Panzerfaust* or American Bazooka, firing projectiles with cone-like hollow heads that created a stream of molten metal once they hit their target. The infantry also benefited from increased firepower in terms of more portable machine guns such as the British Bren and German MG-42, as well as sub-machine guns like the Soviet PPSh or American M-3, while towards the end of the war the Germans were even producing semi-automatic assault rifles. These were of limited use as the enemy had more devastating firepower available; a favorite ploy of the Soviets was to concentrate artillery, including *Katyusha* multi-barreled rocket launchers, to swamp enemy defenses before the infantry and armor went in.

Technological developments at sea normally took longer to effect, chiefly because of the enormous lead-time required. As a result, most naval weapons were refinements of existing designs, although this did not mean they were any less dramatic. By 1939 the Germans had developed new acoustic and magnetic mines, designed to respond to the noise or metal construction of surface ships and later on they extended the acoustic capability to torpedoes. The Allies managed to counter magnetic mines by "degaussing" their ships, passing an electric current round the vessel to reverse its polarity, while acoustic weapons could be confused by extraneous noise, but the real threat came from U-boats that became more sophisticated as the war went on. By 1944 the Germans had developed the *Schnorkel* device to enable submarines to take in air while still submerged, and had perfected new turbine engines that allowed the U-boats to travel quietly. This was important because the one area in which the Allies had a clear advantage was submarine detection using sonar, which worked by bouncing sound waves off underwater objects. Once detected, moreover, the submarines could be attacked using depth charges, set to explode close to a submerged vessel. Other technological changes affecting naval forces included the construction of light carriers, capable of escorting convoys and providing air protection, and amphibious vessels, essential for the campaigns fought in the Pacific, the Mediterranean and North-West Europe. Battleships remained as powerful members of any fleet, but the war in the Pacific showed beyond doubt that the true war-winner was the aircraft carrier.

Airpower went through dramatic changes in World War II, not in terms of its basic use – most air roles were firmly established in World War I – but in its impact on almost every aspect of the conflict. When war broke out in 1939 many combatant powers were still deploying biplanes that would not have looked out of place in the earlier conflict, although most had developed more modern designs. Bombers were seen as potent weapons, capable of destroying industrial and urban centers using high explosives and gas. As the war regressed, it became obvious that bombing could not win wars on its own, although this did not prevent the Germans, British and Americas from conducting strategic bombing campaigns. In all cases, technology was harnessed to increase the impact. The Germans used special radio beams to enhance navigation over England in 1940, and when the RAF moved onto the offensive they too experimented with various aids to navigation and bomb-aiming. By 1942 "Gee" and "H_2S" were available, the latter allowing a navigator to see a radar image of the ground beneath him, and this was followed by "Oboe", a more sophisticated version of radio-beam technology. The Americans, dedicated to daylight bombing which did not require such an ability to read radar images, deployed the Norden bomb-sight, hailed as the ultimate in bombing accuracy, but even they had to explore the capabilities of radar when their B-29s shifted to night-time bombing over Japan in early 1945.

But there was more to airpower than bombing. As the Americans discovered, the deployment of effective fighter aircraft was just as important, in their case to escort the daylight bombers to their targets. The reason was that it was now possible to defend against incoming bombers, partly by using radar and partly by committing fighters that were faster and more agile than their opponents. The Battle of Britain in 1940 showed the potential, when monoplanes such as the Spitfire and Hurricane were guided to the bomber streams by ground controllers using radar, upon which the fighters could take on and defeat the enemy escorts and shoot down the bombers. The Germans came up with the same basic solution when they suffered Allied bombing. At night against the RAF, radar was used to guide specially-equipped night-fighters towards the bomber streams, after which on-board radars could guide the interceptor to an individual target. Many bombers were shot down using *Schräge Musik* → upward-firing cannon that could rake the undefended belly of an aircraft. By 1945 the Germans had developed jet- and rocket-powered fighters such as the Messerschmitt Me-262 and Me-163 to disrupt daylight bomber streams. They had also developed VI pilotless planes and V2 surface-to-surface missiles, designed to hit targets in England or liberated Europe without risking loss of aircrew. Finally, most combatant powers developed fighter-bombers for support of ground forces, as well as transport aircraft and gliders for resupply and airborne landings.

These weapons all pointed the way to the future, particularly if used together, but were eclipsed by the Allied (predominately American) invention of the atomic bomb, used on Japan in August 1945. The ability to take out a city using one bomb carried by a single bomber showed just how far technology had developed in six years of war.

PART V
The Allies Victorious, December 1944 – September 1945

Wars rarely end easily. Despite all the advantages enjoyed by the Allied powers in December 1944, the fighting was by no means over; indeed, some of the most costly and bitter battles had yet to be fought. The remnants of the Axis alliance – essentially Germany and Japan – may have lost all rational hope of victory, but their fanaticism, coupled to an Allied desire to root out all aspects of their beliefs, ensured that the war would not be over until those countries were occupied and their leaders either dead or imprisoned. Nor was this an argument confined to the theorists of total war, for as the conflict came to an end evidence of the cruelties inflicted by both the Germans and Japanese came to light. In Europe, Allied soldiers witnessed first-hand the realities of the "Holocaust" when they liberated concentration camps full of emaciated bodies and starving survivors; in the Far East, news of the Japanese disregard for the rights of prisoners of war and civilian internees did nothing to lessen the widespread desire for revenge. One of the promises made by the Allied powers was that all "war criminals" would be brought before an International Tribunal as soon as peace was restored.

Before that could be done, however, the final campaigns had to be fought and won. In Western Europe, this involved an advance to and a crossing of the River Rhine before thrusting deep into Germany, and the success of that operation in early 1945 showed just how far the Western Allies had come in terms of war-fighting. Not only was great flexibility displayed on the American side in response to the unexpected seizure of an intact bridge at Remagen, but British troops showed during their assault crossings that the lessons of inter-service and all-arms cooperation had been absorbed. The ease of the assault crossings was dimmed in their aftermath by the decision not to go for Berlin, but nothing could disguise the fact that the Western Allies had developed new techniques. The same was true of the Soviets, whose campaign to advance from the Vistula to the Oder, leaving them less than 60 miles from Berlin by February, was masterful. It was dependent not on "brute force and ignorance", as post-war analysts sometimes presumed, but on a refined and much improved version of German *blitzkrieg*, involving surprise to catch the enemy wrong-footed and all-arms momentum to keep him that way. By early 1945 the Germans were being out-thought and out-fought in the East on a regular basis, culminating in their failure to hold Berlin. By then, of course, Hitler was dead and the Western Allies were closing in from the Rhine and from northern Italy, but the final battle was, perhaps fittingly, fought and won by the Soviets. Their losses during four years of war – an estimated 25 million military and civilian dead – show just how much of the fighting they had endured.

Similar casualty figures were not suffered by the Western Allies, although fears of heavy losses as the Americans approached the Japanese Home Islands were very real. As the campaign to liberate the Philippines developed, it was obvious that the Japanese were not going to give in easily – the 100,000 civilian dead in Manila alone, most of them caused by the Japanese, proved that – while landings to take Iwo Jima and Okinawa suggested that casualties would be more severe among the attackers the closer they got to Japan itself. Estimates of half a million dead to take the southern islands of Japan in 1945–46 were commonplace, particularly as the phenomenon of the kamikaze warrior, prepared to commit suicide in battle for his Emperor, emerged. In such circumstances, President Harry Truman's decision to use the atomic bombs when they were offered to him by the Manhattan Project scientists in July 1945 seemed to be justified. Even then, the destruction of Hiroshima and Nagasaki in August did not end the war in the Pacific at a stroke; it took a realization that Japan was no longer able to use her sea-lanes, coupled to a Soviet declaration of war and invasion of Manchuria, to force surrender. Defeat in Burma and stalemate in China clearly did much to exacerbate the Japanese problems.

But Allied victory against the Axis powers created new problems. The decision to fight for "unconditional surrender" meant that enemy states would have to be occupied and all vestiges of their previous governments rooted out. In Europe, the Allies had decided as early as the

Tehran Conference in 1943 that Germany should be divided into zones of occupation, each under the control of one of the victorious powers (Britain, France, the U.S.A. and Soviet Union), and by 1945 this had also been extended to Austria and Berlin. The last-named caused an immediate problem, for it lay inside the Soviet zone, and it was not until July 1945 that Western troops were allowed to enter the city. By then, much of the wartime friendliness between the Allies was already strained, suggesting that common hatred of fascism had been all that had held them together. It would not take long for a new confrontation, this time between communism and liberal democracy, to emerge, dividing Europe into two armed camps until the collapse of the Soviet Union through essentially internal pressure in the early 1990s. The Cold War, with its ever-present threat of nuclear conflict between Superpowers, was one of the more obvious results of World War II, it was fueled in the Pacific by an American insistence that, despite the Soviet invasion of Manchuria in 1945, the occupation of Japan should be a Western (predominantly American) responsibility.

As in 1918, however, peace in 1945 brought a degree of hope for the future. Not only had the world been freed from fascist tyranny but it had also recognized the advantages to be gained from collective international action. The Cold War may have undermined its effectiveness, at least until the 1990s, but the United Nations, created in 1945, was designed to avoid many of the problems associated with the now defunct League of Nations. It acted as a forum for debate and a means of absorbing new states, many of them ex-colonial, into the international system without recourse to conflict. Most of all, it reinforced the general desire to avoid a repetition of total war and the enormous costs involved.

Churchill, Roosevelt and Stalin at The Yalta Conference, February 1945.

Battle of the Bulge DECEMBER 1944 – JANUARY 1945

As early as September 1944, Hitler began to prepare a counterattack in the West, designed to disrupt the Allied advance and allow a concentration of German troops against the Soviets. Serious planning began in October, by which time a stalemate had set in and the Western Allies' dispositions were clear. A glance at the map showed that the two U.S. armies of Bradley's 12th Army Group were advancing on divergent axes, split by the thinly-held Ardennes. Attracted to the region by memories of the success of May 1940, Hitler aimed to break through, cross the River Meuse and recapture Brussels and Antwerp. Split in two, the Allies would be forced onto the defensive; indeed, if the operation, codenamed *Wacht am Rhein* ("Watch on the Rhine"), did enough damage to their morale, they might even collapse.

German forces were moved into position in great secrecy, taking advantage of winter weather and Allied complacency. By mid-December 1944 a total of 25 divisions (10 of them armored) were in place, divided into three armies. In the north, SS General Josef "Sepp" Dietrich's Sixth Panzer Army was to advance on Antwerp; in the center General Hasso von Manteuffel's Fifth Panzer Army was to attack towards Brussels; in the south General Erich Brandenberger's Seventh Army was to protect the flank of the main assault. With more than 275,000 troops and nearly 1000 armored vehicles available, the German force was formidable. Facing it were about 83,000 Americans, strung out along a 60-mile front from Monschau in the north to Echternach in the south. Part of Lieutenant-General Courtney H. Hodges' U.S. First Army, they were a mixture of formations – some were resting, others were

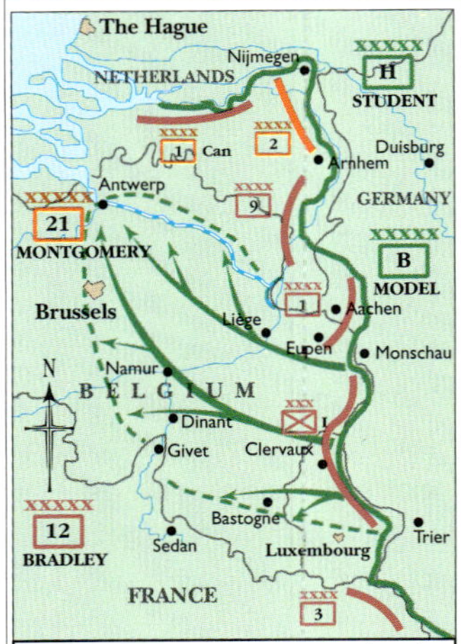

1/The German Plan
'Wacht am Rhine' December 1944
- Allied positions, 15 Dec
- German front line, 15 Dec
- Planned German offensive

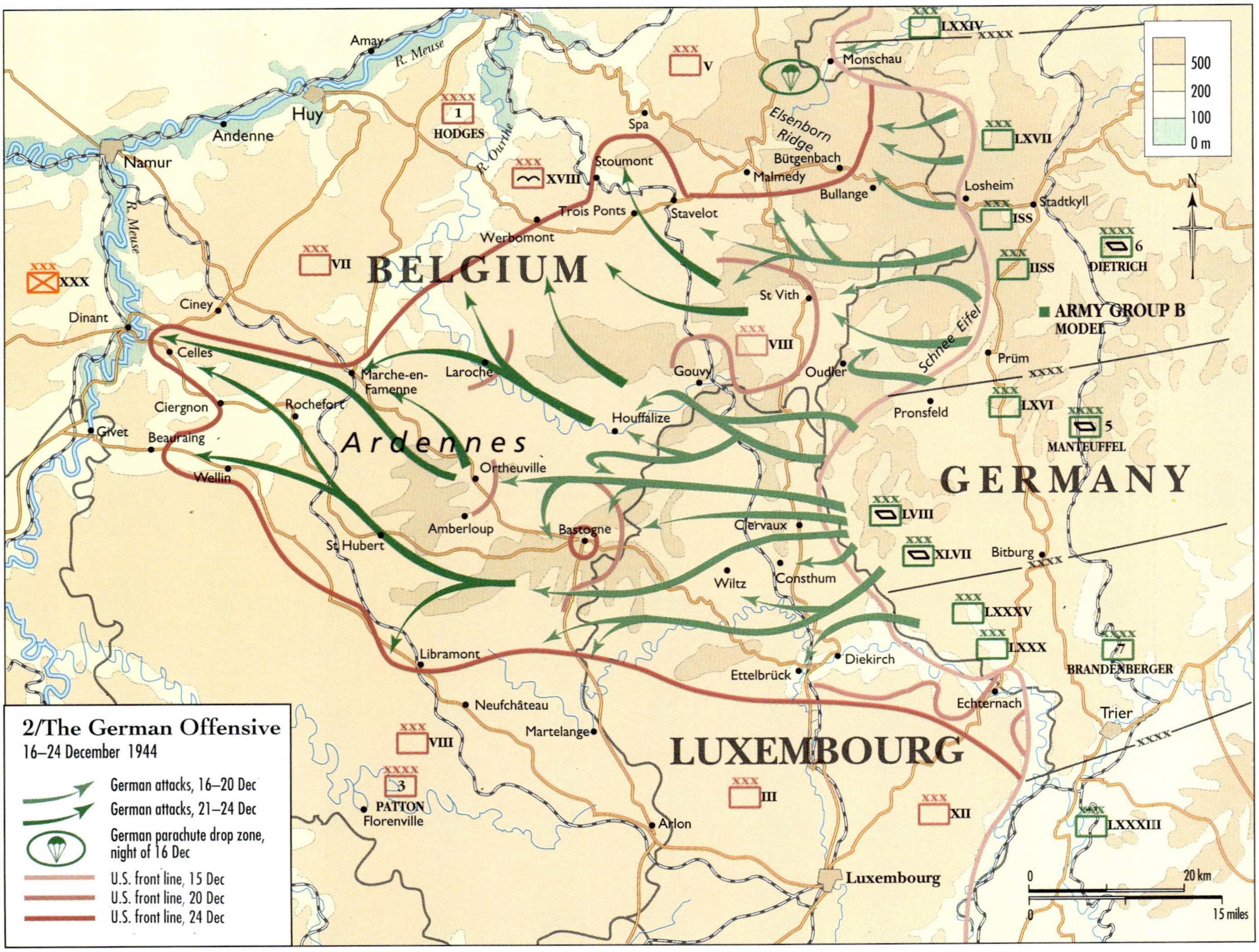

2/The German Offensive
16–24 December 1944
- German attacks, 16–20 Dec
- German attacks, 21–24 Dec
- German parachute drop zone, night of 16 Dec
- U.S. front line, 15 Dec
- U.S. front line, 20 Dec
- U.S. front line, 24 Dec

new to the European Theater. They were supported by no more than 420 armored vehicles.

The attack began early on 16 December with a short artillery bombardment. Denied air cover because of overcast skies, the Americans could do little to prevent a breakthrough, although enough of them held out in isolated pockets to disrupt German momentum. In the north, where a parachute assault behind American lines was scattered by high winds, the U.S. 2nd and 99th Infantry Divisions pulled back to the Elsenborn Ridge, creating a "shoulder" that held firm. To their right, the spearhead of the 1st SS Panzer Division – *Kampfgruppe* Peiper – made some progress on 17 December, but was soon contained. Dietrich's only real success came on the Schnee Eifel, where the inexperienced U.S. 106th Infantry Division was overwhelmed. Manteuffel achieved more, approaching St Vith and Bastogne – vital road junctions in the Ardennes – after pushing through the U.S. 28th Infantry Division along "Skyline Drive", but to his south Brandenberger failed to make much progress. By 18 December, a "bulge" had developed in the Ardennes and the assault was running out of steam.

Eisenhower refused to panic. Moving reserves into the threatened region, he divided responsibility for its defense between Bradley and Montgomery. At the same time, he ordered Lieutenant-General George S. Patton, south of the "bulge", to mount a counterattack. St Vith held out until 21 December, by which time Montgomery had consolidated the defense of the northern sector, and although Bastogne, held by the U.S. 10th Armored and 101st Airborne Divisions, was surrounded, it stood like a rock in the stream of the German advance. Some German units bypassed Bastogne, but ran out of fuel before reaching the Meuse. By 26 December, Patton had broken through to relieve Bastogne from the south, creating a new focus for German attention. Although there was still much fighting left to do, the crisis had passed.

Once the assault had been contained, the Allies squeezed the "bulge" from north and south. Hitler wasted his remaining reserves in an abortive assault in the Vosges Mountains (Operation *Nordwind*) on 31 December, leaving little with which to face the Allied onslaught. On 15 January 1945 the Americans linked up at Houffalize in the center of the "bulge"; by the end of the month the battle was over. In the process, the Germans had lost nearly 120,000 men and a wealth of irreplaceable equipment.

"On this day four Germans in one of our jeeps, dressed in American uniforms, were killed, and another group of seventeen, also in American uniforms, were reported by the 35th Division as follows: 'One sentinel, reinforced, saw seventeen Germans in American uniforms. Fifteen were killed and two died suddenly."

General Patton, Commander Third Army, 30 December 1944

American prisoners are rounded up by German paratroopers, many of whom were veterans of the Russian Front and therefore used to fighting in extreme weather conditions. This helped them to gain the upper hand in the early days of the campaign, when they attacked weakly-held Allied lines and forced an American retreat.

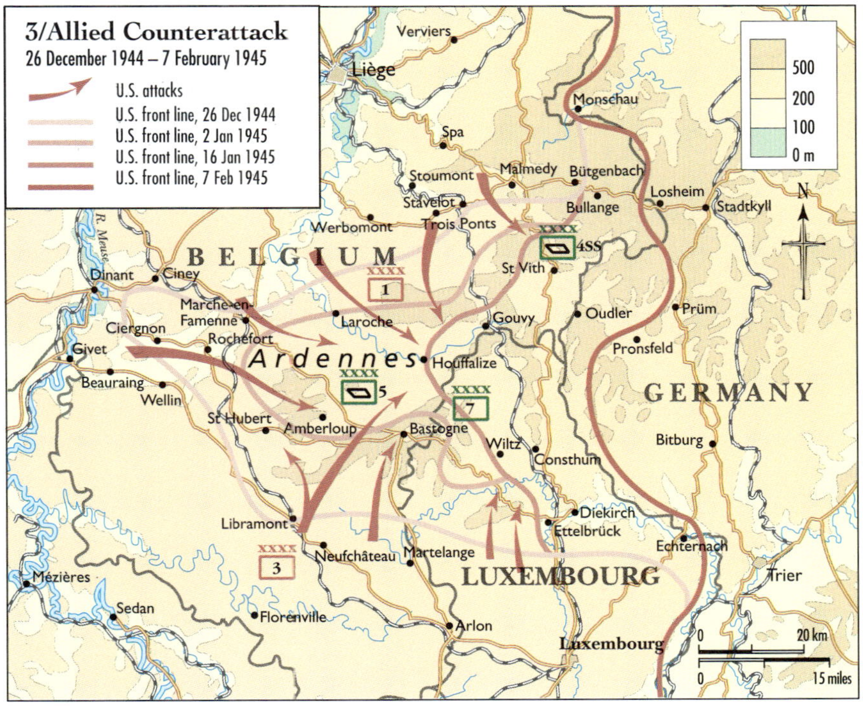

Sherman tank crews of the U.S. 3rd Armored Division prepare to venture into the "witches' lair" of the Hürtgen Forest southeast of Aachen. Covering 32 square miles (80 square kilometers) and strewn with mines, barbed wire and pillboxes, it was the scene of dreadful casualties on the four occasions that U.S. infantry divisions were sent in.

Advance to the Rhine FEBRUARY – MARCH 1945

The German attack in the Ardennes delayed Allied plans for an advance towards the Rhine – the last great barrier to the enemy heartland. Eisenhower favored a "broad-front" offensive, whereby all armies would push forward in unison before crossing the river, but he could not order this to begin while the Germans still occupied the "bulge". Once that battle was over, however, German losses meant that the advance could be initiated with some confidence.

According to Eisenhower's plan, the main attack was to take place in the north, where Montgomery's 21st Army Group, comprising the British Second, Canadian First and U.S. Ninth Armies, would mount two offensives – Operation *Veritable* to close to the Rhine opposite Wesel and Operation *Grenade* to sweep north-east from the River Roer to link up. Further south, Lieutenant-General Omar Bradley's 12th Army Group, containing the U.S. First and Third Armies, would move forward in Operation *Lumberjack* to reach the Rhine between Cologne and Koblenz, while Lieutenant-General Jacob Devers' 6th Army Group, comprising the U.S. Seventh and French First Armies, would attack the industrial area of the Saar and take Mannheim in Operation *Undertone*. Only then would assault crossings be made: one in the north under Montgomery and one in the south under Bradley, designed to split enemy defenses and encircle the Ruhr before thrusting deep into Germany.

Veritable began on 8 February 1945, when the British XXX Corps, under command of the Canadian First Army, attacked south-eastwards down a narrow corridor between the rivers Meuse and Rhine in the eastern Netherlands. To begin with, good progress was made, but when the British entered a heavily-wooded area known as the Reichswald, they came across fortified villages defended by hardened veterans of General Alfred Schlemm's First Parachute Army. Warmer weather led to extensive flooding, which disrupted the movement of reinforcements and supplies, and it took until 16 February for the Reichswald to be cleared. British and Canadian troops took the defended towns of Kleve and Goch, eventually consolidating on the Rhine between Emmerich and Xanten by 21 February. But *Grenade*, designed to take place simultaneously, had not even begun. The U.S. Ninth Army, commanded by Lieutenant-General William H. Simpson, had been delayed by enemy destruction of dams on the River Roer, which led to extensive flooding, and the advance could not start until 23 February. German reserves had been committed to oppose the attack further north, however, so Simpson's men encountered little real resistance. They took Mönchengladbach on 1 March, reaching the Rhine near Düsseldorf the following day. By then, the British and Canadians had squeezed out the last of the pockets on the west bank and Schlemm had pulled back across the river, destroying bridges as he went.

Further south, *Lumberjack* achieved a breakthrough on a broad front, breaching the supposedly impregnable Siegfried Line with ease and racing for the Rhine. It was during this advance that men of the U.S. 9th Armored Division, spearheading the extreme right of Lieutenant-General Courtney H. Hodges' U.S. First Army, approached the river at Remagen on 7 March. They knew that a railway bridge across the Rhine existed there but, quite naturally, expected it to have been destroyed. At about midday, they were surprised to see it still intact, and although the Germans tried to blow it up, the bridge stubbornly resisted their efforts. Just before 4 p.m. Lieutenant Karl Timmermann of the U.S. 27th Armored Infantry Battalion led his men onto the bridge to achieve the totally unexpected – a crossing of the river in the central sector. This was not part of Eisenhower's plan, but he immediately diverted everything he could to Remagen. As Bradley's troops were by now in possession of the west bank from Cologne to Koblenz, enough forces were available to make the most of the opportunity. Meanwhile, Devers' troops had cleared German forces from the Colmar "pocket" and, in cooperation with elements of Patton's U.S. Third Army, they advanced through the Saar to take Mannheim and complete Operation *Undertone*. By late March, the Western Allies were in place all along the Rhine, poised for their final campaign.

American artillerymen prepare for an attack on German positions across the Rhine. The swift-flowing river was a huge obstacle for the Allies. On the opposite side, German troops withdrew as they found themselves bombarded by 9½-inch (244mm) shells.

Three infantrymen watch for snipers among the ruins of Stein, one of the twelve German villages captured by the British during their advance towards the Rhine. Across the river lay Germany's industrial heartland, the Ruhr Valley, which the Allies hoped to conquer.

> *"In this, the twilight of their gods, the defenders of the Reich displayed the recklessness of fanaticism and the courage of despair ... they fought with special ferocity and resolution, rendering the battles in the Reichswald and Hockwald forests grimly memorable in the annals of this war."*
>
> **Colonel C.P. Stacey**

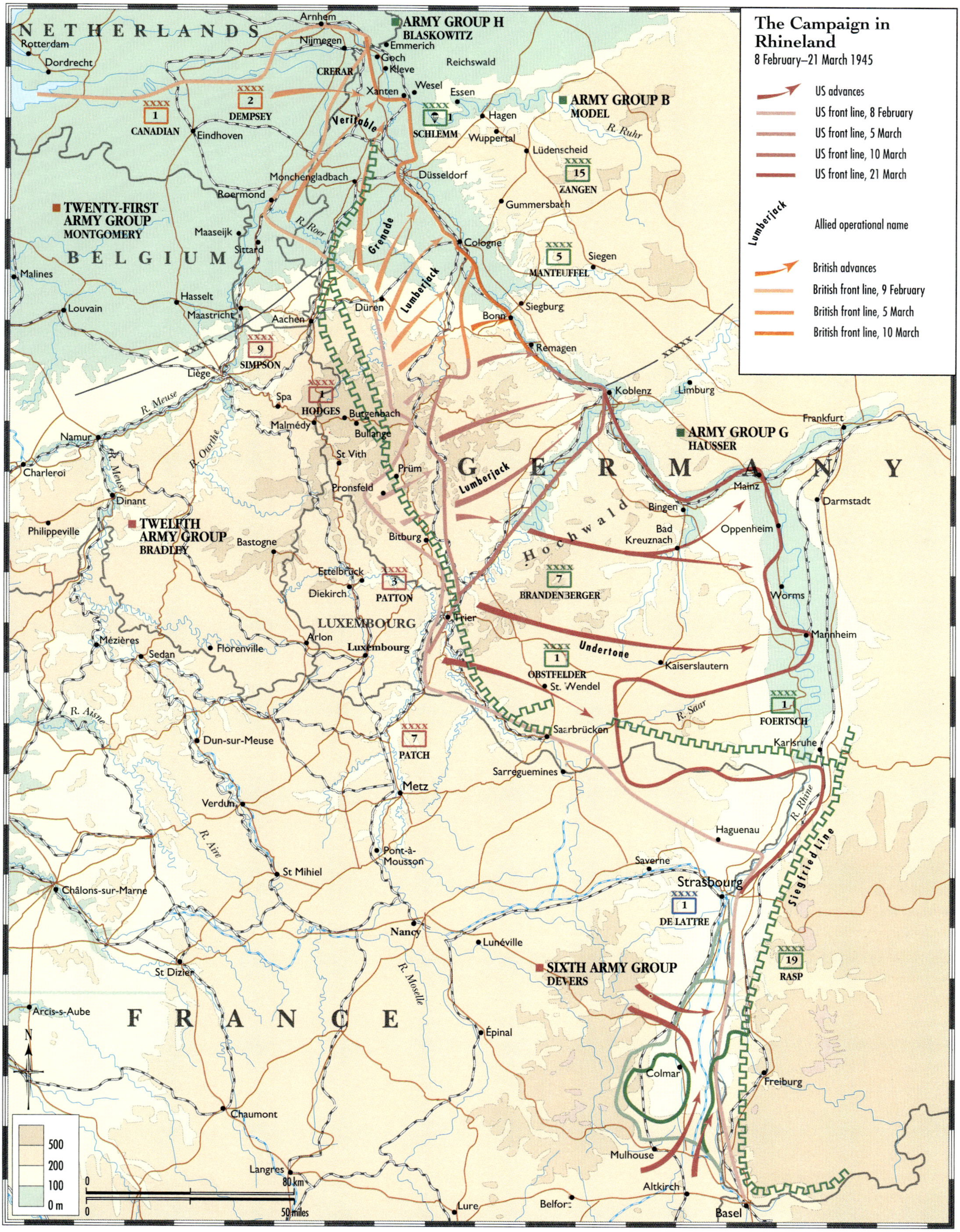
The Campaign in Rhineland
8 February–21 March 1945
US advances
US front line, 8 February
US front line, 5 March
US front line, 10 March
US front line, 21 March
Lumberjack
Allied operational name
British advances
British front line, 9 February
British front line, 5 March
British front line, 10 March
NETHERLANDS
BELGIUM
GERMANY
FRANCE
LUXEMBOURG
ARMY GROUP H
BLASKOWITZ
ARMY GROUP B
MODEL
ARMY GROUP G
HAUSSER
TWENTY-FIRST ARMY GROUP
MONTGOMERY
TWELFTH ARMY GROUP
BRADLEY
SIXTH ARMY GROUP
DEVERS
1 CANADIAN
2 DEMPSEY
CRERAR
1 SCHLEMM
15 ZANGEN
5 MANTEUFFEL
9 SIMPSON
1 HODGES
3 PATTON
7 BRANDENBERGER
1 OBSTFELDER
7 PATCH
1 FOERTSCH
1 DE LATTRE
19 RASP
Veritable
Grenade
Lumberjack
Undertone
Hochwald
Siegfried Line
R. Roer
R. Ruhr
R. Meuse
R. Ourthe
R. Aisne
R. Aire
R. Moselle
R. Saar
R. Rhine
Rotterdam
Dordrecht
Arnhem
Nijmegen
Emmerich
Goch
Kleve
Reichswald
Wesel
Xanten
Essen
Hagen
Wuppertal
Lüdenscheid
Eindhoven
Düsseldorf
Monchengladbach
Roermond
Maaseijk
Sittard
Gummersbach
Cologne
Siegen
Malines
Hasselt
Louvain
Maastricht
Aachen
Düren
Bonn
Siegburg
Remagen
Liège
Spa
Malmédy
Butgenbach
Bullange
Koblenz
Limburg
Frankfurt
Namur
St Vith
Prüm
Pronsfeld
Charleroi
Dinant
Mainz
Darmstadt
Bingen
Bad Kreuznach
Oppenheim
Philippeville
Bastogne
Bitburg
Ettelbrück
Diekirch
Worms
Trier
Mannheim
Mézières
Sedan
Florenville
Arlon
Luxembourg
Kaiserslautern
St. Wendel
Saarbrücken
Karlsruhe
Dun-sur-Meuse
Sarreguemines
Metz
Verdun
Haguenau
Pont-à-Mousson
Saverne
St Mihiel
Strasbourg
Châlons-sur-Marne
Nancy
Lunéville
St Dizier
Arcis-s-Aube
Épinal
Colmar
Freiburg
Chaumont
Mulhouse
Langres
Altkirch
Lure
Belfort
Basel
N
500
200
100
0 m
0
80 km
0
50 miles

Crossing the Rhine MARCH 1945

Despite the unexpected seizure of an intact bridge across the River Rhine at Remagen on 1 March 1945, the Allied plan for breaching the Rhine barrier did not change. Eisenhower had always intended to mount the main assault in the north, where Montgomery's Anglo-Canadian 21st Army Group had consolidated positions along the west bank of the river by early March. Other crossings would clearly be valuable further south, in the sector covered by Bradley's U.S. 12th Army Group, but they would be subsidiary, aiming merely to split German defenses and threaten the southern approaches to the Ruhr industrial area. Thus, although Eisenhower and Bradley did all they could to reinforce the bridgehead at Remagen, they recognized that a breakout into central Germany through the hills of the Wester Wald was impracticable, while crossings any further south, in the sectors covered by Patton's U.S. Third Army and Devers' Franco-American 6th Army Group, were just too far away from what was still the main objective, Berlin.

Montgomery had been planning his assault crossings (codenamed Operation *Plunder*) for some time. They were scheduled to take place on the night of 23/24 March, after massive air and artillery bombardments had prepared the way. On the left, elements of Lieutenant-General Sir Miles Dempsey's British Second Army would seize a bridgehead between Rees and Wesel, while on the right men of Lieutenant-General William H. Simpson's U.S. Ninth Army would cross between Wesel and Duisburg. As soon as the infantry had reached the east bank, engineers would construct bridges to enable reinforcements (including armor) to pour over the river, where they would be joined on 24 March by forces belonging to Major-General Matthew B. Ridgway's U.S. XVIII Airborne Corps (comprising the British 6th and U.S. 17th Airborne Divisions) in Operation *Varsity*. The aim was to create a bridgehead some 40 miles long and 10 miles deep, out of which 21st Army Group could advance to begin the encirclement of the Ruhr industrial area, eventually linking up with U.S. forces from the Remagen sector. Canadian troops, on Montgomery's extreme left, would cross the Rhine at Emmerich once the main assault was complete, moving north and west to trap German units in northern Holland.

Patton stole a march on his rival Montgomery by crossing the Rhine at Oppenheim on 22/23 March, but nothing could substitute for *Plunder*. At 6 p.m. on 23 March the British artillery barrage, involving more than 2000 guns, began and lead battalions of infantry boarded an assortment of amphibious craft. After a seven-minute crossing just after 9 p.m., men of the 51st (Highland) Division landed to the south-east of Rees against minimal opposition. An hour later the 1st Commando Brigade carved out a bridgehead to the south of Wesel, just in time to witness a devastating air attack on the town by RAF bombers, while battalions of the 15th Scottish Division crossed in the center, between Rees and Wesel. At 2 a.m. on the 24th, after a short artillery bombardment, troops of the U.S. 30th and 79th Infantry Divisions landed around Walsum and Orsoy. By dawn, the Allies had a firm hold on the east bank.

The Germans were in chaos, made worse when, at 10 a.m. on 24 March, Operation *Varsity* began. Witnessed by British Prime Minister Winston Churchill, who had arrived the previous day, an armada of 1700 transport aircraft and 1300 gliders deposited Ridgway's two divisions around Hamminkeln, from where they seized the towns of Diersfordt and Dinlaken before advancing east to cross the River Issel. Despite heavy fighting in Rees, where the 51st (Highland) Division suffered casualties clearing the town, the bridgehead was secure. By the end of March, Montgomery had 20 divisions and over 1000 tanks across the river.

To his intense disappointment, he was denied the opportunity to take Berlin. Political agreements between the Allies at Yalta in February had assigned the capture of the city to the Soviets, and on 28 March Eisenhower issued a new directive to his armies which shifted the emphasis of their attack further south. Montgomery had to be content with an advance into northern Germany and Holland. Even so, the end was clearly in sight.

US armor is unloaded from landing craft after crossing the Rhine. In 1945 the Rhine was not fortified and was only weakly garrisoned with troops who were already battle-fatigued. Opposition to the crossings was minimal.

"A river is welcome as a tactical obstacle, but operationally, however, it cannot be held for long … When the Allies had crossed the Rhine the last illusory obstacle was lost and with it the war."

General Blumentritt

A tank of the US 9th Army is ferried across the Rhine on a floating Bailey raft. Various means of crossing the river were devised by the Allies, including Buffalo amphibious vehicles used by the British commandos and pontoon bridges which replaced the permanent bridges destroyed by the retreating German forces.

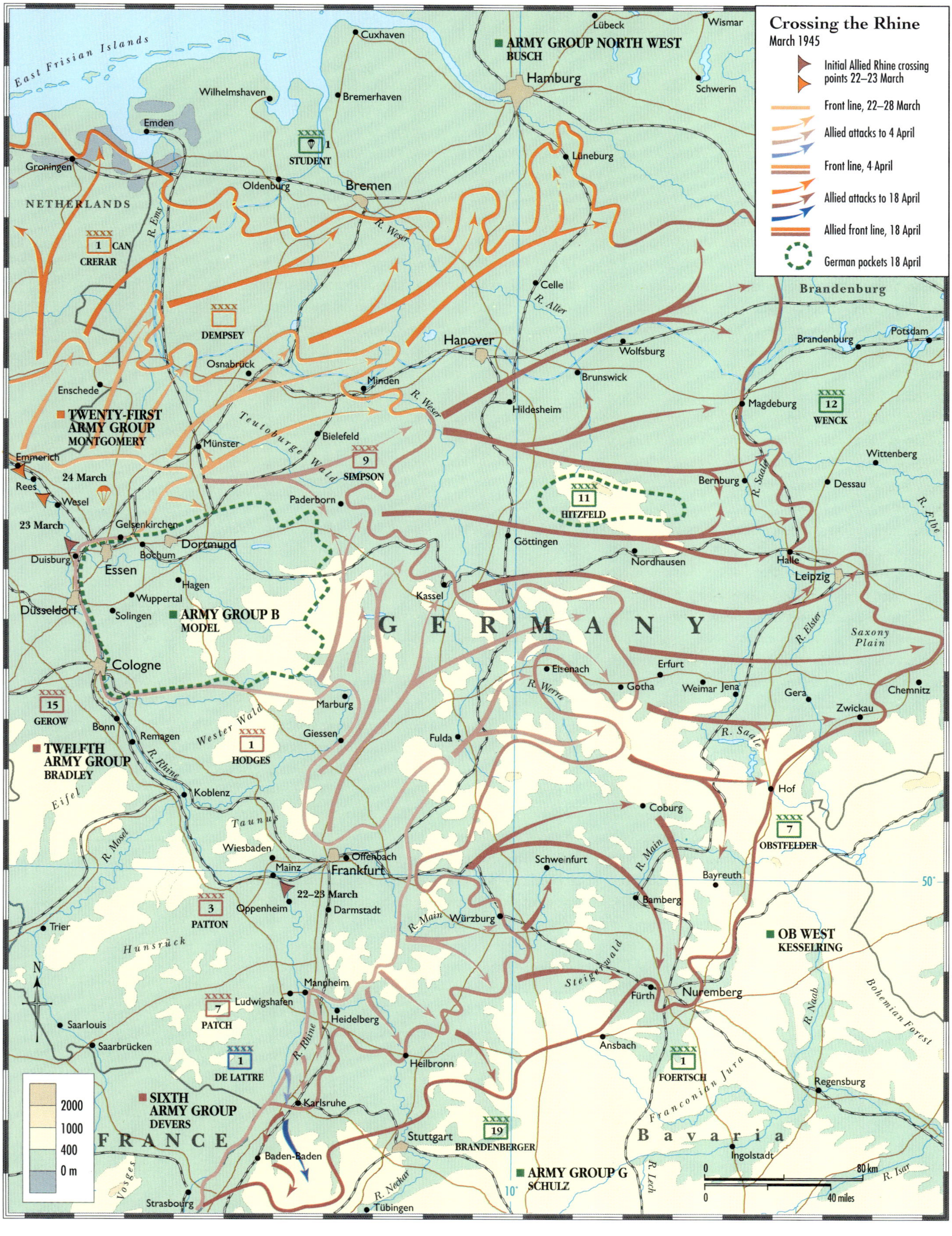
Crossing the Rhine
March 1945
Initial Allied Rhine crossing points 22–23 March
Front line, 22–28 March
Allied attacks to 4 April
Front line, 4 April
Allied attacks to 18 April
Allied front line, 18 April
German pockets 18 April
ARMY GROUP NORTH WEST
BUSCH
TWENTY-FIRST ARMY GROUP
MONTGOMERY
ARMY GROUP B
MODEL
TWELFTH ARMY GROUP
BRADLEY
SIXTH ARMY GROUP
DEVERS
OB WEST
KESSELRING
ARMY GROUP G
SCHULZ
1 CAN
CRERAR
DEMPSEY
1 STUDENT
9 SIMPSON
11 HITZFELD
12 WENCK
15 GEROW
1 HODGES
3 PATTON
7 PATCH
1 DE LATTRE
19 BRANDENBERGER
1 FOERTSCH
7 OBSTFELDER
24 March
23 March
22–23 March
East Frisian Islands
NETHERLANDS
GERMANY
FRANCE
Brandenburg
Saxony Plain
Bavaria
Teutoburger Wald
Wester Wald
Eifel
Taunus
Hunsrück
Steigerwald
Franconian Jura
Bohemian Forest
Vosges
R. Ems
R. Weser
R. Aller
R. Elbe
R. Saale
R. Elster
R. Werra
R. Rhine
R. Mosel
R. Main
R. Naab
R. Neckar
R. Lech
R. Isar
Cuxhaven
Lübeck
Wismar
Hamburg
Schwerin
Wilhelmshaven
Bremerhaven
Emden
Groningen
Oldenburg
Bremen
Lüneburg
Celle
Hanover
Wolfsburg
Brunswick
Potsdam
Brandenburg
Magdeburg
Osnabrück
Enschede
Minden
Hildesheim
Bielefeld
Münster
Emmerich
Rees
Wesel
Paderborn
Wittenberg
Bernburg
Dessau
Gelsenkirchen
Dortmund
Bochum
Duisburg
Essen
Göttingen
Nordhausen
Halle
Leipzig
Hagen
Wuppertal
Kassel
Düsseldorf
Solingen
Cologne
Eisenach
Erfurt
Gotha
Weimar
Jena
Gera
Chemnitz
Zwickau
Bonn
Remagen
Marburg
Giessen
Fulda
Koblenz
Hof
Coburg
Wiesbaden
Offenbach
Mainz
Frankfurt
Schweinfurt
Bayreuth
Oppenheim
Darmstadt
Bamberg
Würzburg
Trier
Mannheim
Ludwigshafen
Fürth
Nuremberg
Heidelberg
Saarlouis
Saarbrücken
Ansbach
Heilbronn
Regensburg
Karlsruhe
Stuttgart
Ingolstadt
Baden-Baden
Strasbourg
Tübingen
2000
1000
400
0 m
0
80 km
40 miles
50°
10°
N

Bombing of Germany AUGUST 1944 – MAY 1945

As Allied armies broke out from the Normandy beachhead in August 1944, the need to devote heavy bombers to support the ground forces declined. Although Eisenhower retained the right to call for such support until the end of the war, both Air Chief Marshal Sir Arthur Harris, C-in-C of RAF Bomber Command, and his counterpart in command of the Eighth USAAF, Lieutenant-General Carl Spaatz, were free to resume the strategic bombing offensive against Germany. Despite the "Pointblank Directive", issued in June 1943, which ordered the RAF to bomb cities and the USAAF to go for more precise targets, it was decided on 25 September 1944 that the resumed offensive would concentrate on the destruction of synthetic oil and transportation, with the area-bombing of urban centers a less urgent priority. Harris remained unconvinced, believing that the RAF, by now capable of fielding over 1000 bombers a night on a regular basis, was in an ideal position to hammer the enemy flat, taking out industrial targets within the cities and helping to crush the spirit of the civilian population. This, he argued, would shorten the war by undermining German resistance to ground forces. Spaatz believed that the destruction of oil and transport targets would do just the same.

The result was an Allied campaign that was not fully coordinated, although the size of the bomber fleets, combined with a steady deterioration of German defensive measures, meant that the impact was still devastating. Indeed, as 1944 drew to an end, the RAF resumed some daylight raids, beginning operations that were to culminate on 14 March 1945, when specially designed six-ton "earthquake" bombs destroyed the Bielefeld viaduct on the Hamm-Hannover railroad. Nevertheless, Harris' preference for city bombing was apparent, citing the reason that poor weather rendered more accurate attacks impossible. A second "Battle of the Ruhr" was conducted in fall 1944, after which the RAF shifted to smaller cities such as Darmstadt, Freiburg and Ulm. Meanwhile, Spaatz concentrated on synthetic-oil factories, particularly around Leipzig, and took every opportunity to disrupt communications within the *Reich*. It was during these operations that the Eighth AAF first experienced a new German weapon – the Messerschmitt Me-262 twin-jet fighter, capable of flying at more than 500 mph. If this had appeared earlier, the B-17s and B-24s under Spaatz's command would have had a hard time. As it was, they suffered losses but never enough to halt the campaign.

There were occasions on which the two air forces did cooperate. The most controversial of these was the bombing of Dresden in mid-February 1945. For some months, the British Air Ministry had been contemplating a series of heavy raids on German cities, designed to create chaos and consternation. Codenamed Operation *Thunderclap*, the plan was revived when Winston Churchill attended the Yalta Conference in early February and promised to help the Soviets by bombing cities in the path of their advance. Dresden was targeted and the Americans were persuaded to take part. On the night of 13/14 February over 800 RAF bombers dropped more than 3000 tons of high explosives and incendiaries on the city, producing a "fire-storm" that killed between 25,000 and 50,000 people. The Americans stoked the fires further on 14 and 15 February. When the scale of destruction was realized, Churchill began to query the need for such raids now that the war was drawing to a close. By the end of March, few targets remained, and both the British and American bombers were diverted to supporting the military.

The strategic bombing campaign therefore ended on something of a sour note, suggesting that heavy aircrew losses – 55,500 RAF and over 63,000 USAAF personnel were killed – were wasteful. This is unjust. Although pre-war theories about the capabilities of bombers to win the war on their own, without the need for land campaigns, were clearly wrong, the bombing offensive did enormous damage to the German war economy and contributed in no small measure to Allied victory. By early 1945, German front line forces were desperately short of fuel and munitions, lacking the factories to produce such resources and transportation to get them forward, and civilian morale, although not broken, was battered enough to reduce resistance.

"... if the Tommies are allowed to go on bombing us like this, soon there will be nothing left of Western Germany."

Anonymous German citizen

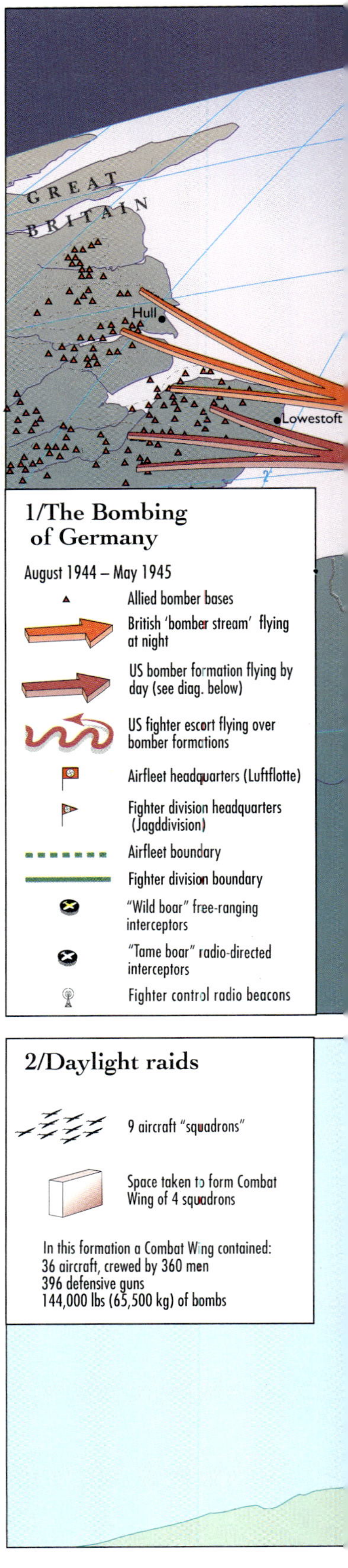

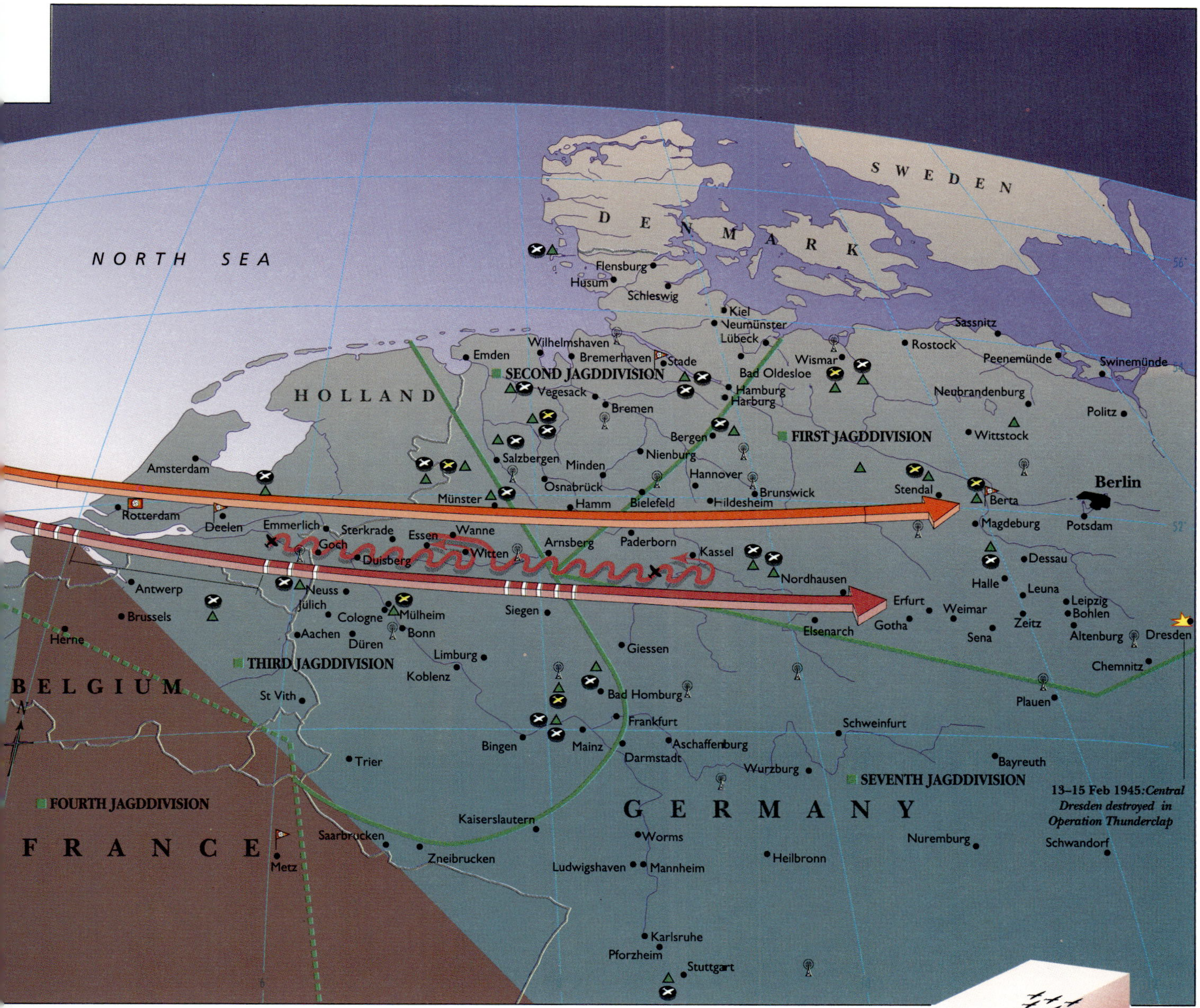

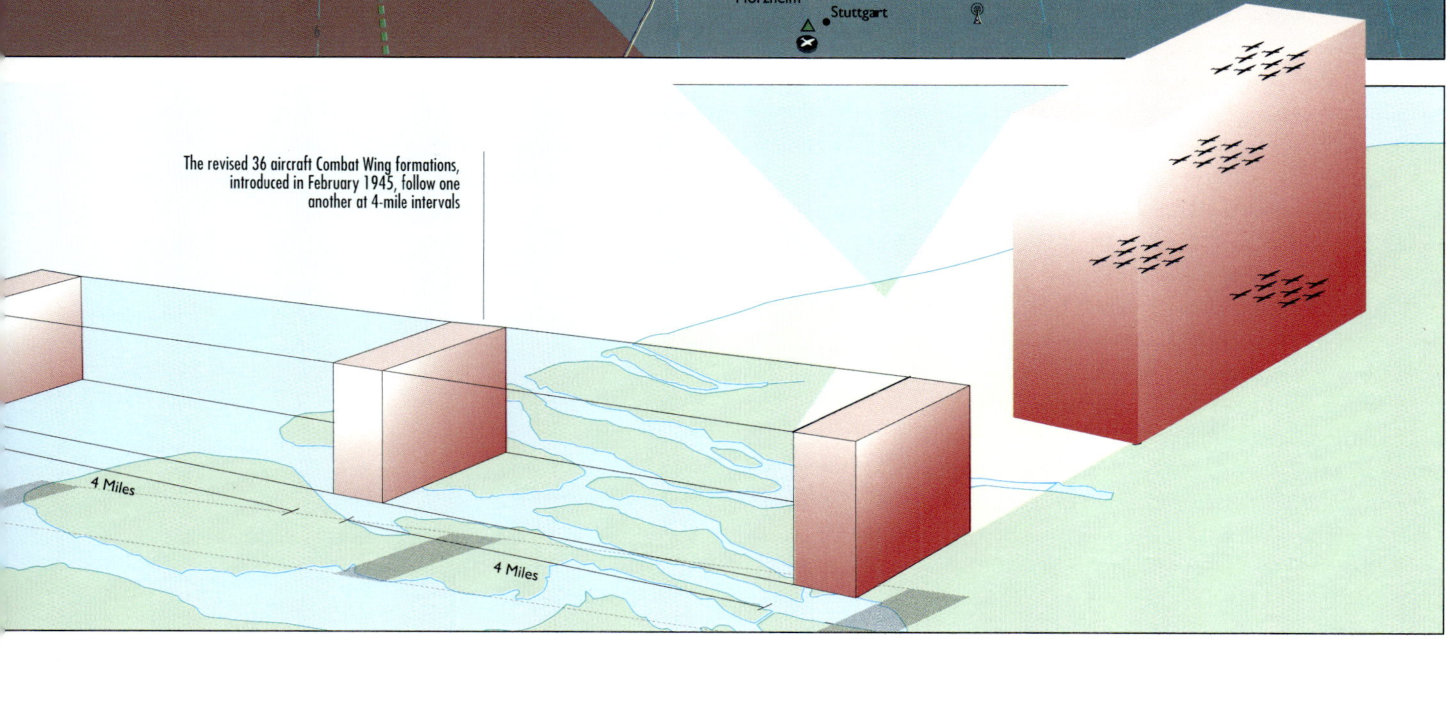

The revised 36 aircraft Combat Wing formations, introduced in February 1945, follow one another at 4-mile intervals

The End in Italy APRIL – MAY 1945

Appalling winter weather effectively stopped all Allied offensives in Italy by December 1944. Field Marshal Sir Harold Alexander, newly appointed Supreme Allied Commander in the Mediterranean, ordered Lieutenant-General Mark Clark, now commander of the 15th Army Group (comprising the U.S. Fifth and British Eighth Armies), to concentrate on patrolling and training, in preparation for a renewed assault on German positions in the spring. The Allies were holding a line from north of Viareggio on the west coast, through the Apennines to the banks of the River Senio in the east, from where they faced General Heinrich von Vietinghoff's Army Group C (comprising the Tenth and Fourteenth Armies). Vietinghoff planned to fight a delaying action along the Rivers Po and Adige before making a stand in the Alps, but Hitler refused to sanction any further withdrawals. The two sides spent the winter in uneasy stalemate.

Alexander planned his offensive for early April 1945. The initial attack was to take place in the east, where Eighth Army, commanded by Lieutenant-General Sir Richard McCreery, would seize the shores of Lake Comacchio before advancing north-west across the Rivers Senio and Santerno. The area had been extensively flooded by the Germans, leaving only one relatively dry route, through the so-called "Argenta Gap", so the fighting was expected to be hard. Once the Germans had been engaged around Argenta, however, a major assault would begin in the west, where Major-General Lucien Truscott's U.S. Fifth Army would drive north to Bologna and Modena. The ultimate objective was to establish positions in the Po Valley, although if the enemy collapsed there was every intention of advancing further. Alexander was aware that SS General Karl Wolff, head of the SS and police in northern Italy, had already approached U.S. officials in Switzerland with a view to negotiating surrender, but he could not depend on this coming to fruition.

The offensive began on 1 April, when British commandos, together with the 24th Guards Brigade, seized a thin strip of land between Lake Comacchio and the coast. This enabled the commandos to mount amphibious operations across the lake, timed to coincide with the main assault on 9 April. The Germans, caught between the two forces, beat a hasty retreat. Argenta fell to Eighth Army on 17 April, opening the route to Ferrara and the River Po. By then, Truscott had joined in, committing his men to a direct attack on Bologna. Despite tough fighting in mountainous terrain, Fifth Army broke through to the suburbs on 20 April, allowing the Polish II Corps (part of Eighth Army) to enter the city from the south-east the following day. Vietinghoff, staring defeat in the face, ordered his troops to retreat across the Po. By 23 April they had succeeded in doing so, but much of their heavy equipment was left behind.

As Truscott pushed forward to take Modena and crossed the Po to the west of Ostiglia, Vietinghoff met with Wolff and other commanders to discuss future moves. Despite Hitler's orders to stand fast, they realized that all was lost and, on 29 April, representatives traveled to Alexander's headquarters at Caserta to sign an unconditional surrender of all German forces in Italy. It came into effect on 2 May, by which time Allied troops had advanced against minimal opposition to take Venice and Trieste in the east, Verona in the center, and Milan and Turin in the west. On 4 May, as the war in the rest of Europe drew to a close, they entered the Brenner Pass and linked up with men of Lieutenant-General Alexander M. Patch's U.S. Seventh Army, advancing from the Rhine.

This completed one of the toughest campaigns of the war for the Western Allies, fought the length of Italy through some of the most difficult terrain imaginable and against a determined enemy. In the process, German formations that would otherwise have reinforced the Western or Eastern Fronts were tied down and the fascist government overthrown. Benito Mussolini, head of that government and its German-controlled puppet successor, was killed in Milan by Italian partisans on 28 April 1945 and his body, together with that of his mistress, Clara Petacci, strung up for all to see.

"We were thrust out... if not like the proverbial sore thumb, certainly like an aggressive forefinger, reaching out for the enemy's throat along the line of the Santerno."

Geoffrey Cox, New Zealand Intelligence officer

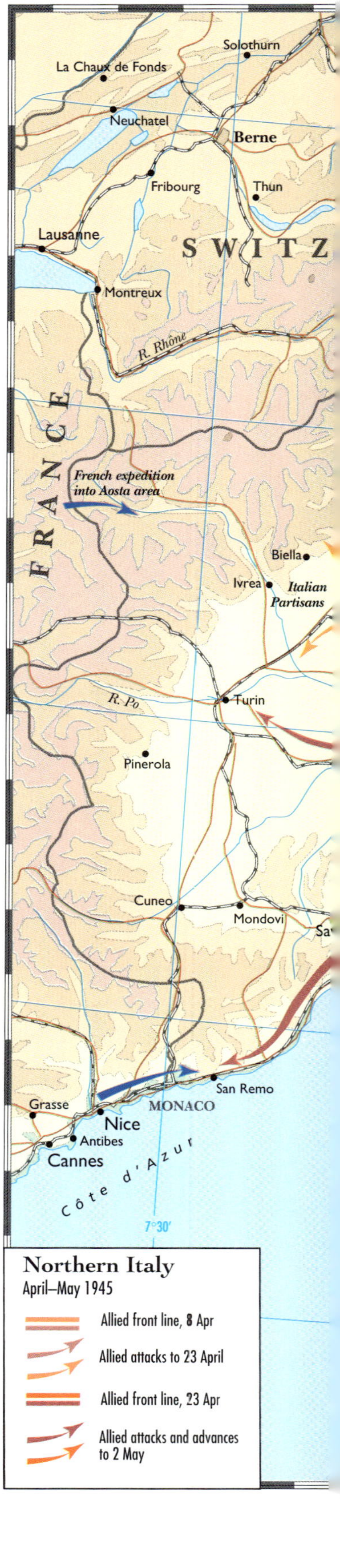

AUSTRIA
Alps
Apennines
ARMY GROUP C
VIETINGHOFF
ARMY GROUP SOUTH WEST
KESSELRING
FIFTEENTH ARMY GROUP
CLARK
14 LEMELSEN
10 HERR
5 TRUSCOTT
8 McCREERY
Alpine Line
Adige (Venetian) Line
Po Line
4 May 1945
2 May 1945: Surrender official
26 April 1945: Mussolini captured by Partisans
30 April
Italian Partisans
Tito's Partisans
Brenner Pass
Lake Constance
Lake Garda
Lake Comacchio
R. Rhine
R. Adige
R. Santerno
R. Senio
R. Tiber
Gulf of Venice
Gulf of Genova
ADRIATIC SEA
LIGURIAN SEA
Corsica
Elba Is.
SAN MARINO
Zürich
Winterthur
St Gallen
Herisau
Dornbirn
Kempten
Salzburg
Innsbruck
Predlitz
Villach
Klagenfurt
Ljubljana
Bolzano
Trento
Rovereto
Belluno
Udine
Trieste
Koper
Motovun
Novigrad
Parenzo
Rovigno
Pola
Fiume
Labin
Rasa
Varese
Como
Busto Arsizio
Milan
Bergamo
Brescia
Schio
Vicenza
Treviso
Verona
Padova
Venice
Chioggia
Lodi
Pavia
Mantova
Cremona
Ostiglia
Rovigo
Alessandria
Piacenza
Parma
Reggio
Modena
Ferrara
Codigoro
Argenta
Bologna
Imola
Lugo
Ravenna
Forli
Rimini
Genova
La Spezia
Carrara
Pistoia
Prato
Viareggio
Lucca
Pisa
Florence
Livorno
Volterra
Siena
Arezzo
Citta di Castello
Cortona
Perugia
Gubbio
Fabriano
Urbino
Pesaro
Fano
Ancona
Iesi
Macerata
Fermo
Foligno
Ascoli
Teramo
Orvieto
Grosseto
Piombino
Portoferraio
Bastia
LXVI
XIV
LI
(MTN)
IV
II
VIII
X
V
1
3000
2000
1000
400
200
0 m
80 km
50 miles
47°
46°
45°
44°
43°
10°30'
12°
13°30'

Advance into Germany APRIL – MAY 1945

The decision to leave Berlin to the Soviets, taken by the Supreme Allied Commander, Eisenhower, on 1 March 1945, dictated the course of the final weeks of the war on the Western Front. Eisenhower's aim was to split Germany in two by sending elements of Lieutenant-General Omar Bradley's U.S. 12th Army Group from its bridgeheads on the east bank of the Rhine to Dresden on the Elbe, although this did not prevent advances to the north and south of that line. In the north, Montgomery's Anglo-Canadian 21st Army Group, stripped of responsibility for the U.S. Ninth Army, which joined Bradley, was to liberate northern Holland and strike north-east towards the Baltic. In the south, Lieutenant-General Jacob Devers' Franco-American 6th Army Group, with help from Patton's U.S. Third Army (part of 12th Army Group), was to push east towards Czechoslovakia and Austria and south-east into the Alps. Bradley was ordered to go no further than the River Elbe, where a link would be forged with the Soviets.

The first priority was to capture the industrial center of the Ruhr, vital to what remained of Germany's war economy. On 2 April, lead elements of the U.S. Ninth Army made contact with the U.S. First Army at Lippstadt, cutting off more than 325,000 German troops belonging to Field Marshal Walther Model's Army Group B. The Americans then turned inwards to clear the Ruhr, encountering some resistance. Model's position was hopeless, however, and when he committed suicide on 21 April, the survivors of his force surrendered. Meanwhile, the British Second Army under Lieutenant-General Sir Miles Dempsey captured Osnabruck on 4 April and advanced as far as Bremen by the 17th. In the process, men of the 11th Armored Division liberated the concentration camp at Belsen. By the end of the month, Dempsey's troops were approaching Lübeck on the Baltic coast, having crossed the Elbe to the south of Hamburg. To their left, Lieutenant-General Henry Crerar's first Canadian Army had taken Arnhem and pushed north as far as Groningen, isolating the German Twenty-Fifth Army in Amsterdam and forcing a local ceasefire.

Further south, the Americans had made spectacular gains. As part of the U.S. Ninth Army helped to seize the Ruhr, the rest of that formation advanced to take Hannover on 10 April, before crossing the Elbe at Magdeburg. To their right, the U.S. First Army bypassed a German force in the Harz Mountains and captured Leipzig on 19 April, sending patrols forward toward the Elbe. On 25 April one of these patrols made contact with men of Marshal Ivan Konev's 1st Ukrainian Front near Torgau, creating a link between the Western and Eastern Fronts. Germany was now in a hopeless position, made worse as Patton's U.S. Third Army raced toward Czechoslovakia and into northern Austria. South-west Germany was cleared by Devers' 6th Army Group: as men of the U.S. Seventh Army moved through Stuttgart and Munich, liberating the concentration camp at Dachau on 29 April, the French First Army reached the Swiss border and entered western Austria.

Hitler's suicide in Berlin on 30 April meant that it was only a matter of time before the remnants of his once-powerful armies surrendered. On 3 May Admiral Hans von Friedeburg, representing Hitler's successor, Grand -Admiral Karl Dönitz, arrived at Montgomery's headquarters on Lüneburg Heath to the south-east of Hamburg, hoping to arrange a local ceasefire. this was refused by Montgomery, who demanded the unconditional surrender of all forces in northern Germany. After consultations with Dönitz, Friedeburg accepted, signing the documents on 4 May. He then traveled to Eisenhower's headquarters at Rheims, where he tried to organize a surrender just to the Western Allies. He had no more success, even when joined by General Alfred Jodl: Eisenhower insisted on a complete and unconditional surrender of all enemy forces, including those facing the Soviets. Jodl signed such an agreement early on 7 May, to be effective from one minute after midnight on the 9th. Included in the surrender were German garrisons in Norway, Denmark and the Channel Islands, although local documents had to be signed in each case. The Western Allies celebrated VE- (Victory in Europe) Day on 8 May, marking the end of nearly six years of war.

Reichsmarschall Hermann Goering obeys Allied orders to remove his decorations. Brought to trial at Nuremberg, Goering confessed to his crimes but evaded execution by poisoning himself.

"When the people saw what the camp was like and were led through the torture chambers and past the ovens, men and women screamed out and fainted... All swore that during the past years they had had no idea of what had been going on in the camp just outside their town ... I never knew what to believe."

Lester Atwell,
British Infantryman

Once the scene of a fervent reception for the Führer, the Bavarian city of Nuremberg, including the old walled inner city, was badly damaged in an air raid in 1944. As its jail and courthouse remained intact, the city was later the location for the trial of many of Germany's war criminals.

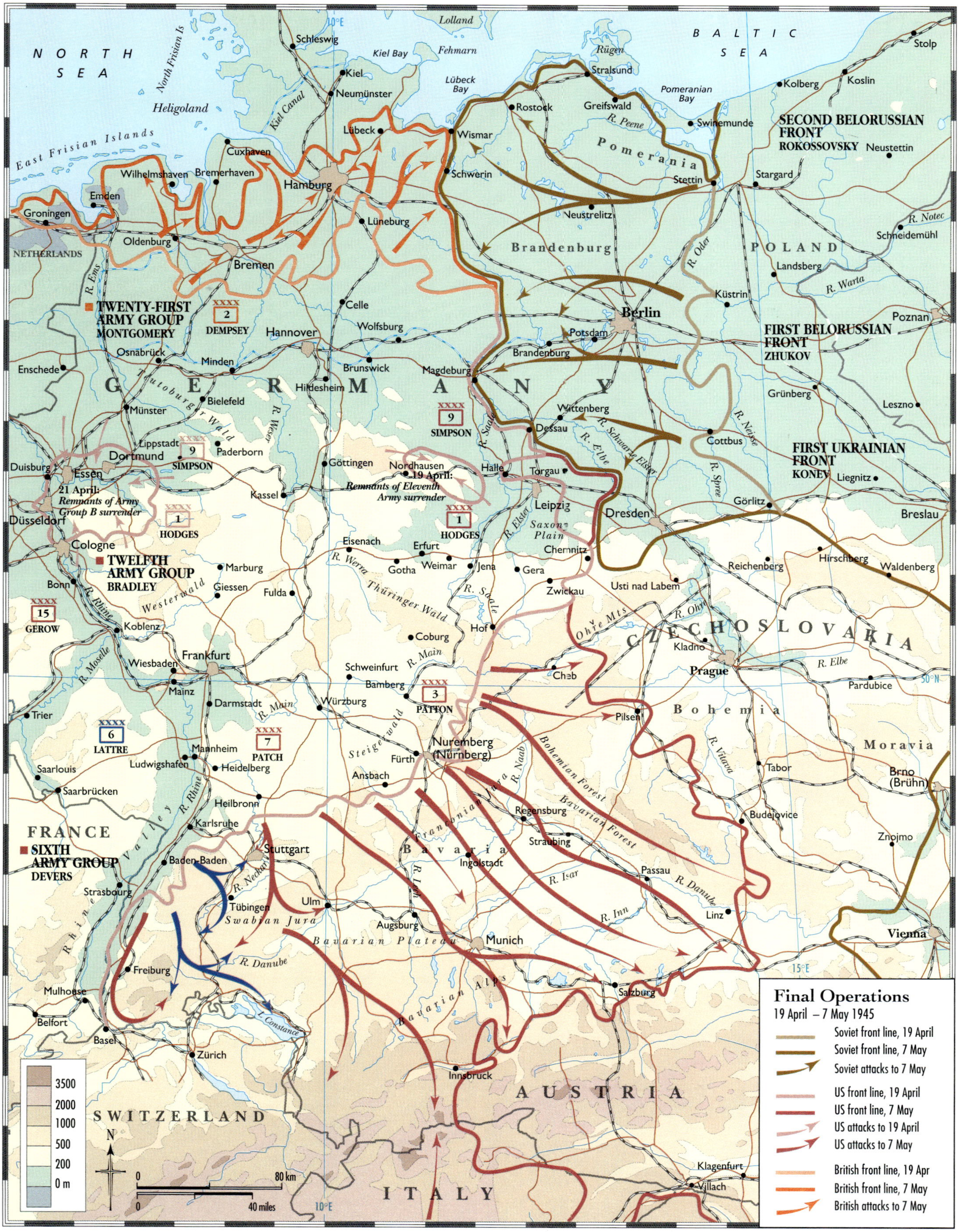
Final Operations
19 April – 7 May 1945
Soviet front line, 19 April
Soviet front line, 7 May
Soviet attacks to 7 May
US front line, 19 April
US front line, 7 May
US attacks to 19 April
US attacks to 7 May
British front line, 19 Apr
British front line, 7 May
British attacks to 7 May
NORTH SEA
BALTIC SEA
North Frisian Is
Heligoland
East Frisian Islands
Kiel Canal
Kiel Bay
Lolland
Fehmarn
Lübeck Bay
Rügen
Pomeranian Bay
Schleswig
Kiel
Neumünster
Lübeck
Wismar
Rostock
Stralsund
Greifswald
R. Peene
Swinemunde
Stolp
Kolberg
Koslin
SECOND BELORUSSIAN FRONT
ROKOSSOVSKY
Neustettin
Pomerania
Stettin
Stargard
Cuxhaven
Wilhelmshaven
Bremerhaven
Hamburg
Schwerin
Emden
Groningen
Lüneburg
Neustrelitz
R. Notec
Schneidemühl
NETHERLANDS
Oldenburg
Bremen
Brandenburg
R. Oder
POLAND
Landsberg
R. Warta
R. Ems
TWENTY-FIRST ARMY GROUP
MONTGOMERY
2
DEMPSEY
Celle
Küstrin
Berlin
Poznan
Hannover
Wolfsburg
Potsdam
FIRST BELORUSSIAN FRONT
ZHUKOV
Osnabrück
Minden
Brunswick
Magdeburg
Enschede
GERMANY
Hildesheim
Teutoburger Wald
Bielefeld
R. Weser
Münster
9
SIMPSON
Wittenberg
Grünberg
Leszno
Lippstadt
Paderborn
R. Saale
Dessau
R. Elbe
R. Schwarze Elster
Cottbus
R. Neisse
R. Spree
FIRST UKRAINIAN FRONT
KONEV
Liegnitz
Duisburg
Essen
Dortmund
Göttingen
Nordhausen
19 April:
Remnants of Eleventh Army surrender
Halle
Torgau
21 April:
Remnants of Army Group B surrender
Kassel
Leipzig
Dresden
Görlitz
Breslau
Düsseldorf
HODGES
1
R. Elster
Saxon Plain
Cologne
TWELFTH ARMY GROUP
BRADLEY
Eisenach
Erfurt
Gotha
Weimar
Jena
Gera
Chemnitz
Reichenberg
Hirschberg
Waldenberg
Bonn
Marburg
Giessen
Fulda
R. Werra
Thüringer Wald
Zwickau
Usti nad Labem
Westerwald
R. Rhine
15
GEROW
Koblenz
R. Moselle
Coburg
R. Saale
Hof
Ohre Mts
R. Ohre
CZECHOSLOVAKIA
Kladno
Prague
Wiesbaden
Frankfurt
Mainz
R. Main
Schweinfurt
Bamberg
Cheb
R. Elbe
Pardubice
3
PATTON
Darmstadt
Würzburg
Pilsen
Bohemia
Trier
6
LATTRE
7
PATCH
Mannheim
Ludwigshafen
Heidelberg
Steigerwald
Fürth
Nuremberg (Nürnberg)
Ansbach
R. Naab
Bohemian Forest
R. Vltava
Moravia
Tabor
Brno (Brühn)
Saarlouis
Saarbrücken
Heilbronn
Regensburg
Bavarian Forest
Budejovice
FRANCE
Karlsruhe
Franconian Jura
Straubing
Znojmo
SIXTH ARMY GROUP
DEVERS
Baden-Baden
Stuttgart
Bavaria
Ingolstadt
R. Lech
R. Isar
Passau
R. Danube
R. Neckar
Tübingen
Ulm
Swabian Jura
Augsburg
R. Inn
Linz
Strasbourg
Bavarian Plateau
Munich
Vienna
R. Danube
Freiburg
Bavarian Alps
Salzburg
Mulhouse
Belfort
L. Constance
Basel
Zürich
Innsbruck
AUSTRIA
SWITZERLAND
ITALY
Klagenfurt
Villach
3500
2000
1000
500
200
0 m
N
0
80 km
40 miles
10°E
15°E
50°N

The Vistula–Oder Campaign JANUARY – FEBRUARY 1945

By January 1945, the central sector of the Eastern Front had been relatively quiet for nearly five months. The stunning Soviet advance to the River Vistula – Operation *Bagration* – had run out of steam in August 1944 and both sides had taken the opportunity to regroup. Hitler's armies were by then in a bad way. Short of reinforcements and supplies, they were stretched out along a front from East Prussia in the north to Hungary in the south, while at the same time facing threats from the Western Allies in France and in northern Italy. By comparison, the Soviets enjoyed numerical superiority and, once the problems of movement through war-ravaged countryside had been solved, virtually unlimited logistic support. This gave them the ability to mount simultaneous attacks which forced the Germans to spread themselves even more thinly in an effort to cope.

The next stage of the Soviet offensive was clearly to advance toward Berlin, but Hitler remained obsessed with other fronts. This suited the Soviets, who mounted attacks in both Hungary and East Prussia to keep the enemy tied down, while actively preparing a major assault in the center, where three bridgeheads across the Vistula – at Magnuszew, Pulawy and Sandomierz – gave them ideal jumping-off points. By early January 1945 more than 2.5 million Soviet troops, backed by enormous weights of artillery and armor, were ready to attack. In response to a request from Churchill, Stalin agreed to bring the date of the offensive forward to 12 January, relieving pressure on the West in the aftermath of the Battle of the Bulge.

On 12 January, Marshal Konstantin Rokossovsky's 2nd Belorussian Front attacked northwestwards towards Danzig, severing the link between Army Group Center and the rest of Germany. There was little the Germans could do to prevent the advance, particularly as they were under simultaneous attack from Marshal Ivan Bagramyan's 1st Baltic and General Ivan Chernyakovsky's 3rd Belorussian Fronts. By early February the remnants of Army Group Center – about 500,000 men – had been surrounded with their backs to the Baltic. Although many were saved by the German Navy and some held out in isolated pockets until the end of the war in May, they had been effectively neutralized.

But this was only the beginning. At the same time as Rokossovsky's attack, Marshal Ivan Konev's 1st Ukrainian Front mounted a full-scale offensive out of the Sandomierz bridgehead further south, catching elements of Army Group A by surprise. An artillery bombardment was followed by an infantry assault, upon which the Germans rushed to plug the gap. At that precise moment, another artillery barrage came down, presaging an armored assault that was overwhelming. By the end of the day, Konev's men had penetrated to a distance of 12 miles; by 17 January they had crossed the River Warta and pushed about 100 miles beyond the Vistula along a 160-mile front. Meanwhile, on 14 January, Marshal Georgi Zhukov's 1st Belorussian Front attacked out of the Pulawy and Magnuszew bridgeheads, encountering weak opposition from Army Group A, the bulk of which had been moved to the north and south. Warsaw fell on 17 January and, as Soviet momentum built up, enormous tracts of territory were seized. By the end of the month Zhukov's leading units had reached the River Oder at Zehden, less than 50 miles from Berlin, while further south Konev's troops had taken Czestochowa and virtually cut off the Silesian industrial area (which was, as a result, captured intact). The only stubborn German resistance was encountered in Poznan, designated a "fortress city" by Hitler, but even that has been reduced by 23 February.

Zhukov and Konev consolidated along the Oder in February, while Rokossovsky maintained the pressure on Army Group Center. In March, he and Zhukov pushed into Pomerania, taking Gdynia and Danzig and forcing the withdrawal of the newly created Army Group Vistula, commanded by the inexperienced Heinrich Himmler, head of the SS. Isolated pockets of Germans held out in places such as Kolberg and, further south, Breslau, but it was only a matter of time before they would be forced to surrender. Berlin lay exposed.

Soviet troops inspect equipment captured from the retreating German Army during the advance toward the Vistula.

"Marching all night to cross the Oder before bridges blown ... Intense cold, six refugee children died on route – many falling out of ranks exhausted – frostbite gets a grip."

Sergeant Webster, Prisoner-of-War

A member of the Waffen SS prepares to use his Panzerfaust (anti-tank missile launcher) against approaching Soviet armor. Obsessed with thoughts of cowardice and betrayal, Hitler undermined the morale of even his most fanatically loyal troops by stripping them of their decorations and regimental insignia when they failed to fulfill his desperate and impossible orders.

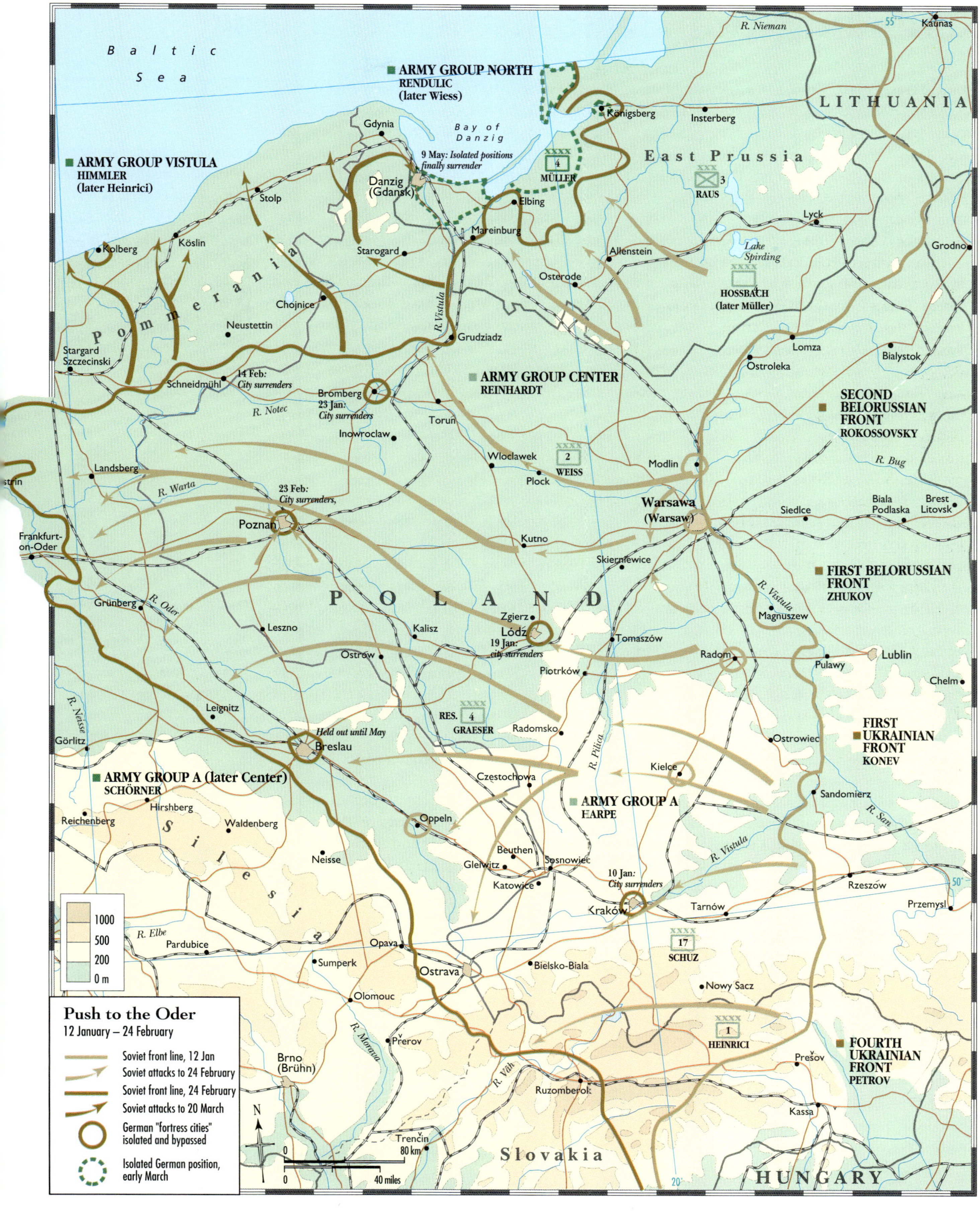
Baltic Sea
ARMY GROUP NORTH
RENDULIC
(later Wiess)
ARMY GROUP VISTULA
HIMMLER
(later Heinrici)
Bay of Danzig
9 May: Isolated positions finally surrender
Königsberg
Insterberg
LITHUANIA
R. Nieman
Kaunas
East Prussia
MÜLLER
RAUS
Gdynia
Danzig (Gdansk)
Elbing
Stolp
Köslin
Kolberg
Mareinburg
Starogard
Allenstein
Lyck
Lake Spirding
HOSSBACH (later Müller)
Grodno
Osterode
Pommerania
Chojnice
Neustettin
Stargard Szczecinski
R. Vistula
Grudziadz
Lomza
Bialystok
Ostroleka
Schneidmühl
14 Feb: City surrenders
Bromberg
23 Jan: City surrenders
R. Notec
Torun
ARMY GROUP CENTER
REINHARDT
SECOND BELORUSSIAN FRONT
ROKOSSOVSKY
Inowroclaw
Wloclawek
WEISS
Plock
Modlin
R. Bug
Landsberg
R. Warta
23 Feb: City surrenders,
Poznan
Warsawa (Warsaw)
Siedlce
Biala Podlaska
Brest Litovsk
Frankfurt-on-Oder
Kutno
Skiernewice
FIRST BELORUSSIAN FRONT
ZHUKOV
POLAND
Grünberg
R. Oder
Leszno
Kalisz
Zgierz
Lódz
19 Jan: city surrenders
Tomaszów
Magnuszew
Ostrów
Radom
Lublin
Pulawy
Piotrków
Chelm
R. Neisse
Leignitz
RES.
GRAESER
Radomsko
R. Pilica
Ostrowiec
FIRST UKRAINIAN FRONT
KONEV
Görlitz
Held out until May
Breslau
ARMY GROUP A (later Center)
SCHÖRNER
Czestochowa
Kielce
ARMY GROUP A
HARPE
Sandomierz
R. San
Hirshberg
Reichenberg
Silesia
Waldenberg
Oppeln
Neisse
Beuthen
Gleiwitz
Sosnowiec
Katowice
R. Vistula
10 Jan: City surrenders
Rzeszów
Kraków
Tarnów
Przemysl
R. Elbe
Pardubice
Opava
SCHUZ
Sumperk
Ostrava
Bielsko-Biala
Nowy Sacz
Olomouc
R. Morava
Prerov
HEINRICI
FOURTH UKRAINIAN FRONT
PETROV
Presov
Brno (Brühn)
R. Váh
Ruzomberok
Kassa
Trencin
Slovakia
HUNGARY
1000
500
200
0 m
0 80 km
0 40 miles
Push to the Oder
12 January – 24 February
Soviet front line, 12 Jan
Soviet attacks to 24 February
Soviet front line, 24 February
Soviet attacks to 20 March
German "fortress cities" isolated and bypassed
Isolated German position, early March

Clearing the Balkans DECEMBER 1944 – MAY 1945

One of the reasons for the Germans' inability to stand firm against Soviet offensives out of the Vistula bridgeheads in January 1945 was that they were also under attack further south. Despite pleas from General Heinz Guderian, by now Army Chief of Staff, that Hitler should reinforce the approaches to Berlin, the Führer remained obsessed with the situation in Hungary, where Marshal Rodion Malinovsky's 2nd Ukrainian Front was laying siege to Budapest and threatening vital oilfields to the south-west of the city. At the beginning of January 1945 Hitler sent an SS Panzer Corps to relieve Budapest, and when it failed, he withdrew SS General "Sepp" Dietrich's Sixth Panzer Army from the Ardennes as reinforcement. It took time for Dietrich to move across central Europe; he did not arrive in Hungary until 13 February, just in time to witness a massive Soviet offensive which took Budapest. The Sixth Panzer Army withdrew to a line running from the River Danube to south of Lake Balaton.

Hitler ordered Dietrich, together with remaining elements of Lieutenant-General Hermann Balck's Sixth Army, to mount counterattacks to north and south of Lake Balaton to create a defensive barrier around the oilfields. Codenamed Operation *Frühlingserwachen* ("Spring Awakening"), it began on 6 March, at a time when it was expected that the ground would still be frozen. Unfortunately, an early thaw reduced the terrain to a sea of mud, while Soviet defenses proved strong. It was the last formal German offensive of the war and it failed miserably. Dietrich pulled back without authorization, incurring Hitler's wrath. In a temper, he ordered the SS officers involved to be stripped of their decorations, further undermining their morale. By then, Sixth Panzer Army had been reduced to less than 50 tanks and was in no position to prevent a Soviet seizure of the oilfields in early April.

Meanwhile, Malinovsky had maintained the pressure. On 16 March he thrust toward Bratislava in southern Czechoslovakia, cutting Army Group South off from other German forces in the north. At the same time, Marshal Fedor Tolbukhin's 3rd Ukrainian Front took the oilfields and pushed into Austria, approaching Vienna from the south-east. Hitler's response was typical – he sacked the commander of Army Group South and replaced him with General Lothar Rendulic, an Austrian officer. But Rendulic could only continue the withdrawal, leaving Malinovsky and Tolbukhin to surround Vienna. They entered the city on 6 April and captured it after four days of bitter fighting. Dietrich, by now in danger of being outflanked, managed to extricate the majority of his troops to establish a new line to the west of the River Traisen. He eventually surrendered to American forces, advancing from the west. His comment that his command was called Sixth Panzer Army because it only had six tanks left was painfully close to the truth.

By then, Malinovsky had shifted the emphasis of his advance to the north, aiming for Brno and Prague. This took him towards the remnants of Army Group Center, pushed south by the Soviet advance towards the River Oder and for a time it seemed as if that formation, under Field Marshal Ferdinand Schörner, might hold out. But Schörner was effectively surrounded. On 8 May, as Malinovsky advanced from the south-east, General Ivan Petrov's 4th and Marshal Ivan Konev's 1st Ukrainian Fronts attacked from east, north and west. As they approached Prague, local people rose in open revolt, disrupting German communications and helping to ensure liberation of the city on 9 May. Elsewhere, the fighting had finished – Hitler was dead and Berlin was in Soviet hands – but Schörner held on, refusing to surrender until 11 May. By then, with American troops in south-western Czechoslovakia and approaching Vienna from the west, he had nowhere left to go. His surrender was the last act of the European war.

"Soldiers of the German front in the east! The hordes of our Judeo-Bolshevist foe have rallied for the last assault. They want to destroy Germany and to extinguish our people... He who at this moment does not do his duty is a traitor to the German nation. The regiments or divisions that relinquish their posts are acting so disgracefully that they must hang their heads in shame ... Berlin must stay German. Vienna will be German again. And Europe will never be Russian."

Hitler's Last Order of the Day, 16 April 1945

"If the war is lost, the German nation will also perish ... There is no need to take into consideration the basic requirements of the people ... Those who will remain after the battle are those who are inferior; for the good will have fallen."

Hitler to Albert Speer, March 1945

One of the last of Hitler's generals to be promoted to the rank of field marshal, Friedrich Schörner was both respected and feared by his men. An early convert to Nazism and a holder of the Pour le Mérite, Schörner was inordinately ambitious but his willingness to obey even the most impossible orders recommended him to the Führer's attention. In Hitler's will he was appointed as Commander-in-Chief but he had only ten days in which to enjoy his new honours.

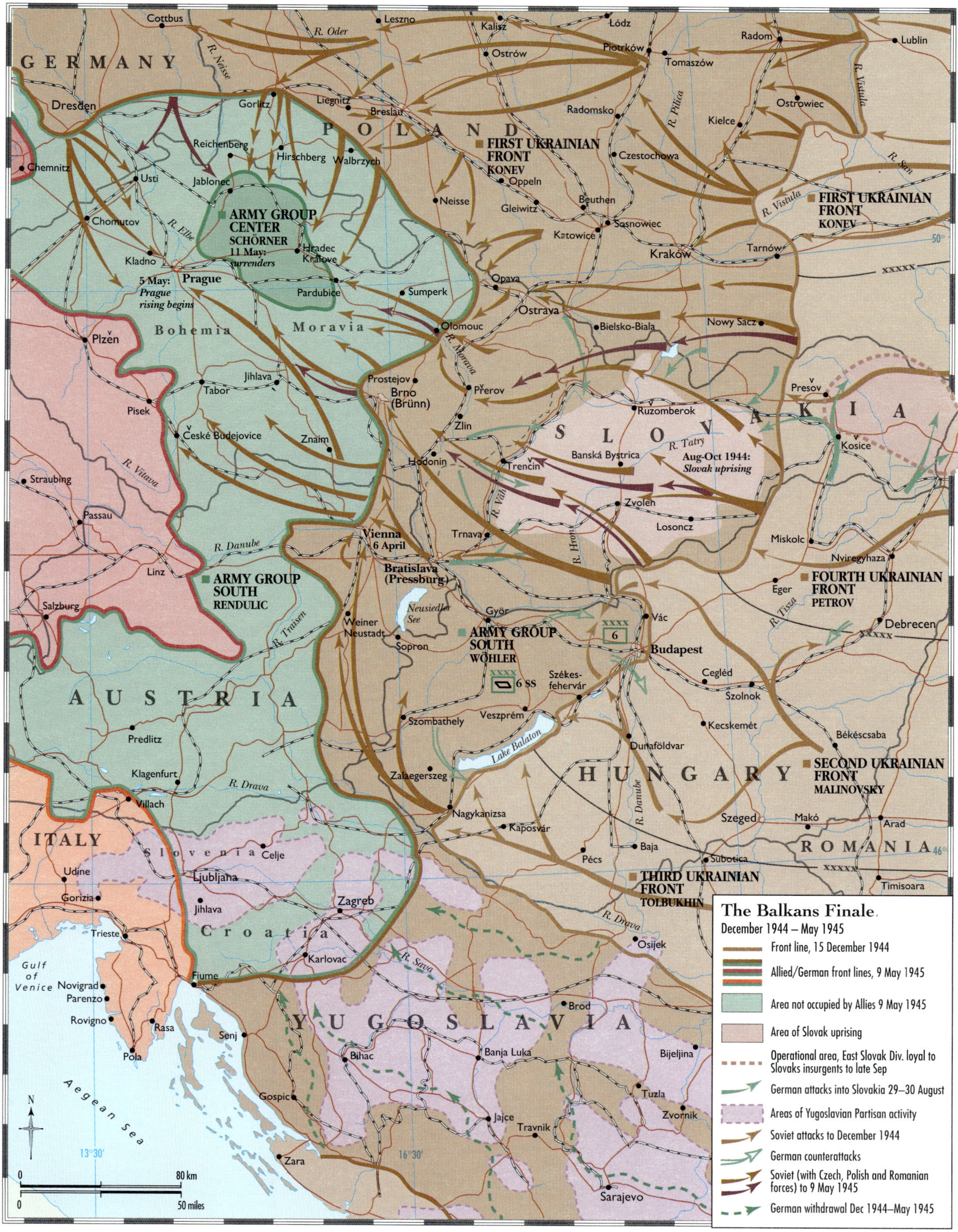
GERMANY
POLAND
FIRST UKRAINIAN FRONT
KONEV
ARMY GROUP CENTER
SCHÖRNER
11 May: surrenders
5 May: Prague rising begins
Bohemia
Moravia
SLOVAKIA
Aug-Oct 1944: Slovak uprising
ARMY GROUP SOUTH
RENDULIC
AUSTRIA
ARMY GROUP SOUTH
WÖHLER
6 SS
Vienna 6 April
Bratislava (Pressburg)
FOURTH UKRAINIAN FRONT
PETROV
SECOND UKRAINIAN FRONT
MALINOVSKY
HUNGARY
ROMANIA
THIRD UKRAINIAN FRONT
TOLBUKHIN
ITALY
Slovenia
Croatia
YUGOSLAVIA
Gulf of Venice
Aegean Sea
Prague
Budapest
Lake Balaton
R. Danube
R. Drava
R. Sava
R. Vistula
R. Oder
R. Elbe
80 km
50 miles
The Balkans Finale
December 1944 – May 1945
Front line, 15 December 1944
Allied/German front lines, 9 May 1945
Area not occupied by Allies 9 May 1945
Area of Slovak uprising
Operational area, East Slovak Div. loyal to Slovaks insurgents to late Sep
German attacks into Slovakia 29–30 August
Areas of Yugoslavian Partisan activity
Soviet attacks to December 1944
German counterattacks
Soviet (with Czech, Polish and Romanian forces) to 9 May 1945
German withdrawal Dec 1944–May 1945

Berlin APRIL – MAY 1945

The Soviet offensive to take Berlin began on 16 April 1945. Zhukov's 1st Belorussian Front, facing the city along the River Oder, with a bridgehead at Küstrin less than 35 miles from its eastern suburbs, enjoyed significant advantages. Comprising over a million men, it faced elements of Army Group Vistula, commanded by General Gotthard Heinrici. The Germans had constructed lines of defense, the first of which – along the Seelow Heights – was strong, but they lacked trained manpower, ammunition and fuel. In addition, Zhukov was not alone. Rokossovsky's 2nd Belorussian Front threatened the area to the north of Berlin, while Konev's 1st Ukrainian Front was poised to advance toward Leipzig and Dresden further south. German forces around Berlin were as weak as those defending the direct approaches to the city, with the added problem of having to face simultaneous attacks from the west.

But Zhukov did not have an easy passage. Reports from the east that Soviet soldiers were being allowed to loot and rape gave the final battle a desperate nature. Enough fanatical Nazis remained to ensure that ordinary German soldiers – including *Volkssturm* (Home Guard) battalions – stayed at their posts out of fear, while the thought of what might happen if they surrendered to the Soviets was sufficient to guarantee a fight to the death. This became apparent on 16 April when Zhukov encountered the Seelow Heights, for although he managed to seize them on the 17th, casualties were high. Moreover, once through this obstacle, he hit a second line of defense that appeared to be just as strongly held. By the evening of the 17th, Stalin was sufficiently concerned about lack of progress to order Konev, whose assault the previous day had gathered momentum, to divert two of his tank armies north to help out. This meant that Berlin was being approached from two directions and that many of the German forces to the south-east of the city were encircled. On 20 April Rokossovsky joined in, thrusting west then north towards the Baltic to trap most of von Mauteuffel's Third Panzer Army around the Stettiner Haff, a large lake near the coast. The Germans had little left with which to defend their capital – the city garrison itself, plus General Walther Wenck's Twelfth and SS General Felix Steiner's Eleventh Armies. Both armies were virtually static due to crippling shortages of fuel.

Hitler remained in Berlin, occupying a bunker beneath the *Reichskanzlei*, and on 22 April he took personal charge of the defensive battle. On 21 April Zhukov and Konev broke into the northern and southern suburbs respectively and, three days later, linked up to the south-east of the city. Their final assault began on the 26th; within 24 hours the defenders had been confined to a narrow corridor less than three miles across and 10 miles long, extending east–west through the city center. By 29 April Soviet troops had cut this corridor in at least two places and were approaching the *Reichstag*. After bitter hand-to-hand fighting, that building was taken late on the 30th.

The Soviets were now less than 300 yards from the *Führerbunker*, but Hitler was already dead. At about 3.30 p.m. he shot himself. Political leadership was transferred to Grand Admiral Karl Dönitz in Flensburg (Schleswig-Holstein), but he could do nothing to save Berlin. On 2 May General Karl Weidling, Commandant of Berlin, let the Soviets know that he was willing to surrender unconditionally. By the end of that day, the battle was over. It had cost the Soviets an estimated 100,000 men to take the city, which lay in ruins around them. Fighting continued elsewhere for a few more days but the Third Reich no longer existed.

Russian Illyushin IL-2 "Sturmovik" ground attack aircraft launched a series of heavy raids on the city of Berlin but it took a further week of fierce street fighting to totally eradicate all vestiges of German resistance.

"German men and women... Our Führer, Adolf Hitler, is dead... he died a hero's death in the capital of the German Reich, after having led an unmistakably straight and steady life."

Admiral Dönitz

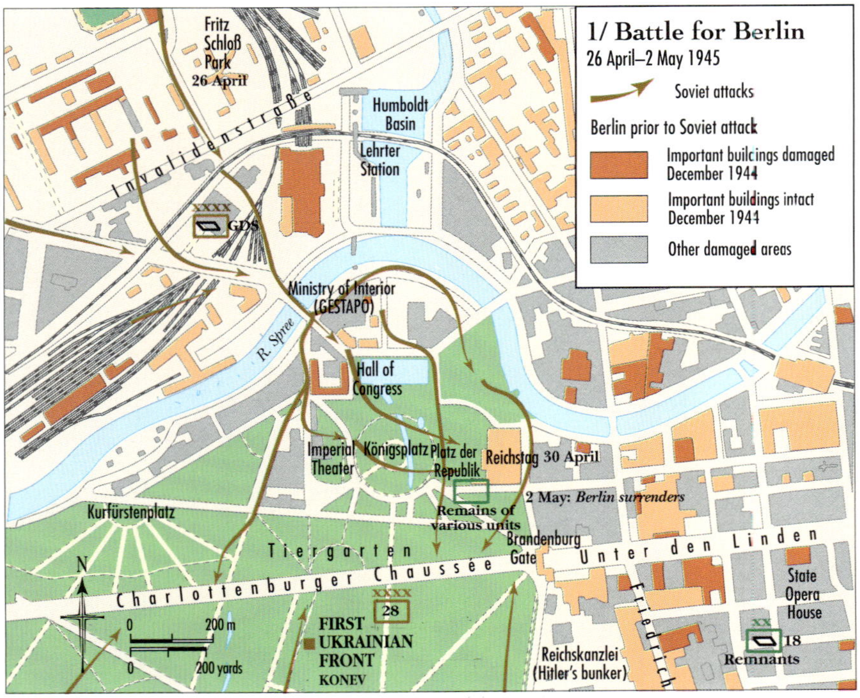

2/Link Up of the Allies
15 April – 6 May
Soviet front line, 15 April
Soviet attacks to 18 April
Soviet front line to 18 April
Soviet attacks to 25 April
Soviet front line to 25 April
Soviet attacks to 6 May
German defensive line
German counterattacks
German pockets
British attacks to 6 May
US attacks to 6 May
Polish attacks 15 April-6 May
BALTIC SEA
DENMARK
Fehmarn
Rügen
Lübeck Bay
Pomeranian Bay
Stettiner Haff
Pomerania
Meckenburg
Brandenburg
Saxony
Saxony Plain
ARMY GROUP VISTULA
HEINRICI
(TIPPELSKIRCH)
SECOND BELORUSSIAN FRONT
ROKOSSOVSKY
FIRST BELORUSSIAN FRONT
ZHUKOV
FIRST UKRAINIAN FRONT
KONEV
ARMY GROUP CENTER
SCHÖRNER
WENCK
Polish
25 April: Soviet and US troops meet at Torgau
Berlin
Ribnitz
Stralsund
Rostock
Greifswald
Peenemünde
Demmin
Wismar
Güstrow
Swinemünde
Anklam
Ueckermunde
Schwerin
Friedland
Neubrandenburg
Waren
Pasewalk
Stettin
Stargard
Parchim
Ludwigslust
Prenzlau
Neustrelitz
Pritzwalk
Wittstock
Templin
Dömitz
Lenzen
Schwedt
Angermünde
Wittenberge
Zehdenick
Neuruppin
Oranienburg
Eberswalde
Bernau
Wriezen
Küstrin
Stendal
Tangermünde
Rathenow
Seelow
Ketzin
Potsdam
Genthin
Brandenburg
Frankfurt an der Oder
Fürstenwalde
Beelitz
Burg
Zossen
Beeskow
Markisch Buchholz
Magdeburg
Belzig
Baruth
Luckenwalde
Jüterbog
Lubben
Gubin
Zerbst
Luckau
Wittenberg
Schlieben
Cottbus
Dessau
Forst
Herzberg
Torgau
Finsterwalde
Spremberg
Elsterwerda
Hoyerswerda
Halle
Horka
Leipzig
Riesa
Grossenhain
Kamenz
Bautzen
Görlitz
Colditz
Meissen
Dresden
R. Peene
R. Oder
R. Warta
R. Elbe
R. Schwarze Elster
R. Spree
R. Neisse
R. Elster
2 SHOCK
3 SHOCK
5 SHOCK
2GDS
8 GDS
1GDS
3 GDS
3GDS
5 GDS
N
0 65 km
0 40 miles
54°
52°
12°
15°

Liberation of Burma NOVEMBER 1944 – AUGUST 1945

By November 1944 Lieutenant-General Sir William Slim's British/Indian Fourteenth Army, having defeated the Japanese at Imphal and Kohima, had advanced as far as the River Chindwin. Despite poor weather, British engineers immediately constructed pontoon bridges to secure crossings for IV Corps at Sittaung in the north and XXXIII Corps at Mawlaik and Kalewa further south. These were complete by 4 December, enabling Slim to begin an advance, codenamed *Extended Capital*, that was designed to capture the Shwebo Plain and close to the next major obstacle, the River Irrawaddy. On 15 December, elements of IV Corps made contact with Chinese forces at Banmauk, while in a separate operation the British/Indian XV Corps advanced into Arakan, seizing Akyab on 4 January 1945. The Japanese, badly mauled at Imphal and Kohima, could do little to prevent these attacks. The Fifteenth Army, now commanded by Lieutenant-General Shihachi Katamura, desperately needed time in which to regroup, using the Irrawaddy as a barrier against Slim's advance.

If Slim was to exploit his success, therefore, he had to move fast and he had to cross the Irrawaddy, keeping the enemy off balance. His situation was made worse by the withdrawal of part of his air support to China and by the imminence of the monsoon, due in May. By 11 January the 19th Indian Division, part of IV Corps, had reached the river at Thabeikkyin, having pushed south along the railway from Indaw, but when a crossing was attempted, it was apparent that the Japanese Thirty-Third Army, defending the area to the north of Mandalay, was still in good condition. In such circumstances, a more elaborate plan was needed, and Slim already had one prepared. His aim was to use 19th Indian Division and the whole of XXXIII Corps as a decoy, drawing Japanese forces north, while the rest of IV Corps moved south through the Kabaw Valley and Pondaung Mountains to approach the Irrawaddy around Pakokku, threatening to cut behind the enemy. On 12 February XXXII Corps opened up another bridgehead at Ngazun, to the west of Mandalay, where it encountered the expected stiff opposition; 24 hours later the bulk of IV Corps crossed at Myaungu, to the south of Pakokku, against only light resistance. As 17th Indian Division pushed east to take the railhead at Meiktila on 3 March, the Japanese suddenly realized that they had been out-maneuvered.

But the battle had only just begun. Katamura, aware of the danger, hastily moved units from Mandalay to reinforce the Meiktila sector. Seventeenth Indian Division, joined by elements of other formations, dug in and waited for the onslaught. It was not long in coming. On 5 March the Japanese retook the village of Taungtha, severing the link between Meiktila and the bridgehead at Myaungu, and surrounded Meiktila itself. The fighting was to continue until 29 March, but it had the effect of drawing enemy forces south leaving Mandalay exposed. The city was taken on 20 March. By then, Katamura had already begun to withdraw towards Rangoon.

Slim immediately initiated a pursuit, sending XXXIII Corps down the Irrawaddy and IV Corps down the Sittang, racing for Rangoon against the monsoon. They did not quite make it in time, for when the rains began on 1 May, XXXIII Corps was still approaching Prome (which fell on 3 May) and IV Corps, despite having pulled ahead, was only on the outskirt of Pegu. But Rangoon was taken. Slim, aware of the shortage of time, had ordered XV Corps in Arakan to carry out Operation *Dracula*, sending 26th Indian Division by sea to land to the south of Rangoon on 2 May. *Dracula* was spearheaded by 50th Indian Parachute Brigade, which landed at Elephant Point on 1 May in high winds, although in the event such a large-scale landing was unnecessary. When 26th Indian Division arrived, it was able to advance into Rangoon with ease, the Japanese garrison having already been withdrawn. Four corps linked up at Hlegu on 5 May.

The campaign was not yet over, even though the liberation of Rangoon represented a major defeat for the Japanese. Lieutenant-General Hyotaro Kimura, commander of what remained of the Burma Area Army, pulled back to the east of the River Sittang and it was to take until August 1945 for the last pockets of his force to be flushed out. By then, the British were actively preparing for operations to liberate Malaya and Singapore, although these were rendered unnecessary by the Japanese surrender.

Indian machine-gunners on Pagoda Hill during the battle for Fort Dufferin in Mandalay. Many of the troops who fought the Japanese in Burma were Indian, and around half of these were Sikhs hailing from the Punjab. India lost more than 40,000 men in the campaign in Burma.

"The population in thousands welcomed our men with a relief and joy they made no attempt to restrain. We were back!"

General Slim, upon entering Rangoon

In a five minute ceremony in Rangoon, a Japanese delegation surrenders to Allied representatives.

The Road to Mandalay
4 December 1944–6 May 1945
Allied advances:
Dec 1944 – 21 Feb 1945
Chinese advance to 7 March
US advance to 7 March
21 Feb – 30 Mar 1945
Front line, 9 Apr 1945
31 Mar – 6 May 1945
British parachute landing
Japanese counterattacks
3500
2000
1000
500
200
0
INDIA
CHINA
FRENCH INDOCHINA
BURMA
SIAM (THAILAND)
Bay of Bengal
Gulf of Martaban
Arakan Mountains
Pondaung Mountains
R. Chindwin
R. Irrawaddy
R. Sittang
R. Thaungyin
Kerenni States
ELEVENTH ARMY GROUP
LESSE
CEF ARMY GROUP
WEI
Northern Combat Area Command
SULTAN
BURMA AREA ARMY
KIMURA
14 SLIM
33 STOPFORD
4 MESSERVY
15 CHRISTISON
33 HONDA
15 KATAMURA
28 SAKURAI
19 Indian
20 Indian
7 Indian
5 Indian
17 Indian
26 Indian
71 Indian
36
2
28 East African
82 West African
81 West African
18-30 Dec 1944: British 4th Corps changes to right front
7 March 1945: After capture of Lashio most Chinese and US troops recalled to China
3 May 1945: Rangoon occupied without resistance
1 May 1945: Airborne landings
2 May 1945: Operation "Dracula" landings South of Rangoon
Tamanthi
Myitkyina
Kohima
Hopin
Paoshan
La-Meng
Imphal
Homalin
Bishenpur
Banmauk
15 Dec 1944
Indaw
Bhamo
Wanting
Sittaung
4 Dec 1944
Pinlebu
Katha
Namhpakka
Tiddim
Mawlaik
Yazagyo
Namhkan
Kalewa
24 Dec 1944
Shwegyin
Thabeikkyin
Lashio
26 Feb 1945
Yeu
Hsipaw
Shwebo
5 Jan 1945
Kyaumyaung
14 Jan 1945
Gangaw
10 Jan 1945
Maymyo
Myinmu
21 Feb 1945
Mandalay
Keshi Mansam
Tilin
Pauk
Myingyan
30 Mar 1945
Kyaukse
26 Jan 1945
Nyaungu
Pakokku
Mong Nawng
Paletwa
Keng Tung
21 Feb 1945
Letse
Taungtha
5 Mar 1945
Thedaw
Taung Gyi
Seikpyu
Meiktila
4 Mar 1945
Thazi
Mong Pawn
23 Dec 1944
Donbaik
Myohaung
Mong Nai
25 Apr 1945
Yamethin
Akyab
4 Jan 1945
Magwe
Mawk Mai
Kangan
An
Taungdwingyi
Minhla
Tamandu
Chiang Rai
21 Jan 1945, 0942 hrs
Loika
Ramree
9 Feb 1945
Thayetmyo
5 May 1945
Allanmyo
28 Apr 1945
Taungup
Chiengmai
Meng Lampun
Kama
22 Apr 1945
Toungoo
2 May 1945
Prome
Paungde
Pyu
Papun
Chengmai
Sandoway
Shwegyin
Letpadan
Daiku
Madauk
Henzada
Tharrawaddy
Gwa
Pegu
29 Apr 1945
Taikkyi
Kamamaung
Bilin
Hlegu
5 May 1945
Pang Kyon
Tak Rahaeng
Rangoon
Thaton
Kunzeik
Kawkareik
Bassein
Thongwa
Kado
Kyauktan
Martaban
Kungyangon
Myawaddy
Myaungmya
Pyapon
Thanbyuzayat
Meng Nakawn Sawan
N
0
160 km
0
100 miles
95°
100°
25°
20°
15°

Liberation of the Philippines JANUARY – AUGUST 1945

Having secured the bulk of the Filipino island of Leyte, General Douglas MacArthur looked towards Luzon, and in particular the symbolic city of Manila, as his next objective. In December 1944 the Western Visayan Task Force, commanded by Brigadier General William C. Dunckel, secured the southern part of the island of Mindoro and constructed airfields that would act as forward bases for the Luzon assault, on 9 January 1945. That assault took place when 200,000 men of Lieutenant-General Walter Krueger's U.S. Sixth Army, supported by the U.S. Third and Seventh Fleets, braved Japanese *kamikaze* (suicide) air attacks to land on the shores of Lingayen Gulf, in northwest Luzon. The Japanese Fourteenth Area Army offered little initial resistance: Lieutenant-General Tomoyuki Yamashita had already decided to fight delaying actions on the Central Plain before pulling back into the mountains.

MacArthur's primary aim was to liberate Manila, but before he could risk a direct assault, the threat posed by Yamashita's forces on his left flank – 152,000 men of the *Shobu* Group, dug in among the Caraballo Mountains – had to be contained. Thus, although Major-General Oscar Griswold's U.S. XIV Corps moved south towards Manila in late January, the early fighting was done by Major-General Innis Swift's U.S. I Corps, advancing step-by-step into the mountains. Griswold, up against 30,000 men of the Kembu Group, made slow progress, and it was not until 31 January that Clark Field was secured. By then, MacArthur had ordered formations belonging to Lieutenant-General Robert Eichelberger's U.S. Eighth Army to land to the north and south of Manila Bay, effectively encircling the capital. On 3 February a "flying column" from XIV Corps entered the northern suburbs to liberate internees held in the Santo Tomas prison camp.

Manila should have been wide open. Yamashita had no intention of holding the city, but he had little control over its garrison, made up of naval personnel under Rear Admiral Sanji Iwabuchi. By early February they had begun systematically to burn parts of Manila and to massacre Filipino civilians, while ensuring that the city was strongly defended. Bridges were blown, streets mined and almost every building transformed into a fortress, defended by Japanese marines who were determined to fight to the death. As Griswold's men crossed the River Pasig into the heart of Manila, they entered a nightmare. The only way to deal with the defenses was to bring up heavy artillery, which inflicted enormous damage and killed Filipinos. It was not until 3 March that the shattered remains of the city were firmly in American hands, including the fortress of Corregidor in Manila Bay, taken by airborne assault in mid-February. By then, over 100,000 Filipinos had been killed, along with more than 16,000 Japanese and 1000 Americans.

Meanwhile, other American units had continued to fight Yamashita, who still had 172,000 soldiers at large on Luzon. Elements of Krueger's army moved to the east of Manila to engage the *Shimbu* Group – 80,000 men defending dams that provided water to the capital – but it took until the end of May to clear the area. To the west of Manila, the smaller *Kembu* Group posed less of a problem, but to the north, where Yamashita had his headquarters at Baguio, the fighting was long and bitter, taking place over some of the worst terrain on the island. Yamashita held out until ordered to surrender by the Emperor in early September, having tied down four American divisions for the best part of nine months.

The rest of the Philippines were left to Eichelberger, who conducted more than 50 amphibious landings between February and June 1945. Some islands, such as Palawan and Panay, proved to be easy to capture, not least because of the activities of Filipino guerrillas, but others involved hard fighting. The invasion of Mindanao, for example, began well enough on 17 April but took over two months to complete, at the cost of more than 13,000 Japanese and 820 American lives. MacArthur was criticized for ordering such attacks when it was obvious that the Japanese garrisons posed little direct threat, and a similar argument was used when he sent Australian divisions to liberate Borneo in May. The fact remains, however, that Japanese defeats in the Philippines and Borneo prepared the way for what many saw as the inevitable next step – the invasion of Japan.

A flamboyant self-publicist, General Douglas MacArthur frequently provoked the disapproval of his colleagues. Having lost the Philippines in 1942, he had vowed to return at the earliest opportunity to liberate the Filipino people. Before the war he had spent several years in the Philippines as an adviser to the government.

"I cannot recall, even in a life filled with emotional scenes, a more moving spectacle than my first visit to the Santo Tomas camp ... It was a wonderful and never-to-be-forgotten moment – to be a life-saver, not a life-taker."

General MacArthur

Members of the Philippine Fifth Column, who worked as snipers for the Japanese, are rounded-up by Filipino soldiers of the U.S. Army. The battle for the Philippines was bitter and over 100,000 civilians were killed.

2/Allied Operations in the Philippines
February–August 1945
Allied movements (Australian and US)
PACIFIC OCEAN
SHOBU GROUP YAMASHITA
Surviving Japanese forces fight on until ordered to surrender Sept 1945
S.W. PACIFIC AREA MACARTHUR
U.S.A.F.P.A.C MACARTHUR (from 6 Apr)
KRUEGER
EICHELBERGER
South China Sea
Mindoro Strait
Luzon
Manila
Quezon City
Palawan
Sulu Sea
Mindanao
Davao Gulf
Moro Gulf
Celebes Sea
Molucca Sea
Halmahera
BRITISH NORTH BORNEO
BRUNEI
BRITISH SARAWAK
Morshead
Martin
Irving
Guer
1/Allied Operations on Luzon
January–August 1945
Allied movements:
9 January – 5 February
5 February – 26 June
Japanese front lines :
15 March
15 March– 1 July
1 July– 15 August
15 August onwards
Babuyan Channel
Filipino guerrilla units operate against Japanese positions
SHOBU GROUP YAMASHITA
Kembu
Shimbu
PHILIPPINE ISLANDS
Lingayen Gulf
Manila
Manila Bay
Sierra Madre
Baler Bay
Dingalen Bay
Polillo Strait
SOUTH CHINA SEA
SIBUYAN SEA
Mindoro
Bicol Peninsula
Lagonoy Gulf
KRUEGER
SWIFT
GRISWOLD
HALL
EICHELBERGER
2000
1000
200
0 m

Iwo Jima and Okinawa FEBRUARY – JUNE 1945

On 3 October 1944 Admiral Chester Nimitz received instructions to support General Douglas MacArthur's advance on Luzon by taking an island in the Bonin-Volcano group, to the north-west of the Marianas. He chose Iwo Jima, a small volcanic outcrop dominated by Mount Suribachi, that could be used as a base for fighter aircraft escorting B-29s bombing Japan. The Japanese garrison, commanded by Lieutenant-General Tadamichi Kuribayashi, comprised about 22,000 troops, well established in a honeycomb of tunnels, pillboxes and caves. Nimitz planned to subject the island to a 75-hour air and naval bombardment, after which the 4th and 5th U.S. Marine Divisions of Major-General Harry Schmidt's V Amphibious Corps would storm ashore.

Landings began at 9 a.m. on 19 February 1945. The preliminary bombardment seemed to have worked: as the Marines struggled ashore across soft, black volcanic ash, resistance was sporadic. Twenty minutes later, however, the Japanese opened fire from concealed positions. Casualties mounted alarmingly – 566 Marines were killed and 1755 wounded on 19 February – but the Japanese strategy was flawed. Enough American forces had been put ashore to establish a strong beachhead, and by the end of the day over 30,000 Marines had been committed. They fought for the island inch by inch, taking Mount Suribachi on 23 February (an event immortalized by the famous "flag-raising" photograph) and then turned north-east. The last Japanese stronghold at Kitano Point was taken on 26 March, by which time all but a handful of the defenders had been killed, along with a total of 5885 Marines.

Nimitz's next objective was Okinawa in the Ryukyu group, less than 350 miles from the southern tip of Japan and administratively part of the Home Islands. Okinawa contained a large civilian population, defended by 130,000 men of Lieutenant-General Mitsuru Ushijima's Thirty-Second Army. Ushijima, like Kuribayashi, made the most of prepared defenses, concentrated primarily in limestone escarpments in the south of the island. Despite orders from Tokyo to defend landing beaches, Ushijima decided to let the Americans come ashore and then engage them in a war of attrition. Rear Admiral Raymond Spruance was in overall command of Operation *Iceberg*, with Lieutenant-General Simon Bolivar Buckner commanding the two Marine and four Army divisions that comprised the U.S. Tenth Army, responsible for seizing the island. Air attacks took place between 14 and 31 March, with a naval bombardment added from the 23rd, during which the Japanese launched 196 *kamikaze* (suicide) missions in an attempt to disrupt the invasion fleet. Between 23 and 29 March, the U.S. 77th Infantry Division secured outlying islands, isolating the Japanese garrison.

The assault began on the west coast of Okinawa at 8.30 a.m. on 1 April 1945. It seemed to be an anti-climax. Units of the III Amphibious and XXIV Corps established beachheads with ease before moving inland against minimal opposition to secure Kadena and Yontan airfields. On the following day, they reached the east coast, splitting the island in half, and then moved north and south. In the north, Marines advanced steadily, clearing the Motobu Peninsula by 20 April, but their Army compatriots had a tougher time, encountering the defenses of the Shuri Line to the north of Naha on 9 April. By 3/4 May, after heavy fighting in a maze of cave defenses, the Americans were subjected to a sudden Japanese counterattack which, when combined with heavy rains that turned the ground to mud, stopped them in their tracks. It was not until 21 May, after bitter hand-to-hand engagements, that Tenth Army achieved a breakthrough. Even so, it took until 21 June for the final strongholds to be secured. By then, 12,281 Americans (including Buckner) had been killed; the Japanese lost over 110,000, although more than 7,000 chose to surrender. At sea, the Americans lost 36 ships (most of them to kamikaze attack), but on 7 April they destroyed the Japanese battleship Yamato, sent on a hopeless mission to Okinawa. In the air, the Americans lost 763 aircraft whilst the Japanese lost 4155.

All this implied that an assault on the Japanese Home Islands, Operation *Olympic*, would be expensive. It was anticipated that the landings would be opposed with all the suicidal dedication displayed at Okinawa and figures of up to half a million casualties were mooted. In the event, the landings proved unnecessary, but the final stages of the conflict in the Pacific left no-one in any doubt that this was, indeed, a war to the death.

U.S. landing craft head for the beaches of Iwo Jima, 19 February 1945. Using General Harry Schmidt's 30,000-strong Amphibious Corps, the Americans intended to capture both Suribachi and one of the Japanese airfields on the island. Japanese resistance was fanatical and despite its superior numbers the American assault force failed to achieve either of its objectives on the first day.

"He saw me and charged with his bayonet-tipped rifle aimed at my stomach. I dropped my bayonet and grabbed my rifle. I squeezed off four rounds before he hit me."

Charles J. Leonard, Marine

1/Landings on Iwo Jima
19 February – 26 March 1945

2/The Fall of Okinawa
1 April – 21 June1945

Bombing of Japan JUNE 1944 – AUGUST 1945

When Lieutenant-Colonel James Doolittle led his B-25 Mitchell bombers to Tokyo on 18 April 1942, he gave notice to the Japanese that the Americans intended to carry out a strategic bombing campaign. But this was easier said than done. By early 1942 all U.S. airbases within range of Japan had been lost, necessitating the development, from scratch, of new aircraft capable of flying extremely long distances. American technology provided the answer in the Boeing B-29 Superfortress, the prototype of which flew as early as 21 September 1942. With a range of 3250 miles carrying a 5000 lb. bomb-load, this was an impressive machine, but mechanical problems delayed deployment. The first squadrons were not ready until early 1944.

The decision was taken to deploy the bombers, now formally part of Brigadier General Kenneth B. Wolfe's XX Bomber Command, to south-central China, around Chengdu. This necessitated flying the aircraft from India, then across the Himalayas, carrying all their fuel, bombs and spare parts to airfields that were vulnerable to Japanese attack. The first raid was not carried out until 14 June 1944, when 68 B-29s bombed Yawata, on the island of Kyūshū. It was not a success. Only 47 of the aircraft arrived over Yawata, seven failed to return and the target was barely touched. Wolfe was recalled and, in late August, replaced by Major-General Curtis LeMay, fresh from the bombing campaign against Germany. He introduced a number of changes and, very gradually, the raids began to have an effect, but the losses incurred were crippling: by the end of the year 147 B-29s had been destroyed. By then, the Americans had decided to shift the bombers to the newly-captured Mariana Islands in the central Pacific. The last raid from China took place on 15 January 1945.

The Marianas were closer to Japan – about 1500 miles south-south-east of Tokyo – but the problems of the campaign were not solved by the decision to move there. Early "shake-down" missions by the newly-activated XXI Bomber Command, principally against targets on Truk and Iwo Jima, proved that the B-29 still had mechanical problems, and it was not until 24 November 1944 that the first raid on Japan could take place. The target was an aircraft-engine factory outside Tokyo, but only 24 out of a total of 111 B-29s dropped their bombs accurately from operating altitudes of 27– 32,000 ft. The factory was revisited no less than 10 times during the next few weeks, but the results were similar on each occasion and the bombers were beginning to lose heavily to enemy air defenses. In January 1945 LeMay was moved from China to take charge. On 19 February he introduced new tactics, moving away from daylight, high-altitude precision bombing to night-time, lower-altitude incendiary attacks, using the newly-invented napalm. The results were dramatic. On the night of 9–10 March 279 B-29s arrived over Tokyo to swamp Japanese defenses and create a "fire-storm" in which an estimated 84,000 people died.

LeMay now began a deliberate policy of destroying Japan's major cities. Raids later in March devastated Nagoya, Osaka and Kobe, killing 120,000 civilians, and between then and mid-June, Tokyo was revisited and Kawasaki and Yokahama added to the list, by day as well as by night. All were burned out in raids involving anything up to 500 B-29s, escorted during daylight by P-51 Mustangs from Iwo Jima. Between mid-June and mid-August smaller cities such as Kagoshima, Omuta, Hamamatsu and Toyohashi were destroyed, while LeMay also used his bombers for mining operations off the coast of Japan. By August he was running out of targets.

But Japan did not surrender, raising the prospect of costly seaborne landings by the Allies. This above all persuaded the Americans to use the new atomic bombs – the fruits of the Manhattan Project – when they became available in early August 1945. First tested at Alamogordo in New Mexico on 16 July, two such weapons, nicknamed "Little Boy" and "Fat Man", were transported in great secrecy to the Marianas, where the specially-trained 509th Composite Group of modified B-29s was waiting. On 6 August Colonel Paul W. Tibbetts flew a B-29 known as "Enola Gay" to drop "Little Boy" on Hiroshima. Just after 8.15 a.m., in a blinding flash of atomic power, the city was devastated and 78,000 people killed. Three days later, Major Charles W. Sweeney dropped "Fat Man" on Nagasaki from the B-29 "Bochscar"; a further 35,000 people died. The end of the war was in sight.

British servicemen hunt for souvenirs among the debris of Hiroshima. The densely-populated city was targeted because it contained large military supply bases, shipyards and industrial plants. The blast, equivalent to 12,500 tons of TNT, vaporized thousands of people within seconds.

"Mother was completely bedridden, the hair of her head had almost all fallen out, her chest was festering, and from a two-inch hole in her back a lot of maggots were crawling in and out. The place was full of flies and mosquitoes and fleas, and an awfully bad smell hung everywhere."

A nine-year-old boy in Hiroshima

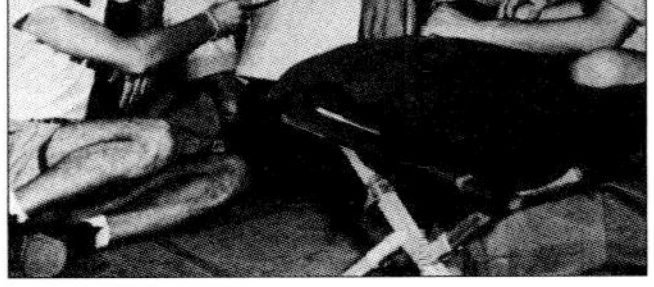

U.S. troops in the Pacific read the first newspaper reports of the atomic raids on Japan.

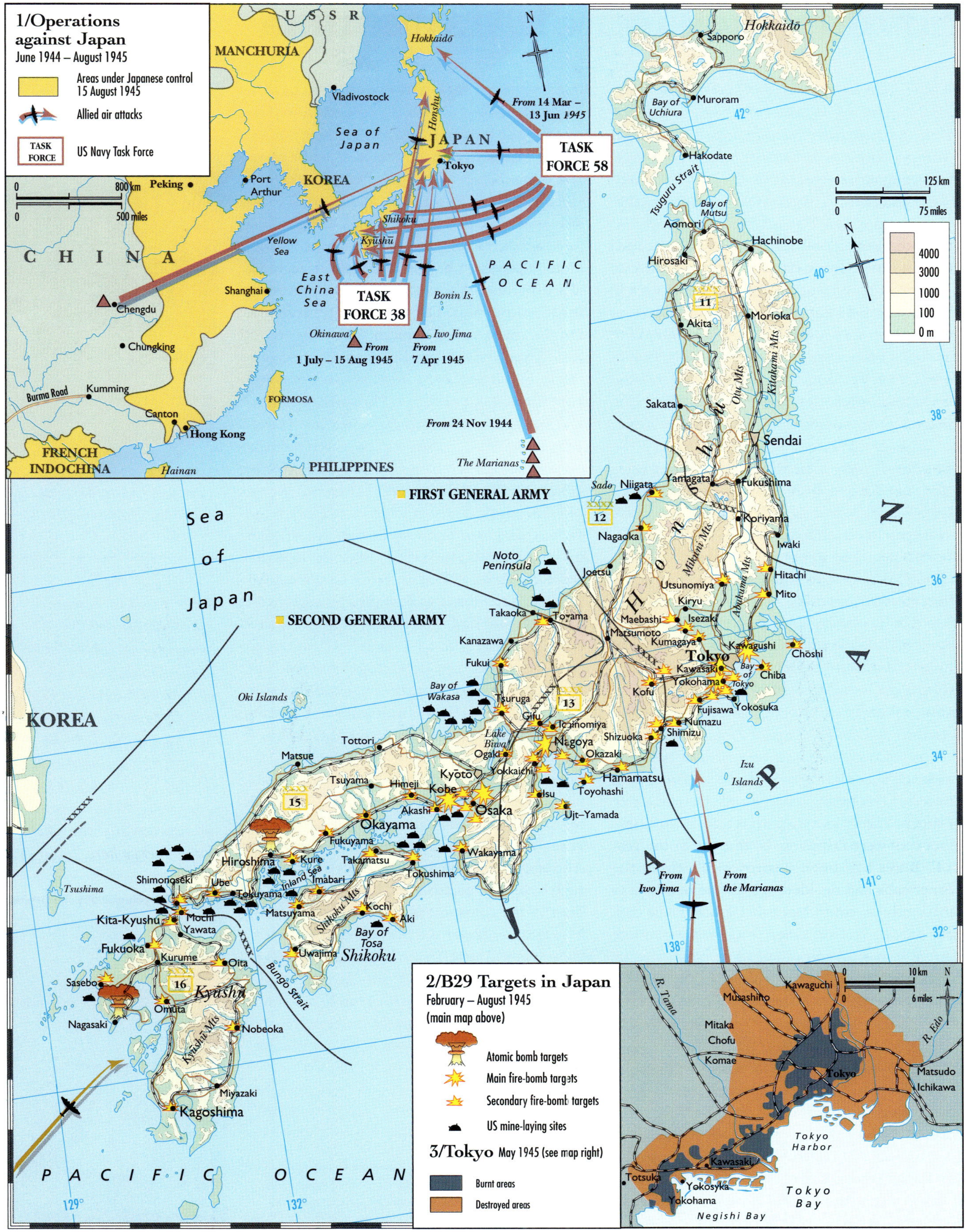
1/Operations against Japan
June 1944 – August 1945
Areas under Japanese control 15 August 1945
Allied air attacks
US Navy Task Force
TASK FORCE 58
TASK FORCE 38
From 14 Mar – 13 Jun 1945
From 1 July – 15 Aug 1945
From 7 Apr 1945
From 24 Nov 1944
USSR
MANCHURIA
CHINA
KOREA
JAPAN
Vladivostock
Peking
Port Arthur
Shanghai
Chengdu
Chungking
Kumming
Burma Road
Canton
Hong Kong
Hainan
FRENCH INDOCHINA
FORMOSA
PHILIPPINES
Sea of Japan
Yellow Sea
East China Sea
PACIFIC OCEAN
Okinawa
Iwo Jima
Bonin Is.
The Marianas
Hokkaidō
Honshu
Shikoku
Kyushu
Tokyo
800 km
500 miles
FIRST GENERAL ARMY
SECOND GENERAL ARMY
Sea of Japan
PACIFIC OCEAN
JAPAN
KOREA
Sapporo
Muroran
Bay of Uchiura
Hakodate
Tsugaru Strait
Bay of Mutsu
Aomori
Hachinobe
Hirosaki
Morioka
Akita
Kitakami Mts
Ou Mts
Sakata
Sendai
Sado
Niigata
Yamagata
Fukushima
Koriyama
Iwaki
Nagaoka
Mikuni Mts
Abukuma Mts
Hitachi
Mito
Noto Peninsula
Joetsu
Utsunomiya
Kiryu
Maebashi
Isezaki
Takaoka
Toyama
Matsumoto
Kumagaya
Kawagushi
Chōshi
Kanazawa
Fukui
Tokyo
Kawasaki
Yokohama
Chiba
Bay of Tokyo
Kofu
Yokosuka
Fujisawa
Numazu
Shimizu
Shizuoka
Bay of Wakasa
Tsuruga
Gifu
Ichinomiya
Nagoya
Okazaki
Lake Biwa
Ogaki
Hamamatsu
Toyohashi
Izu Islands
Oki Islands
Tottori
Matsue
Kyōto
Yokkaichi
Tsu
Ujt–Yamada
Tsuyama
Himeji
Kobe
Akashi
Osaka
Okayama
Fukuyama
Wakayama
Hiroshima
Kure
Takamatsu
Tokushima
Shimonoseki
Ube
Inland Sea
Imabari
Tokuyama
Tsushima
Kita-Kyushu
Mochi
Yawata
Matsuyama
Shikoku Mts
Kochi
Aki
Bay of Tosa
Shikoku
Fukuoka
Kurume
Oita
Uwajima
Bungo Strait
Sasebo
Kyushu
Omuta
Nagasaki
Kyushu Mts
Nobeoka
Miyazaki
Kagoshima
From Iwo Jima
From the Marianas
125 km
75 miles
4000
3000
1000
100
0 m
2/B29 Targets in Japan
February – August 1945
(main map above)
Atomic bomb targets
Main fire-bomb targets
Secondary fire-bomb targets
US mine-laying sites
3/Tokyo May 1945 (see map right)
Burnt areas
Destroyed areas
10 km
6 miles
R. Tama
R. Edo
Kawaguchi
Musashino
Mitaka
Chofu
Komae
Tokyo
Matsudo
Ichikawa
Tokyo Harbor
Kawasaki
Totsuka
Yokosyka
Yokohama
Tokyo Bay
Negishi Bay

Soviet Invasion of Manchuria AUGUST 1945

By early August 1945, Japan was close to collapse. American forces were closing in on the Home Islands, having taken Iwo Jima and Okinawa, and Japanese cities were little more than smouldering ruins from the B-29 bombing raids. In addition, Japan's navy had virtually ceased to exist and her merchant fleet, without which she could not survive economically, had been crippled. Surrender seemed the only option, but the Japanese government, led by Prime Minister Kantaro Suzuki, still refused to accept the unconditional terms demanded by the Allies. Even when news came through of the atomic raid on Hiroshima on 6 August, debate continued. As the Japanese prevaricated, the Americans dropped their second atomic bomb on Nagasaki, although it was probably a sudden declaration of war by the Soviet Union that clinched the decision to open negotiations. Early on 9 August, as the Americans were preparing for the Nagasaki raid, Soviet armies invaded Japanese-occupied Manchuria.

Stalin had been planning the attack for some time, having promised the Western Allies in 1943 that he would join in the war against Japan soon after the Germans were defeated. By early August 1945, more than 1.6 million Soviet troops, equipped with 5550 tanks and 28,000 artillery pieces, had been transferred to the Far East using the Trans-Siberian railway. Commanded by Marshal Aleksandr Vasilevsky, they faced just over a million men of Japan's Kwantung Army in Manchuria, although the figures were deceptive. Many Japanese units were of inferior quality, equipped with fewer than 1200 obsolete tanks and 5400 artillery pieces between them; they also lacked air cover. Moveover, they were deployed to protect the central plain and the approaches to Korea, ignoring border areas which, it was assumed, could not be crossed because of mountains and river barriers.

This gave the Soviets the opportunity to catch the Japanese by surprise. In the west, Marshal Rodion Malinovsky's Trans-Baikal Front, comprising 45 divisions with 2400 tanks and nearly 10,000 guns and mortars, prepared to cross the Great Hingan Mountains and the Gobi Desert, neither of which was well defended. At the same time, in the east, Marshal Kiril Meretskov's 1st Far Eastern Front, containing 37 divisions, nearly 2000 tanks and 12,000 guns and mortars, planned to attack from the direction of Vladivostok through a wild landscape of hills and deep valleys to link up with Malinovsky, trapping the bulk of the Kwantung Army in the central plains. To fix the Japanese while these attacks took place, General Maxim Purkayev's 2nd Far Eastern Front, with 17 divisions, 1200 tanks and 6000 guns and mortars, was to cross the Rivers Amur and Ussuri in the north.

The campaign ran like clockwork. Early on 9 August the Sixth Guards Tank Army spearheaded Malinovsky's assault by entering the Great Hingan Mountains, seizing the strategic Khorokhon Pass within 48 hours. At the same time a mixed Soviet–Mongolian cavalry corps under Colonel-General Issa Pliev advanced into the Gobi Desert, while to the north the Thirty-Sixth Army diverted Japanese attention by striking towards Hailar along a predictable route. Malinovsky's men entered Changchung and Mukden on 21 August; a few days later Pliev made contact with communist troops of Mao Tse-tung's army to the north of Peking. By then, Meretskov's 1st Far Eastern Front had breached Japanese defenses around Suifenho and taken Matuankiang, while thrusting south towards Korea. Purkayev's 2nd Far Eastern Front completed the campaign by taking Tsitsihar and Harbin, linking up with the Trans-Baikal Front on 21 August. The Soviet navy joined in to seize the Kurile Islands by early September. It was a comprehensive victory.

Many of these operations in fact post-dated the Japanese decision to surrender. On 15 August Emperor Hirohito, in an unprecedented move, broadcast by radio to the Japanese people (most of whom had never heard his voice before) to announce his acceptance of Allied terms. Japan was to be occupied and, although the Emperor was to remain, his power was to be curtailed. On 2 September 1945 Foreign Minister Mamoru Shigemitsu, along with representatives of the Japanese armed forces, signed the documents of surrender on board the U.S. battleship *Missouri* in Tokyo Bay. The nightmare was over.

Two thousand Allied planes staged a fly-past and the Star-Spangled Banner rang out as Foreign Minister Shigemitsu and General Umezu arrived on board the USS Missouri *in Tokyo Harbor. Their surrender was accepted by General Douglas MacArthur on behalf of the Allies.*

"We call upon the Government of Japan to proclaim now the unconditional surrender of all the Japanese armed forces, and to provide proper and adequate assurances of their good faith in such action. The alternative for Japan is complete and utter destruction."

Allied ultimatum to Japan

As the Japanese delegates signed the formal articles of surrender on 2 September 1945 on USS Missouri, *General MacArthur expressed his hope that "a better world shall emerge out of the blood and carnage of the past – a world dedicated to the dignity of Man and the fulfilment of his most cherished wish – for freedom, tolerance and justice."*

Soviet Attacks on Manchuria, Sakhalin and the Kurile Islands
August–September 1945
Soviet attack and advance
Front line, 1st September
Japanese front line in China, 1st September
TE38 U.S. Naval task force operating off Japanese coastline
Sea of Okhotsk
FAR EASTERN COMMAND
SECOND FAR EASTERN FRONT
PURKAYEV
TRANS-BAIKAL FRONT
MALINOVSKY
FIRST FAR EASTERN FRONT
MERETSKOV
KWANTUNG ARMY
1 AREA
3 AREA ARMY
17 AREA
WESTERN PACIFIC FLEET
SOVIET-MONGOLIAN CAV MECHANISED ARMY
FIRST GENERAL ARMY
SECOND GENERAL ARMY
CHINA EXPEDITIONARY FORCE
Red Banner
MONGOLIA
CHINA
KOREA
JAPAN
USSR
Siberia
Manchuria
Sakhalin
Kurile Islands
Hokkaido
Honshu
Shikoku
Kyushu
Gulf of Tartary
Sea of Japan
Korea Strait
Korea Bay
Yellow Sea
East China Sea
Gobi Desert
Lake Baikal
Hingan Mountains
Quelpart I.
R. Amur
R. Shilka
R. Songari
R. Ussuri
R. Hwang Ho
Okha
Nikolayevsk-na-Amure
Aleksandrovsk-Sakhalinsk
Shikka
Sovetskaya-Gavan
Toyohara
Wakkanai
Asahigawa
Sapporo
Hakodate
Aomori
Hachinohe
Morioka
Akita
Sendai
Niigata
Nagaoka
Tokyo
Toyama
Yokohama
Nagoya
Kyoto
Kobe
Osaka
Okayama
Hiroshima
Kitakyushu
Fukuoka
Nagasaki
Kagoshima
Ust-Maisk
Aldan
Chulman
Bodaibo
Tynda
Zeya
Stoyba
Skovorodino
Chegdomyn
Moho
Magocha
Sryetensk
Belogorsk
Blagoveshchensk
Aigun
Sunwu
Khabarovsk
Chita
Borzja
Petrovsk
Ergun Zuoqi
Nunkianghsien
Bei'an
Hegang
Shuangyashan
Dalnerechensk
Dalnegorsk
Hailar
Manzhouli
Tsitsihar
Harbin
Suifenho
Nin Guin
Vladivostok
Barskotun
Nonmohan
Arxan
Horqin-Youyi Qianqi
Taonan
Kirin
Changchung
Siping
Tongliao
Linxi
Abagnar Qi
Mukden
Funshun
Anshan
Mubultin
Erenhot
Ah Tung
Pyongyang
Kanko
Wensan
Seoul
Chemulpho
Taiden
Fusan
Masan
Koshu
Tyedyu
Kalgan
Peking
Jining
Wuyan
Hokow
Bashkulchai
Tang Tai
Luda
Che-Foo
Wei-Hsien
Tsing-Tao
Jinan
Yulin
Cheng Tiung Pu
Tai Yuan Fu
Yan-An
Su Chow Fu
Huainan
Hefai
Wuxi
Nanking
Soochow
Shanghai
101
16
LVI
2
10
4
36
15
3
35
1
5
25
39
6
53
44
17
30
34
11
12
13
TE38
500 km
250 miles
3500
2000
1000
500
200
0 m

The Legacy of War

The human cost of World War II was staggering. Although precise figures are not known for all combatant states, it is estimated that up to 60 million people lost their lives between 1937 and 1945 as a direct result of conflict. In purely military terms, the Soviet Union suffered the most, losing 7.5 million service personnel, but Germany (3.25 million), Japan (1.5 million) and China (an estimated 1.3 million) did not escape lightly. By comparison, British service losses were 326,000 and American 292,000. But it was civilians who suffered the most. Recent research suggests that more than 10 million Chinese civilians died, as did 16 million Soviets, 6 million Poles, 3.6 million Germans and 1.4 million Yugoslavs. On top of this, 5.9 million Jews were murdered by the Nazis. It is an endless and deeply disturbing catalogue.

Nor did the suffering end with the surrender of the Axis powers, for many people, particularly in Europe, no longer had anywhere to go. Some had lost everything as a result of bombing or land fighting, others chose to return to countries now under foreign (predominantly Soviet) occupation. By the end of 1945 the refugee problem in Europe was acute, forcing the victorious powers to spend time and scarce resources on trying to resettle and rehouse an estimated 10 million civilians. To them were added enormous numbers of demobilized Axis soldiers, who arrived back in civilian life with few marketable skills and little prospect of work. It soon became clear to the Allied powers that one of the by-products of fighting a war for the total destruction of an enemy state was having to put that state back together again so that the victorious armies could go home.

In order to do that effectively, it was important to ensure that all vestiges of the previous governments were destroyed and new ones created in the image of the victors. In eastern Europe this often meant the summary execution or imprisonment of all fascists under the communist regimes; in the western sectors of Germany it involved a laborious process of "denazification" based on investigation and re-education. All the victors were agreed on one thing, however, and that was that war criminals – those regarded as responsible for having started and conducted aggressive war as well as the men and women involved in deliberate mass murder – should be publicly tried and, if found guilty, suitably punished. In Europe, this led to the International War Crimes Trials at Nuremburg, the most important of which, involving 21 leading members of the German General Staff, government and Nazi Party, lasted from November 1945 until April 1946. Judges were provided by the Allied powers and 18 of the defendants, including Hermann Goering, Rudolf Hess, Wilhelm Keitel and Karl Dönitz, were sentenced either to death or to long terms of imprisonment. International trials were also held in Tokyo in 1946–47, with similar results. Elsewhere, traitors such as Philippe Pétain and Vidkun Quisling were tried by their own countries and collaborators were hunted down and punished, often in ways that suggested personal vendettas. Those who had suffered needed to lay the blame and exact revenge. In the process, some important war criminals escaped, although they continued to be hunted down. The seizure of Adolf Eichmann in Argentina by Israeli agents and his subsequent trial and execution for involvement in the holocaust occurred nearly 20 years after the war was over. More recently, the French tried and punished Klaus Barbie, the so-called "Butcher of Lyons", for his wartime activities.

Revenge may have been understandable, but it did little to solve the more pressing problems of the world. In 1945, the map of Europe was altered to reflect new realities of power. Not only was Germany split into zones of occupation by the Allies, but territory was taken away from the country in an effort to prevent a resurgence of trouble in the future. Poland, under Soviet influence, was literally shifted westward, losing land to the Soviet Union in the east and gaining commensurate amounts from what had been Germany in the west. The intention here, as elsewhere in what would soon be called the Eastern Bloc, was to create more solid, communist-controlled buffers around the Soviet Union, although the way in which it was done, often by force, served only to alienate the West. As early as July 1945, when the Soviets did all they could to delay the movement of Western troops into their allotted sectors of Berlin – a city well within the Soviet-controlled part of Germany – politicians in Washington, London and Paris were beginning to distrust the motives of their erstwhile ally. To many, the Soviets seemed intent on further expansion, raising fears that would lead, in 1949, to the creation of the North Atlantic Treaty Organization (NATO), dedicated to the protection of Western Europe. Six years later when NATO permitted a rearming of the Federal Republic of Germany and welcomed that state into the alliance, the Soviets created their own military bloc, the Warsaw Pact. Europe was divided into two armed camps that continued to stare belligerently at each other until the collapse of the Soviet Union in the early 1990s. The last symbol of this division – the presence of Allied troops in Berlin – did not end until 1994, nearly 50 years after the end of World War II.

East–West rivalry was not confined to Europe. Although the Americans were sure in 1945 that the Soviets would have no share in the occupation of Japan – instead , General Douglas MacArthur was appointed Supreme Commander Allied Powers and given virtually unlimited authority to demilitarize and modernize Japan – the spread of communism in the Far East and Pacific suggested a global strategy orchestrated by Moscow. In Korea, where the country was occupied by Soviet and Americans troops, meeting on the 38th parallel, a communist government was set up in Pyongyang; in China Mao Tse-tung's victory over the Nationalists in October 1949 was widely blamed on the Soviets. At the same time, communist insurgencies in the Philippines, Malaya and French Indo-China seemed to fit the perceived pattern. The Cold War, in which the "superpowers" – the U.S.A. and Soviet Union – vied for global influence beneath an umbrella of nuclear weapons, was one of the long-term effects of World War II. It was also the most dangerous, leading on more than one occasion to crises that came perilously close to war.

But many of the problems had more complex motivation. The spread of communism to colonial areas was not a Soviet ploy to undermine the West (although politicians in Moscow undoubtedly exploited the situation for their own ends), for one of the results of the fighting in World War II had been a growth of nationalism in regions hitherto controlled by Western powers. Britain, France and the Netherlands had all tapped the manpower and economic resources of their respective empires and raised armies within them that had, on occasions, borne the brunt of the fighting. French colonial troops recruited in North-West Africa, for example, fought in the desert campaign, in Italy and in the liberation of France itself, while Dutch soldiers raised in the East Indies found themselves pitted against the Japanese in 1942 long after the mother country had succumbed to Nazi occupation. By the same token, without units recruited in India and Africa, the British Army would have been unable to cope with the campaign in Burma, given that it was already conducting major operations in the Mediterranean and, from 1944, in North-West Europe. But it was no good using men from such areas to contribute to a "war for democratic freedoms" if they did not enjoy such freedom themselves. Many colonial ex-servicemen returned to their homes after 1945 imbued with ideas of democracy and determined to gain their independence from imperial rule. In those areas where the colonial authorities had been defeated by the Japanese, European credibility was already seriously compromised, particularly if native resistance to Japanese rule had been effective. In such circumstances, calls for independence enjoyed popular support and, if those calls were ignored, armed action seemed a viable alternative. By the 1960s most of the European empires had been disbanded, often without a need for violence, producing a plethora of new states.

Most of these found a voice and a place in the international political system through the United Nations (UN), set up formally at San Francisco in July 1945. Based on the now discredited League of Nations, the new organization was designed to act as a forum for discussion and as a "world policeman", controlled by the five permanent members of the Security Council (the U.S.A., Soviet Union, Britain, France and China). From the start, the Security Council fell foul of the Cold War and, with the exception of the Korean Conflict (1950–53), when the Soviets were boycotting the council and could not use their veto to prevent Western aid to South Korea under the UN auspices, any attempt to act out the policing role proved impossible, at least until the demise of the Soviet Union in the early 1990s. But this does not mean that the UN was a failure. Its willingness to act in a peacekeeping role, committing troops from selected member states to stand between warring factions and defuse crises, helped to prevent escalation, while the General Assembly gave new states the voice they demanded. It was (and still is) one of the more positive results of World War II.

Index

Picture and map page references are shown in **bold** and quote references are shown in *italics*

GENERAL

A

B

C

D

E

F

G

PLACES

Select Bibliography and Acknowledgements

Allen, Louis, *Burma, The Longest War 1941–45* (J.M. Dent and Sons, London, 1984)

Barnett, Correlli, *The Desert Generals* (George Allen and Unwin, London, 2nd edition, 1983)

Bullock, Alan, *Hitler and Stalin – Parallel Lives* (Fontana Press edn., 1993)

Calvocoressi, Peter, Wint, Guy and Pritchard, John, *Total War, The Causes and Course of the Second World War*, 2 vols. (Viking Press, London, 1989)

Craig, William, *The Fall of Japan* (Penguin Books, London, 1979)

Costello, John, *The Pacific War* (William Collins and Son Ltd., London, 1981)

D'Este, Carlo, *Decision in Normandy: The Untold Story of Montgomery and the Allied Campaign* (Collins, London, 1983)

Ellis, John, *The Sharp End of War, The Fighting Man in World War II* (David and Charles, London, 1980)

Erichson, John, *The Road to Stalingrad* (Weidenfeld and Nicolson, London, 1975)

Erichson, John, *The Road to Berlin* (Weidenfeld and Nicolson, London, 1983)

Falk, Stanley L., *Seventy Days to Singapore, The Malayan Campaign 1941–42* (Robert Hale, London, 1975)

Gilbert, Martin, *Second World War* (Weidenfeld and Nicolson, London, 1989)

Keegan. John, *The Second World War* (Penguin, London, 1989)

Russell, Paul, *Wartime, Understanding the Behaviour in the Second World War* (Oxford University Press, Oxford, 1989)

Hastings, Max, *Bomber Command* (Michael Joseph, London, 1979)

Hastings, Max, *Overlord, D-Day and the Battle for Normandy 1944* (Michael Joseph, London, 1984)

Horne, Alistair, *To Lose a Battle, France 1940* (Macmillan, London, 1969)

Jackson, W.G.F. *Battle for Italy* (Batsford, London, 1967)

Jukes, Geoffrey, *Hitler's Stalingrad Decisions* (University of California Press, Berkeley, 1985)

Lewin, Ronald, *Ultra Goes to War* (Hutchinson, London, 1978)

Macdonald, Charles B., *The Battle of the Bulge* (Weidenfeld and Nicolson, London, 1984)

Man, John, *Atlas of D-Day* (Penguin, London, 1994)

Manstein, Erich von, *Lost Victories* (Presidio Press, California, 1982)

Middlebrook, Martin and Everitt, Chris, *The Bomber Command War Diaries* (Viking, London, 1985)

Milward, Alan S., *War, Economy and Society 1939–1945* (Allen Lane, London, 1977)

Morison, Samuel B., *The Two-Ocean War, A Short History of the United States Navy in the Second World War* (Little, Brown and Company, Boston, Mass. 1963)

Overy, Richard J., *The Air War 1939–1945* (Macmillan, London, 1980)

Spector, Ronald H., *Eagle Against the Sun, The American War Against Japan* (Macmillan, New York, 1985)

The World at Arms, The Reader's Digest Illustrated History of World War II (Reader's Digest, London, 1989)

Thomas, Gordon, and Morgan-Witts, Max, *Ruin From the Air, The Atomic Mission to Hiroshima* (Hamish Hamilton, London, 1977)

Weigley, Russell F., *Eisenhower's Lieutenants, The Campaigns in France and Germany, 1944–1945* (Sidgwick and Jackson, London, 1981)

Weinberg L. Gerhard, *A World at Arms* (Cambridge University Press, Cambridge, 1994)

Willmott, H.P., *The Great Crusade, A New Complete History of the Second World War* (Michael Joseph, London, 1989)

Wilson, Dick, *When Tigers Fight, The Story of the Sino-Japanese War, 1937–1945* (Viking Press, London, 1982)

The Publishers would like to thank the following:

Picture Credits

Hulton Deutsch Collection

Imperial War Museum

Peter Newark's Military Pictures

Popperfoto

Robert Hunt Library

and from private collections

"Losses" by Randall Jarrell
reproduced courtesy of Faber and Faber Ltd.

Concept, Design and Layout:
Malcolm Swanston

Editorial:
Rhonda Carrier,
Stephen Haddelsey
and Elizabeth Wyse

Indexing:
Jean Cox and Barry Haslam

Maps compiled and produced by:
Andrea Fairbrass
Peter Gamble
Elsa Gibert
Elizabeth Hudson
Thekla Kampelmann
Isabelle Lewis
David Murphy
Peter Smith
Andrew Stevenson
Simon Yeomans
Sunita Yeomans

Typesetting:
Jeanne Radford